Read This First

The information in this book is as up to date and accurate as we can make it. But it's important to realize that the law changes frequently, as do fees, forms and procedures. If you handle your own legal matters, it's up to you to be sure that all information you use—including the information in this book—is accurate. Here are some suggestions to help you:

First, make sure you've got the most recent edition of this book. To learn whether a later edition is available, check the edition number on the book's spine and then go to Nolo's online Law Store at www.nolo.com or call Nolo's Customer Service Department at 800-728-3555.

Next, even if you have a current edition, you need to be sure it's fully up to date. The law can change overnight. At www.nolo.com, we post notices of major legal and practical changes that affect the latest edition of a book. To check for updates, find your book in the Law Store on Nolo's website (you can use the "A to Z Product List" and click the book's title). If you see an "Updates" link on the left side of the page, click it. If you don't see a link, that means we haven't posted any updates. (But check back regularly.)

Finally, we believe accurate and current legal information should help you solve many of your own legal problems on a cost-efficient basis. But this text is not a substitute for personalized advice from a knowledgeable lawyer. If you want the help of a trained professional, consult an attorney licensed to practice in your state.

1st edition

Your Crafts Business:

A Legal Guide

by Attorney Richard Stim

First Edition	JANUARY 2003
Editor	ILONA BRAY
Illustrations	SASHA STIM-VOGEL
Book & Cover Design	TERRI HEARSH
Proofreading	JOE SADUSKY
CD-ROM Preparation	JENYA CHERNOFF
Index	ELLEN DAVENPORT
Printing	CONSOLIDATED PRINTERS, INC.

Stim, Richard
   Your crafts business: a legal guide / by Richard Stim.--1st ed.
     p. cm.
   Includes index.
   ISBN 0-87337-838-5
   1. Artisans--United States--Handbooks, manuals, etc. 2. Handicraft industries--Law
and legislation--United States--Popular works. 3. Handicraft--Law and
legislation--United States--Popular works. I. Title.

KF390.A69 S75 2002
346.73'0787455-dc21   2002071789

For information on bulk purchases or corporate premium sales, please contact the Special
Sales Department. For academic sales or textbook adoptions, ask for Academic Sales. Call
800-955-4775 or write to Nolo, 950 Parker Street, Berkeley, CA 94710.

Dedication & Thank You

This book was inspired by my sister Barbi Jo who, if you met her, you'd realize is really an inspiring person. I once wondered whether she could support herself and her daughter on a crafts artist's income, and I'm happy to report that I don't wonder anymore. Not only did she motivate me to write this book, she also provided invaluable aid by patiently answering my questions and referring me to other artists who provided helpful insights. So thanks, BJ (and please don't become a dental technician)!

For their helpful thoughts and comments, I owe thanks to many crafts artists, including my wife, Andrea, (whose hookywooky crocheted tank tops I hope to soon see adorning indy film stars), Valerie Stainton, Maira Dizgalvis, Lisa Graves, Andrea Serrahn, Susan Brooks, Marge Heard, Alison Antelman, Crispina ffrench, Paul Lubitz, Martha Wilkes, Rebecca Yaffe and Lori Sanstedt.

Many of the chapters of this book were inspired by or borrowed from articles originally published in *The Crafts Report,* and I am grateful to *The Crafts Report* and my editor, Bernadette Finnerty, for editing and encouraging these columns.

Portions of this book relating to workspace leasing, employees and taxes were borrowed from, inspired by or donated by other authors at Nolo including Steve Fishman, Janet Portman, Lisa Guerin and Amy Delpo, all great writers and cool people!

I lucked out with my editor, Ilona Bray. She's got a devious sense of humor, and she added a lot of life into my otherwise dry style. I also lucked out to have Terri Hearsh at Nolo design this book and its cover. Thanks, Nolo!

About the Author

Richard Stim is an attorney and editor at Nolo and the author of 12 books including *Getting Permission, Music Law* and *License Your Invention*. He is the legal columnist for *The Crafts Report Magazine* and has represented crafts artists, photographers, and musicians for over ten years. He has no crafts skills.

Cover Credits

1 Tapestry Quilt, by Quilted Artistry 2002

2 Crocheted cotton hat, by hookywooky 2002

3 Gourd lamp, by Firefly Lamps 2002

4 Stoneware hatched vase, by Richard Urban Ceramics 2002

5 Eye of Isis choker, by Maira Dizgalvis 2002

6 Forged steel vessel, by Andrew Bergman 2002

7 Leather and metal eyeglass/cell phone necklace pouch, by Barbini/Barbi Jo Stim 2002

8 Sterling silver brooch with blue chalcedony drusy and moonstone, by Alison B. Antelman 2002

Table of Contents

Introduction

1 Business Forms: What's Right for Your Crafts Business?

2 Your Workspace

3 Selling: Consignments, Sales, Shows and Collections

4 Go Live: Taking Your Business Online

5 Employees and Independent Contractors

6 Trademarks and Trade Dress

7 Design Patents

8 Copyright

9 Licensing

10 Sales Representative Agreement

11 Lawyers, Lawsuits and Liability

12 Taxes

Appendixes

A How to Use the CD-ROM

B Tear-Out Forms

Index

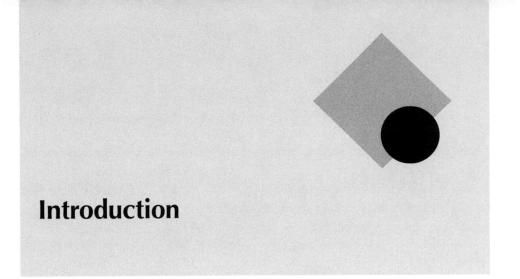

Introduction

he first time Maira Dizgalvis spotted a stranger wearing her jewelry, she had a mini-epiphany—the realization of knowing that someone appreciated what she was doing.

Since that night, many more strangers have purchased Maira's work (check out her designs at www.baltic shop.com), and she's discovered that selling jewelry is tough! Along the way, she's learned a few lessons, too. For example, the arty photographs she took of her jewelry (see Figure I-1) didn't send the right message to festival juries. "The photos handicapped me," says Maira. "Juries prefer plain backgrounds and sloping perches."

But when I asked Maira if there were any particular areas that created legal or business problems for her—for example, consignments, retail sales, taxes or studio problems—she said there was nothing significant. In the ten years she's been making her sterling silver Latvian-influenced jewelry, Maira has been fortunate to have had only minor problems; she's avoided major legal or business disputes.

It would be my wish that every crafts artist I spoke with could have the same "no major problems"

response as Maira. Unfortunately, the fast-growing crafts industry has stirred up a hornet's nest of small business problems. Bankruptcies, design thievery, tax disputes, poorly written studio leases, workspace safety and employer liability have become prevalent concerns as hand-made crafts penetrate malls, catalogs and online retail outlets.

This book is my attempt to provide a real-world view of running a small crafts business and to offer tips for steering your business on a "no problems" course. I've tried to incorporate the experiences of various crafts artists as well as my own experience working with crafts clients.

This book will guide you through the following types of issues:

- **Determining the form of your crafts business.** Chapter 1 discusses the advantages and disadvantages of basic business forms such as sole proprietorships, partnerships, LLCs and corporations, and explains how to create these business forms.
- **Securing your workspace.** Chapter 2 provides information on the legalities of a home studio

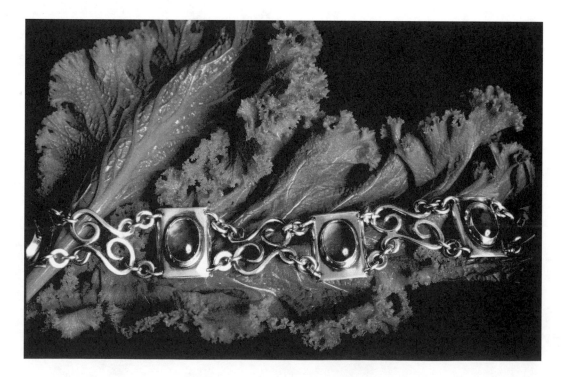

Figure I-1: Bracelet by Maira Dizgalvis

and explains how to examine and negotiate a studio lease.

- **Selling your work.** Chapter 3 analyzes consignment, retail, wholesale and commissioned sales and provides model sales agreements.
- **Going online.** Chapter 4 takes your business online and suggests how to protect yourself when choosing a domain name, setting up a shopping cart and choosing a Web host.
- **Working with employees and contractors.** Chapter 5 helps you sort through your legal obligations and rights with employees and independent contractors.
- **Protecting trademarks and business names.** Chapter 6 explains how to register and protect your trademarks.
- **Protecting your work with design patents.** Chapter 7 offers information about registering a design patent.
- **Avoiding copyright problems.** Chapter 8 covers the world of copyrights and explains how to register and protect crafts copyrights.
- **Licensing your crafts.** Chapter 9 provides information about how to license a crafts work and how to analyze a license agreement.
- **Dealing with sales reps.** Chapter 10 discusses sales reps and offers a model sales rep agreement.
- **Avoiding liability and legal problems.** Chapter 11 helps you find a lawyer, examine your insurance options and avoid expensive contract disputes and rip-offs.
- **Paying taxes.** Chapter 12 helps demystify the frightening world of income taxes for the self-employed.

In addition to this information, you'll find a dozen agreements and sample letters that you can modify on the CD-ROM included at the back of this book. I hope you find all of this helpful and not too daunting. I look forward to receiving feedback so that I can provide even more useful information in future editions.

Icons Used in This Book

To aid you in using this book, we use the following icons:

 The caution icon warns you of potential problems.

 This icon indicates that the information is a useful tip.

 This icon refers you to helpful books or other resources.

 This icon refers you to a further discussion of the topic somewhere else in this book.

 This icon tells you that the form or document indicated is available on the CD-ROM at the back of this book.

 This icon refers you to related information in another chapter of this book.

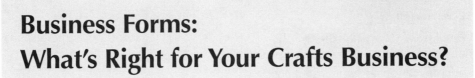

Business Forms:
What's Right for Your Crafts Business?

*V*alerie Stainton always dreamed of opening a crafts gallery. One day, she took the plunge, gave notice to her employer of 22 years and leased space for *Valerie's Gallery* in nearby Newburyport, Massachusetts.

One of Valerie's biggest concerns was how to structure her enterprise—that is, as a sole proprietorship, partnership, corporation or limited liability company (LLC). She knew something about business —she had been the business manager at her former job—and learned more by reading books and researching on the Net. (One helpful source was Score (www.score.org), where retired businesspersons counsel new businesses.)

Armed with this information, and with the help of an attorney, Valerie decided to form an LLC. "I'm a conservative person," says Valerie, "and one of [the LLC's benefits] is the protection of personal assets." In other words, creditors would be blocked from attempting to collect on business debts by reaching into Valerie's personal bank account or going after her house.

Forming an LLC or a corporation will shield you from personal liability—but is it the right choice for your crafts business? That depends. Personal liability isn't the only issue to consider. This chapter provides a full analysis of the various business forms, including:

- how your choice affects your personal liability— whether you'll risk getting stuck for business debts, bankruptcy and damages from lawsuits (see Section A)
- the tax implications of each business form (see Section B)
- how to establish each business form (see Section C), and
- what you'd gain by forming a cooperative, a unique business structure that's popular for crafts businesses (see Section D).

It's possible that your business is doing well and you've never given much thought to your business form. Perhaps you started as a sole proprietor and never changed. Great! There may be no reason to change anything now. But whether you're just starting out or you've been operating for years, you should learn about business forms if any of the following are true:

- you want to operate a business with others
- you're worried that you may be personally liable for business debts or other liabilities, or
- you'd like to know more about how each type of business is taxed.

Biz Form Basics

A "business form" is the legal structure under which a business operates. Here's a snapshot of what distinguishes the four most popular business forms. I'll talk about each in more detail later in the chapter.

- **Sole proprietorship.** One person (or a husband and wife) owns and operates the business and is personally liable for business debts.
- **Partnership.** Two or more people own and operate the business, sharing expenses, responsibilities and profits. Each partner is personally liable for all partnership debts.
- **Corporation.** One or more persons own and operate the corporation and share corporate profits and losses (as shareholders). Each shareholder's personal liability is limited.
- **Limited liability company (LLC).** One or more persons own and operate the LLC (as members), and profits and losses are shared in predetermined proportions. Each member's personal liability is limited.

Many crafts businesses also operate as cooperatives, discussed in Section D. Cooperatives—depending on state law—must choose to operate as either a partnership, corporation or LLC.

A. Personal Liability: Can They Take My House?

Before talking about how to limit personal liability, let's define what liabilities are. They're basically debts—money you owe. Every business carries some liabilities—for example, ongoing payments to suppliers, rent for your studio, compensation to employees or booth fees at a show. Additional liabilities may arise if your business is devastated by a fire or flood or if you are the victim of a lawsuit—for example, someone is injured in your studio and sues you for damages.

If you operate your business as a sole proprietorship—the most common business form for crafts businesses—then you will be personally liable for all business debts. The same is true for a partnership. A creditor can collect a partnership debt against any partner, regardless of which partner incurred the debt. That means that if your partner orders $50,000 worth of supplies (without telling you) and then moves to Venezuela, you could be on the hook. A written partnership agreement (see Section C3) can apportion liability among partners, but it won't absolve you of personal liability.

1. Corporate Shield

Corporations and limited liability companies (LLCs) are created to shield the owners from personal liability. For a dramatic example of how this shield works to deflect liability, consider the demise of People's Pottery, the 52-store chain that sold made-in-America crafts. The company filed for bankruptcy in 2001, owing millions to crafts businesses. However, the owners were not held personally liable, because they had created a corporate entity that owned the company. In short, if you operate as a corporation or LLC, creditors can—with rare exceptions (see Section A4)—only collect their debts from the business's assets, not from the owners.

But that's not to say you should rush out tomorrow and convert your sole proprietorship or partnership into one of these entities. All this protection comes at a price. To acquire corporate or LLC status, you need to pay fees and file paperwork with your Secretary of State or other state filing office. For example, Valerie Stainton paid $750 in legal fees and $585 in state filing fees. (As I'll explain in Section C, you can cut these fees by preparing your own filing.)

And, regardless of the fees, LLCs and corporations require some legal attention. For example, Valerie

Stainton's LLC was formed in New Hampshire (where she lived), but she then needed to file a foreign corporation statement in Massachusetts in order to do business there. (She would have filed her LLC in Massachusetts, but it is the only state that requires two owners to form an LLC; every other state allows you to form it with just one.)

2. Prudence, Insurance and Contracts: Other Ways to Limit Liability

Many crafts businesses operate comfortably as sole proprietorships or partnerships because they have limited their liability in other ways. For example, you don't need to bother forming an LLC or a corporation if you:

- **Avoid incurring substantial debts.** If you keep your debts to a minimum, you'll have gone a long way toward shielding yourself from creditor liability problems. In other words, take fewer business risks—don't rack up debts without having a good idea of how you'll pay for them. Unfortunately, for crafts workers with an adventurous entrepreneurial streak, this approach may limit business growth.

  Example: Sheila's GlassHouse receives an order for $300,000 worth of glass beads from KnickKnacks, a home furnishings chain (to be paid on a net-90 days invoice). In order to fill this mammoth order, Sheila would have to buy $80,000 worth of supplies. (KnickKnacks won't advance Sheila the cost of supplies.) Sheila decides not to accept the order because she believes her business is not prepared to carry an $80,000 debt for three months. By reducing her personal liability, she's also reduced the need for the protection of a corporation or LLC.

- **Maintain adequate insurance.** Insurance, as I explain in Section A3, below, and in Chapter 11, can provide a suitable umbrella when creditor problems rain on your crafts business. Although insurance coverage will add to your ongoing costs, the addition will be regular and predictable, as opposed to the limitless costs that a natural disaster or a lawsuit could generate.

Example: Jack's pewter business has sufficient insurance to cover injury to visitors, loss of business property and any legal costs related to common business lawsuits. Since Jack's insurance covers most of the predictable disasters, forming an LLC or corporation is probably not worth the hassle.

- **Use liability-shifting techniques when entering into contracts.** Every agreement you sign makes you liable for something—for example, if you fail to pay rent, you're liable for the missing payments; if you wreck your rental car, you're liable for damages. You and your attorney may be able to negotiate changes to some agreements that shift or lessen your liability.

Example: Andrew is licensing his crafts doll design to a toy company. He receives a $20,000 advance, but the license agreement states that Andrew must refund his advance if the company is sued for copyright infringement over the design. Andrew and his attorney modify the agreement so that Andrew refunds the advance only if the lawsuit results in a final verdict—in other words, if infringement is proven, not just claimed. This substantially shifts the liability away from Andrew and makes him less likely to have to pay back the $20,000.

3. Combining Insurance and Limited Liability Business Forms

INSURANCE, n. An ingenious modern game of chance in which the player is permitted to enjoy the comfortable conviction that he is beating the man who keeps the table.

Ambrose Bierce, *The Devil's Dictionary*

If forming a corporation or LLC can limit your liability, why bother with insurance? Or vice versa? In terms of liability, the difference between the two is that the corporate or LLC form only protects you when your business goes under—that is, it's an end game protection. If your business's debts become so burdensome that you must declare bankruptcy, having an LLC or corporate structure will shield you from personal loss. But until you cry "bankruptcy," your business must find a way to pay its debts—which, if you're uninsured, could leave you writing some hefty checks.

Insurance allows your business to take a licking and keep on ticking.

Example 1: Leslie operates his Western-inspired jewelry business as an LLC. While at a show, his studio burns to the ground, causing the loss of $90,000 in supplies and $30,000 in inventory. At the time of the fire, Leslie owes creditors some $45,000. Because he has an LLC, Leslie's business can declare bankruptcy and avoid paying the $45,000 in debts. His personal assets are unaffected. Still, he has lost the tools of his livelihood, his workspace and goodwill among suppliers, who are now wary of offering him credit.

Example 2: If Leslie had instead maintained fire insurance, he would receive compensation for his supplies and possibly rental costs for a temporary studio. He would be able to return to work and hopefully repay creditors without declaring bankruptcy.

Insurance has its drawbacks: periodic payments, annoying deductibles and hard-to-read policies. (I offer suggestions for choosing insurance for your crafts business in Chapter 11.) But insurance is the best way to protect against business disasters such as fire, theft, injury to visitors, workplace injuries, injuries resulting from the use of your crafts goods and even claims that you stole someone else's design.

Sometimes your business *must* get insurance—for example, because state laws require obtaining workmen's compensation coverage, or because you sign a lease requiring you to have business and personal property coverage. In other cases, insurance may prove too expensive and you'll have to forego it. A good insurance agent can help you make the right decisions. Here are some additional tips on choosing and using your insurance wisely:

- Maintain enough property and liability coverage to protect yourself from common claims—for example, fire, theft or accidental injury.
- Buy insurance against serious risks, that is, those that would cost you the most if they occurred (so long as the insurance is reasonably priced for your business).
- When possible, keep insurance costs down by selecting high deductibles.
- Do your best to reduce hazards or conditions that can lead to insurance claims.

Chapter 11, Section H offers advice on determining your insurance needs and locating insurance agents.

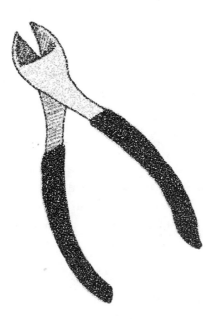

4. When the Corporate Shield Can't Protect You

Your corporation or LLC cannot always protect your personal assets. For example, you won't be shielded if:

- You are negligent (that is, you're careless in a way that's unreasonable).

    Example: Phil, carrying a large case of pottery, runs to catch the departing UPS driver. He trips and drops the pottery on Francis, injuring her foot. Even if Phil's business operates as an LLC, he can be held personally liable for Francis's injury.

- You sign a guarantee promising to be liable for a debt. For example, a bank lends money to your LLC but demands that you personally guarantee the loan.

    Example: Sarita's fabric business operates as a corporation. The business borrows $80,000 from a bank to cover the cost of supplies for a large order. The bank requires that Sarita and her husband personally guarantee the loan. Operating as a corporation offers little help from this liability.

B. How Your Business Will Be Taxed

Okay, now that you've analyzed business forms from a liability perspective, let's look at another money issue: how these various business forms are taxed. In fact, one of the reasons Valerie Stainton chose the LLC business form was because of its tax benefits. "[With the LLC], you avoid double taxation," says Valerie.

Valerie had compared the corporation and the LLC. She discovered that both limited her personal liability, but that with the corporate business form, her business income would have been taxed twice—once when the corporation filed its income tax form and a second time when the shareholders filed their individual tax returns. We'll see that the LLC is a more flexible tax entity. We'll also see that double-taxation is not necessarily as bad as it sounds.

Below, I summarize the tax attributes of each business form. More detailed information regarding taxation of your crafts business is provided in Chapter 12. However, it's best to seek advice from your accountant or tax preparer before making a final decision.

Flow-Through and Entity Taxation, Defined

We use two common tax terms in this article—flow-through (or pass-through) taxation and entity taxation (which is related to double taxation).

Flow through occurs when your business profits and losses are reported on your individual tax return—that is, they pass through the business to you. Sole proprietorships, partnerships and, in most cases, LLCs operate as flow-through businesses.

Entity taxation occurs when the IRS considers your business as a separate tax-paying creature. (Corporations and some LLCs operate this way.) Under an entity taxation business form, the corporation or LLC must pay taxes and file a tax return.

A great source of information regarding business taxation is *Tax Savvy for Small Business*, by Frederick W. Daily (Nolo).

1. Sole Proprietorships' Tax Obligations

If you own your business (or if you and your spouse own it) and you haven't formed an LLC or corporation, you're classified by the IRS as a sole proprietorship. Here's a brief summary of the applicable tax rules:

- You must report your business income or loss on a Schedule C, filed with your individual or joint tax return.

- You must pay quarterly estimated income taxes, as well as self-employment tax for Social Security and Medicare contributions.
- You are eligible for tax-sheltered retirement plans.

2. Partnerships' Tax Obligations

If two or more people own a crafts business—and they haven't formed an LLC or corporation—the business is classified as a partnership by the IRS. Below are the most important partnership tax rules:

- Partnerships, though not taxed separately, must prepare and file a Form 1065, usually filed on April 15.
- The partnership must issue a K-1 form showing each partner's share of the income or loss. The K-1 is filed with each partner's individual return.
- Each partner must pay a tax based on his or her "distributive share," not on what the partner may have actually received. Unless a partnership agreement says otherwise, all partners are presumed to have an equal distributive share in the partnership.
- Even if the partnership leaves profits in the business, the partners must pay taxes on those profits. (If your partnership is able to retain profits each year, consider forming a corporation.)
- Partners must pay quarterly estimated income taxes, as well as self-employment tax for Social Security and Medicare contributions.

3. LLCs' Tax Obligations

The LLC—which has become wildly popular among small business owners—offers flexible tax choices:

- The owners of an LLC can choose either pass-through or entity taxation. (Most choose pass-through.) Your tax advisor can help you make that decision.
- If the owners choose pass-through taxation, the LLC operates like a general partnership and prepares and files a Form 1065. The LLC must

also issue its members K-1 forms to be included with their individual returns.

- If the LLC has only one owner (and pass-through taxation has been chosen), the owner operates like a sole proprietorship and files a Schedule C to report the LLC's income.
- Although no federal tax is paid for a pass-through LLC, some states, such as California, impose taxes on LLCs.

4. Corporations' Tax Obligations

Corporations—known as C corporations because they operate under Subchapter C of the IRS code—have more tax reporting responsibilities than any other business form. So, get ready for paperwork. Here's a brief summary:

- Since corporations are separate tax entities, the owners must prepare a tax return for the corporation and pay corporate taxes, if any are owed.
- If you're an employee of the corporation or receive income from the corporation, you must report that on your individual tax return.

You can avoid the burden of double taxation through legal accounting methods. For example, you could pay higher salaries to shareholders, thereby reducing profits. Or, you could reinvest the business's profits. An accountant can assist you in legally avoiding corporate income taxes.

There are some advantages to being not only an owner, but an employee of a corporation. Health benefits are 100% deductible by the business. (Not so with a sole proprietorship, in which instance less than 70% of the health premiums can be deducted.). Another benefit to forming a C corporation is that its retained profits are taxed at a lower rate than those of other business forms. In other words, a C corporation may be the best choice if your business annually retains substantial income.

Choices for Smaller Businesses: S Corporation vs. LLC Status

Any C corporation with fewer than 75 owners can elect to change its tax status to an S corporation. This effectively allows the owners to claim the tax benefits available to partnerships—that is, the company goes from entity taxation to pass-through status. You get the limited liability advantages of a corporation and the tax advantages of a partnership.

But wait, isn't that what an LLC is supposed to provide? Yes, and compared to S corporations, LLCs do it better and with less formality.

For example, a one-person S corporation must file a federal and state corporate tax return. A one-person LLC only files a Schedule C with the individual return. (An LLC with more than one person can file a fairly simple partnership Form 1065.) Similarly, an S corporation—like a C corporation—must file and pay employment taxes on its employees. In addition, the S corporation has none of the "retained income" advantages of a C corporation. All in all—and your accountant can provide further advice—it makes sense to choose an LLC over an S corporation.

C. Forming Your Business

The final factor that may affect your choice of business structure is how hard it is to create that type of business. For example, creating and maintaining a corporation requires some diligence and paperwork. However, creating a sole proprietorship is easy; just sell some crafts and you've done it.

You can create each type of business without the help of an attorney. (Nolo (www.nolo.com), the publisher of this book, offers books on forming partnerships, corporations, nonprofits and LLCs.) However, even if you decide to use an attorney's services, continue reading this section so as to inform yourself on what you're getting into.

Also read this section if you already operate a crafts business and want to change its structure. If, for example, you want to convert a sole proprietorship to an LLC, the rules are generally the same as if you were starting from scratch. The exception is that you'll need to formally transfer the assets of the old business to the new one, and you may have to modify your tax reporting information. Again, you can accomplish these tasks on your own. But if you prefer crafting to filling out legal and tax forms, then leave these tasks to a professional.

1. Required Paperwork for All New Businesses ...

If you're starting a new business from scratch, you'll have to take care of some paperwork no matter what business form you choose. Many businesses will need to obtain one or more of the following:

- **EIN.** An Employer Identification Number (EIN) is required for partnerships, LLCs and corporations. (If you're a sole proprietor without employees, you can use your Social Security number.) To obtain an EIN, complete IRS Form SS-4 (download it from the IRS website at www.irs.gov).
- **DBA.** If you're doing business under an assumed name, most local governments require that you file a DBA ("doing business as") statement. You can find out the details from the county clerk at your local courthouse. If you're doing business under your own name (that is, your last name—for example *Wellhausen's Welding Studio*), you won't need to file. If, however, you're using only your first name in your business name—for example, *Valerie's Gallery*—you will have to file a DBA. (For more information on business names, read Chapter 6.)
- **Local Permits.** In addition to filing a DBA, your local or state government may have other permit or licensing requirements. You can usually find out those details at your county clerk's office.

There's competition for business names. Registering your business name as a DBA with your county clerk or filing incorporation papers does not guarantee your right to use your name in business or to use that name to identify your products. Before choosing a name for your crafts business, review the rules regarding trade names and trademarks in Chapter 6.

2. How to Create a Sole Proprietorship

Eighty percent of the businesses in the United States are sole proprietorships. It's easy to see why they're so popular. Forming one is effortless. All you have to do is sell (or diligently make an attempt to sell) your crafts. If you're running your business by yourself—that is, without anyone sharing the expenses and profits—you've already created a sole proprietorship.

3. How to Create a Partnership

Like a sole proprietorship, you don't have to do anything other than sell your crafts—together with one or more other people—to create a partnership. No written agreement is required among the partners—although a written agreement is strongly recommended. One reason for an agreement is to establish each partner's share of the income; another is to guarantee the continued existence of the partnership in the event one partner leaves or dies. Without an agreement, the departure of a partner ends the partnership. Below is a sample partnership agreement.

You'll also find copies of the Partnership Agreement in Appendix B and on the CD-ROM at the back of this book.

a. Completing the Partnership Agreement

The explanation below will help you when you and your partners sit down to think through and complete the partnership agreement.

- **Partners.** Insert the names of all partners.

Partnership Agreement

Partners. _____
(the "Partners"), agree to the following terms and conditions.

Partnership Name. The Partners will do business as a partnership under the name of _____
_____ .

Partnership Duration. The partnership _[choose one]_ ☐ began ☐ will begin   on _____ .
It will continue:

   [Choose one]

   ☐ indefinitely until it is ended by the terms of this agreement.

   ☐ until _____ , unless ended sooner by the terms of this agreement.

Partnership Office. The main office of the partnership will be at _____
_____ . The mailing address will be:

   [Choose one]

   ☐ the above address.

   ☐ the following address: _____
_____ .

Partnership Purpose. The primary purpose of the partnership is_____
_____ .

Capital Contributions. The Partners will contribute the following capital to the partnership on or before
_____ .

   A. Cash Contributions

Partner's Name	Amount
_____	$ _____
_____	$ _____
_____	$ _____
_____	$ _____

   B. Noncash Contributions

Partner's Name	Description of Property	Value
_____	_____	$ _____
_____	_____	$ _____
_____	_____	$ _____
_____	_____	$ _____

Capital Accounts. The partnership will maintain a capital account for each Partner. The account will consist of the Partner's capital contribution plus the Partner's share of profits less the Partner's share of losses and distributions to the Partner. A Partner may not remove capital from his or her account without the written consent of all Partners.

Profits and Losses.

A. The net profits and losses of the partnership will be credited to or charged against the Partners' capital accounts:

[Choose one]

☐ in the same proportions as their capital contributions.

☐ as follows: _____

_____

_____ .

B. The partnership will only make distributions to the Partners if all the Partners agree.

Salaries. No Partner will receive a salary for services to the partnership.

Interest. No interest will be paid on a Partner's capital account.

Management. Each Partner will have an equal say in managing the partnership.

[Choose one]

☐ All significant partnership decisions will require the agreement of all the Partners.

☐ Routine partnership decisions will require the agreement of a majority of the Partners. The following partnership actions will require the agreement of all the Partners:

☐ borrowing or lending money

☐ signing a lease

☐ signing a contract to buy or sell real estate

☐ signing a security agreement or mortgage

☐ selling partnership assets except for goods sold in the regular course of business

☐ other: _____

Partnership Funds. Partnership funds will be kept in an account at _____

_____ , unless all Partners agree to another financial institution.

Partnership checks:

[Choose one]

☐ may be signed by any Partner.

☐ must be signed by all the Partners.

☐ must be signed by _____ Partners.

Agreement to End Partnership. The Partners may unanimously agree to end the partnership.

Partner's Withdrawal.

[Choose one]

☐ The partnership will end if a Partner withdraws by giving written notice of such withdrawal to each of the other Partners.

☐ Upon the withdrawal of a Partner, the other Partners will, within 30 days, decide either to end the partnership or to buy out the withdrawing Partner's interest and continue the partnership. A decision to buy out the withdrawing Partner's interest and continue the partnership requires the unanimous consent of the remaining Partners.

Partner's Death.

[Choose one]

☐ The partnership will end if a Partner dies.

☐ Upon the death of a partner, the other Partners will, within 30 days, decide either to end the partnership or to buy out the deceased Partner's interest and continue the partnership. A decision to buy out the withdrawing Partner's interest and continue the partnership requires the unanimous consent of the remaining Partners.

Buyout. If the remaining Partners decide to buy the interest of a withdrawing or deceased Partner, the remaining Partners, within _____ days after that Partner's withdrawal or death, will pay the withdrawing Partner or the deceased Partner's estate:

[Choose one]

☐ the amount in the capital account of the withdrawing or deceased Partner as of the date of withdrawal or death.

☐ the fair market value of the interest of the withdrawing or deceased Partner as determined by the partnership's accountant.

☐ other: _____.

General Provisions.

Entire Agreement. This is the entire agreement between the parties. It replaces and supersedes any and all oral agreements between the parties, as well as any prior writings. Modifications and amendments to this agreement, including any exhibit or appendix, shall be enforceable only if they are in writing and are signed by authorized representatives of both parties.

Successors and Assignees. This agreement binds and benefits the heirs, successors and assignees of the parties.

Notices. Any notice or communication required or permitted to be given under this agreement shall be sufficiently given when received by certified mail, or sent by facsimile transmission or overnight courier.

Governing Law. This agreement will be governed by the laws of the State of _____.

Waiver. If one party waives any term or provision of this agreement at any time, that waiver will only be effective for the specific instance and specific purpose for which the waiver was given. If either party fails to exercise or delays exercising any of its rights or remedies under this agreement, that party retains the right to enforce that term or provision at a later time.

Severability. If a court finds any provision of this agreement invalid or unenforceable, the remainder of this agreement will be interpreted so as best to carry out the parties' intent.

Attachments and Exhibits. The parties agree and acknowledge that all attachments, exhibits and schedules referred to in this agreement are incorporated in this agreement by reference.

[Optional]

☐ **Arbitration.** Any controversy or claim arising out of or relating to this agreement shall be settled by arbitration in _____ *[county]*, _____ *[state]*, in accordance with the rules of the American Arbitration Association, and judgment upon the award rendered by the arbitrator(s) may be entered in any court having jurisdiction. The prevailing party shall have the right to collect from the other party its reasonable costs and attorney's fees incurred in enforcing this agreement.

Date signed: _____

By: _____

Printed Name: _____

Address: _____

_____

By: _____

Printed Name: _____

Address: _____

_____

By: _____

Printed Name: _____

Address: _____

_____

By: _____

Printed Name: _____

Address: _____

_____

Partnership Agreement (Page 4)

- **Partnership Name.** Insert the name of the partnership. If you're going to use a business name for your partnership that's different from the names of the partners—for example, Miraculous Windchimes instead of Furry, Brown and Nemir—it's wise to conduct at least a local name search to see whether some other business is already using the name. For more information on choosing a name, see Chapter 6.

- **Partnership Duration.** Insert the date the partnership began or is to begin. Then check one of the boxes to indicate when the partnership will end. If you check the second box, insert a date for the end of the partnership—for example, "June, 2005."

- **Partnership Office.** Insert the address where partnership records will be kept. Usually this will be the partnership's main business location. If the partnership's mailing address is the same as the partnership office, check the first box. If you have a separate mailing address—a post office box, for example—check the second box and fill in the mailing address.

- **Partnership Purpose.** Insert the purpose of the partnership—for example, to manufacture and distribute handmade crafts and to operate one or more retail stores for the sale of crafts.

- **Capital Contributions.** Insert the date when the partners are to contribute their start-up capital—the funds or property given to the partnership to enable it to begin operations.
  - A. If partners will be contributing cash, fill in their names and the amount each will contribute.
  - B. If partners will contribute property, insert the partners' names. Then describe the property and what value it will be given on the partnership's books.

- **Capital Accounts.** You don't need to insert anything here. A capital account is a bookkeeping technique for keeping track of how much of the partnership assets each partner owns. Your capital account starts out with the amount you invest in the partnership. To that figure, you

add your share of the profits and deduct your share of the losses. If you're getting bogged down on these calculations, consult an accountant.

- **Profits and Losses.**
  - A. Check the first box if you want the partners' shares of profits and losses to be proportionate to the capital they put into the partnership. Here are two examples of the results of making this choice.

    Example 1: Three partners put in the same amount of capital: $10,000 each. All profits will be added equally to each partner's capital account (in other words, a $15,000 profit would result in a $5,000 addition to each partner's account), and losses will be equally subtracted.

    Example 2: One partner puts in $20,000 and two partners put in $10,000 each. The profits and assets will be allocated 50%/25%/25%. (Therefore, a $15,000 profit would result in additions of $7,500 to one partner's account and $3,750 to the other two partners' accounts.)

    Check the second box and insert a different formula if you don't want profits to be divided according to capital contributed. For example, if you agree that one partner will be spending more time than the others working on the partnership business, you may decide to allocate proportionately more profits to that partner.

    Example: Since Linda Smith will be handling bookkeeping duties for the partnership in addition to her other partnership duties, she and her two partners decide that 40% of the net profits should be credited to her capital account and 30% of the net profits should be credited to the capital account of each of the other two. Net losses, however, will be charged equally against the partners' capital accounts.

Of course, this isn't the only way to recognize the contribution of a partner who's doing extra work. You could, for example, agree to pay this partner a salary for keeping the books, making it fair to simply allocate profits in proportion to contributions.

- **Salaries.** You don't need to insert anything here unless you want to. Generally, a partner's reward for doing work for the partnership is a share of the partnership profits. But as suggested in the instructions, there's no legal or tax reason why the partners can't agree to hire one or more partners as employees who will receive a salary for their services. If you decide to follow such an arrangement, spell out the details in the partnership agreement.

- **Interest.** You don't need to insert anything here. Again, the benefit a partner receives from investing money in a partnership is a share of partnership profits. If you agree that a partner is to receive interest, it's better to have the partner lend money to the partnership. Document the loan by creating a promissory note.

- **Management.** Approach this section—describing how management decisions are made—with a healthy dose of skepticism. The reality is that for a small partnership to succeed, the partners need to have both shared goals and confidence in one another's judgment. If those elements don't exist, pages of rules detailing how decisions should be made won't help. Or, put more bluntly, if you don't trust your partners and enjoy working with them, don't bother creating a partnership in the first place.

It's difficult to define how day-to-day decisions will or should be made in a partnership. Certainly, when it comes to making important decisions, talking the matter over with all the partners and respecting each other's opinions is wise. But unanimity on everything may be as unnecessary as it is hard to achieve—making it impractical to select the first option in this paragraph (agreement of all partners on all partnership decisions).

Checking the second box—requiring a majority vote on routine decisions—allows you more flexibility. Unanimity is only required on the major business decisions specified.

- **Partnership Funds.** Insert the name of the financial institution where you'll keep the partnership funds.

Then check a box to indicate who will be permitted to sign partnership checks. If you check the last box, insert the number of partners who must sign a single check. In a three-person partnership, for example, you may want to require that all checks be signed by two partners.

The financial institution where you keep the partnership account will also have a form for you to fill out to indicate who has signing authority.

- **Agreement to End Partnership.** You don't need to insert anything here. This paragraph makes it clear that the partnership can be ended if all the partners agree.

- **Partner's Withdrawal.** This section deals with what happens if one of the partners wants to leave the partnership. It raises two major legal points for you to think about: First, unless your partnership has a written agreement stating otherwise, the law says your partnership will end if any partner decides to leave. Second, if your partnership has no agreement to the contrary, a partner isn't free to transfer his or her partnership interest to someone else. In short, unless you agree in writing to a different plan, if one partner leaves, the partnership assets will be liquidated, bills will be paid and the partners will be cashed out. Check the first box if this scenario is what you want.

Check the second box if you want to give the remaining partners the chance to keep the partnership alive by buying out the interest of the withdrawing partner. Technically, this means the remaining partners will create a new partnership, but the business will continue as if there had been no change.

- **Partner's Death.** As with a partner's withdrawal, a partner's death will end the partnership unless you agree to another outcome. Check the first box if you want the partnership to end automatically after a death. Once the partnership assets have been liquidated, the dead partner's share of the assets will be paid to that partner's estate.

  Check the second box if you and the remaining partners will want the chance to keep the partnership alive by buying out the interest of the deceased partner. (Technically, the remaining partners will then have a new partnership.)

- **Buyout.** Complete this optional paragraph only if you've provided for a buyout of a withdrawing partner's interest (paragraph 14) or of a deceased partner's interest (paragraph 15). Check one of the first two boxes if it contains an acceptable formula for fixing the buyout price. If not, check the third box and fill in your chosen method of setting the buyout amount.

  If you haven't provided for a buyout in paragraph 14 or 15, either cross out this paragraph (in which case, all partners should initial the deletion) or insert the words, "Not Applicable." (Or, assuming you're doing this on a computer, you can just delete the paragraph and renumber the paragraphs that follow.)

- **Standard Clauses.** The remainder of the agreement contains the standard clauses I discuss in Chapter 11. The only thing you'll need to fill in here is the name of the state whose law will apply to the contract, in the paragraph called "Governing Law."

- **Date and Signatures.** Fill in the date the agreement is signed. Each of the partners must sign his or her name. Their respective names and addresses should be typed in.

4. How to Create a Corporation

Each state's incorporation laws may differ. Therefore, providing detailed instructions for incorporating in your state is beyond the scope of this book. However, here are the basic rules followed in most or all states.

One person, or many, can incorporate a business. The process starts when an incorporator—any of the owners—prepares and files articles of incorporation with the state's corporate filing office, usually the Secretary of State. Bylaws, rules that establish the voting, directors, equity and other rules, must be prepared (but not filed).

Once the state certifies the articles of incorporation, the corporation's board of directors is chosen, the bylaws are adopted and stock is issued to the owners (one person can own 100% of the stock). The directors manage the business and choose officers who manage the day-to-day operations.

All of this may sound frightfully complex, but rest assured, you can accomplish these tasks by yourself if you wish—the process has been simplified by various books, websites and incorporating services (check at www.nolo.com).

5. How to Create a Limited Liability Company

You can form an LLC with just one member in every state except Massachusetts (which requires at least two members). Like a corporation, creating an LLC requires formal filing procedures, and the rules differ from state to state. Again, I can only provide some basics.

Creating an LLC requires filing a document, called articles or certificate of organization, with the state's corporate filing office, usually the Secretary of State. The owners (known as members) can manage the business or designate others to do so. In general, there is far less formality to maintaining an LLC than a corporation.

Business Forms: Pros and Cons

The table below summarizes the advantages and disadvantages of each business form.

Business Form	Description	Advantages	Disadvantages	Type of crafts business
Sole Proprietorship	One person runs the business.	Easy to create and operate. Owner reports profits and losses on individual tax return.	Owner is personally liable for business debts and liabilities.	Suitable for most one-person crafts businesses whose exposure to liability is limited.
Partnership	Partners contribute money and/or time to the business and share in profits and losses.	Easy to create and operate. Partners report profits and losses on individual tax return.	Partners are all personally liable for business debts.	Suitable for small crafts ventures with two or more people and limited exposure to liability.
C Corporation	Owners (shareholders) receive shares in the business, and payments are based on share of ownership. Officers run the day-to-day business.	Owners have limited personal liability for business debts and the potential for a lower overall tax rate.	More expensive to create and operate than partnership or sole proprietorship. Requires filing separate corporate tax return.	Recommended for large businesses, particularly those with many (over ten) employees or considerable retail sales activity.
Limited Liability Company (LLC)	A hybrid, in which member-owners enjoy benefits of corporate and partnership rules.	Owners (members) have limited personal liability for business debts.	More expensive to create and operate than a partnership or sole proprietorship. Requires strict compliance with IRS rules.	Recommended for small crafts businesses with one or more owners, moderate retail activity and not many employees.

Adapted from *Legal Guide for Starting and Running a Small Business*, by Fred S. Steingold (Nolo).

Honey, I Incorporated the Kids: Family-Owned Businesses

If you're one of the many family-owned crafts businesses, you may wonder how your family fits into the world of business forms. Here are some things to consider.

A husband and wife can operate a business as a sole proprietorship. In other words, they report the business income on their joint return using a Schedule C. The spouses can also operate as a partnership. However, if the couple plans to file a joint return anyway, there are no tax advantages to operating as a partnership. If spouses file separate returns, there may be tax advantages. Check with your accountant or tax preparer.

If family members other than a husband and wife are owners, the business has no choice but to operate as a partnership, corporation or LLC. One of the advantages of the corporate business form is that the family can provide and fully deduct employee health benefits.

D. The Cooperative

By 1844, the Industrial Revolution and its mechanized looms had devastated the British weaving trade. Weavers in Rochdale, England worked 16-hour days for less than the modern equivalent of $1.25 a week. Unable to petition the government or organize labor unions or strikes, these crafts workers tried a radical experiment—creating a store to sell food and supplies. Unlike a traditional business that earned profits for investors, the Rochdale co-op was democratically owned and controlled. Its members—not outside investors—acquired benefits. The Rochdale experiment was a success, and the three principles it popularized became the tenets of modern cooperative business:

- **The user-owner principle.** Members own the business and provide the necessary financing.
- **The user-control principle.** Members control the business democratically, elect the board of directors and approve changes in the business's structure and operation.
- **The user-benefit principle.** Members receive benefits—money, discounts or goods—based on their contributions to the business.

American crafts workers, like their predecessors in Rochdale, often utilize the cooperative system to market their work, share studio space and expensive equipment and save money when making bulk purchases.

1. Every Cooperative Needs a Business Form

The cooperative is a great way for crafts workers to participate together in a business. Unfortunately, the cooperative structure is not a distinct legal business form like the partnership, corporation or LLC. In other words, it's not enough to band together and call your business a cooperative. Cooperative members must also adopt a traditional business form such as a partnership or corporation, and legal help may be needed during the organizing and formation stages.

Many cooperatives operate informally as partnerships without filing or preparing any written agreements. Some adopt a formal partnership agreement. Some cooperatives operate as corporations (either for-profit or nonprofit, depending on state law) or as LLCs.

State laws often permit (or require) incorporation in order to claim cooperative benefits. For example, in New Mexico five or more natural persons or two or more associations may incorporate as a cooperative association for any legal purpose to buy, sell or produce goods or services.

It may seem odd to form a corporation or LLC when the underlying principles of corporations and cooperatives differ dramatically. But the union of these strange bedfellows is beneficial for cooperatives, because under corporation laws, the directors, managers and members are generally shielded from personal liability for business debts. The same is not true in a partnership, where any partner may be individually liable for debts or liabilities of the partnership.

Just as with any incorporation, the cooperative must file articles of incorporation with the state government and must prepare bylaws (establishing voting, equity, refunds and retained capital for each member or "patron"). Again, each state's laws may differ.

2. Decision-Making Practices

Whether a co-op chooses to be a partnership, corporation or LLC, it typically opts for voting rights based on the Rochdale rule: one member, one vote. A small percentage of crafts co-ops make decisions based on a consensus (unanimity) of members.

The cooperative's voting system may establish rules for resolving conflicts, but sorting out disputes often depends more on the personalities than the paperwork. Earthworks Cooperative in Berkeley, California provides a good example. Founded 30 years ago, the members pool resources for rent, shows and heavy equipment. "There are occasional squabbles," says potter Jiri Minarik, "but that's inevitable whenever people work together." For most of its history, Earthworks relied on consensus in its decision-making, but two years ago it switched to a three-quarters majority. "So far we haven't had to use [the three-quarters majority]," points out Minarik.

An attorney (or accountant) may be needed for advice on other cooperative formation issues such as acquiring property, capitalizing the co-op (that is, getting money to start the business) and writing contracts with suppliers and members (see below). A co-op may also benefit by retaining an attorney's services to ensure continuing compliance with state laws.

Once the initial formalities are completed, the directors of the co-op, elected by the members, must chart a course of action. Even though co-ops are not run for profit in the traditional sense, some states require that they file as regular corporations; others require that they file as nonprofit corporations. Whatever money or assets the co-op accumulates (after its expenses and obligations have been paid) will ultimately be returned or distributed (as "patron-age dividends") to members in proportion to the amount of work transacted by that member. For example, if you worked more days managing the store or more of your glasswork was sold at the co-op outlet, that might translate into a larger dividend.

Cooperatives receive an exemption under federal tax law, by excluding from their gross income any patronage dividend payments made to members. That's great for the co-op, but individual members must pay taxes on this income when preparing their individual income tax returns.

3. A Standard Membership Agreement

Although it's not mandatory, it's strongly recommended that each cooperative have a membership agreement—a document that is distinct from other business form documentation such as your articles of incorporation. This document establishes the legal relationship between the co-op and the member.

Under the agreement, the potential member:

- agrees to be bound by the co-op's rules
- appoints the co-op as its agent to sell crafts
- agrees to deliver products, and
- agrees to provide capital as required by the by-laws.

In return, the co-op:

- agrees to act as the agent for marketing the products, and
- agrees to account to the member in accordance with the co-op rules.

A lawyer should create or review the cooperative's standard membership agreement (sometimes referred to as a membership application). Most member agreements also describe what happens when members break the agreement. Often an agreed-upon payment (known as liquidated damages) must be paid for a breach. Courts have generally upheld these payments unless they don't accurately reflect the damage suffered by the co-op.

Membership agreements are usually open-ended in how long they last. Some extend for a year or two, after which either party can cancel by giving notice. In some states, the membership contract must be filed at the local county recorder's office.

Starting a co-op is a great way for craft artists to keep control of the selling of their work, but the legalities can be complicated.

While I recommend that you obtain legal and financial assistance from professionals when creating a cooperative, many online sources can also help you get started. See, for example:

- the National Cooperative Business Association (www.ncba.org)
- Cooperative Solutions (www.co-opbuilders.com)
- the Center for Cooperatives at UC Davis (http://cooperatives.ucdavis.edu; the University of California Davis website), and
- the University of Wisconsin Center for Co-ops (www.wisc.edu/uwcc).

Should You Form a Nonprofit?

Any business created to benefit the public can be classified as a nonprofit corporation. The business can earn a profit, but the primary purpose has to be beneficial, like offering educational or charitable assistance. Most nonprofits incorporate because they thereby gain significant tax benefits. This book is aimed at for-profit crafts businesses, but if you'd like more information, review *How to Form a Nonprofit Corporation* (National Edition), by Anthony Mancuso (Nolo).

Chapter

2

Your Workspace

*J*eweler and fine artist Susan Brooks (www. susanbrooks.com) knows something about crafts studios. She grew up in one, among a family of artisans. As an adult, she operated her first studio in her home, then later leased workspaces in the Bay Area. She has firsthand knowledge of other artist's studios as well, having directed the Berkeley Artisans Holiday Open Studios program (www. berkeleyartisans.com) since 1991. And like many crafts artists, she's familiar with commercial lease agreements—and has "heard every [lease] horror story in the book."

Brooks's number one suggestion for a crafts artist leasing a workspace is to find a studio that's in a building with other crafts artists. "You'll find that quite often you need the cooperation or assistance of other artists. That's very important. For example, if you want to do an open house or participate in an open studio event, the more artists in the building, the more success you are likely to have."

"And," adds Brooks, "remember that leasing space in an 'artist' building doesn't necessarily mean you will be working amongst other crafts artists. The 'Use' provision of the building lease may say 'Artists Only,' but that can also mean graphic artists, Web designers and, in some cases, architects or even engineers. These people may make good neighbors, but for purposes of selling your work or sharing ideas, you'll be better off working amongst other artisans. So check out the tenants before committing to an artist building."

Should you take a short-term or long-term lease? Brooks suggests trusting your intuition. "Do what you think is right. I've always wanted long-term leases, but in one instance I was glad I had a short-term lease because I was able to leave."

Brooks also suggests checking out the landlord. "You don't need for them to be your friend. You're in a business relationship. You just want to make sure you can do honest business with the landlord or the management company. Find out what people are saying about the landlord and their experience in the building. Is the landlord concerned about safety, etc.? Talk to tenants in the building. In some cities, you can go to the Planning Commission and learn about problems with landlords."

What about operating a home studio? "I did it for many years," says Brooks. "The only problem was that I didn't know when to stop working. And, of course, you have to be careful that your home studio creates a professional atmosphere. It shouldn't smell like dinner."

No doubt about it, establishing your studio is often one of the most difficult activities of establishing a crafts business. Home studios may run afoul of neighbors and zoning restrictions. Leases may require enormous financial commitments and produce anxiety over keeping up on the rent. In this chapter I discuss workspace issues, including:

- establishing a studio in your home (see Section A)
- finding a studio to lease, with a reasonable rent, security deposit, level of needed improvements and length of lease (see Section B)
- evaluating the essential elements of a lease agreement (see Section C)
- agreeing on the rent in a commercial lease (see Section D), and
- learning to maintain safety in your workspace (see Section E).

Most of the information in this chapter is derived from *Leasing Space for Your Small Business,* by attorneys Fred Steingold & Janet Portman (Nolo). If you want to save money on attorney fees I suggest reading this plain-English explanation of negotiating strategies and legal rules regarding commercial leasing.

A. Working From Home

There are many tempting reasons to operate your crafts business out of your home. It's convenient and economical—no studio rent, a potential home office tax deduction and, best of all, no commuting. As long as your business is small, quiet and doesn't create traffic or parking problems or violate local zoning rules, operating in your home is usually legal. But before setting up a home studio, review the laws that restrict a person's right to operate a business from home.

1. Zoning Laws

Municipalities have the legal right to establish rules about what types of activities can be carried out in different geographical areas. For example, they often establish zones for stores and offices (commercial zones), factories (industrial zones) and houses (residential zones). In some residential areas—especially in affluent communities—local zoning ordinances absolutely prohibit all types of business. In the great majority of municipalities, however, residential zoning rules allow small nonpolluting home businesses, as long as any home containing a business is used primarily as a residence and the business activities don't negatively affect neighbors.

To determine the zoning rules that apply to your home, get a copy of your local ordinance from your city or county clerk's office, the city attorney's office or your public library. Read it carefully; zoning ordinances are worded in different ways to limit business activities in residential areas. Some are extremely vague, allowing "customary home-based occupations." Others allow homeowners to use their houses for a broad—but, unfortunately, not very specific—list of business purposes (for example, "professions and domestic occupations, crafts or services"). Still others contain a detailed list of approved occupations, such as "law, dentistry, medicine, music lessons, photography, cabinet making." If you read your ordinance and still aren't sure whether your business is okay, you may be inclined to ask zoning or planning officials for the last word. But until you figure out what the rules and politics of your locality are, it may be best to do this without identifying and calling attention to yourself.

In most areas, zoning and building officials don't actively search for violations. Hundreds of thousands of home-based businesses exist in violation of zoning laws but go undetected by local officials. The majority of home-based businesses that run into trouble do so when a neighbor complains—often because of noise or parking problems, or even because of an unfounded fear that the business is doing something illegal—for example, a neighbor smells chemical solvents or soldering and thinks illegal drugs are being manufactured. Your best approach is to explain your business activities to your neighbors and make sure that your activities are not worrying or inconveniencing them.

Many ordinances, especially those that are fairly vague as to the type of business you can run from your home, also restrict how you can carry out your business. The most frequent rules limit your use of on-street parking, prohibit outside signs, limit car and truck traffic and restrict the number of employees who can work at your house on a regular basis (some prohibit employees altogether). In addition, some zoning ordinances limit the percentage of your home's floor space that can be devoted to the business. Again, you'll need to study your local ordinance carefully to see how these rules will affect you.

2. Contractual Limitations

Your legal right to set up a home studio may be affected by your property and lease agreements. If you rent your home or apartment, your written lease (if you have one), may prohibit you from using the premises for business purposes. Your only means of resolving this is for you and your landlord to amend the lease.

If you live in a subdivision, condo or planned unit development that required you to agree to special rules when you moved in—typically called Covenants, Conditions and Restrictions (CC&Rs)—these will govern aspects of property use. CC&Rs pertaining to home-based businesses are often significantly stricter than those found in city ordinances.

Keep the noise down. One of the most common triggers for neighbor complaints is noise. Frequent use of your band saw will likely result in zoning investigations and may violate local municipal noise ordinances. Before operating noisy machinery, check your local noise ordinance at your local library. For information on noise ordinance violations throughout the nation, check out the Noise Pollution Clearinghouse (www.nonoise.org).

You might not have to take no for an answer. In many cities and counties, if a planning or zoning board rejects your business, you can appeal—usually to the city council or county board of supervisors. This can be an uphill battle, but it is likely to be less so if you have the support of all affected neighbors. In some communities, people are working to amend ordinances that have home-based business prohibitions to permit those that are unobtrusive. For more information on home-based businesses and zoning, consult Entrepreneuer.com (www.entrepreneur.com; click "Home Biz" on the home page).

3. Insuring Your Home Studio/Office

Don't rely on your homeowner's or renter's insurance policy to cover your home-based crafts business. These policies often exclude or strictly limit coverage for business equipment and injuries to business visitors. For example, if your inventory is stolen, your home studio is destroyed in a fire or a client trips and falls on your steps, you may not be covered. Fortunately, it's easy to avoid these nasty surprises. Sit down with your insurance agent and disclose your planned business operation. You'll find that it's relatively inexpensive to add business coverage to your home-owner's policy, and it's a tax-deductible expense. Some insurance companies provide special cost-effective policies designed to protect your home and home-based business.

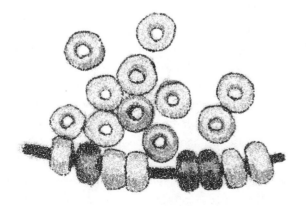

If you operate your business from home and qualify under IRS rules, you may be able to deduct part of your rent from your income taxes. If you own your home, you may be able to take a depreciation deduction. You may also be eligible to deduct a portion of your total utility, home repair and maintenance, property tax and house insurance costs, based on the percentage of your residence you use for business purposes. For information on claiming the home office deduction for your home studio, read Chapter 12, Section D.

For more home business information check out BizOffice (www.bizoffice.com), BusinessTown.com (www.businesstown.com), Home Office Association of America (www.hoaa.com) and Nolo's online resources (www.nolo.com).

It Gets Lonely ...

According to the 2001 survey of the Craft Organization Directors Association (CODA), 64% of crafts artists work alone in a studio, 18% work with a partner or family member and 16% work with paid employees.

B. Finding the Right Space at the Right Price

If your crafts sales won't rely on foot traffic—for example, you don't wish to operate a retail space—your best bet is to search out convenient, low-cost, utilitarian surroundings, preferably among other crafts artists. Even if people will visit your location, a low-cost, offbeat location may make more sense than a high-cost, trendy one. The basic concepts of leasing space for your studio are described in this section.

The major issues to consider first are the obvious ones. Figure out the maximum rent your business can afford to pay per month, determine what type of security deposit you can pay and consider how much money you can afford to spend to alter the space to fit your studio needs.

⚠ **Don't assume your landlord will tell you about zoning rules.** As with a home office, you'll need to be sure that there are no zoning laws that would prohibit you from using your leased space for your studio or retail use—usually, a simple matter of getting appropriate documentation from your landlord. *Never sign a lease without being absolutely sure you will be permitted to operate your business at that location.*

1. Rent

When you lease commercial space, calculating the monthly rent is more complicated than what you're used to when paying monthly rent for an apartment or house. That's because many landlords charge you not only for square footage, but also for other regular expenses such as real estate taxes, utilities and insurance. If you rent in a multitenant building, you're likely to be asked to pay your share of common area maintenance, too. If you rent the entire building, you may be asked to foot the entire bill for these costs. How to determine the cost of a rental space is explained in detail in Section D. For now, understand that your rent figure may need to be big enough to cover multiple, recurring expenses.

2. Deposits

Many commercial landlords require tenants to pay one or two months' rent up front as a security deposit. The landlord will dip into this deposit if the tenant fails to pay the rent or other sums required by the lease (such as insurance or maintenance costs). The amount of the deposit for commercial rentals is not regulated by law, but is instead a matter of negotiation. Landlords tend to demand high deposits from new or otherwise unproven businesses—which are often the least able to produce a large chunk of cash.

3. Improvements and Expenses

Security deposits aren't the only up-front costs that tenants may face during the first few months in a new location. Unless you are fortunate enough to find space that was previously owned by a crafts

person in the same field as yourself, you'll need to modify the space to fit your needs and tastes. These modifications are known as "improvements."

There are several ways that landlords and tenants can allocate the cost of improvements. You might find a landlord willing to foot the entire bill. But for now, don't count on it. The tenant usually pays for this work. You'll need to determine what it would cost to make your space usable.

4. Length of the Lease

The "term" of your lease means its chronological life. Your lease could be as short as 30 days (in a "month to month" agreement), or run for one, five or ten years. As long as you satisfy the important conditions of the lease (such as paying rent and other costs), you have the right to remain in the space until the lease is terminated or expires. And unless the other terms of the lease provide otherwise, they, too, are guaranteed for the life of the lease. For example, your landlord's promises to provide on-site parking and janitorial services can't be ignored. You'll need to decide whether to pursue a short-term or long-term lease.

a. Short-Term Leases

Occasionally, a small business that's just starting out will do better with a lease permitting it to occupy the space for a limited period—either from month to month or for a short fixed term. This might seem attractive if you just want to test the waters, are feeling uncertain about your business's prospects for success or wouldn't mind leaving on short notice.

If you want the most flexibility, look for space that's offered on a month-to-month basis (month-to-month leases are also called "rental agreements"). A month-to-month rental is automatically renewed each month unless you or your landlord gives the other the proper amount of written notice to terminate the agreement. Under a month-to-month agreement, the landlord can raise the rent or change other terms with proper written notice. You can negotiate how much notice is required. If you don't address the issue in your rental agreement, the law in your state will dictate the amount of notice required. In most states, this is 30 days.

Another way to set up a short-term tenancy is to sign a lease for a short but fixed period of time—say, 90 days or six months. This type of lease terminates at the end of the time period you've established. Unlike a month-to-month tenancy, it's not automatically renewed. You and the landlord can, however, negotiate lease language specifying what happens at the end of the fixed period covered by the lease. You could provide, for example, that if you stay in the space beyond the stated period, your tenancy becomes a month-to-month tenancy. A fixed-term lease, even for a short term, gives you the assurance that the landlord can't boot you out on short notice. It also means, of course, that you're obligated to pay rent throughout the lease term, unless you can negotiate an escape clause that gives you the right to end the lease earlier.

b. Long-Term Leases

Many small businesses and landlords prefer the protection of a lease that lasts a year or more. There are many solid business reasons why both sides look for long-term commitment, such as:

- **Minimizing transaction costs.** It takes a lot of time (and money) to find and secure good rental space. It's better to minimize the number of times you go through these leasing courtships.
- **Minimizing improvement costs.** Chances are that you'll have to pay to alter your space to fit your studio needs. You may not want to do it again soon.
- **Locking in a good deal.** If the space is desirable, you may want to make sure that you'll have it for some years to come.

Of course, there are drawbacks to signing a multi-year lease. The most obvious is that you will, indeed, be legally obligated to lease this space for a considerable length of time. But keep in mind that even a long-term lease can be quite flexible if it lets both you and the landlord make adjustments depending on the success of your business or the overhead costs of the landlord. Likewise, you can turn a short lease into a long one by the use of an option to renew.

You'll get more in the way of improvements with a long-term lease. If you go for a short-term lease, the landlord probably won't do much to fix up the space—maybe just slap on a coat of fresh paint. Any other improvements will probably have to be done at your expense. With a longer lease, the landlord is much more likely to pay for substantial improvements, or at least pick up a good chunk of the tab.

5. Fresh Air, Amenities, Security and Comfort

In addition to the business terms, you'll need to evaluate elements of the property that are important to you personally and in the operation of your studio, such as:

- **Open windows.** Fresh air may be free but it's not always available in today's buildings. Many landlords feel that windows, ones that open and close, will compromise the efficiency of the building's heating, ventilating and air-conditioning system, known in the trade as HVAC. (And if the heater is blasting while the windows are wide open, you, too, will bear some of the cost, since tenants typically pay for a portion of the HVAC costs.) Still, there are buildings around that do contain operating windows, so if you highly value fresh air on demand, make this a priority.
- **Soundproofing.** Good sound insulation between rooms within your space and in the walls separating your space from that of adjacent tenants may be very important—especially if you're the one who will be making noise with machinery or tools.
- **Control of heating and cooling.** In some buildings, you have to take whatever the HVAC system happens to be pumping out. In others, you may have one or more thermostats within the space you lease. Individual control of your work climate will be a high priority if you or employees work on weekends or nights, when building-wide ventilation and heating controls are typically turned off.

- **Storage space.** Some buildings have extra storage space for tenants in a basement or other out-of-the-way area. If you need space for items that you use only occasionally, access to a separate storage area may be a priority. This can reduce clutter and free up your rental space for important uses.

- **Private restrooms.** Many buildings offer restrooms that are shared by several tenants. (This is a far cry better than no restrooms at all, as some artists have suffered.) However, if you're willing to pay a higher rent, it may be important to you to have restrooms within your leased space for the exclusive use of employees and customers.

- **Other tenants and services in and near the building.** As discussed at the opening of this chapter, there are many advantages to being in a building with other crafts tenants.

- **Parking.** If parking is a necessity for you, your landlord may impose an additional charge for on-site parking. You won't be guaranteed a specific number of spaces or spaces at a designated location unless the lease says so.

- **Security.** If you're concerned about security, check on the neighborhood. Your local police department is a good source of information on the safety of various areas in your town. Also check on the internal building security—flimsy locks on doors or windows are invitations to opportunists. Reasonable security steps may include adequate outside and inside lighting, strong locks, limited entry, alarm systems and even security guards.

Subleasing Space

Sometimes, the ideal space for your business may be within an area that someone else is renting. If you rent space directly from another tenant, you're subleasing from that tenant (and you're called the subtenant). Nevertheless, you must abide by the terms and conditions that the landlord has set up with the tenant.

You may be able to get a great deal as a subtenant. Tenants who are willing to share their space usually need to do so—their projected requirements for space didn't pan out as hoped, or their income is insufficient to cover the rent. As long as the tenant's own lease allows it, subleasing is one way to cut the overhead.

There are, however, downsides to being a subtenant. For one, you're dealing with someone who is not in the business of being a landlord and may not know or care about treating a tenant—that is, you—properly and legally. For instance, you may not find your "landlord" reacting as promptly and conscientiously as you might wish when it comes to requests for repairs.

If you are considering renting from another tenant, take the following protective measures first:

- Check to see if the landlord's consent is needed for subletting the space or assigning the lease. If it is, don't finalize your agreement with the tenant until the landlord has consented in writing.

- Look out for clauses in the prime lease (the lease between the landlord and the original tenant) that require the landlord's consent for a use change or alterations of the space. Assuming that your use will trigger this clause, don't sign up unless the landlord gives the needed approvals, in writing.

- Scrutinize the prime lease for charges in addition to rent, such as pass-through charges for common area maintenance, taxes and insurance. Find out if the tenant will be passing these costs on to you.

- Get written confirmation from the landlord and tenant that the tenant's lease is in good standing, and that as long as you pay your rent and other required charges, you can continue to occupy your space.

- Include a clause in your lease allowing you to cancel the sublease if the landlord fails to provide building services and repairs. The last thing you want is to be stuck in the middle of a fractious relationship between the landlord and the tenant.

- **Ability to expand space.** In worrying about failure, some craftspeople forget to plan for success. After the first year or two, you may need more space. Depending on your expectations for growth, you may feel that the ability to take over additional space in the building is a high-priority factor. You'll want to nail down your right to occupy additional parts of the building in a lease clause giving you the right of first refusal when space opens up.

C. Elements of a Lease

The lease that you and your landlord sign defines your legal relationship. It's a contract in which:

- you agree to pay rent and abide by other conditions (such as using the space for production purposes only or not displaying outside signs unless the landlord first approves them), and
- your landlord agrees to let your business occupy the space for a set amount of time, perhaps with a number of listed amenities such as on-site parking and weekly janitorial service.

Along with your insurance policy and your loan documents, your lease will be one of the most important legal documents in your filing cabinet. You must make sure you understand everything in the lease before you sign it. Typically, you'll be working with a lease that's been written by the landlord or the landlord's lawyer—and you can bet that neither one of them will be looking out for your best legal or economic interests. So treat the landlord's proposed lease as the starting point from which you'll negotiate changes.

1. There Are No "Standard" Leases

Don't fall for the line that "this is a standard lease" —there's no such thing. Even if the landlord starts with a lease that's widely used in your community, printed and distributed by a big real estate management firm or accepted by other tenants who lease from this landlord, it can always be modified.

2. How Leases Are Organized

Leases are usually organized by numbered paragraphs or clauses. Often, the Arabic or Roman number is followed by a title (such as "II. Term"), but the title may not alert you to what the clause covers (consider "III: Subordination"). To compound matters, lawyers often dress the body of these clauses in dense legal verbiage or burden them with mile-long sentences.

3. You Are the Tenant

Your business, typically, will be the tenant. When you identify your business as the tenant in a lease—both at the beginning of the lease and at the end where you sign—make sure that you correctly name the business. You must also designate its legal form (partnership or corporation, for instance). For an explanation of how to identify your business, see Chapter 1.

The legal nature of your business entity, for example, sole proprietorship, partnership, corporation or LLC, determines whether or not you'll be personally responsible for paying rent and meeting the other obligations stated in the lease. (If you're not personally responsible, creditors can reach the assets of your business but no more.) See Chapter 1 for more information on business forms.

4. Describing the Leased Space

Somewhere near the beginning of your lease, often right after the Parties clause, you'll see a clause that identifies the space that you'll be occupying. This clause is often titled "Premises." You might think that a Premises clause is just about as straightforward as a lease clause could be. As long as you've seen the space and understand how the square feet have been calculated, what could complicate or concern you about a simple description of your space? Well, leave it to ingenious landlords (or their lawyers) to bury a few potential surprises in this innocent clause. Here are the common wrinkles.

a. Changing the Common Areas

Landlords often write clauses that give them the right to change the common areas at will. For example, in order to create a larger space for another tenant, the landlord might someday want to narrow the entryway to your store or chop into the lobby area outside of your office. Changes in the common areas can make your own space less convenient, prestigious or usable. If you see language in a premises clause that gives the landlord the right to adjust the common areas as he sees fit, try to eliminate it or at least build in a bit of protection—for example, by having the landlord agree in writing not to reduce the access to your space or make your space less visible from the street.

b. Changing Your Space

Believe it or not, some landlords will write a premises clause that gives them the right to substitute other space—whether in the building or elsewhere—for the space described in the clause. Most of the time, such a move will be a giant pain in the neck for you. Even if the lease requires the landlord to pay for the cost of a move, it's usually a poor idea to agree to such a deal.

5. The Use Clause

A use clause can be either a restriction on how you do business—telling you what you can't do—or a prescription, telling you what you must do. The limitations can be as broad as what business you'll conduct there, as narrow as what specific services or products you'll offer or as nebulous as the quality level of your operation. In general, you'll want to avoid strict restrictions on your use of the rented space. Most of the time, you'll count yourself lucky if the lease handed to you by the landlord does not include a use clause.

a. Restricted Use Clause

This type of use clause states what you're prohibited from doing. The landlord includes a list of every forbidden use—for example, a prohibition against use of kilns or ovens, or even all retail sales. You're free to do anything that's not on the list. If you look at a restricted use clause and don't see anything that you could imagine doing, it's probably going to be okay with you.

b. Permitted Uses Only

This type of clause puts the burden on you to come up with every conceivable use you can think of at the time you sign the lease. If you later want to do something that's not on the list, too bad. In addition, a use clause will hamper your ability to sublet or assign.

6. Landlord's Remedies If You Fail to Pay Rent or Breach the Lease

Not surprisingly, the landlord's lease is likely to be pretty thin when it comes to explaining what you can do if he messes up. His list of permitted reactions to your failures, however, will be long, detailed and punitive. Below are the common remedies for failure to pay rent.

a. Notice and Cure: Your Second Chance

Since most landlords understand that a tenant breach may be inadvertent, they agree in the lease to notify you of the problem (called "notice") and give you a specified amount of time to rectify (or "cure") the problem before they take sterner measures. And even when it comes to deliberate breaches—such as failing to pay the rent because you can't—landlords typically extend the same second chance. They'd rather get their money late than have to start over with a new tenant. Typically, the notice and cure period will be rather short for monetary misdeeds (such as failure to pay the rent), but longer for problems that take more time to fix.

b. Landlord Self-Help: Doing It for You

If you fail to live up to a lease obligation during the notice and cure period, the landlord may decide to "fix" your error. Known as a landlord's right of "self-help," it means that the landlord can correct your breach of the lease, then sue you for his expenses (or deduct them from your security deposit, which you will then have to top off). For example, if you're late with the rent, the landlord will take it from the security deposit (and then demand that you bring the deposit back up to its original sum). Or, a tenant who doesn't maintain the property as required in the lease, or who parks in others' spaces, may find the maintenance done or his car towed—and a bill from the landlord for the work or the services of the tow truck.

Landlords have a particularly harsh method of dealing with tenants who fail to reimburse the landlord for money he's spent on self-help measures. Careful landlords will specify that any sums they have to spend on self-help will be designated "additional rent"—in other words, it's lumped together with your monthly rent bill. Giving the debt this label makes it easier for the landlord to sue you for the unpaid bill. Here's why: You know what happens when you don't pay the normal rent—the landlord can terminate and evict in a court proceeding that is quickly scheduled and very short. By contrast, a typical civil suit over an unpaid bill takes forever. When the unpaid self-help bill is designated as "rent," it means that the landlord can bypass the slow civil suit and instead sue to evict in order to collect—a powerful incentive for you to pay up.

c. Terminating the Lease

The next weapon in the landlord's arsenal is his right to terminate the lease. If the landlord terminates, you'll have to move out. If you don't, the landlord may file an eviction lawsuit against you. Clearly, neither would be a welcome event. Even if you plan never to let matters get to this extreme, it's wise to pay attention to this clause.

A harsh clause will allow the landlord to terminate for any lease violation, but many leases permit termination only for "material" or "significant" breaches. These are slippery concepts, that should be nailed down in the lease. You wouldn't want the landlord to jump to termination over a breach that looks major to him but minor to you.

Although your lease clause probably won't address it, be sure you understand what happens after the landlord terminates the lease. Contrary to what you might expect, you won't normally just walk away without financial consequences. In fact, depending on market conditions, you might end up paying a considerable amount of money in damages. Here's why.

When you and the landlord signed the lease, you promised to pay a certain amount of rent for a specified number of years. The landlord is legally entitled to that money, regardless of the fact that your misbehavior caused him to terminate the lease. In most states, however, the landlord cannot sit back and sue you for unpaid rent as it becomes due. Usually, the landlord must take reasonable steps to rerent the space. Once the space is re-rented, the landlord credits the new rent money against your debt. If the new rent doesn't cover what you owe, you pay the difference. In legal jargon, the landlord's duty to rerent and credit your debt is called "mitigation of damages."

You can see that your continued responsibility for rent will depend on market conditions. If you were paying below-market rates, or if the new tenant was simply unable to negotiate as low a rent as you did, you may end up with no rent liability, since the new tenant's rent will cover (or exceed) what the landlord had been charging you. But if the value of the location has gone down or the income from the new tenant doesn't match yours, you'll pay the difference.

You might think that a termination of your lease—and the possibility that a new tenant's rent won't cover your obligation to pay the balance of your rent—would be the worst thing that could happen if you fail to honor your lease and it's terminated. Actually, there's a variation on this move that could be even more devastating. If the landlord's remedies clause has a provision allowing "recapture," you could be in for more grief. Recapture allows the landlord to take over your space and lease it out to another tenant *without* terminating your lease. Or, to add insult to injury, the clause might also allow him to take over your business and run it himself. Either way, you remain obligated under the terms of the lease for rent and everything else, such as insurance obligations, repair responsibilities and maintenance. If the new tenant (or the landlord, now running your shop) honors your obligations—in particular, pays the rent on time—you might not be too put out. But if the new operation falls short with respect to any lease obligation, you will be on the hook to satisfy the lease provision until the lease runs out.

Check Your Current Lease Before You Leap

If you're currently renting space and plan to move elsewhere, check your lease first. Here's what to look for:

- **The exact termination date.** Try to begin your search for new space well enough in advance so that you won't feel rushed. If the termination date is too far off, however, you may be forced to begin your new lease before the old one is over. It's a delicate balance—you don't want to be responsible for a period of double rents, nor do you want a gap between lease periods.

- **The possibility of a buyout.** If you need to move before the current lease expires, look to see if you can leave early by paying a "buyout amount." This is money that the landlord accepts in exchange for letting you out of your lease early.

- **Staying longer.** If your new space isn't ready on time—a common problem—it would be smart to find out if you can continue to occupy your current space after the stated termination date. You might be able to negotiate a short-term extension of your current lease. If the landlord won't give you an extension, check to see whether your lease imposes onerous "holdover" provisions. Landlords typically charge big rents to those tenants who don't leave on time.

- **Options and sublets.** An option clause in your current lease could significantly affect your decision and ability to move. Your lease may give you the option to renew, and perhaps pick up additional space as well. If you nevertheless want to move, it may be wise to investigate whether you can exercise the option—but instead of using it yourself, sublet the space at a profit and move your operation to a new location.

Consider arbitration and attorney fees provisions. Your lease may include ways you can iron out problems using mediation and arbitration and a provision explaining who pays for attorney fees and court costs if the dispute boils over into litigation. These provisions, common to many agreements, are discussed in Chapter 11.

D. Agreeing on the Rent in a Commercial Lease

If you're preparing to lease a commercial space for your crafts studio, your biggest concern is probably the rent. Determining the monthly payment can be fairly complicated in a commercial lease—much more complicated than in a residential lease. By understanding how commercial rents are typically worked out, you'll be able to negotiate for a reasonable alternative, or at least make sure the landlord doesn't slip up in his calculations.

For example, let's say you're considering a 500–square-foot studio. The landlord tells you it's $10 per square foot per month plus utilities. Sounds good—right within your budget! But before you sign on the dotted line, let's review some of the legal rules regarding rent.

Square footage isn't everything. In addition to the factors listed in this section, there are many more lease elements that can affect your rent payments—for example, use restrictions, length of the lease, security deposits, improvements, code compliance and options to renew or sublet. Review Section C for more information on these topics.

1. Square Footage

First, if your rent is tied to the square footage—for example, $10 per square foot—you should find out how the square footage is measured. Some landlords measure square footage from the outside of the walls—so that you end up paying for the thickness of the walls—while others measure from the inside. In addition, some landlords use a complicated system (known as the "loss factor") to reduce the amount of space you rent based on the common area space you can use (hallway, lobbies and so on.). For example, under a "loss factor" lease you may be paying for 500 feet but really only occupying 475 square feet because one-fifth of the building is common space.

2. Net Lease or Gross Lease

Second, you should find out if you have a "gross" lease or a "net" lease." A gross lease is one in which you have a fixed monthly rate with periodic increases. The increases may be based on a flat percentage— for example, 3% a year—or $.10 per square foot per year. Or, the increase may be variable and tied to increases in a national indicator, commonly the Consumer Price Index. In this case, if you're paying $5,000 a month and the CPI jumps 5% in one year, your payments will jump to $5,250.

Often there is no way around this type of increase, but if you have the power to negotiate you should ask your landlord for a minimum annual increase and a cap on the CPI increase, for example a minimum of 2% per year and a maximum of 3%. In that case, if the CPI jumps 4%, you will only have to pay 3%.

Under a net lease, you pay a base rent—say, $10 per square foot—as well as additional periodic expenses such as taxes, insurance and maintenance. (You may also have to pay periodic increases, such as CPI tied to the base rent.) Some of the issues you face with a net lease are highlighted below.

3. Allocation of Taxes

Many net leases state that if property taxes increase during the lease, the tenant must pay some percentage of that increase. Usually, your tax payment is tied to the percentage of space you are leasing—for example, if you rent one-fifth of the total space in the building, you may be obligated to pay one-fifth of any increase. The only problem with this approach is that property tax evaluations take into account any improvements made by other tenants in the building. So if one of your neighbors upgrades the wiring and provides special ventilation, the property value may

increase, and you will be obligated to pay the resulting tax increase. If you have the bargaining power— and most small business tenants leasing space do not—try to negotiate your tax obligation based on your pro-rata share of the taxable value of the property. Also, try to limit the amount of tax increase you must pay. This type of cap may protect you if the property tax jumps drastically or the building is reassessed and sold.

4. Insurance

Insurance policies protect the landlord from property damage from fires or other disasters and from claims made by third parties who are injured at the building. Most net leases require that the tenant contribute to the insurance for the building (in addition to purchasing separate insurance policies that the tenant needs to cover its own business). Like tax obligations, you want to make sure you are only paying a contribution to the landlord that is based on how much space you take up—for example, if you're occupying one-fifth of the building, you should only have to pay one-fifth of the insurance. If possible, you want to avoid having to split insurance costs with a tenant whose business causes the building insurance rates to go up—for example, the insurance costs may jump if another tenant opens a martial arts studio. An attorney or insurance adjuster's help may be needed to make this assessment.

5. Common Area Maintenance

Most net lease tenants must pay for common area maintenance (CAM). If you lease a whole building, you'll get stuck with all of the maintenance costs for the common areas. If you lease a portion of a building, you often must pay a percentage of the costs to maintain the lobbies, hallways, garages and elevators. Sometimes you must pay for maintenance of the heating and ventilation system. CAMs can really come back to haunt a tenant, particularly if the landlord can pass through operating costs without limitation. One way to head off problems is to have your lease specifically include (or exclude) the improvements that can be passed through. For example, you may negotiate to pass through janitorial, landscaping and security services or to exclude parking lot maintenance, accounting fees and legal fees. If possible, you also may want to negotiate for the ability to amortize such expenses over the life of the item. Imagine, for example, that you have one year left on a five-year lease and your landlord is suddenly billing you for your percentage of the cost of a new roof. If the roof can be amortized over five years, you will only have to pay your percentage of one-fifth of the cost. Again, it makes sense for your CAM cost to be allocated fairly, based on your portion of the leased property.

E. Studio Safety

Many an artisan has looked at his craft as a means to support life and raise a family, but all he has got from it is some deadly disease, with the result that he has departed this life cursing the craft to which he has applied himself.

> Dr. Bernadino Ramziini, 1713
> (quoted by Charles Lewton-Brain
> in "Safety in the Studio," *The Crafts
> Report,* January 2000).

Twenty-five years ago, jewelers used asbestos fibers, cadmium solder (now banned) and carcinogenic solvents including tri-chloroethylene, benzene and carbon tetrachloride—often without suitable ventilation. Fortunately, there's been progress in crafts safety standards since then, much of it led by crafts artists themselves. It goes without saying that it is absolutely essential for your studio to maintain adequate safety standards. Not only can it affect your short- and long-term health, but ignoring these standards may violate the law and lead to lawsuits by employees and neighbors.

In 1998, Engineer Milt Fischbein wrote four basic principles for maintaining studio safety:

- understand the hazards associated with each chemical, tool and machine in your studio
- design your studio to minimize hazards
- use safe procedures for each of your work processes, and
- make absolutely sure that each safety procedure is followed and that no shortcuts are taken.

Because of the wide range of crafts activities, it's beyond the scope of this book to provide specific safety advice for your crafts studio. Chances are good that you are already aware of the recognized risks within your field—risks that come with the territory when working with and around polishing machines, rolling mills, infrared radiation, dermatitis-causing dust, propane tanks and so on. Determining what is right for your crafts business requires research. Before you snap on your safety goggles (with side shields), review the resources below to best identify dangers and prevent injuries:

- *The Artist's Complete Health and Safety Guide,* by Monona Rossol (Allworth Press).
- *Health Hazards Manual for Artists* and *Artist's Beware: The Hazards of Working With All Art and Craft Materials and the Precautions Every Artist and Photographer Should Take,* both by Michael McCann (The Lyons Press)
- *The Jewelry Workshop Safety Report,* by Charles Lewton-Brain (Brain Press Publications). Order it on the web at www.ganoksin.com. Two helpful articles by Charles Lewton-Brain are online at www.craftsreport/com/april00/ studioissues.html and www.craftsreport/com/ june00/studioissues.html.
- *Safe Practices in the Arts and Crafts: A Studio Guide,* by Julian Waller (College Art Association of America; out of print but available used from online booksellers).
- *CROETweb* (www.ohsu.edu/croet/). Under Occupations and Industries, click "Artists." An excellent set of links for all occupational hazards to artists and crafts workers. Also divides safety hazards by crafts. ■

Selling: Consignments, Sales, Shows and Collections

few blocks from the Pacific Ocean in San Francisco's Sunset District, you'll find The Last Straw, a tiny shop with an eclectic mix of crafts. Marge Heard has operated the shop for 27 years, buying and selling crafts from local artisans and from trade shows. Heard has defied many of the rules of retail crafts success—in some cases contradicting the advice provided in this chapter! For example:

- She doesn't require ID from customers writing checks: "I tell people, 'What am I going to do? Go out and chase you?' If a check bounces I call the person, and they usually come right over. In the history of the shop, I don't think I've lost more than $100 total."

- She doesn't accept credit cards: "People say that they would buy a lot more if I would accept credit cards, but I don't want to. I feel people will spend more than they can afford."

- She allows people to take items home and pay for them in installments: "It works well for the more expensive stuff. I tell them, pay when you can, and please don't die in the meantime!"

- She operates in a working class neighborhood with very little foot traffic. "Most of my business is word of mouth, although," she adds, "some customers *don't* tell others because they want it for themselves."

Most crafts artists make retail sales, and many operate small retail shops or studios. In this chapter, you will find information on standard business procedures and on avoiding legal problems when dealing with customers and making sales. But, as The Last Straw proves, running a problem-free business can be accomplished by using common sense, developing business radar and doing business with people you trust. "The thing is," says Heard, "customers and artists who come into the shop become my friends. I don't know if *they* feel like my friends, but that's the way I feel—that we're attracted to the same kind of things."

Of course, no matter how you operate your crafts business, not everyone you deal with may treat you as a friend. In this chapter you'll find suggestions for preventing trouble and dealing with common sales issues, including:

- **Wholesale marketing.** Section A offers suggestions on how to fill orders and extend credit to wholesale customers without getting over-extended.
- **Retail sales.** Section B tells you about accepting checks and credit cards, paying sales tax and giving refunds.
- **Crafts shows.** Section C alerts you to common ways in which crafts show agreements work to the crafts vendor's disadvantage.
- **Consignments.** Section D advises you about placing your work in galleries for sale on consignment.
- **Custom orders.** Section E covers negotiating and drafting an agreement with a customer placing a custom order.
- **Shipping.** Mail order rules, in particular time limits you'll need to meet, are provided in Section F.
- **Collections.** You'll find strategies for dealing with past due accounts in Section G.

How the Crafts Dollars Break Down

According to the Craft Organization Directors Association (CODA) survey, published in 2001, crafts sales profits in the U.S. total $12.3 to $13.8 billion per year. The average craftsperson derives 52.9% of annual sales from direct retail accounts, 27% from wholesale marketing and 11.2% from consignments to galleries.

A. Selling on the Wholesale Market

In a wholesale transaction, you sell quantities of your work to a dealer or a retailer, usually at a discount. That person then resells your work to the general public. Wholesale transactions can take place at crafts shows, directly between galleries and artists or sometimes with the aid of agents who broker deals with retail outlets.

However, don't expect to get a check as soon as the deal is made. Payments for wholesale sales are traditionally made 30, 60 or 90 days after the goods have been transferred. In effect, the crafts business is extending credit to the retail outlet. You may not feel like you're extending credit—after all, you're just waiting for payment—but from a legal perspective, you're making an unsecured loan to the store or gallery. (The intricacies of unsecured loans are explained in Section A2, below.) Your "creditor" status can have a significant impact on your business, particularly if you extend a lot of credit to a store that has financial problems. (For information about collection practices, see Section G, below).

1. Extending Credit: Net 30, 60 or 90?

The length of time for which you extend credit will be one of the terms of the deal that you negotiate with the buyer. You'll naturally want to get paid as soon as possible—after all, you've already laid out for the labor and materials that went into producing the goods. However, this won't always be possible. To help you determine a particular payment date, ask yourself how much credit your business can afford at any one time, and then how much credit your business can afford with any one customer. When banks extend credit they look at four variables known as the "4 Cs of Lending." These are:

- **Condition of the business.** If you are considering placing a lot of your eggs in one retail basket, you will want to verify the retailer's banking references. You do this by asking the retailer to complete a credit report application.
- **Collateral.** Collateral is any property pledged by the retail outlet to support other loans. If the retailer owns assets that can be used as collateral, that's good. However, if most of the retailer's assets are already pledged to a secured lender, you will have a harder time collecting your debt, particularly in the event of credit problems such as bankruptcy. See Section A2, below, for more on collateral and secured loans.
- **Character.** Who is it you're extending credit to? Can you trust the retailer and its ability to

manage the debt? What is the retailer's background and reputation? If you're not getting satisfactory answers, trust your intuition and don't make the sale.
- **Capacity to repay.** What are the retailer's payment practices? Does it pay within terms, stretch terms to the limit or even go beyond terms? If other artists report that the retailer stretches Net 60 to Net 90 (or more), the retailer may turn out to be a problem account.

Finding out the answers to the 4 Cs requires some investigation. For starters, ask for a completed credit application and seek bank references. You can investigate the information on your own or use a credit research company.

Use the Web for research. You can find credit and business information about businesses on the Internet, although you may have to pay for the research from companies such as Dun & Bradstreet (www.dnb.com), BusinessCreditUSA (www.business creditusa.com) or Equifax (www.equifax.com).

2. What Happens If a Retailer Goes Bankrupt?

When People's Pottery, the 47-store chain specializing in American-made crafts, filed for bankruptcy in December 2001, it claimed $20 million in debts. That sum included $3 million that remained owing to approximately 250-300 crafts vendors. An attorney working on the case told one of the crafts artists that it would be a victory if the crafts businesses got 1% of the amount owed them.

What happened to the $8 to $10 million in assets that the company still had when it declared bankruptcy? It was used to pay secured creditors—lenders who had demanded that their loans be secured with property. If the debt wasn't paid, the secured creditors could demand that the bankruptcy court sell the assets and turn the proceeds over to the creditors. Crafts artists who had used Net 30 or Net 60 terms were considered unsecured creditors and would only be paid if money remained after paying the secured creditors. In other words, the crafts artists were left holding an empty bag!

It would be difficult, perhaps impossible, for a small crafts vendor to avoid the results of the People's Pottery debacle. Unless a crafts business has somehow secured its loan, that is, required in writing some collateral as a condition of a wholesale purchase, the purchaser's bankruptcy will effectively wipe away the debt.

Since there's not much you can do once a store goes into bankruptcy, you'll need to minimize your risks beforehand. Below are some suggestions:

- **Avoid putting all your eggs in one basket.** In the case of People's Pottery, crafts artists who had a range of retail accounts suffered less than those who had relied exclusively on People's Pottery. On the same note, don't ditch your smaller retailers because of large orders from one retailer. Loyal smaller accounts give a business a constant, reliable source of income.
- **Don't wait to pursue those who owe you money.** Some vendors managed to successfully pursue People's Pottery before it went under. Manufacturers Credit Cooperative (MCC) began taking claims against People's in the summer of 2001. "We had 16 clients," said Jim Dempster, CEO of MCC (www.mcccredit.com), "and all of them obtained some payments. Four collected in full. The earlier they came in, the greater percentage they received."
- **When in doubt, don't extend credit.** Some larger retailers will promise you anything to get your merchandise into the store under a Net 30 or 60 arrangement. That's because the store may have an "asset-based" loan with its bank. Under this arrangement, the more merchandise in the store, the more money the store can borrow. Don't play into a failing store's problems. As discussed in subsection 1, above, there's no sense extending credit when you have doubts. In these cases, obtain prepayment or payment upon receipt of the goods.

3. The Wholesale Order Form

When selling wholesale, you don't need a custom-made wholesale order form. Perfectly suitable carbonless order forms can be purchased at an office supply store. You can personalize these forms, if you wish, with a rubber stamp with the name of your business. Alternatively, many business software suites such as *QuickBooks* or *PeachTree Classic Accounting* include customizable forms and invoices. In the event you want to create your own custom invoice, I have provided a template.

A copy of the invoice is also available in the Appendix and on the CD-ROM at the back of this book.

At a minimum, your order form should include
- information about your company, that is name, address, phone and so on.
- date of the order
- information about the buyer, including customer account number, "ship to" address, sales tax number and "bill to" person
- purchase order number
- ship date and method of shipping, and
- order information including quantity, item number, description, price each and total cost.

It's normal to include a statement in the invoice that the order cannot be canceled. After all, a deal is a deal, and most stores understand that. If you want, you can seek compensation in the event of cancellation. For example, in the sample invoice, check the box, "Buyer agrees that in the event the order is cancelled, there is a cancellation fee of ___% of balance due." Although some crafts businesses use such language, always keep in mind that if a store fails to pay it, you must go to court to enforce the agreement. The same is true for the optional statements regarding interest payments and collection fees. When preparing your own invoices, you can decide whether to use this language (or delete it from) in your invoice.

Invoice

_____

_____

_____

_____

_____

_____

Bill to: _____   Ship to: _____

_____   _____

_____   _____

_____   _____

Date	Your Order #	Our Order #	Sales Rep.	Ship Via	Terms

Item Number	Description	Quantity Ordered	Quantity Shipped	Retail Price	Discount	Unit Price	Total

☐ If payment is late, interest shall accrue from the date the payment was originally due, and the interest rate shall be 1.5% of the unpaid balance.

☐ If this account is delinquent, it shall be referred for collection, and Buyer shall pay all collection fees and costs including reasonable attorney fees.

[Choose one]

☐ This order may not be canceled.

☐ In the event the order is canceled, there is a cancellation fee of _____% of balance due.

Subtotal	
Tax	
Shipping	
Miscellaneous	
Balance Due	

B. Selling on the Retail Market

Retail sales are sales made directly to the public, whether at a crafts fair, an open studio or as the result of special order (see Section E, below). Such sales are the bread and butter of the crafts industry and the source of more than half of the money made by crafts artists. The good news is that you probably won't need much legal advice for retail sales. All you need is a trusty receipt book and a system for accounting for your income. This section provides advice on the few areas of retail sales that sometimes raise legal red flags—sales tax, handling checks and credit cards and returns.

1. Sales Tax

Did you ever dream of working as a tax collector? If your state has a sales tax law and you sell directly to customers, then your dream has come true. Whenever you make an in-state retail sale to a customer, you must collect sales tax and pay it to the appropriate state agency. This is true whether you operate as a business or as a hobby (see Chapter 12, Section B). But you don't need to collect and pay sales taxes for:

- wholesale or consignment sales (though you will need a valid resale permit), or
- out-of-state customer purchases made directly via phone, mail order or the Internet and shipped to a location outside your state.

In order to collect the tax, you will need a sales tax certificate and sales tax number, usually issued by the state department of revenue, sales tax division. To learn your state's sales tax requirements and whether registration is required, check with your state department of revenue. You can also find state tax rates online at the Tax and Accounting Sites Directory (www.taxsites.com/state.html) or the Federation of Tax Administrators' website (www.taxadmin.org).

Being a tax collector does have some benefits. You can use your sales tax number to bypass paying sales tax on any materials used to create your crafts products—for example, wool, solder, gemstones, glass or wood. You still have to pay sales tax on office supplies, instructional manuals and other studio expenses.

If you travel out of state for a crafts fair, the promoter will usually either help you obtain a temporary sales tax certificate for that state or will require that you report your sales to the promoter at the end of the show (who will then collect the tax from you and remit the payment).

In addition to state sales tax, you'll need to watch out for taxes in:

- large cities, some of which have separate sales taxes, and
- areas close to state borders, particularly if you live on the border between two states or regularly sell in a neighboring state—some states have arrangements with neighboring states for combined tax certificates.

Myth: Sales tax cuts into crafts profits. As Kathryn Caputo points out in *How to Start Making Money With Your Crafts* (Betterway), sales tax money you pay to the state is *not* taken from your profits (it just feels that way). The tax is added to your selling price, usually after you ring the item up.

2. Accepting Checks

Considering that 450 million checks bounce each year, it's best to follow these common-sense procedures for minimizing your risks:

- Avoid taking checks that lack the person's name or address.
- Require ID, preferably a driver's license—and really look at it, for example, by comparing the address on the ID with the address on the check.
- Never accept a postdated check.
- Never accept two-party checks (checks written by someone other than your prospective buyer).
- Never accept the following as identification: membership cards, library cards, any card or ID that appears to be altered, Social Security cards or temporary driver's licenses.

- Record the buyer's license number and phone number on the check.

⚠ **Check your state's law regarding what ID you can demand.** Some states, such as California, have established limits on the types and number of identification that can be requested from a customer. For information, check with your state attorney general's office.

3. Accepting Credit Cards

Though some retailers such as Marge Heard don't like to use them, many small crafts businesses find that accepting credit cards is a business necessity. More and more customer's wallets contain only plastic, and the ATM machine may be nowhere in sight at your local crafts fair.

Handling credit cards is fairly straightforward when the customer is physically present. The customer—who has obtained a credit card from an *issuing bank*—hands you the card; you pass it through a terminal. Phone lines to a processing firm—the transaction clearinghouse—connect the terminal, and within seconds, you get verification that the card is valid and that the customer has sufficient credit to cover the transaction. Later, the money is sent to the bank that has authorized you to accept credit card payments—the *merchant bank*. Transaction fees and charges are deducted from your merchant bank account. The charge is added to the customer's monthly bill. The mechanics of person-to-person retail transactions are usually easy and smooth. It's also simple to prove, if necessary, that the customer actually made the purchase, because you have a signed charge slip.

Nevertheless, when accepting credit cards in person, here are some precautions:

- If at all suspicious, require proof of identity, check a "Hot Sheet" (a list of bad cards) or telephone the issuing bank for authorization.
- Avoid any transaction where a card has been altered, has expired, is not yet valid or shows a signature that doesn't look like the one the customer writes on the sales slip.

- Always be careful processing an order from a new customer—especially if the customer places a large order or wants overnight delivery.
- Consider rejecting purchases when a bank in a foreign country has issued the credit card. This may seem harsh, but foreign credit cards are reported to have a higher fraud rate than those issued by U.S. banks.
- When you ship merchandise, choose a shipment method that requires the card owner to sign upon receipt. This approach adds some expense to the transaction, but you'll know whether or not the shipment arrived—thereby preventing claims by the customer that it didn't.

When you do business over the phone, by mail order or online, the mechanics are more cumbersome and avoiding fraud is more difficult. For one thing, you have no credit card to swipe through a terminal and no signature. So, you need something approximating a card swipe machine. In addition, in online transactions, you need a *gateway* that links your website to the credit card processing network. (Online credit transactions and shopping cart systems are discussed in Chapter 4.)

When taking phone, mail order or online orders, always obtain:

- type of card (for example, Visa or Discover)
- card number
- name on card
- expiration date, and
- billing address.

It can also be useful to ask for the name of the bank that issued the card. And you might also ask for a phone number so you can call the customer if something seems fishy.

No doubt in coming years, technology will provide consumer-friendly online payment methods that reduce the chances of your business being defrauded. Several new systems—variously dubbed *digital cash, virtual escrow, digital wallets* and *virtual credit cards*—are on the drawing board or being tested. No one can tell you which, if any, will become the system of choice for businesses and consumers.

Gateway software and services can help keep you from being a victim of online credit card fraud. For example, the software or service can do a comparison to make sure that the shipping address is the same as the customer's billing address. If not, you're given a chance to decide whether you want to check further before completing the transaction.

You may want to speak to the customer by phone to make sure that everything's on the up and up before you ship out the merchandise. Of course, you'll need to exercise some judgment to determine if you're speaking to the true card owner. Sometimes it's a tough judgment call, because there are perfectly valid reasons why a customer wants to have an order shipped to an address other than the billing address. For example, the merchandise being shipped may be a gift. Or the billing address may be the customer's home and the customer may prefer to receive the product at work, where he or she will be present to receive it during normal delivery hours.

Gateway software or a transaction clearinghouse can also provide additional fraud protection services. Some popular software add-ons include:

- **Fraud protection.** This system lets you rate the chances that a particular transaction will be fraudulent based on criteria that you select. If a transaction is flagged as especially risky, you can seek further information from the customer or reject the transaction entirely.
- **AVS.** This system (short for Address Verification Service) takes the first five numbers of the street address and the ZIP code information from the customer's stated billing address and compares that data to the billing address the card issuer has. You're told if there's a good match. If not, you can decide to reject the sale.
- **CIC.** Every credit card has a Card Identification Code, a three- or four-digit number that's printed on the credit card in addition to the 16-digit embossed number. You can minimize fraud by including a feature that checks this number, since only someone who actually has the card in hand will know the number. Some companies call the number a CVV2, CVC2 or CID.

The process of setting up to accept credit cards can take two to four weeks, so plan accordingly. You should begin by entering into a written agreement with the merchant bank. Check it carefully and make sure that the fees are as agreed.

Look out for excessive *chargeback* fees—the money a bank takes out of your business account when a customer disputes a transaction. Disputes about online transactions can pop up in several ways. For example, a customer may order merchandise, get it and keep it—but dispute that it was ever received. Or a customer may have some other complaint about the transaction. Unfair as it may seem, a bank typically can take a chargeback in any situation in which the customer is dissatisfied. In a retail store, chargebacks are rare, accounting for a mere 0.14% of credit transactions; but at an online store it's 1.25% of transactions. In other words, chargebacks are nine times more frequent in online transactions than in traditional store transactions. So compare chargeback rates at merchant banks before signing with a merchant bank. (See sidebars "Comparison Shop Before Picking Your Providers," below.)

In addition, the merchant bank agreement will require that you comply with advertising restrictions set by the credit card companies—governing, for example, how the images of the cards are displayed at your store, gallery or studio or on your website. If you don't comply, you lose your merchant accounts.

Comparison Shop Before Picking Your Providers

Credit card fees can eat into your profits, so you need to check them thoroughly before you sign up to be a credit card merchant. You can do comparison shopping on the Web at MerchantWorkz (www.merchantworkz.com), a site that provides clearinghouse and merchant bank fees, merchant bank profiles and advice on gateways and the other necessary elements for setting up an online credit card account.

Credit Card Lingo

Here are some terms you'll need to get used to when handling credit card transactions:

- **Authorization.** Confirmation from the consumer's credit card company that the credit card is in good standing and the necessary funds are available for the transaction.
- **Chargeback.** Taking the money out of your account because of a disputed transaction (for example, one in which the customer claims you never sent the goods). You may have to pay a fee of $15 to $25 to the merchant bank for each disputed transaction.
- **Gateway.** For online purchases, the gateway is the method of connecting your online business to the transaction clearinghouse. You can have a company (a gateway service) provide this, or you can purchase gateway software on disk or in hardware that acts as the digital equivalent of the card-swipe machine used in a store. Gateways allow for real-time checking of the credit card information so that the customer knows, at the time of purchase, whether the transaction has been approved.
- **Issuing bank.** This is the bank that issues the credit card to the customer.

- **Merchant bank (sometimes called acquiring bank).** To accept Visa, MasterCard and many other credit cards (but not American Express or Discover), your business must open a *merchant account* through a *merchant bank*. (Note, not all merchant banks support use of their services for online transactions.)
- **Return.** The opposite of an authorization. Money is taken from your merchant bank account and credited to the consumer's credit card bank. This usually happens when the consumer returns goods to you.
- **Settlement.** A process in which funds from the consumer's credit card bank are transferred into your merchant bank account.
- **Transaction clearinghouse.** To collect money from a customer, you don't deal directly with the customer's issuing bank. Instead, you deal with an intermediary known as a *transaction processor* or *clearinghouse* that handles credit card transactions for your merchant bank. The transaction processor checks the validity of the customer's card and okays (or rejects) the purchase.

Selling Overseas

If you're interested in selling your crafts overseas, here are a few tips:

- **Get the payment up front.** You don't have the ability to chase down rubles, drachmas or pesos in a far away land, so demand payment up front for all international transactions. These payments can be made by credit card, bank transfers or bank letters of credit. If accepting payment by credit card, keep in mind that it is very difficult to avoid credit card fraud from non-U.S. credit card providers. Therefore, if possible, check with your merchant bank to verify that payment was made and that the card is not fraudulent or involved in disputes. To avoid confusion about currency conversion, keep your dealings in U.S. dollars.

- **If you can't get payment up front, get references.** If it's impossible to get payment up front, check all business references before shipping an international order.
- **Your price quote should reflect shipping costs.** Your price quote should reflect the added costs of shipping internationally, which will not only be higher than ordinary shipping but may include extra insurance and tariffs. DHL, FedEx and UPS can advise you on international ordering.

For more information on exporting your crafts goods, check out The Export Institute (www.exportinstitute.com), the U.S. Bureau of Export Administration (www.bxa.doc.gov) and the U.S. Trade Information Center (www.trade.gov/td/tic).

4. Returns and Refunds

The legal rules for returns and refunds are straight-forward: Once a sale is complete, you don't have to give a refund. The only exceptions are if:

- there's been a significant breach of the sales contract, for example, your crafts goods were defective or seriously flawed, or
- you had an agreement with the customer allowing a refund.

That said, many crafts businesses have adopted a policy of giving customers the option of returning merchandise for either a cash refund or at least a credit toward another online purchase. If you want to provide refunds and impose conditions on when merchandise can be returned, you should post your return and refund policy prominently at the point of sale (for online sales, post the policy prominently on your website). Your state law may require this type of posting. Even if it's not the law in your state, it's a good practice. Typical conditions might require the customer to return the merchandise within a certain number of days, to return only unused merchandise or to submit a receipt or other proof of purchase along with the return.

Of course, galleries and stores that sell consigned or special orders should not offer returns for those goods unless they're flawed; all sales of such items should be final.

Refunds: California, Florida, New York and Virginia

Four states have laws governing refund policies. If your crafts business is in California, you must post your refund policy *unless* you offer a full cash refund or credit refund within seven days of purchase. If you don't post your policy as required, the customer is entitled to return the goods for a full refund within 30 days of purchase. In Florida, if a crafts business does not offer refunds, that fact must be posted. If the statement isn't posted, the customer can return unopened, unused goods within seven days of purchase. In New York, if a crafts business offers cash refunds, that policy must be posted and the refund must be given within 20 days of purchase. Virginia crafts businesses that don't offer a full cash refund or credit within 20 days of purchase must post their policy.

Selling jewelry? The Federal Trade Commission has established rules for advertisements and catalog sales of jewelry containing diamonds, gemstones and pearls. For more information, call the FTC toll-free at 1-877-FTC-HELP (382-4357), or read the guidelines online at www.ftc.gov. Click "Business Guidance."

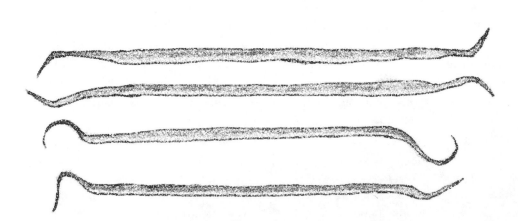

The Pricing Dilemma: How Much Do You Charge?

Author Christopher Morley wrote, "When you sell a man a book you don't sell him just 12 ounces of paper and ink and glue." Although this maxim applies to crafts works as well, there are times when you may need to dissect the costs of your raw materials in order to determine the proper retail price. Imagine you spent $8 per product on materials and your per-product overhead is $7 (the average per-day cost for rent, utilities and services divided by the number of products you make per day). Each product is costing you $15 in materials and overhead. After you figure out how much time you spend on each item and factor in what your time is worth, you'll have an idea of what you've invested in each product. A good analysis of pricing and a template for determining a pricing formula is provided in Chapter 5 of Wendy Rosen's *Crafting As a Business* (Sterling Publishing).

A common mistake is to price your work based on your own wallet. As Barbara Brabec, author of *Handmade for Profit* (M. Evans & Co.), explained, "Beginners look at their product and say 'I wouldn't spend more than $10 for this ....' which is a very big mistake because most crafters aren't very rich. What they have to do is research the marketplace and see what others who are making similar products are charging for their wares."

For some crafts artists, formulas don't work. "I have no formula for pricing," says jeweler Susan Brooks. "I may do a little bit of market research, but I rely more on intuition. Through trial and error, I hit a price that's comfortable for galleries."

little or no sales. The crafts show promoters explained that they could do nothing, since the law guaranteed the man the right of free speech in a public place. At another outdoor crafts show, I watched sales dissipate when the smoke from a nearby barbecue stand poured through a line of booths. Another time, my sister called from a crafts fair to report that she had spent many hours in the dark after the electricity blew in the convention center.

It's difficult, if not impossible, to resolve disputes like these during the two to three intense days of a crafts show. An artist who has paid hundreds of dollars in booth fees and traveled quite a distance wants to generate revenue, not get embroiled in battles with a promoter. And once the show is over, most artists don't want to chase promoters or sue, because they can't afford it, they don't want to waste time traveling to an out-of-state courtroom or they don't want to endanger their relationship with the promoter. The tendency is to chalk it up to a bad show, express an opinion on a crafts message board, and factor the experience into the decision whether to attend next year.

Crafts Fairs and Trade Shows

Although this book, like many crafts artists, uses the terms crafts fairs and trade shows interchangeably, the term "crafts fair" often refers to a retail show where the artist sells directly to the consumer. "Trade show" commonly refers to wholesale shows where the artist takes wholesale orders to be completed and delivered at some future date.

C. Crafts Shows

While attending an outdoor crafts show where my sister had a booth, I watched the customers quickly disappear as a Bible-toting evangelist confronted them about sin and damnation. For two hours he continued while the ten booths in the vicinity saw

And there's more bad news for the crafts vendor. Many crafts show agreements contain provisions that relieve the promoter from damages in situations like those I've described. For example, one promoter's agreement states:

I agree not to hold [Promoter] responsible for personal injuries or property damage and I agree not to be party to any legal action against [Promoter]. All exhibit personnel, merchandise fixtures, etc. on the premises are my sole responsibility and I agree to indemnify and hold harmless [Promoter] from all liability stemming from their presence or their acts.

Note: The statement "and I agree not to be party to any legal action against [Promoter]" may not be enforceable in some states. In such cases, the provision would probably be severed from the agreement.

Other promoter's agreements shield the promoter from lawsuits through what is known as a Force Majeure (or "Acts of God") contract provision. For example, one promoter's agreement says:

[Promoter] will not be liable for refunds, loss of profits and out of pocket expenses or any other liabilities whatsoever for the failure to fulfill this contract due to any of the following reasons:
a. The facility in which the exhibition to be produced is destroyed by fire or other calamity.
b. By an act of God, public enemy or strikes, the requirements of statutes, ordinances or any legal authority or any cause beyond the control of [Promoter].
c. The bankruptcy or insolvency of the facility.

Just in case such broadly written clauses don't cover enough, many contracts itemize the ways in which the promoter holds all the cards, such as:
- **Prohibition on refund of booth fees.** Most crafts show agreements contain a provision stating that there will be no refund of exhibit space fees.
- **Penalties for unqualified exhibitors.** Some exhibitors have been known to violate show rules. The rules usually set certain qualifying criteria, for example that the crafts are handmade or that the artist be present at the booth. Crafts show agreements often contain language allowing the promoter to remove the exhibit if it is not "up to show standards." In reality, most promoters will not act on infractions during the show; they will wait until after the show to decide how to investigate and resolve the matter. An article in The Crafts Report by Carrie Groves, *Show Rule Enforcement, Whose Job Is It?* (May 2001) concluded that enforcement of show rules by promoters was inconsistent.
- **No recourse for lack of promotion.** If a show is not properly promoted, there's not much that a crafts artist can do. Crafts show agreements sometimes contain statements indicating that the promoter makes no promises as to sales or attendance.

Why Can't We All Just Get Along?

Not all crafts show disputes are between promoters and artists. At an Australian crafts fair in 2000, a jeweler clobbered the artist in a nearby booth with a coffee cup, resulting in an assault conviction and an $800 fine.

For practical advice about entering and exhibiting at crafts fairs, check out the *Crafts Fair Guide* (www.craftsfairguide.com) or read *Crafting as a Business,* by Wendy Rosen (Sterling Publishing) or *How to Start Making Money With Your Crafts,* by Kathryn Caputo (Better Way).

D. Selling on Consignment

A consignment occurs when an artist provides work to a gallery (the "consignee"), who agrees to pay the artist the proceeds from a sale minus the consignee's commission (usually 40 to 50% of the sale price). If the work doesn't sell, the consignee can return the work to the crafts artist. Under this arrangement, the consignee takes very little risk since it does not have to purchase the goods. The advantage of consignment for many crafts workers is that it gives them access to sales outlets that might not otherwise be open to them.

Consignments to galleries are the third-largest method of craft sales in the United States according to the Craft Organization Directors Association (CODA) Survey, published in 2001. Consignments account for over $3 billion in annual U.S. crafts sales. After stores and galleries collect their 25 to 50%, America's crafts workers pocket approximately $1.5 to $2 billion in consignment revenue. On average, craft consignments represent over $8,300 in revenue per artist.

Consignment obviously comes with risks and obligations. What if the store doesn't pay? How do you retrieve unsold merchandise? Who's responsible when crafts are damaged? And—dread of dreads—what do you do when a gallery goes belly up?

Consider the crafts people left holding the bag when a Minneapolis gallery filed for bankruptcy while owing artists a total of $97,000. Said one crafts artist at the time, "We're the canaries down the coal mine. When the gas comes we're the first to die."

So what's a crafts person to do?

Below is a discussion of three types of legal protection for consignors: the Uniform Commercial Code, state consignment laws and written consignment agreements. You may find some of these legal principles difficult to comprehend, inconsistent and expensive to enforce. Of the options provided below, I would recommend the use of written agreements as the best option.

Never forget to do some research and trust your common sense. Ask other crafts persons about their experiences with specific stores and galleries. Avoid large orders until you have built a level of trust with an unknown shop. And if you have doubts about a consignment, ask the store for references from other crafts people. If you've got a funny feeling about a shop, trust your intuition and don't hand your work over to it.

1. The Uniform Commercial Code

The Uniform Commercial Code (UCC) is a set of laws adopted by every state except Louisiana. Under the UCC, if damage to your consigned crafts results from the store's negligence, the store must pay for the loss. If the damage is not the fault of the store—for example, there's a flood or fire—the store may or may not be liable, depending on how the courts in that state interpret the UCC.

Normally, under the UCC, if a store files for bankruptcy, the store's creditors can seize your consigned goods as payment for debts. In other words, anyone owed money by the store can take your crafts as payment. You must stand in line behind the other creditors and hope that the judge awards you some compensation. However, the UCC gives crafts artists ways to prevent the creditor of a gallery from claiming your work as payment in the event of the gallery's insolvency or bankruptcy. You can avoid this unhappy outcome by fulfilling one of three requirements:

- file a UCC form (known as UCC Form 1) at the time of the consignment, in the county where the store is located
- have the store owner post a sign telling the public that the goods are consigned (not applicable in all states), or
- prove that the creditors were aware that the gallery sold consigned goods.

These efforts are referred to as "perfecting a security interest." Having a security interest gets you certain rights over other creditors—for example, you can seize the property if the gallery doesn't pay you. Although crafts people rarely use these cumbersome UCC requirements, you may find it worthwhile, in the case of high-ticket one-of-a-kind crafts items, to file the UCC form. The filing creates a lien (a legal claim over property) elevating you to the level of a "secured creditor" and putting you at the head of the line in bankruptcy court. If you do file the form and obtain the lien, you must remove the lien at the time of any sale.

Having the store or gallery post a sign—the second UCC requirement—is a troublesome request. In general, galleries prefer not to post such notices. However, some galleries are complying with such requests, and I have included an optional provision in the sample consignment agreement for this purpose. It requires that the gallery post a notice such as "Crafts At This Gallery Are Sold Under The Terms Of

A Consignment Agreement." As noted, this may not be effective in all states.

Most crafts workers will find the third requirement difficult to accomplish. It requires some legwork when it comes to obtaining proof that creditors of the store were aware of the consignment. Some consignors have accomplished this by sending creditors a copy of the consignment agreement. As you can imagine, the average crafts worker—who does not know who the store's creditors are and who may not have a written consignment agreement—would find this impractical.

Keep in mind that in the event of a store bankruptcy you must prove to a bankruptcy court that you have met one of these three conditions—which usually means hiring an attorney.

2. State Consignment Laws

Because the UCC has proven to be a frightening trapdoor for crafts people, many states have passed special consignment laws to protect artists from gallery abuses and bankruptcy. So far, 31 states have passed art consignment laws—Alaska, Arizona, Arkansas, California, Colorado, Connecticut, Florida, Georgia, Hawaii, Idaho, Illinois, Iowa, Kentucky, Maryland, Massachusetts, Michigan, Minnesota, Missouri, Montana, New Hampshire, New Jersey, New Mexico, New York, North Carolina, Ohio, Oregon, Pennsylvania, Tennessee, Texas, Washington and Wisconsin.

Each of these laws is unique, but all of them operate under one basic presumption: Whenever art is handed over to a gallery, store or dealer, it's presumed to be a consignment unless the artist is paid by the time of delivery. Most of these laws provide two benefits:

- any art held under a consignment arrangement or any money from a consignment sale is held in trust by the gallery for the artist (that is, the artist always owns the work and the proceeds), and
- the artist is shielded from bankruptcy, because creditors are prohibited from seizing consigned goods. (In reality, enforcing these laws usually

requires hiring a lawyer and filing claims in bankruptcy court.) Half of the state laws require a written consignment agreement as a condition for enforcing the law.

The problem for crafts artists in these states is proving that their work qualifies as "art" under state laws. The determination can be confusing. Some state consignment laws apply only to "fine art." Fine art is traditionally defined as a painting, sculpture, drawing, graphic art or print, but not multiples. Many states—for example, Arizona and Ohio— specifically include crafts in the definition of "artwork" (defining them as any work made from clay, textile, fiber, wood, metal, plastic or glass). Some statutes are vague, and it's not clear whether crafts are covered.

Tad Crawford and Susan Mellon's *The Artist-Gallery Partnership: A Practical Guide to Consigning Art* (Allworth Press) offers the best all-around guide to art consignment laws.

3. Landing Consignment Accounts and Avoiding Consignment Problems

"Consignments can be an ideal situation for my riskier work," says jeweler Alison Antelman (www.antelman.com), who has built her business with a combination of wholesale and consignment sales. "Galleries sometimes perceive some of my work as being a riskier sell. By taking it on consignment, the gallery takes less risk, and these works are available in outlets that might not buy wholesale. I also like consignments because I can pull back items or switch my line if I choose." But, Antelman adds, "It's a shared responsibility. The gallery has to make payments on time and has to keep track of the inventory, too."

Antelman locates consignment accounts the old fashioned way, by visiting shops and investigating their inventory. "I check out galleries to see if my work fits with their taste and what they are trying to promote."

"Never assume they can see you when you drop in. I always ask if I can make an appointment. If they're willing to see me then, that's fine, too. I bring samples of my work and slides and literature such as an artist statement, bio, contact information and tear sheets from magazine articles. The important thing is to always maintain a professional approach."

And what about rejection or rudeness? "I always, always, act friendly and calm, leave and thank them for the time. You can't be insulted personally. You have to be thick-skinned. After all, my work is not suitable for all galleries."

Here are some tips for assessing a gallery before committing to a consignment:

- If you can't visit a gallery, ask someone you know in the area to check out the customer traffic and report back to you.
- Get names of other artists exhibiting at the gallery, preferably on your own rather than through the gallery owner. Then contact the artists and ask about the gallery's practices.
- Be wary of a gallery that won't give you financial or credit information.
- Check online about a gallery at crafts chat rooms (for example, www.craftsreport.com).
- After placing your work in the gallery, stay in contact. Regular communication may alert you to any financial problems and will also prepare you for success. You may need to get to work and build up stock to ship out because of ongoing sales.

In those rare cases when you have a problem, either because of late payments or suspicions that the gallery is having financial problems, follow Antelman's simple strategy: "Take your work out. Put all of your energy and talent in another place."

4. Written Consignment Agreements

Traditionally, consignments are made by written agreements, often furnished by the gallery, or through oral agreements. I recommend, when possible, using a written consignment agreement. It can provide benefits for you, obligations for the gallery and, most important, it is required under many state consignment laws. A consignment agreement should cover:

- the inventory being consigned
- the retail prices for the goods
- the store or gallery's responsibility for damage to the goods
- the gallery's fees for consigned goods
- who pays for shipping
- whether discounting is permitted
- promotional responsibilities, if any, and
- the gallery or store's obligation to post a sign regarding consignment (a condition that may protect you in the event of consignee bankruptcy).

I also recommend including an attorney fee provision (requiring that the loser pays the winner's attorney fees) and an arbitration provision (requiring settlement by a private arbitrator, not a judge). These provisions create incentives for rapid settlement of all (nonbankruptcy-related) disputes. (A discussion of these provisions is provided in Chapter 11.)

Many galleries furnish their own consignment agreements. If you are furnished one of these agreements, compare it to the sample agreement below, or compare it to model consignment agreements such as those prepared by the Society for North American Goldsmiths (a copy of which is posted at their website, www.snagmetalsmiths.org). It is possible that a gallery may refuse to modify its consignment agreement. If the agreement compares unfavorably to model consignments, you will have to decide whether there is any risk in proceeding. Usually, however, galleries are flexible about negotiating some terms and conditions.

How do you convince a gallery to use your consignment agreement? The best approach is to bring up the subject in your introductory conversation. Ask the gallery if they have a contract. If they do, ask them to send or fax it, and then compare it to the professional guidelines. If it's unacceptable, or if the gallery doesn't have a contract, tell the gallery you have a contract and ask if they're comfortable reviewing your agreement.

⚠ **Don't use the sample agreement for vanity galleries or auctions.** The agreement below is not intended for vanity galleries or auctions. Under a vanity gallery arrangement, the artist pays a fee for the right to exhibit works and may pay to rent the space, install his work and use the gallery's mailing list. The consignment agreement is also not intended for use at auctions. Auctions often involve more specialized financial arrangements covering advances or loans to an artist, catalog costs, reserves and estimates of minimum payments. For more information on your legal rights in auctions, read *Legal Guide to Buying and Selling Art and Collectibles*, by attorney Armen R. Vartian (Bonus Books).

Discounts: What Are They? Who Needs Them?

Discounts are used by galleries to provide special customers with an incentive to make regular purchases. For example, a gallery might give a favorite collector a 10% discount. When the practice started, discounts were usually only offered to collectors of higher priced crafts works, for example works valued at $10,000 or more. That's changed, and galleries now may attempt to inflate prices to cover the discounts.

If the consignment price is not inflated to absorb the "discount", who absorbs this loss? Many artists believe that the gallery, not the artist, should take the hit because the discount reflects the relationship between the gallery and the collector. They reason that the artist and the collector usually don't have an ongoing business or personal relationship. Obviously this is a matter of negotiation between the artist and gallery. The sample consignment agreement in this chapter provides three choices for the artist, ranging from no discounts to splitting the loss.

---

a. Sample Crafts Consignment Agreement

📀 You'll find copies of the Consignment Agreement in Appendix B and on the CD-ROM at the back of this book.

b. How to Fill Out the Sample Consignment Agreement

Here are certain important provisions of the consignment agreement shown below:

- **Introductory paragraph.** Insert your name as artist and insert the name and street address of the gallery.
- **Appointment of Gallery.** This provision establishes whether your relationship with the gallery is exclusive or nonexclusive, and establishes the geographic area within which the gallery will represent your works. Exclusive means that while the agreement is in force, only the gallery (not you or another gallery) can represent the sale of the artwork within the territory you define. If the agency relationship is nonexclusive, then others (including you) could solicit potential sales within the territory. If it's exclusive, insert a statement in the territory section to reflect the regions in which you have granted rights, for example, "New York State."
- **Fees and Payments.** Under this provision, the gallery receives a percentage of all works that are sold. The audit statement permits you or your representative to audit the gallery's books.
- **Discounts.** The sample agreement provides two choices: subjecting all discounts to your prior approval, or having the artist and gallery split the difference. Check the choice that's applicable.
- **Shipping:** Three choices are provided for shipping costs: an open choice in which you can describe your arrangement; the traditional approach of "whoever ships, pays;" and a negotiated approach that is established by using Attachment B. Check the choice that's applicable.
- **Insurance.** This is standard language, requiring that the gallery's insurance cover and protect your works.
- **Termination.** After the initial period of sale (within a reasonable time period that you establish), this agreement is drafted to permit

Consignment Agreement

_____ ("Artist")
is the owner of the original works and accompanying rights in the works listed in Attachment A (referred to as
the "Works"). Artist desires to have _____ (the
"Gallery") located at _____
_____ represent Artist with regard to the exhibition and
sale of the Works. From time to time, the parties may revise the list of Works specified in the inventory listing
and such revisions, if executed by both parties, shall be incorporated in this agreement.

Appointment of Gallery; Agency Relationship. Artist appoints Gallery as its: _[Choose one]_

☐ exclusive agent for the sale and exhibition of the Works in _____
    (the "Territory").

☐ nonexclusive agent.

Gallery shall use its best efforts to promote and sell the Works and to provide attribution of the Works to Artist.

Fees and Payments. Gallery shall sell the Works at the retail prices established by Artist in this agreement. All
income paid as a result of the sale of any Works by the Gallery shall be paid directly to Gallery, and Gallery
shall issue payment to Artist within _____ days of Gallery's receipt of such income along with
any accountings, including identifying inventory numbers.

For sales of Works, Gallery shall receive a commission of _____ % of any sales income.

[Optional]

☐ Gallery shall keep accurate books covering all transactions relating to the Works, and Artist or Artist's
    authorized representatives shall have the right, upon five days' prior written notice and during normal
    business hours, to inspect and audit Gallery's records relating to the Works.

☐ No payments may be made on credit or approval without the permission of Artist.

☐ Gallery shall provide Artist with the name and contact information for purchasers of the Works.

Discounts.
[Choose one]

☐ Gallery will obtain Artist's approval before changing retail prices or offering the Works at discount.

☐ Gallery may offer discounts to selected customers up to _____% and Gallery and Artist will split the
    discount equally, provided that Artist does not receive less than _____% of the sale price.

Custom Order Commissions.
[Choose one]

☐ In the event of custom orders resulting from exhibition at Gallery, Gallery shall receive a commission of
    _____% of any sales income.

☐ Gallery shall not be entitled to any commission on custom orders resulting from exhibition.

Shipping.

[Choose one]

☐ Costs for shipping shall be as follows: _____.

☐ Costs for shipping: (a) from Artist to Gallery shall be paid by Artist; (b) from Gallery to Artist shall be paid by Gallery; and (c) from Gallery to anywhere other than Artist (for example, to customers) shall be paid by Gallery.

☐ Costs for shipping shall be as set forth in Attachment B.

Insurance. Gallery shall maintain adequate insurance for the wholesale value of the Works (the retail price minus potential commission) and shall pay all deductibles.

Termination. This Agreement may be terminated at any time on or after _____ at the discretion of either Artist or Gallery. This Agreement shall automatically terminate if Artist dies or if Gallery becomes insolvent, declares bankruptcy or moves from the Territory. In the event of termination, all Works in Gallery's possession shall be promptly returned to Artist at Gallery's expense.

Ownership; Loss or Damage; Security Interest. Gallery agrees and acknowledges that the delivery of the Works to Gallery is a consignment and not a sale of the Works to Gallery. As Artist's agent, Gallery shall have a duty to protect the Works and shall be strictly liable for any damage to the Works once in Gallery's possession and until returned to Artist. If Works are destroyed while within Gallery's possession, Gallery shall pay Artist the full value as established by the retail price. Artist shall retain full title to all Works consigned to Gallery and shall in no event be subject to claims by creditors of Gallery. Title of the Works shall pass directly from Artist to purchaser, and, in the event of default or breach by Gallery, Artist shall have all rights of a secured party under the Uniform Commercial Code and Gallery agrees to execute all forms necessary to perfect such interest.

☐ **Posting Consignment Notice.** Gallery agrees to prominently post the following notice in its gallery: "Crafts at this gallery are sold under the terms of a consignment agreement."

General Provisions

Entire Agreement. This is the entire agreement between the parties. It replaces and supersedes any and all oral agreements between the parties, as well as any prior writings. Modifications and amendments to this agreement, including any exhibit or appendix hereto, shall be enforceable only if they are in writing and are signed by authorized representatives of both parties.

Successors and Assignees. This agreement binds and benefits the heirs, successors and assignees of the parties.

Notices. Any notice or communication required or permitted to be given under this agreement shall be sufficiently given when received by certified mail, or sent by facsimile transmission or overnight courier.

Governing Law. This agreement will be governed by the laws of the State of _____.

Waiver. If one party waives any term or provision of this agreement at any time, that waiver will only be effective for the specific instance and specific purpose for which the waiver was given. If either party fails to exercise or delays exercising any of its rights or remedies under this agreement, that party retains the right to enforce that term or provision at a later time.

Severability. If a court finds any provision of this agreement invalid or unenforceable, the remainder of this agreement will be interpreted so as best to carry out the parties' intent.

Attachments and Exhibits. The parties agree and acknowledge that all attachments, exhibits and schedules referred to in this agreement are incorporated in this agreement by reference.

No Agency. Nothing contained herein will be construed as creating any agency, partnership, joint venture or other form of joint enterprise between the parties.

☐ **Attorney Fees and Expenses.** The prevailing party shall have the right to collect from the other party its reasonable costs and necessary disbursements and attorney fees incurred in enforcing this agreement.

☐ **Jurisdiction.** The parties consent to the exclusive jurisdiction and venue of the federal and state courts located in _____ [county], _____ [state], in any action arising out of or relating to this agreement. The parties waive any other venue to which either party might be entitled by domicile or otherwise.

☐ **Arbitration.** Any controversy or claim arising out of or relating to this Agreement shall be settled by arbitration in _____ in accordance with the rules of the American Arbitration Association, and judgment upon the award rendered by the arbitrator(s) may be entered in any court having jurisdiction. The prevailing party shall have the right to collect from the other party its reasonable costs and attorney's fees incurred in enforcing this agreement.

Signatures.

Each party represents and warrants that on this date they are duly authorized to bind their respective principals by their signatures below.

GALLERY:

_____

Signature

_____

Typed or Printed Name

_____

Title

_____

Date

ARTIST:

_____

Signature

_____

Typed or Printed Name

_____

Title

_____

Date

Attachment A

Title of Work	Inventory No./Description	Retail Price
		$
		$
		$
		$
		$
		$
		$
		$
		$
		$
		$
		$
		$
		$
		$
		$
		$
		$
		$
		$
		$
		$
		$
		$
		$

Date

Consignee

Attachment A to Consignment Agreement

Attachment B (Optional)

Expenses. Gallery shall pay expenses as listed in this Attachment B. In the event that an expense shall be shared between Artist and Gallery, the relative percentage of Gallery's payment shall be set forth below, and Artist shall be responsible for the remainder. For any shared expenses, Gallery shall provide an estimate of the expense and, in the event the actual amount of the expense exceeds the estimate, Gallery shall pay the difference.

Expense	Percentage paid by Gallery	Estimate	Deductible by Gallery
Promotional mailing	_____	_____	☐ Yes ☐ No
Advertising	_____	_____	☐ Yes ☐ No
Party/event (opening)	_____	_____	☐ Yes ☐ No
Frames	_____	_____	☐ Yes ☐ No
Installations	_____	_____	☐ Yes ☐ No
Catalog*	_____	_____	☐ Yes ☐ No
Photographic reproductions	_____	_____	☐ Yes ☐ No
Shipping to purchasers	_____	_____	☐ Yes ☐ No
Shipping to artist	_____	_____	☐ Yes ☐ No
Other _____	_____	_____	☐ Yes ☐ No
Other _____	_____	_____	☐ Yes ☐ No
Other _____	_____	_____	☐ Yes ☐ No
Other _____	_____	_____	☐ Yes ☐ No
Other _____	_____	_____	☐ Yes ☐ No
Other _____	_____	_____	☐ Yes ☐ No
Other _____	_____	_____	☐ Yes ☐ No
Other _____	_____	_____	☐ Yes ☐ No

*Gallery shall furnish Artist with ten copies of catalog.

Attachment B to Consignment Agreement (Optional)

your immediate termination of the consignment agreement.

- **Ownership; Loss or Damage.** This provision establishes the gallery's legal liability for any damage that occurs to your work while it is consigned to the gallery. The reference to "secured parties" and the Uniform Commercial Code is to prevent the gallery's creditors from seizing your work to pay the gallery's debts.
- **Miscellaneous provisions.** The assorted provisions at the end of the agreement—"Entire Agreement," "No Joint Venturer" and so on—are explained in Chapter 9, Section B24.
- **Attachment A: Inventory Listing.** Complete the inventory listing. It's important to provide a detailed description of the artworks and to establish the price at which each item will be sold. You may need to determine the price with the assistance of the gallery, since the gallery is likely to better know the market and prices within the territory. But keep in mind that the final decision as to the price is up to you, not the gallery. If you are submitting this sheet when modifying consignments, for example, supplying new work, it's wise to have the gallery sign and send back the new Attachment A (you don't need to sign it). I have included an optional signature section on this Attachment.
- **Attachment B: Expenses.** This optional section establishes how any applicable expenses will be paid (or split, as the case may be). It's more likely you will use this attachment if you are dealing with a lot of high-ticket crafts or if the gallery is providing a special exhibition, not merely offering your work for sale. You and the gallery should agree on estimates for each expense and insert that sum in the attachment. If certain estimates are inapplicable, insert "N/A." You can also request approval of any expenses over a certain amount (for example, over $500).

Send two signed copies of the agreement to the gallery. One copy is for the gallery's records, and the other is to be returned to you with the gallery's signature.

E. Custom Orders

"I love your work," a customer tells you at a crafts fair, "but could you make it in mauve with chartreuse green trim?" Assuming you're willing to prepare the work according to the customer's specs, the best method of following up on the sale is with a commission agreement (also known as special or custom order).

Prior to pulling out any paperwork, you'll need to agree on the basic terms, that is, get an agreed-upon estimate, schedule and payment plan. Sometimes a custom order will cost more than the pieces you're currently selling, for example, if it involves a limited production method or more expensive raw materials. Crafts artists often must explain how a work is made in order for a buyer to understand custom order prices. Once you've agreed on that, you should sign an agreement.

Below we have provided a basic sample Commission Agreement, drafted in terms that are fair for both the buyer and the artist.

You'll find copies of the Commission Agreement in Appendix B and on the CD-ROM at the back of this book.

Explanation for Commission Agreement

Below I help you understand the provisions of the Commission Agreement and give you some tips on filling it out.

- **Basic information.** Include the names of the parties (you and the buyer), the relevant job information (delivery dates and fee) and a description of the job.
- **Payment.** Choose the method of payment that you have agreed upon with the buyer. Sometimes, in the case of larger, more expensive commissions, a buyer may spread the payment over several installments and also insist upon the right to approve the progress of the work at each stage.

Commission Agreement

Number: _____ Job Number: _____

To: _____ ("Buyer")

From: _____ ("Artist")

Delivery Date(s): _____ Fee: _____

Job Description ("Work"):

_____

_____

_____

Payment. Buyer shall pay Artist as follows:

☐ An initial nonrefundable payment of $_____ upon signing this agreement and the remainder upon receipt of the Work.

☐ Payment in full within _____ (_____) days of signing this agreement.

☐ **Additional Expenses:** Artist shall be remunerated for the following expenses:

_____

_____

_____

Buyer shall also pay all applicable sales taxes due on this assignment.

☐ **Credit.** All publications or displays of the Work by Buyer shall contain the following statement:

_____ .

☐ **Termination; Cancellation.** In the event this agreement is canceled by Buyer for any reason other than Artist's breach of this agreement or inability to complete the work as agreed upon, Buyer shall pay to Artist the cancellation fee of $_____ along with expenses incurred. In the event of termination by Buyer, Artist shall retain all works in progress and any payments already made.

Liability. Neither party shall be liable for incidental or consequential damages, nor for any claims in tort (or for punitive damages) which may arise from any breach of this agreement or any obligation under this agreement.

Reservation of Rights; Ownership of Original. Artist retains copyright and all other intellectual property rights in all artwork furnished under this agreement.

☐ **No Destruction or Alteration.** Buyer agrees not to intentionally destroy or modify the Work.

General Provisions

Entire Agreement. This is the entire agreement between the parties. It replaces and supersedes any and all oral agreements between the parties, as well as any prior writings. Modifications and amendments to this agreement, including any exhibit or appendix hereto, shall be enforceable only if they are in writing and are signed by authorized representatives of both parties.

Successors and Assignees. This agreement binds and benefits the heirs, successors and assignees of the parties.

Notices. Any notice or communication required or permitted to be given under this agreement shall be sufficiently given when received by certified mail, or sent by facsimile transmission or overnight courier.

Governing Law. This agreement will be governed by the laws of the State of _____.

Waiver. If one party waives any term or provision of this agreement at any time, that waiver will only be effective for the specific instance and specific purpose for which the waiver was given. If either party fails to exercise or delays exercising any of its rights or remedies under this agreement, that party retains the right to enforce that term or provision at a later time.

Severability. If a court finds any provision of this agreement invalid or unenforceable, the remainder of this agreement will be interpreted so as best to carry out the parties' intent.

Attachments and Exhibits. The parties agree and acknowledge that all attachments, exhibits and schedules referred to in this agreement are incorporated in this agreement by reference.

No Agency. Nothing contained herein will be construed as creating any agency, partnership, joint venture or other form of joint enterprise between the parties.

☐ **Attorney Fees and Expenses.** The prevailing party shall have the right to collect from the other party its reasonable costs and necessary disbursements and attorney fees incurred in enforcing this Agreement.

☐ **Jurisdiction.** The parties consent to the exclusive jurisdiction and venue of the federal and state courts located in _____ [county], _____ [state], in any action arising out of or relating to this agreement. The parties waive any other venue to which either party might be entitled by domicile or otherwise.

☐ **Arbitration.** Any controversy or claim arising out of or relating to this agreement shall be settled by arbitration in _____ [county], _____ [state], in accordance with the rules of the American Arbitration Association, and judgment upon the award rendered by the arbitrator(s) may be entered in any court having jurisdiction. The prevailing party shall have the right to collect from the other party its reasonable costs and attorney's fees incurred in enforcing this agreement.

Signatures

Each party represents and warrants that on this date they are duly authorized to bind their respective principals by their signatures below.

BUYER:

_____
Signature

_____
Typed or Printed Name

_____
Title

_____
Date

ARTIST:

_____
Signature

_____
Typed or Printed Name

_____
Title

_____
Date

Commission Agreement (Page 2)

- **Additional Expenses.** If you are to be paid for additional expenses that you incur in filling this custom order, insert the supplies and services for which you seek compensation. If the buyer is to pay for shipping, include that information here. Also included is a reference to repayment of sales tax.
- **Credit.** If the work will be shown and you wish to be credited, insert the appropriate statement. Although it is not mandatory to include any notice, the use of a copyright notice may provide some benefits in the event you are involved in an infringement lawsuit.
- **Termination; Cancellation Fee.** If you wish to give the buyer the opportunity to terminate after making the order, insert an amount that is equitable, usually one-fourth or more of the amount for the total job.
- **Liability.** This "legalese" section limits the amounts that buyer and artist would have to pay if a dispute arises under the agreement. With this provision, the only amounts due in the event of a breach would be the sum that would correct the problem, usually the fee paid for the artwork.
- **Reservation of Rights; Ownership of Original.** This provision makes it clear that you own the copyright in the work. If the buyer wants to own the copyright, that is a fundamental change to the agreement that can only be accomplished by adding an assignment provision (an example is provided in Chapter 8) or, if the work qualifies, making it a work made for hire (see Chapter 5, Section F).
- **No Destruction or Alteration.** In the case of certain high-ticket, one-of-a-kind crafts works, the artist may choose this optional provision that establishes that the works cannot be destroyed or modified. For some crafts works, this right may also be acquired without the contract under some federal or state laws (see Chapter 8, Section T).
- **Miscellaneous Provisions.** The remaining provisions are explained in Chapter 9, Section B24.

F. Shipping and Delays

If you take orders by mail or fax, over the phone or online, you must follow the shipping and refund rules of the Federal Trade Commission's Mail or Telephone Order Merchandise Rule (also known as the "30-day Rule"). In a nutshell, the rule mandates the following: When you advertise merchandise, you must have a reasonable basis for stating or implying that you can ship within a certain time. If you make no shipment statement, you must have a reasonable basis for believing that you can ship within 30 days.

If, after taking the customer's order, you learn that you cannot ship within the time you stated or within 30 days, you must seek the customer's consent to the delayed shipment. If you cannot obtain the customer's consent to the delay, you must, without being asked, promptly refund all the money the customer paid you for the unshipped merchandise. So if you can't ship within the time promised or within the 30 days, you must obtain consent or provide a refund. If there's going to be a shipping delay and you don't want to seek the customer's consent, you can simply cancel the order. If you decide to cancel, you must promptly notify the customer and refund the payment.

If you take an order by phone, you can satisfy the FTC's requirements by telling the customer of the delay during the conversation. It's a bit more complicated, however, when a customer orders online. Legally, the online order is complete when the customer clicks it along to you. So you'll have to notify the customer of the delay by email, phone, fax or regular mail. When you notify the customer, keep a record of how you gave the notice, when you gave it and how the customer responded.

The rules are a little different if your customer is applying to you to establish a new credit account or to increase an existing credit line to pay for the merchandise being ordered. In that case, if you make no shipment representation when you solicit the order, you are allowed 50 (instead of 30) days to ship the order. The extra 20 days is to enable you to process the credit application. Of course, if you want to use

Importing Your Crafts for Sale in the U.S.

Have you ever traveled to another country and thought, "This is an inspiring place to create hand-crafted works!"? That's what happened to designer Andrea Serrahn when she traveled to India in 1990. "When I got there, I felt like I had *arrived*." Inspired by the vivid colors and fabrics, she worked with Indian tailors to create her unique clothing. There was only one catch—bringing her radiant designs back to the U.S. to sell.

"I think the average traveler would be daunted by what you have to go through to bring work from India to the U.S.—the red tape and bureaucracy. There's a lot of protocol, and you can't just walk into the post office and ship it back with the same expediency as one would in the States. On both sides—U.S. and India—you have to hire people to move it in and out. Textiles need proper visas, and the U.S. government is a stickler. There's also a quota for fabrics. One way to do it is to find an exporter, or another way is to use a courier. Sometimes I've actually dragged it back (over 100 kilograms) on the plane with me."

"Be prepared for surprises when you ship," warns Serrahn. "I've had packages broken into. Nothing is missing, but everything is rearranged. And customs agents slice not only the boxes with their cutters! People want to look through it for antiques or drugs."

Andrea was able to fund part of her work when she qualified for a Fulbright Foundation grant for artists that gave her "cachet and clout, which goes a long way for a woman trying to do business in India."

After 10 years of shuttling back and forth, Serrahn decided to open a shop in Oakland, California. At her shop, called Serrahna (www.serrahna.com), she offers her passionate, colorful clothing designs for men and women.

"You've got to have a couple of screws loose to try something like this," says Serrahn. "It really takes a true dedication to bring your work in from a foreign country. I think you could benefit from taking a course on import/export, but I did it through the school of hard knocks."

For more information on importing and exporting, check out:

- the U.S. Small Business advisor website (www.business.gov). Click "International Trade."
- U.S. Customs (www.customs.gov). Click "Importing & Exporting" or
- the U.S. Commercial Service (www.usatrade.gov).

this provision of the FTC rule, you must have a reasonable basis to believe you can ship in 50 days.

For more information about the FTC rules, call the Federal Trade Commission at (877) FTC-HELP or visit their website (www.ftc.gov). You also may get helpful information from the Direct Marketing Association (www.the-dma.org).

G. Collecting From Customers

One of the most frustrating aspects of running a crafts business is dealing with customers who are slow in paying. You want to be paid in full, but quite often you also want to continue doing business with the customer. Should you pursue the debt aggressively, or write it off as a waste of time?

Get busy on delinquent debts. Based on a recent survey of members of the Commercial Collection Agency Association (www.ccascollect.com), the probability of collecting a delinquent account drops severely over time. After only three months, the probability of collecting a delinquent account drops to *73%*. After six months, the probability of collecting drops to *57%*. After one year, the chance of ever collecting on a past due account is a dismal *29%*.

You can learn collection tips from *The Check Is Not in the Mail: How to Get Paid More in Full, on Time, at Less Cost and Without Losing Valued Customers,* by collection expert Leonard Sklar (Baroque Publishing), or *Collect Your Money: A Guide to Collecting Outstanding Accounts Receivable for Your Business,* by Cody Flecker (Cobra).

1. Strategies for Avoiding or Reducing Losses

Collection experts recommend the following:
- Send bills promptly and rebill at least monthly. There's no need to wait for the end of the month.

- Make sure your bills clearly describe the goods sold or the services provided. Include on the bill a request to the customer to contact you if there are problems with the goods or services. If the customer fails to do so and later tries to excuse the failure to pay by claiming the goods or services were unsatisfactory, you have a good argument that the customer is fabricating a phony excuse.
- Enclose a self-addressed envelope (preferably stamped) to facilitate payment.
- Keep a record of the checking account that the customer uses to pay you.
- Send past due notices promptly when an account is overdue. Ask clearly for payment. Many people worry that the word "pay" sounds too blunt. If it makes you squirm, try alternate phrasing such as "Please bring your account current."
- Telephone to ask what's wrong. The customer needs to know that you follow these matters closely.
- Do not extend more credit, no matter what the hard luck story. This is particularly important. Lots of businesses facing tight finances pay only when they need more merchandise. If you let them have it without payment, you're teaching them that you're a pushover.
- Have a series of letters to use in routine cases. These letters should escalate in intensity as time goes by.
- If the customer has genuine financial problems, find out what the customer realistically can afford. Consider extending the time for payment if the customer agrees in writing to a new payment schedule. Call the day before the next scheduled payment is due to be sure the customer plans to respect the agreement.
- Save copies of all correspondence with the customer, and keep notes of all telephone conversations.
- Watch out for checks for less than the full amount that say "Payment in Full." In some states, if you deposit the check, especially if the amount owed is in dispute, you may have

wiped out the balance owing. Learn the law in your state before you deposit such a check.

- Continue to keep in contact with the customer, but don't harass him or her.

- If an account is unpaid for an extended period and you're doubtful about ever collecting, consider offering in writing a time-limited, deep discount to resolve the matter. This way, the customer has the incentive to borrow money to take advantage of your one-time, never-again offer to settle.

- When collection starts to put heavy demands on your time, and your chances of recovery are slim because you know the customer is on the skids, consider turning the debt over to a collection agency. This allows you to get on with more productive activities.

2. Collection Options

Suppose you can't get the customer to pay up voluntarily. What next? If you're not willing to write off the debt (which is sometimes the wisest thing to do), you have three collection options:

- **Sue in small claims court.** Small claims court is inexpensive and speedy. The downside is that it can take a good chunk of your time. Furthermore, any judgment that you receive may be worthless if the debtor lacks a job or a bank account. For an excellent guide to using small claims court and collecting after you win, see *Everybody's Guide to Small Claims Court*, by Ralph Warner (Nolo).

- **Hire a lawyer.** Lawyers can be effective, but they're expensive. Consider using a lawyer to write dunning letters. Many lawyers are willing to do this for a nominal charge.

- **Turn the account over to a collection agency.** Collection agencies are good at tracing elusive debtors, but they take a big percentage of what they collect for you (see sidebar, "Seven Reasons to Send an Account to Collections," below).

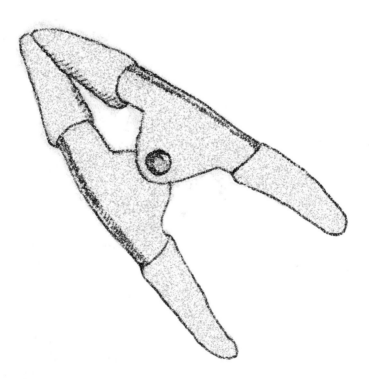

Seven Reasons to Send an Account to Collections

The Commercial Collection Agency Association (www.ccascollect.com) provides seven reasons to send an account to collections. We reprint them below, with permission from the CCAA. They include:

1. Two or more broken promises of payment. Payments were promised, but no checks have been received, and customer will not send immediate payment by overnight delivery.

2. Customer's telephone is disconnected. Double-check with the information operator, and if no new listing can be obtained, place the account in collections immediately.

3. The customer repeatedly requests documentation, even though they have been supplied the documentation previously. This common practice is used to delay payment of the account.

4. Your customer indicates that they do not adhere to your terms of sale. For example, they may indicate that they pay bills in sixty or ninety days and not according to the agreed-upon terms of sale. If you did not have an agreement with the customer before shipment for extended terms, this is just a delaying tactic. Explain to your customer your terms of sale and request immediate payment. If they refuse or fail to send a check as promised, place the account with a certified collection agency.

5. Your customer indicates an inability to pay and refuses to provide a specific date for payment or to initiate a realistic payment schedule. This is a sure indication of a serious cash flow problem, and immediate steps should be taken to protect your interests.

6. Your customer states they will "take care of the account," but refuses to make a realistic commitment for payment or to work out a payment schedule. This is another indication of a serious cash flow problem.

7. Your customer suddenly indicates, in response to your requests for payment, a dispute regarding the merchandise shipped or your terms of sale. Such a dispute was not raised previously. If your investigation shows the dispute groundless and the customer will not take steps to make payment or resolve the matter, the account should be placed with a CERTIFIED collection agency.

3. Sending Collection Letters

You may find it useful to develop a set of past due notices to use when customers fall behind in their payments. Your first letter may suggest that perhaps the bill was overlooked, and that payment should be sent now so that the customer can maintain a good credit rating. Your second and third letters should be polite but increasingly firm. Vary the format of your letters; each one should look a little different. Samples are shown below.

 You'll find additional copies of these sample collection letters in Appendix B and on the CD-ROM at the back of this book.

Debtor have rights, too. Don't threaten to use physical force, use obscene language, harass the debtor or accuse the debtor of criminal behavior. Any of these activities may violate your state's debt collection laws.

Account No. _____

Dear _____ :

Our records show that you have an outstanding balance with our company of $_____.
This is for _____

_____

_____ *(describe the goods or services).*

Is there a problem with this bill? If so, please call me so that we can resolve the matter. Otherwise, please send your payment at this time to bring your account current. I'm enclosing a business reply envelope for you to use.

Until you bring your account current, it's our policy to put further purchases on a cash basis.

Sincerely,

_____

P.S. Paying your bill at this time will help you to maintain your good credit rating.

Collection Letter #1

Re: Overdue Bill ($_____)

Account No. _____

Dear _____ :

Your bill for $_____ is seriously overdue. This is for the _____

_____

_____ *(describe the goods or services furnished)* we supplied to
you last _____ *(state the month).* More than 60 days have gone by since we sent
you our invoice. You did not respond to the letter I sent you last month.

We value your patronage but must insist that you bring your account up to date. Doing so will help you protect your reputation for prompt payment.

Please send your check today for the full balance. If this is not feasible, please call me to discuss a possible payment plan. I need to hear from you as soon as possible.

Sincerely,

_____

Collection Letter #2

Re: Collection Action on Overdue Bill ($_____)

Account No. _____

Dear _____:

We show an unpaid balance of $_____ on your account that is over 90 days old. This is for the _____

that we supplied you over _____ days ago.

I have repeatedly tried to contact you, but my calls and letters have gone unheeded.

You must send full payment by _____ or contact me by that date to discuss your intentions. If I do not hear from you, I plan to turn over the account for collection.

Collection Letter #3

Chapter

4

Go Live:
Taking Your Business Online

*H*olly Yashi Jewelry, founded in 1981, produces stylish jewelry with luminous colors and innovative materials. The company had considerable success in the marketplace. When the Internet exploded in the late 1990s, Holly Yashi considered its options and decided on a slow, steady approach to entering the online business world.

The company site (www.hollyyashi.com) debuted in 2000. At first, it basically reproduced Holly Yashi's print catalog. "We shot with a digital camera," says owner Paul Lubitz, "so that made it easier to transfer our images to the Web." The company later added some handy features (Figure 4-1) including tips on cleaning jewelry, Holly Yashi's top 20 styles, gift ideas and a search feature called Find A Retailer (Figure 4-2). This search feature allows the customer to locate nearby stores selling Holly Yashi Jewelry's products. Although the search feature wasn't cheap—it cost approximately $1,000—it served a secondary purpose: allowing HollyYashi to avoid publishing a list of all its retailers, which would have been easy for competitors to copy.

"In 1998 and 1999, I didn't get the Internet," said Lubitz. "Now, I think it's incredible! I see it as another cost of doing business, just like your electric bill."

No doubt about it, taking your crafts business on the Web can be rewarding. If you're looking for an efficient, relatively inexpensive way to reach customers, clients and fans, establishing a website fits the bill in many respects. Your site can provide images of your work instantly and globally. If you want to invest a little more time and effort, your site can be used for direct sales—an efficient way to increase your profits and reduce your need for agents, galleries and distributors.

If you own a computer and you're willing to learn, you can probably have your website up and running in a few weeks, for a few hundred dollars—or, in some cases, for free. Creating and hosting a website can now be accomplished by even the most tech-challenged crafts worker. If you've got other priorities, you can hire a website developer to custom design the site for you.

In this chapter, I'll discuss the legal and practical issues involved in setting up and running a site, including how to:

- decide what your site will include and who should create it (see Section A)
- choose a Web host to display your site (see Section B)
- choose a domain name and become its rightful owner (see Section C)
- add a direct sales feature to your site (see Section D), and
- protect yourself from disputes and liability by posting certain notices and policies on your site (see Section E).

Note to Web-savvy readers: You may find my discussion too simple. I wrote this chapter primarily for those of you on the fringes of the information highway—interested in committing to a website but confused about the choices and rules.

No, you don't have to have a website. Don't let me (or any other nerds) talk you into a website if you don't really want one. If you're happy with the way you do business or you already have more orders than you can handle, you probably don't need to bother establishing a presence in cyberspace.

HOLLY YASHI Jewelry As Art
1-800-274-2714
help@hollyyashi.com
Our Jewelry
Top 20 Styles
Find a Retailer
Gift Ideas
Care & Cleaning
About Us
Gift Ideas
Find a Retailer
Our Jewelry
Top 20 Styles
Care & Cleaning
About Us
Copyright 2001 Holly Yash

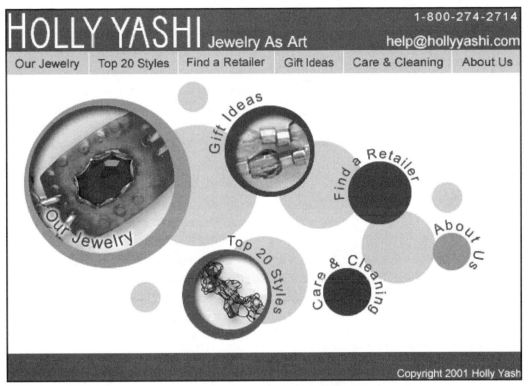

Figure 4-1: www.hollyyashi.com

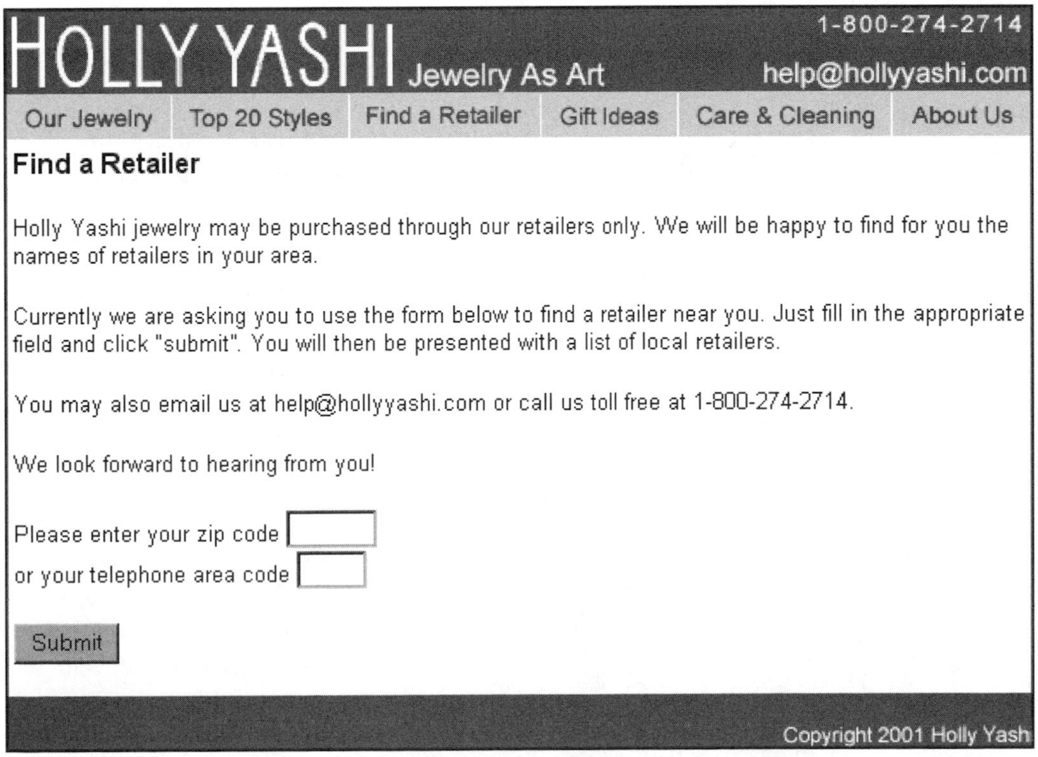

HOLLY YASHI Jewelry As Art
1-800-274-2714
help@hollyyashi.com
Our Jewelry
Top 20 Styles
Find a Retailer
Gift Ideas
Care & Cleaning
About Us
Find a Retailer
Holly Yashi jewelry may be purchased through our retailers only. We will be happy to find for you the names of retailers in your area.
Currently we are asking you to use the form below to find a retailer near you. Just fill in the appropriate field and click "submit". You will then be presented with a list of local retailers.
You may also email us at help@hollyyashi.com or call us toll free at 1-800-274-2714.
We look forward to hearing from you!
Please enter your zip code
or your telephone area code
Submit
Copyright 2001 Holly Yash

Figure 4-2: Find a Retailer

Some Basic Website Terms

Unclear about Internet terminology but afraid to ask? Here are definitions of a few Web terms used throughout this chapter. If you need more tech definitions, you can find reliable ones at Internet.com's Webopedia (www.webopedia.com) and at Whatis.com (www.whatis.com).

- **Domain name registry.** A domain name registry is a company that sells and renews domain names. After you buy a domain name (for $35 or less a month, depending on the registry), the registry will deal with the technical aspects of ensuring that your site is displayed when someone types in your domain name. Domain name registries often provide hosting services as well. I discuss domain names in Section C, below.

- **Internet Service Provider (ISP).** ISPs connect you to the Internet and typically charge a monthly fee for the access. You will need an ISP—for example, Earthlink, Yahoo!, MSN or AT&T—in order to access the Web, receive email and manage and view your website.

- **Server.** Servers are high-capacity, fast-processing computers that store websites. They are connected to the Internet with high-bandwidth connections, and they operate around the clock so that websites are always accessible to Internet users.

- **URL (Universal Resource Locator).** URLs are web addresses, such as www.nolo.com, that point to a Web page or other information on the Internet. The domain name for your website (yourcraftsbusiness.com) is the prominent part of your URL.

- **Website developer.** A person or company that designs and builds websites.

- **Website host.** A company that leases space on its servers to host your website. (Imagine that your website is a movie. The developer would be its director, and the host would be the movie theater.) Usually, you pay a fee of $20 or more per month for hosting services. Hosts will also often help you register your domain name (by linking you with a domain name registry).

A. Planning and Developing Your Site

Creating a website is an art unto itself, with plenty of possibilities to set your creative gears whirring. However, realize that the more functions you want your site to offer—message boards, shopping carts, streaming video—the more you will need the help of a Web developer. You'll also need to consider the various legal rules that apply to each function. Answering the following questions will help you arrive at a plan that's appropriate to your needs and budget:

- Will you use the site mainly to provide information about your crafts—for example, as a supplement to your printed brochure, to enable stores or galleries to see your work or to direct customers to retail outlets? If so, you should be able to design it yourself. The related legal issues are trifling.

- Will you take orders online? As long as customers will be looking at your products, it might be nice to capitalize on their impulses to click and buy. However, adding a so-called shopping cart will probably require the help of a developer. You will also have to familiarize yourself with the federal mail order laws discussed in Chapter 3 and decide how to maintain and use the private information collected from your customers. In addition, your ongoing costs will increase, because most hosting services charge $50 or more per month to provide shopping cart access.

- Will you provide links to other sites? You'll find it easy to set up links, and they can help you—for example, linking to retail websites selling your work. With minor exceptions, linking does not raise any legal concerns (see sidebar, "Don't Worry About Links," below).

- Will you provide message boards or chat rooms? Chances are you won't need to set up these features unless you plan on creating an arts community at your site. If that's your intention, you may have to pay more to include these features, and you'll have to familiarize yourself with some chat room rules (see Section E, below).

Razzle v. Dazzle

Flashy sites are often slower, more confusing and less likely to encourage repeat visitors—a lesson that many website owners have learned the hard way. Before envisioning your dream site, stop to consider the following:

- Every Web page at your site should download within seven seconds on a 56K modem. Normal text will do fine, but avoid large images that are saved at high resolutions (above 72 DPI). Despite the hoopla over broadband (see sidebar, "Should You Go Broadband?", below) the majority of Web surfers still use 56K telephone connections.

- Information should fit legibly on a 15- to 17-inch screen. Build your Web page from the left side of the screen, not the center. That way the most important information will be on the left, where it will be visible right away to most users without having to use the horizontal scroll bar. Not everyone owns a huge monitor.

- Users prefer links over scrolling. If you're going to have a long page, create links to sections or headings within the page rather than requiring the user to manually move down the whole page.

- A large percentage of users click right past Flash animation and multimedia add-ons requiring plug-ins (special programs that the user must have installed to view or hear the content). As users get more savvy, they tend to perceive moving pictures and other bells and whistles as roadblocks rather than entertainment.

- Keep it personal. "I didn't want [my website] to be stiff and formal," says polymer clay artist Irene Semanchuk Dean (see sidebar, "Good Site, Irene," below) because I'm selling handcrafted work. Customers get a personal email from me when they place an order, and I email them again to let them know I've shipped their order. I like the personal touch, and judging from the positive responses I get, it seems other people do, too."

Unsure which do-it-yourself website software to buy? The three leading off-the-shelf programs—Macromedia *Dreamweaver,* Adobe's *Go Live* and Microsoft *FrontPage*—all offer tutorial programs to help you create your own site. But don't trust us alone. Read user comments online about Web-creation software at c/net.com (www.cnet.com) or Amazon.com (www.amazon.com).

1. Working With Website Developers

If you'd prefer not to create your site yourself, you can hire someone to develop it for you. Finding a Web developer isn't difficult—everyone from large companies to the kid down the block seems to be getting into the business. However, sorting through the wide range of choices can be confusing. Below I briefly describe the three most common development offers.

a. ISP Package Deals

ISP companies such as AOL and Earthlink have entered the website development business, commonly offering two types of deals: basic ISP website packages and more sophisticated stores. With a basic package deal, the ISP provides website design services and hosts your website for free or for a token charge. These basic sites don't offer shopping carts or sales features. They're primarily for displaying your work. A major disadvantage is that some ISPs force your customers to put up with banner ads—annoying advertisements for other companies' products that pop up above or below your website.

More sophisticated ISP packages provide shopping services, usually within the context of an online shopping mall. To see examples, look at the zShops at Amazon.com or the online stores at Yahoo! These shops provide a low-hassle means of selling your work.

b. Development Services From a Website Host

Some website hosting services offer a convenient, one-stop approach to creating and hosting your site. See Section B, below.

c. Independent Website Developers

Unless you're doing it yourself, working with an independent website developer will give you the most control over the appearance of your site. If possible, choose a developer recommended by others. Since developers range dramatically in price (and competence), ask to see examples of past work, and get the agreement in writing (see subsection 2, below).

2. The Website Development Contract

Most developers provide a standard written contract, with a few blanks to be filled in. Although contracts are, in theory, meant to be written up after both parties have negotiated and agreed on the terms, the developer is more likely to hand you a standard form and say, "Sign here." In other words, developers often offer take-it-or-leave-it deals, with little or no room for modifications. If, after carefully reading the contract, you believe that it's stacked against you, don't bother hiring that developer. (You've got some leverage here: When it comes to developers, it's a buyer's market.) To protect your interests, make sure your contract includes the following:

- **Specifications and timelines.** The contract should lay out exactly what your website will include. Mention, for example, the planned number of Web pages, the subject of each Web page and what shopping cart features, if any, will be added. The contract should also say exactly when the developer will have the site up and running—for example, a beta version (a test version shown to the client) in six weeks and a "go live" website in 12 weeks.
- **Warranties and indemnity.** The developer should promise not to do anything illegal—like infringing someone else's copyright or displaying something libelous—while creating your site.
- **Ownership of the site.** The developer should provide an assurance that you—and not the developer—will own the copyright in the

appearance of your website. (If you're not familiar with copyright principles, read Chapter 8.) Copyright ownership allows you to copy and display the site without getting permission from anyone.

- **Contract assignment.** If you don't want the developer subcontracting the work on your site to another company without your permission, you'll need a clause that prevents assignment of the contract—usually something like, "Developer cannot assign rights under this Agreement without the written permission of the Client." This does not prevent the developer's employees from creating the work, but at least in that case the developer is supervising the work.
- **Objections and approvals.** You'll want a simple system for approving or objecting to the developer's work. For example, the contract could state that if you disapprove the beta version, the developer has two weeks to correct the defects.
- **Termination.** You'll want an escape hatch in case things go sour during the development process. For example, the contract may include a right to terminate the agreement provided you pay for the work that has already been completed. As a basic business principle, be wary of cavalierly terminating any contract. Review your obligations and, if in doubt as to the consequences of termination, consult an attorney.

 Getting confused about the distinctions between developers, hosts and domain name registries? You may be noticing that the tasks and services of website hosts, domain name registries and developers overlap—for example, a domain name registry may provide development services and hosting, or a developer may obtain your domain name and provide hosting. Because of this overlap, always focus on the services being provided rather than on the title of "host," "domain name registry" or "developer."

Can Crafts Make Money Online?

In 2001, *The Crafts Report* magazine surveyed crafts businesses to find out whether they earned money online. Half of the respondents reported earning less than $500 in a year online. A quarter of the respondents reported earnings between $500 and $5,000 in a year, and a mere 3% reported over $15,000 in annual earnings.

One interesting fact—14% of those surveyed stated they spent nothing on their websites but earned between $1,000 and $3,000. On the other hand, every business that spent over $8,000 on their website reported earning that amount or more in return.

Which crafts earned the most online? One-fifth of those businesses earning $8,000 or more per year online were jewelry artists, with ceramics and glass vendors following closely behind.

B. Hosting Your Site

In order for visitors to reach your website, it must be hosted on a server maintained by a website hosting service. You, or your developer, will need to transfer the completed website to the host, who will display it 24 hours a day, seven days a week.

Free hosting is offered by many ISPs such as AOL and MSN. As with all "free" services, however, there are drawbacks. If you switch ISPs—for example, you move your account from AOL to AT&T—you will need to recreate your site at your new ISP, along with a new URL. Also, with free hosting, your domain name will be longer than you might like, since it will have to include the host's address and internal links as well. Even if you wanted a short and sweet name like "Mycrafts.com," you might end up with something like the following: aol.members.com/rstim/mycrafts. It is possible to resolve this by getting a domain name of your own (see Section C, below) and having the domain name registry (the company that sells you the domain name) redirect visitors to your site. Registries perform this function for free—but they'll add a banner ad for their services on your site.

Free hosting also limits your use of email accounts—that is, you can only use your regular ISP account (rwstim@aol.com), and not the five to ten extra mailboxes where you and your employees can receive email as provided by a commercial host.

Most commercial website owners choose a host that charges a fee, usually $10 to $150 a month depending on the plan. Sites such as The List (webhosts.thelist.com) and Find Webspace (www.findwebspace.com) can help you identify hosts that meet your requirements. The cost will depend upon your choices regarding the following features:

- **Disk space.** The hosting agreement permits you to occupy a certain amount of space on the server. Figure on needing roughly 10MB for each 100 pages on your website.

- **Site access.** The hosting agreement will permit you access to the server to modify your site. Ideally, you want 24-hour access, seven days a week.

- **Email accounts.** Basic plans (approximately $20 a month) usually provide five email accounts. More expensive plans ($40 a month or more) provide more email accounts. For example, you may want a separate email account for orders, customer service, information and so on.

- **Data transfer.** Most website hosts will limit the total number of visitors to your site each month. Basic plans usually permit at least 5 gigabytes (GB) of data transfer. That's roughly equivalent to having 60,000 page views. A page view refers to one visitor accessing one page. For example, if 20,000 visitors accessed three pages, that would be 60,000 page views. If you need more than that, you'll have to pay more per month.

- **Shopping carts and credit card processing.** Some hosting plans offer special shopping plans—for example, manual or automatic credit card services. If you choose automatic credit card services, the credit card company receives the information directly from the consumer. If you choose manual credit card services (best suited for craft vendors with five to ten products and approximately 100 transactions per month), you must manually enter the credit card information into your computer after getting it from the customer via email or some other means. You then forward the information to the credit card processing company for authorization.

- **Ending the hosting relationship.** Someday you may decide to switch to another website host. Plan ahead for this by making sure that your website hosting contract permits you to terminate freely and without a reason. Most contracts will require some notice, perhaps 30 days. Find out if the website host will provide a temporary "pointer" that directs users to your new site during the period when you are moving from one host to another.

Special Pages for Viewing by Retailers

It's possible to set up special pages on your site that list wholesale prices and related information for retailers. Your website developer can make these pages password-protected. You supply the password to retailers and they—not the general public—can access the pages.

C. Choosing Your Domain Name

Your domain name serves as your online address. You will find it easy to get one—assuming your choice is not one of the 40 million domain names that have already been taken.

1. what.com?

You're already aware that a domain name looks like this: *yourcraftsbusiness.com*. The "name" part—yourcraftsbusiness—reflects your choice of an identifier. You don't have to choose ".com" as a suffix (although registrations for .coms outpace other suffixes by ten to one). Currently (as of July 2002),

there are eight choices for a domain name suffix, five of which may be suitable for your crafts business:

- .com, for commercial enterprises
- .edu, for educational institutions
- .gov, for governmental agencies
- .net, for network-related entities
- .org, for nonprofit organizations
- .biz, for businesses
- .info, for information providers, and
- .name, for individuals.

(The suffix ".coop" is expected to be available at the end of 2002, as well.)

The guidelines for many of these suffixes are not strictly enforced. For example, anyone can acquire a .com, .net, .org, .biz or .info domain name regardless of the type of business they operate. But strictly enforced standards put the .edu and .gov suffixes beyond your reach. Similarly, the .name extension is for individuals only, not for businesses. When .coop becomes available, its use will be restricted to cooperatives.

Many observers believe that the preference for .com will continue because people seem to feel—rightly or wrongly—that the .com designation provides familiarity to consumers and confers an extra measure of prestige on the business using it.

You can register under multiple suffixes—for example, *yourcraftsbusiness.com, yourcraftsbusiness. net* and *yourcraftsbusiness.org* (see, sidebar, "barbini.net v. barbini.com," below.).

2. Getting Your Domain Name

After you've chosen a name and made certain that no one else already owns it, you will want to obtain the rights to use your domain name. To do so, register it with a domain name registry. For an alphabetical list of approved registries, go to www.internic.net or www.icann.org. You'll need to provide some information to the registry and pay a fee (approximately $35 per domain name).

To check on name availability, go to any domain name registry and use the search feature. If the name is taken, you can learn who owns it by checking at www.whois.net. This can be helpful if you suspect cybersquatting (see Section C3, below) or in case you want to buy the name.

Once you register your domain name, it's yours forever provided you renew it annually. Most registries will warn you months in advance of when it's time to renew. Normally, no one can stop you from using that domain name, unless you infringe someone's trademark and they sue you claiming you're confusing consumers.

3. Battling Cybersquatters

It's not illegal to speculate in domain names—to buy and sell them for profit. But if someone has registered your trademark as a domain name in a bad-faith attempt to profit from it, they may be engaging in an illegal activity known as cybersquatting. You can, however, stop them, if you can demonstrate that the person who purchased the domain name did so to deprive you of your rights to the name and to profit from it.

There are two possible ways to proceed against a cybersquatter. The first is to use the arbitration service offered by the international organization in charge of domain name registrations (ICANN). (For an explanation of trademarks, see Chapter 6.) If you win your dispute, you'll get the domain name.

Your other option is to sue under the federal cybersquatting law. However, this normally requires the help of lawyers and can take several years to resolve. Of the two options, I recommend the ICANN route for resolving domain name disputes, because it's relatively speedy and inexpensive. Usually an ICANN dispute is resolved within 60 days—much faster than any court resolution would take. To see the ICANN dispute resolution rules, go to www.icann.org/udrp/udrp.htm.

If you'd like to get an idea on how the ICANN arbitrators make decisions in different types of domain name cases, check out UDRP Law at www.udrplaw.net. Based upon past ICANN arbitrations, the odds seem to be in favor of the person seeking to transfer the domain name, that is, the person who has or claims to have trademark rights.

barbini.net v. barbini.com

Barbi Jo Stim (my sister) has been selling women's fashion accessories under the trademark "Barbini" for 17 years. A few years ago, she decided to establish a website (Figure 4-3) so that distributors and buyers could view her inventory. Before leaving for a trade show, she learned that *barbini.com* was available, but after returning, she found that it had been acquired. Although she suspected a cybersquatter (someone who had talked to her at the show), she faced an uphill battle demonstrating that the domain name buyer had acted in bad faith. She was also unwilling to spend the time getting involved in arbitration or a court battle. Instead of disputing the name or finding the cybersquatter and paying for it, she simply registered barbini.net and established her website under this domain name. Within a year, I tracked down the owner, a company in Taiwan that offered to sell me barbini.com for $1,500. (Fig 4-4.)

For more information on domain names, see *Domain Names: How to Choose & Protect a Great Name for Your Website,* by Stephen Elias & Patricia Gima (Nolo).

Don't Worry About Links

It's unlikely that you'll get into legal trouble by linking to another site. If you're concerned about upsetting the owners of the site to which you're linking, ask for permission. Two types of links *do* cause problems: those that encourage illegal behavior, for example, linking to illegal downloads; and inline linking, the process of making a picture on someone else's website appear on your site. A federal court of appeals ruled in 2002 that inline linking by a photo-searching engine violated copyright law. (*Kelly v. Arriba Soft Corp.*, 280 F.3d 934 (9th Cir. 2002).)

Figure 4-3: barbini.net

Figure 4-4: barbini.com

What If You Build and They Don't Come?

There's more to attracting visitors to your website than submitting your name to search engines. In fact, many books and Internet sites are devoted to the subject of attracting visitors (see the ecommerce/marketing channel at www.internet.com, for example). I recommend researching some of these tips and working hard at marketing your site. And don't forget to include your website address on your tags, business cards, postcards and brochures and at your trade show booths.

Wilkes (see sidebar, "Artsymartha.com Meets PayPal.com," below.) You don't have to buy the software, or worry about the store being up. It's self-sustaining."

Not counting development services, you pay $49.95 per month for hosting, $0.10 per item listed per month, a 0.5% transaction fee on all transactions and a 3.5% revenue share on transactions that originate on the Yahoo! Network—that is, when someone specifically searches Yahoo! and finds your work. There is no startup fee, and you can cancel whenever you want. Yahoo! will also line you up with a credit card merchant. Amazon's zShops, eBay's stores and MSN's Small Business Services offer similar selling and site options.

D. Setting Up a Sales Site

Most crafts artists sell their work online in one of three ways: by setting up their own online store with a shopping cart system, by building an online store that's affiliated with an online company such as Yahoo! or Amazon or by using PayPal or another credit card intermediary. A fourth alternative—using email to establish a deal and consummating it by regular mail—is disappearing as a sales choice.

⚠ Don't let your quest for short-term profits ruin important business relationships. Despite the greater profit margin, selling directly to consumers may endanger your relationship with loyal retailers—especially if your prices undercut theirs.

1. The ISP-Affiliated Store

Looking for a fast way to sell your work online? An ISP-affiliated store, such as an Amazon zShop or a Yahoo! Shopping store, offers an easy way to launch your goods into cyberspace.

For example, at Yahoo! (store.yahoo.com) you can design your site yourself or pay Yahoo! to develop it. "If you really want to get it started and not have to worry about it, I recommend the Yahoo! Stores," says website programmer and crafts artist Martha

Selling Directly to Retailers Online

If you're interested in selling your work directly to gallery and store owners and other retailers, sites such as WholesaleCrafts.com (www.wholesalecrafts.com) offer an intriguing option. In return for payment of a setup fee ($100) and maintenance fees (approximately $500 a year), WholesaleCrafts provides you with a custom Web page that can be accessed by over 5,000 retailer members. (The public cannot access the site). To qualify, your business must be artist-owned and your work must be original and made in the United States or Canada. You must submit studio-quality photography and you must, at the time of signing up, be successfully supplying at least two retail establishments. You cannot submit work made from commercially produced kits, molds, castings or patterns or embellished work using commercially made products that can be sold separately.

2. Your Own Sales Site

If you have a large inventory, you may benefit from a shopping cart system—a method by which users can collect items throughout the site, then pay and check out. "People who like to shop online really want to just click on "buy this item" instead of having to send an email asking about prices and availability," says crafts artist Irene Semanchuk Dean. "Installing a cart increased my online orders dramatically."

Some savvy crafts workers set up a shopping cart system themselves using shopping cart software such as Miva Merchant (www.miva.com). However, most website owners affiliate with enterprises such as an online credit card company and an online shopping cart service. I suggest that you use the assistance of your website host or an online service that creates shopping cart solutions. (This stuff gets complex!) You can find some help for setting up an online credit card system at sites such as MerchantWorkz (www.merchantworkz.com), MerchantSeek (www.merchantseek.com/) and SwipeSmart (www.swipesmart.com).

The agreements provided by online services are not negotiable, so read the terms carefully to discover any hidden fees. Some companies, for example, will charge you every time they refund money to a disgruntled customer (called a chargeback fee). Some may include financial penalties for transferring your Web host.

3. PayPal and Other Credit Card Intermediaries

If you're only selling a few items, you may be able to avoid the shopping cart system with a simple order form and a link to PayPal or a similar credit card intermediary (see sidebar, "Artsymartha.com Meets PayPal.com," below). For a fee, PayPal (www.paypal.com) will handle all the details of your getting paid. PayPal will process your customers' credit card payments and transfer the money to your bank account. The procedures can be a little clunky for some customers, but sites selling a few items or with modest sales may find it suitable.

ArtsyMartha.com Meets PayPal.com

Fiber artist Martha Wilkes also works as a Web designer. Her website, www.artsymartha.com (Figure 4-5), provides a good example of a practical, personalized and efficient site. Created with Dreamweaver software, Wilkes's site manages to explain and display her work with several short, well-crafted Web pages. It also focuses the user on her two primary products, wands and wreaths.

By using a PayPal business account, Wilkes gives the customer a simple method for paying by credit card (Figure 4-6). "I'm a programmer, but I didn't want to deal with programming a shopping cart. I saw people on eBay using PayPal and signed up for it. I'd much rather have the third party deal with the credit card processing." By clicking either of the PayPal options at the site, the user is directed to PayPal (Figure 4-7) to consummate the transaction.

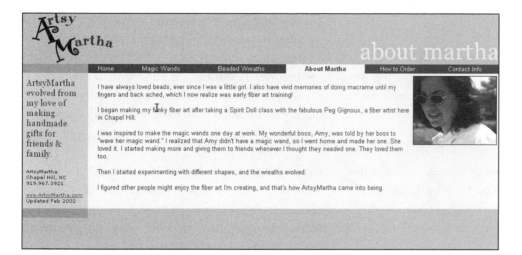

Figure 4-5: www.artsymartha.com

Figure 4-6: Links to PayPal

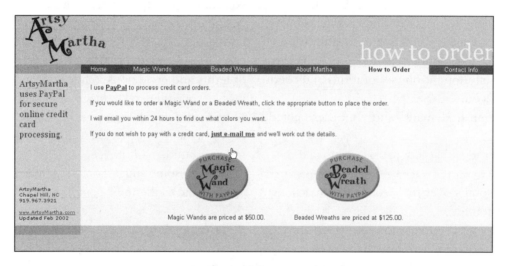

Figure 4-7: PayPal

E. Posting Policies

Every crafts business has rules for customers—like the "Sorry, No Refunds" sign behind the cash register or legal jargon on the back of the order form. With just one major exception, there's no law requiring a website to post similar rules or conditions. Even if you do post them, the law is similarly silent on how and where they should appear. (The exception is the Children's Online Privacy Protection Act (COPPA), which requires you to post a privacy policy if your website is directed to children. See Subsection 3, below.)

But conspicuously posting online notices offers both business and legal benefits. On the business side, being straight with visitors and customers builds trust, a belief in your credibility and loyalty—all of which can help your online business grow. On the legal side, a well-thought-out set of terms and conditions can help you:

- protect your trademarks and your copyrighted content
- limit your legal liability to customers and others, and
- avoid disputes over the details of transactions with customers.

It's true that if a customer sues you, your terms and conditions may not give you 100% protection. But, at least you and your lawyer will have some solid arguing points to present to the court.

Your terms and conditions may include three forms of legal information: transaction conditions, disclaimers and proprietary notices.

- **Transaction conditions** are the terms for doing business with you. For example, you might want to announce that your business won't accept returns more than 30 days after purchase. Your privacy policy—how you handle information that you collect—may also be highly reassuring to potential customers.
- **Disclaimers** are statements that inform customers that you won't be liable for certain kinds of losses they might incur. For example, you may disclaim responsibility for losses that result if pottery breaks when a customer ships it back for return.
- **Proprietary notices** are statements that proclaim the legal status of your intangible business assets. For example, a trademark notice lets users know that you're claiming trademark rights in your name or logo.

Even though the customer doesn't sign on the dotted line, the posted provisions are usually legally enforceable by the business or its customers. If you operate a high-volume crafts business with lots of Web traffic (thousands of hits a day) and are concerned about lawsuits, you can be surer that courts will honor your fine print if you require visitors or customers to click an "I Accept" or an "I Agree" button.

Some e-commerce websites use a lengthy statement of terms and conditions; other sites have short warnings or notices linked to their home page. The amount of fine print you should post depends on your site. As a general rule, you should always include a copyright and trademark notice.

Here are some suggestions for terms and conditions appropriate to the most common types of crafts sites.

1. Display Sites

If your site is primarily a display of your crafts work, you'll need to post only copyright and trademark notices. These warn the world not to rip off the contents of your website or your logo. Consider covering copyrights and trademarks with something like the following:

Copyright © 2002 by [*name of your crafts business*]. All rights reserved. [*Name of your crafts business*] is a trademark.

If your trademark is registered with the federal government, you should replace the second sentence in the example above with: "[*Name of your crafts business*] is a registered trademark."

2. Sales Sites

If your site offers crafts for sale online, you may need notices regarding credit card use, refunds and returns. Here's what a policy for returns and credit cards might look like:

Returns. If you wish to return an item, send it to us at [address]. Enclose a note telling us:

- how you want us to handle the return. We can exchange the item, issue a gift certificate, issue a refund or credit the card originally charged
- why you're returning the item (for example, wrong size, damage in transit and so on)
- the name and address to which we should send your refund or exchange, and
- an email address or fax or phone number so we can contact you if we have questions.

If you need to use freight shipping to return the item to us, call our customer service department at 800-555-1234 and we'll make the necessary arrangements.

Credit cards. YourCraftsBusiness.com wants to make shopping online a convenient and safe experience. Here's our Credit Card Guarantee:

Our computer system safeguards all payment information that you transmit to us while using our site. This includes your user name, password and credit card number and expiration date. We convert your personal information into code that is securely transmitted over the Internet.

If you discover that someone has fraudulently used your credit card information as a result of your making an online purchase from YourCraftsBusiness.com, you must notify your credit card provider in accordance with its rules and procedures. If you do so, and your credit card provider holds you liable for unauthorized charges, we'll reimburse you for up to $50, the limit of your liability under federal law.

3. Chats and Posts

If your site provides space for chats or postings from the Web-surfing public, you'll want to minimize your liability from illegal postings or offensive chat room comments. Here's what a disclaimer might look like:

Disclaimer: Information Posted by Others.
People other than YourCraftsBusiness.com employees supply some of the content on this site. YourCrafts Business.com has no more editorial control over such content than does a public library, bookstore or news-stand. Any opinions, advice or statements expressed by other parties are those of the others and not of Your CraftsBusiness.com. YourCraftsBusiness.com doesn't endorse and isn't responsible for the accuracy or reliability of any opinion, advice or statement made on the site by anyone other than authorized YourCrafts Business.com employees while acting in their official capacities.

If you are gathering information from your customers, including credit card information, you should post a privacy policy detailing how this information will be used or not used (see sidebar, "Good Site, Irene," below.)

If you are catering to an audience under 13 years old, you should learn more about dealing with children at the Federal Trade Commission's website (www.ftc. gov/kidzprivacy). There are many rules regarding gathering information from young Web surfers.

For more information on consumer privacy policies and chat room policies, review *How to Get Your Business on the Web,* by Fred Steingold (Nolo).

Good Site, Irene

Polymer clay artist Irene Semanchuk Dean (author of *The Weekend Crafter-Polymer Clay*) overhauled her website (www.good-night-irene.com; Figure 4-8) in March 2002. She now has a very fresh policies statement that satisfies the legal requirements for shipping, returns, credit cards and privacy. Best of all, it's not written in legalese. For example, she simply says, "I solemnly swear I will never share your name or contact info with any other mailing list, ever." Her disclaimer explains to buyers that they are buying one-of-a-kind items whose appearance may differ slightly from items shown: "Everything here is hand-made, by one person, one at a time. Variations from what you see depicted are almost certainly guaranteed. Know this, accept this, expect this."

Should You Go Broadband?

You can connect to the Internet via dial-up modems (regular phone lines) or over high-speed broadband systems such as DSL phone lines or coaxial cable (the same system that carries cable TV signals). Broadband costs twice as much as dial-up service, and the rates are on the way up (the average monthly broadband bill in January 2002 was $44.22). Over one third of Internet users in the United States connect using broadband connections. (I agree with those who claim broadband is addictive.) I would recommend broadband if you develop and regularly maintain your site or manage the sales on your site.

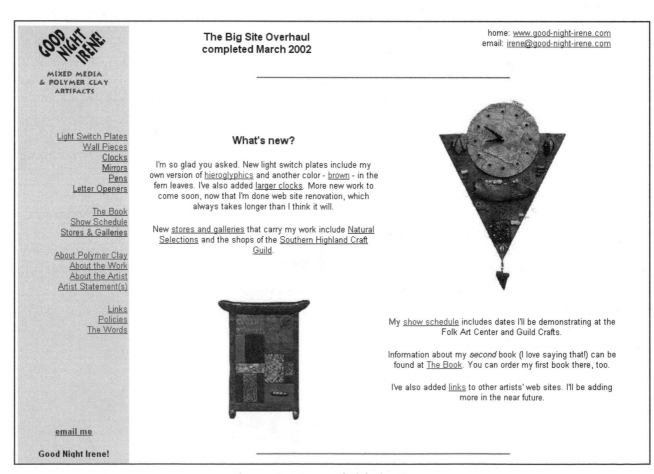

Figure 4-8: www.good-night-irene.com

How Easy Is It to Copy From Your Website?

The short answer: It's fairly easy to copy any image that's on your website. If you don't believe me, click your right mouse button (if you use a PC) on any website image and look at your choices: *"Save Picture As," "Email Picture," "Print Picture."* There are some sophisticated ways to prevent this copying, but—as with all security measures—there are ways around these copy-protection schemes. For example, regardless of such copy protection, it's always possible to capture any portion of a Web page using a program such as Snag-It (www.techsmith.com).

If you're concerned about the copying and reproduction or sale of images from your website, you can try some of the tricks used by the stock art websites. To prevent high-quality reproductions—and to help your pages load faster—only use low-resolution imagery (that is, save your Web pictures at 72 DPI, not 300 DPI).

If you want to display works for your known customers but you don't want them available to general public, there's an easy solution. Create an "unlinked" Web page. A typical visitor to your site will not see the page, because it is not available from any of your linked pages. However, a client who is given the unique URL can find the page. ∎

Chapter 5

Employees and Independent Contractors

*I*n 1984, a dispute arose as to who owned the rights to Hummel figurines, one of the world's most collectible crafts products. At issue was whether the copyright in these cherubic creations was owned by the estate of the creator, Sister Berta Hummel, or by the German convent in which Sister Hummel toiled.

Under copyright law, the creator of the work—with one major exception—is the owner. The exception is that when someone is hired to create a work, the hiring party may, in some circumstances, be the owner. This is known as the "work-made-for-hire" (or "work-for-hire") principle. A manufacturer, trying to preserve its license to manufacture the Hummel figurines in the United States, argued that Sister Hummel was employed by the convent and that the drawings were works made for hire. The manufacturer pointed out that Sister Hummel had taken a vow of poverty and intended that all the fruits of her labors pass to the convent.

The U.S. federal court disagreed with the manufacturer. It was true that Sister Hummel performed artistic work for the convent—designing ecclesiastical vestments and artifacts—but the convent did not ask her to create the secular and spiritual drawings that were to become the basis of the figurines. Even if Sister Hummel was an employee of the convent, spending time on the spiritually inspired figurines was not part of her job description. Sister Hummel had created and controlled the drawings and supervised the creation of the ceramic figures. She, not the convent, owned the rights, and her rights passed to her mother, her only surviving relative. (*Schmid Brothers, Inc. v. Goebel*, 589 F.Supp. 497 (E.D. NY 1984).)

It may seem odd that, 40 years after her death, lawyers are arguing about whether Sister Hummel was an employee when she created her crafts. But the dispute demonstrates the crucial importance of correctly classifying an employee's status. Workers—those people you hire for your crafts business—provide important services and can increase your profit margins. But they can also be the source of disputes over a wide range of issues, including:

- employment tax reporting responsibilities (see Sections A, B and C)
- firing workers (see Section D)
- workers' compensation coverage (see Section E)
- your ownership of patents and copyrights in works created by the worker (see Sections F and G)
- workers' misuse of secret information (see Section H).

Employees Make a $$ Difference

According to the 2001 survey of the Craft Organization Directors Association (CODA), craftspeople that have paid employees have three times the household income and ten times the sales/revenue of those who work alone.

A. Employee or Independent Contractor?

The first question to ask when analyzing your tax and other obligations with respect to people working for you is whether they are your employees or are simply independent contractors. These are the two categories used by the government—there are no other categories in between, although the line between them is far from distinct. Some workers are clearly employees; some are clearly independent contractors. But in between these two extremes, the real world contains a vast middle ground where work relationships have some elements of traditional employment and others of independence. Workers who fall into this uncertain middle ground are often misclassified by their employers, leading to problems with the IRS, state tax authorities, unemployment compensation authorities and other agencies. Here's why it's important to get the classification right:

- **Federal income taxes.** You need to withhold and pay federal payroll taxes for employees—but not for independent contractors—including Social Security tax, federal disability tax and federal income tax.

- **State unemployment compensation.** If the worker is an employee, you will need to pay for state unemployment compensation coverage; not so for independent contractors.
- **State income taxes.** You don't have to withhold state income taxes for an independent contractor. But if your state tax department considers the worker an employee, you will need to withhold state income taxes from the worker's paycheck.
- **Workers' compensation insurance.** You need to provide workers' compensation coverage for employees but usually not for independent contractors.
- **Overtime.** If the U.S. Labor Department considers the worker an independent contractor, you won't need to pay the worker time-and-a-half for overtime. If the worker is an employee, you might have to pay it.
- **Discrimination.** If the worker is considered an independent contractor under federal and state laws outlawing workplace discrimination, the worker will have fewer grounds on which to sue you.
- **Intellectual property ownership.** You're more likely to own the rights in works created by employees than by independent contractors. In both cases, you can guarantee ownership of any intellectual property the worker creates on your behalf by taking certain steps.

While it is possible for a worker to have a hybrid status—that is, to be an independent contractor for some purposes and an employee for others—this can lead to trouble down the road. If a government agency discovers that you're treating a worker as an employee for any purpose, the chances go up that it will conclude that the worker is an employee for its own purposes as well.

1. Workers Who Are Independent Contractors

An independent contractor is a person who contracts to perform services for others, but who does not have the legal status of an employee. Most people who qualify as independent contractors follow their own trade, business or profession—that is, they are in business for themselves. This is why they are called "independent" contractors. They earn their livelihoods from their own independent businesses instead of depending upon an employer to pay their living.

People who own their own businesses usually have certain working characteristics in common. They typically:

- offer their services to the general public, not just to one person or company
- have their own business offices
- invest in tools, equipment and facilities
- take care of their own taxes, and
- make a profit if the business goes well, but risk going broke if it goes badly.

Good examples of independent contractors are the people you hire to paint your office, repair your computer or prepare your taxes. Sometimes it's very easy to tell if workers are or are not in business for themselves.

Example: To fill a large ongoing order, you hire someone to perform soldering at your studio for your metal crafts business for six months. It is clear that a worker in a crafts shop is not in business. He or she is an employee of your business.

In many other cases, however, classifying a worker is more difficult. It can be especially hard where workers perform specialized services by themselves —that is, without the help of assistants.

Example: You hire Heather to perform accounting for your business. Heather has no employees and ends up spending three days a week working at your spare desk on your accounting books. It's difficult to say for sure that Heather is in business for herself while she works for you. An IRS or other government auditor might not be convinced.

2. Applying Legal Tests

Government agencies and courts have developed two main tests to determine whether workers should be classified as employees or independent contractors:

- the *common law* test, which focuses on the physical control of the worker by the hiring firm, and
- the *economic reality* test, which focuses on whether the worker is economically dependent upon the hiring firm.

These tests, discussed in detail below, are designed to reveal how you treat the worker, what roles the worker plays in your business and what roles you play in the worker's economic life.

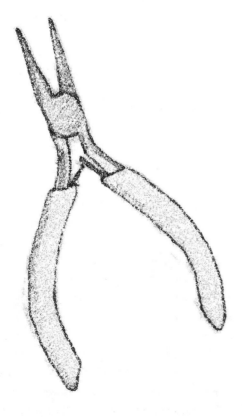

Three Myths About Independent Contractors

A few myths live on about who is and who is not an independent contractor.

Myth #1: Saying a worker is an independent contractor will make it so.

Don't get caught in the trap of thinking workers are independent contractors because that's what you label them. The mere fact that you call a worker an independent contractor will not by itself convince the IRS or other government agency. Government auditors look at the substance of the relationship between the hiring firm and worker, not mere formalities. If you have the right to control a worker on the job, the worker will be considered an employee regardless of how the two of you characterize your relationship.

This is not to say that a written independent contractor agreement can't be helpful in establishing that a worker is an independent contractor. It can be, provided that it's well drafted and reflects reality—that is, those involved actually behave the way the agreement says they will.

Myth #2: People who work for more than one company are independent contractors.

If you have the right to control a worker on the job, the worker will be your employee even if he or she works for others at the same time. It's possible for a worker to have more than one employer at the same time.

Myth #3: Part-time and short-term workers are independent contractors.

Don't think that because you're hiring a person for only a couple of weeks, or for only a few hours a week, the worker must be an independent contractor. To most government agencies, it doesn't make much difference whether a worker works full time or part time. If you have the right of control, a part-time worker will be deemed a part-time employee and a short-term worker a short-term employee.

3. Common Law Test for Independent Contractor Status

The common law test of whether workers are employees or independent contractors is widely used, including by:

- the IRS
- unemployment compensation insurance agencies in many states
- workers' compensation insurance agencies in many states, and
- courts, in determining copyright ownership disputes.

The common law test is based on a very simple notion: Employers have the right to tell their employees what to do. The employer may not always exercise this right—for example, if an employee is experienced and well trained, the employer may not feel the need to closely supervise him or her—but the employer has the right to do so at any time.

Under the common law test, workers are employees if the people for whom they work have the right to direct and control them in the way they work—both as to the final results and as to the details of when, where and how the work is performed.

In contrast, when you hire an independent contractor, you hire an independent businessperson. The hiring firm normally does not have the right to control the way an independent businessperson—an independent contractor—carries out the agreed-upon services. Its control is limited to accepting or rejecting the final results.

To evaluate whether a worker is truly an independent contractor, you need to examine these common law factors. The first 20 factors below make up the famous IRS 20 Factor Test—the test the IRS has historically used to measure control. However, the IRS has simplified and liberalized its test. As a result, not all of the 20 factors are as important as they once were.

To understand the "Instructions" factor (Factor #12), focus on whether you have the *right* to give instructions. Even though you have not given a worker instructions, the IRS could conclude that you have the right to do so and view this factor as indicating employment status. If a worker is running an independent business and you are just one client or customer among many, it's likely you don't have the right to give the worker instructions about how to perform the services. Your right is usually limited to accepting or rejecting the final results.

Treating a worker as an employee for tax purposes (Factor #23)—that is, remitting federal and state payroll taxes for the worker—is strong evidence that you believe the worker to be your employee and you have the right to exercise control over him or her. Indeed, one court has ruled that paying federal and state payroll taxes for a worker is a virtual admission that the worker is an employee under the common law test. (*Aymes v. Bonelli*, 980 F.2d 857 (2d Cir. 1992).)

4. Economic Reality Test

Some courts and government agencies, when reviewing the common law test of employee versus independent contractor status, consider it too restrictive to focus on the hiring firm's right to physically control the worker. These courts and agencies use a different test, called the economic reality test. Under this test, workers are employees if they are economically dependent upon the businesses for which they render services. Economic dependence equals an employment relationship.

Using the economic reality test, a court will include all workers who would be considered employees under the common law test and other workers who government agencies and courts feel need and deserve special protection. These are primarily low-skill, low-paid workers—the type of workers labor and workers' compensation laws were originally intended to help. The factors courts examine to gauge the degree of a worker's dependence on a hiring firm include:

- the skill required to do the work
- the amount of the worker's investment in facilities and equipment
- the worker's opportunities for profit or loss

Common Law Factors

Factor	Employees	Independent Contractors
1. Making a Profit or Loss	Employees are typically paid for their time and labor and have no liability for business expenses.	In addition to the gain or loss ordinarily realized by employees, independent contractors can earn a profit or suffer a loss as a result of the services being performed.
2. Working on Specific Premises	Employees must work where their employers tell them, usually on the employer's premises.	Independent contractors are usually able to choose where to perform their services.
3. Offering Services to the General Public	Employees offer their services solely to their employers.	Since they are independent business-people, independent contractors normally make their services available to the public.
4. Right to Fire	An employee typically can be discharged by the employer at any time.	An independent contractor's relationship with a hiring firm can be terminated only according to the terms of their agreement.
5. Furnishing Tools and Materials	Employees are typically furnished all the tools and materials necessary to do their jobs by their employers.	Independent contractors typically furnish their own tools and materials.
6. Method of Payment	Employees are usually paid by unit of time.	Independent contractors are typically paid a flat rate for a project.
7. Working for More Than One Firm	Although employees can have more than one job at a time, employers can require loyalty and prevent employees from taking some alternative jobs.	Independent contractors usually have multiple clients or customers.
8. Continuing Relationship	Employees have a continuing relationship with their employers.	Independent contractors generally work on one project and then move on.
9. Investment in Equipment or Facilities	Employees generally have no investment in equipment or facilities.	Independent contractors invest in the equipment and facilities appropriate for their businesses.
10. Business or Traveling Expenses	Employees' job-related business and traveling expenses are paid by the employer.	Independent contractors typically pay their own business and traveling expenses.
11. Right to Quit	An employee may normally quit the job at any time without incurring any liability to the employer.	An independent contractor is legally obligated to complete the work he or she agreed to do.
12. Instructions	Employers have the right to give their employees oral or written instructions that the employees must obey about when, where and how they are to work.	Independent contractors need not comply with instructions on how to perform their services; they decide on their own how to do their work.
13. Sequence of Work	Employees may be required to perform services in the order or sequence set for them by the employer.	Independent contractors decide for themselves the order or sequence in which they work.

Common Law Factors (continued)

Factor	Employees	Independent Contractors
14. Training	Employees may receive training from their employers.	Independent contractors ordinarily receive no training from those who purchase their services.
15. Services Performed Personally	Employees are required to perform their services on their own—that is, they can't get someone else to do their jobs for them.	Independent contractors ordinarily are not required to render services personally; for example, they can hire their own employees or even other independent contractors to do the work.
16. Hiring Assistants	Employees hire, supervise and pay assistants only at the direction of the employer.	Independent contractors hire, supervise and pay their own assistants.
17. Set Working Hours	Employees ordinarily have set hours of work (for example, 9 to 5).	Independent contractors are masters of their own time; they ordinarily set their own work hours.
18. Working Full Time	An employer might require an employee to work full time.	Independent contractors are free to work when and for whom they choose—and usually have the right to work for more than one client or customer at a time.
19. Oral or Written Reports	Employees may be required to submit regular oral or written reports to the employer regarding the progress of their work.	Independent contractors are generally not required to submit regular reports; they are responsible only for end results.
20. Integration Into Business	Employees typically provide services that are an integral part of the employer's day-to-day operations.	Independent contractors' services typically are not molded into the hiring firm's overall business as one integrated operation.
21. Skill Required	Workers whose jobs require a low level of skill and experience are more likely to be employees.	Workers with jobs requiring high skills are more likely to be independent contractors.
22. Worker Benefits	Employees usually receive benefits such as health insurance, sick leave, pension benefits and paid vacation.	Independent contractors ordinarily receive no similar workplace benefits.
23. Tax Treatment of the Worker	Employees usually have federal and state payroll taxes withheld by their employers and remitted to the government.	Independent contractors ordinarily pay their own taxes.
24. Intent of the Hiring Firm and Worker	People who hire employees normally intend to create an employer–employee relationship.	People who hire independent contractors normally intend to create an independent contractor–hiring firm relationship.
25. Custom in the Trade or Industry	Workers who are normally treated like employees in the trade or industry in which they work are likely to really be employees.	Workers who are normally treated like independent contractors in the trade or industry in which they work are likely to really be independent contractors.

- whether the worker's relationship with the hiring firm is permanent or brief
- the extent to which the services provided by the worker are an integral part of the hiring firm's business
- whether the hiring firm has the right to control how the work is done, and
- the amount of initiative, judgment or foresight in open market competition with others required for the success of the worker's independent enterprise.

Highly skilled, highly paid workers with substantial investments in tools and equipment are likely going to pass this test so long as they don't work full time for just one firm. You're going to have a very hard time passing the economic reality test if you don't pay a worker very much, the worker is not highly skilled, the worker has no investment in tools or equipment and the worker doesn't have to use much individual initiative to earn a living.

5. Other Tests for Independent Contractor Status

About half the states use a special statutory test, sometimes called the ABC test, to determine if workers are independent contractors or employees. This test is mainly used to determine whether unemployment compensation is owed. The ABC test focuses on just three factors:

- whether the hiring firm controls the worker on the job
- whether the worker is operating an independent business, and
- where the work is performed—meaning, does the worker work where the company says he should work, or does he work where he wants to work?

This test is simpler than the others discussed above, but can be the hardest to satisfy.

The following chart lists most of the factors government auditors use to classify workers, and it shows the differences among the various agencies.

B. Tax Concerns When Hiring Employees

The tax rules you have to follow when you hire helpers differ depending upon whether the workers qualify as employees or independent contractors according to the IRS and other government agencies.

Whenever you hire an employee, you become an unpaid tax collector. You are required to withhold and pay both federal and state taxes for every employee of your business. These taxes are called payroll taxes or employment taxes. You must also satisfy these requirements if you incorporate your business and continue to actively work in it. In this event, you will be an employee of your corporation.

If you hire an independent contractor, you need not comply with these requirements. All you have to do is report the amount you pay the independent contractor to the IRS and your state tax department. However, hiring an independent contractor is not necessarily cheaper than hiring an employee. Some independent contractors charge far more than what you'd pay an employee to do similar work. Nevertheless, many self-employed crafts workers still prefer to hire independent contractors instead of employees because of the lesser tax and bookkeeping burdens.

1. Federal Payroll Taxes

The IRS regulates federal payroll taxes, which include:

- Social Security and Medicare taxes—also known as FICA
- unemployment taxes—also known as FUTA, and
- income taxes—also known as FITW.

IRS Circular E, *Employer's Tax Guide,* provides detailed information on federal payroll taxes. It is an outstanding resource that you should have if you hire employees. You can get a free copy by calling the IRS at 800-TAX-FORM, by calling or visiting your local IRS office or by downloading it from the IRS website (www.irs.gov).

Factors Considered in Classifying Workers

	Unemployment Compensation in states using ABC Test	Unemployment Compensation in states using common law test	Workers' Compensation in states using economic reality test	Workers' Compensation in states using common law test	U.S. Labor Dept.	Copyright Ownership	IRS Test
No training		✓		✓		✓	✓
Assistants can do work		✓		✓		✓	✓
Worker can realize profit or loss		✓		✓	✓		✓
Work not done on hiring firm's premises	✓	✓		✓			
No right to fire worker		✓		✓	✓		
Worker offers services to public		✓		✓			✓
Worker furnishes tools and materials		✓		✓			✓
Payment by the project		✓		✓		✓	✓
Worker has multiple clients or customers		✓		✓		✓	
Worker and hiring firm have no continuing relationship		✓		✓	✓	✓	
Worker has significant investment in equipment and facilities		✓		✓	✓		✓
Worker pays own business expenses		✓		✓			✓
Worker has no right to quit		✓		✓			
Worker sets order or sequence of work		✓		✓			✓
Worker provides own training		✓		✓			✓
Worker need not perform services personally		✓		✓			✓
Worker sets own hours		✓		✓		✓	
Full-time work not required		✓		✓			
Reports not required		✓		✓			✓
Work outside hiring firm's usual business	✓	✓	✓	✓		✓	✓
Custom in the community		✓		✓			
Worker highly skilled		✓		✓		✓	
Initiative, judgment needed to succeed		✓		✓	✓		
Intent of worker and hiring firm		✓		✓			✓
Worker not subject to hiring firm's control		✓		✓	✓		✓
Worker has independent trade or business	✓	✓	✓	✓		✓	✓
Tax treatment of worker		✓		✓		✓	✓
No worker benefits provided		✓		✓		✓	✓
Work typically not supervised		✓		✓			
No right to assign additional projects						✓	

a. FICA

FICA is an acronym for Federal Income Contributions Act, the law requiring employers and employees to pay Social Security and Medicare taxes. The IRS imposes FICA taxes on both employers and employees. If you hire an employee, you must collect and remit his or her part of the taxes by withholding it from paycheck amounts. You must also pay a matching amount.

The amounts you must withhold and pay are listed in the current edition of IRS Circular E. For 2002, for example, employers and employees were each required to pay 7.65% on the first $84,900 of an employee's annual wages. The 7.65% figure is the sum of the 6.2% Social Security tax and the 1.45% Medicare tax.

There is no Social Security tax on the portion of an employee's annual wages that exceeds the $84,900 ceiling. However, the Medicare tax marches on: Both you and the employee must pay the 1.45% Medicare tax on any wages over $84,900. The ceiling for the Social Security tax changes annually. To find out this year's Social Security tax ceiling, see IRS Circular E, *Employer's Tax Guide*; the amount is printed right on the first page.

b. FUTA

FUTA is an acronym for the Federal Unemployment Tax Act; the law establishes federal unemployment taxes. Most employers must pay both state and federal unemployment taxes. But even if you're exempt from the state tax, you may still have to pay the federal tax. Employers alone are responsible for FUTA. You may not collect or deduct it from employees' wages.

You must pay FUTA taxes if:

- you pay $1,500 or more to employees during any calendar quarter—that is, during any three-month period beginning with January, April, July or October, or
- you had one or more employees for at least some part of a day in any 20 or more different weeks during the year. The weeks don't have to be consecutive, nor does the employee have to be the same one each week.

Technically, the FUTA tax rate is 6.2%, but in practice, you rarely pay this much. You are given a credit of 5.4% if you pay the applicable state unemployment tax in full and on time. This means that the actual FUTA tax rate is usually 0.8%. In 2002, the FUTA tax was assessed on the first $7,000 of an employee's annual wages. That brought the FUTA tax to around $56 per year per employee.

c. FITW

FITW is an acronym for federal income tax withholding. When you hire an employee, you're not only a tax collector for the government, but you are a manager of sorts of your employee's income. The IRS fears that employees will not save enough from their wages for their tax bill on April 15. Also, it wants to speed up tax collections. So the IRS tells you, the employer, not to pay the employees their entire wages but to send the money to the IRS—the employee version of the estimated taxes independent contractors must pay.

You must calculate and withhold federal income taxes from all your employees' paychecks. You normally deposit the funds in a bank, which transmits the money to the IRS. Employees are solely responsible for paying federal income taxes. Your only responsibility is to withhold the funds and remit them to the government.

You must ask each employee you hire to fill out IRS Form W-4, Employee's Withholding Allowance Certificate. The information on this form is used to help determine how much tax must be withheld from the employee's pay.

By January 31 of each year, you must give each employee on your payroll the previous year a copy of IRS Form W-2, Wage and Tax Statement, showing how much he or she was paid and how much tax was withheld for the year. You must also send copies to the Social Security Administration.

You can obtain copies of these forms by calling the IRS at 800-TAX-FORM, by visiting your local IRS office or by downloading them from the IRS website.

For detailed information on FITW, see IRS Publication 505, *Tax Withholding and Estimated Tax*. You can obtain a copy by calling the IRS at 800-TAX-FORM, by visiting your local IRS office or from the IRS website (www.irs.gov).

d. Paying Payroll Taxes

You pay FICA, FUTA and FITW either electronically or by making federal tax deposits at specified banks. The IRS will tell you how often you must make your payroll tax deposits. The frequency depends on the total taxes you pay. If you pay by mail, you must submit an IRS Federal Tax Deposit coupon (Form 8109-B) with each payroll tax payment. If you have employees, you must also report these payments to the IRS on Form 941, Employer's Quarterly Federal Tax Return, after each calendar quarter that you have employees. Form 941 shows how many employees you had, how much they were paid and the amount of FICA and income tax withheld.

Once each year you must also file IRS Form 940, Employer's Annual Federal Unemployment Tax Return, or the simpler Form 940-EZ. This form tells the IRS how much federal unemployment tax you owe.

Instead of depositing payroll tax payments by check with specified banks, you may transfer funds straight to the IRS electronically, using the IRS's Electronic Federal Tax Payment System (EFTPS). Using EFTPS, you can make deposits by phone or by using your personal computer. If you pay more than $200,000 in payroll taxes each year, using EFTPS is mandatory. If you pay less than $200,000, using the electronic system is optional. For information on EFTPS or to get an enrollment form, call EFTPS Customer Service at 800-555-4477 or 800-945-8400.

Figuring out how much to withhold, doing the necessary recordkeeping and filling out the required forms can be complicated. Computer accounting programs such as Intuit's *QuickBooks* can help with all the calculations and print out your employees' checks and IRS forms. You can also hire a bookkeeper or payroll tax service to do the work. Payroll tax services are usually not expensive, especially if you only have one or two employees.

e. Penalties for Failing to Pay FICA and FITW

As far as the IRS is concerned, an employer's most important duty is to withhold and pay over Social Security and income taxes. Employee FICA and FITW are also known as trust fund taxes because the employer is deemed to hold the withheld funds in trust for the U.S. government.

If you fail to pay trust fund taxes, you can get into the worst tax trouble there is. The IRS can—and often does—seize a business's assets and force it to close down if it owes back payroll taxes. You can also get thrown in jail, but this rarely happens.

At the very least, you'll have to pay all the taxes due plus interest. The IRS may also impose a penalty known as the trust fund recovery penalty if it determines that you willfully failed to pay the taxes. The agency can claim you willfully failed to pay taxes if you knew the taxes were due and didn't pay them. Good evidence that you knew such taxes were due is that you paid them in the past, but stopped.

The trust fund recovery penalty is also known as the 100% penalty, because the amount of the penalty is equal to 100% of the total amount of employee FICA and FITW taxes the employer failed to withhold and pay to the IRS. This can be a staggering sum. As a business owner, you'll be personally liable for the 100% penalty—that is, you will have to pay it out of your own pocket. This is so even if you've incorporated your business.

For guidance on how to deal with the IRS if you are having trouble meeting your payroll tax obligations, see *Tax Savvy for Small Business*, by Frederick W. Daily (Nolo).

f. Rules for Family Members

Self-employed people often hire family members to help them. An argument in favor of this family togetherness is that if you hire your child, spouse or parent as an employee, you may not have to pay FICA and FUTA taxes.

i. Employing your child

You need not pay FUTA taxes for services performed by your child if he or she is under 21 years old. You need not pay FICA taxes for your child under 18 who works in your trade or business, or in your partnership if it's owned solely by you and your spouse.

Example: Lisa, a 16-year-old, handles the Internet orders for her mother's decorative broom business, which is operated as a sole proprietorship. Although Lisa is her mother's employee, her mother need not pay FUTA until Lisa reaches 21 and need not pay FICA taxes until she reaches 18.

However, these rules do not apply—and you must pay both FICA and FUTA—if you hire your child to work for:

- your corporation, or
- your partnership, unless all the partners are parents of the child.

Example: Ron works in a stoneware business that is half owned by his mother and half owned by her partner, Ralph, who is no relation to the family. FICA and FUTA taxes must be paid for Ron because he is working for a partnership and not all the partners are his parents.

ii. Income tax break for child employees

You must withhold income taxes from your child's pay only if it exceeds the standard deduction for the year. The standard deduction was $4,700 in 2002 and is adjusted every year for inflation. A child who is paid less than this amount need not pay any income taxes on his or her salary.

You might consider getting your child to do some work around the studio instead of paying him or her an allowance for doing nothing. If your child's pay is below the standard deduction amount, it is not only tax-free, but you can also deduct the amount from

your own taxes as a business expense if the child's work is business-related. For example, cleaning the studio, answering the phone or making deliveries are all business-related tasks. However, you can only deduct your child's wages if they are reasonable— that is, what you'd pay a stranger for the same work. Don't try paying your child $100 per hour for cleaning the studio so you can get a big tax deduction.

If you pay your child $600 or more during the year, you must file Form W-2 reporting the earnings to the IRS. No matter how much you pay your child, each year you should fill out and have your child sign IRS Form W-4, Employee's Withholding Allowance Certificate. If you pay your child less than $200 per week, then keep the form in your records. If you pay your child more than $200 per week, keep a copy of the form for your records and file a copy of the form with the IRS.

iii. Employing your spouse

If you pay your spouse to work in your trade or business, the payments are subject to FICA taxes and federal income tax withholding, but not to FUTA taxes.

Example: Kay's husband, Simon, is a sole proprietor pewter sculptor. Kay works as his assistant and is paid $1,500 per month. Simon must pay the employer's share of FICA taxes for Kay and withhold employee FICA and federal income taxes from her pay.

But this rule does not apply—and FICA, FUTA and FITW must all be paid—if your spouse works for:

- a corporation, even if you control it, or
- a partnership, even if your spouse is a partner along with you.

Example: Laura's husband, Rob, works as a glassblower in Laura's hand-blown glass business, a corporation of which she is the sole owner. The corporation must pay FICA, FUTA and FITW for Rob.

iv. Employing a parent

The wages of a parent you employ in your trade or business are subject to income tax withholding and FICA taxes.

Example: Don owns and operates a studio that produces agate candleholders. He employs Art, his father, as a part-time worker. Since the firm is a business, Don must pay the employer's share of FICA taxes for Art and withhold employee FICA and federal income taxes from his pay.

2. State Payroll Taxes

Employers in all states are required to pay and withhold state payroll taxes for employees. These taxes include:

- state unemployment compensation taxes, in all states (see subsection a)
- state income tax withholding, in most states (see subsection b), and
- state disability taxes, in a few states (see subsection c).

a. Unemployment Compensation

All states must, under federal law, provide most types of employees with unemployment compensation, also called UC or unemployment insurance.

Employers are required to contribute to a state unemployment insurance fund. Employees make no contributions except in Alaska, New Jersey, Pennsylvania and Rhode Island where employers must withhold minor contributions from employees' paychecks. An employee who is laid off or fired for other than serious misconduct is entitled to receive unemployment benefits from the state fund. You need not provide unemployment for independent contractors.

If your payroll is very small—below $1,500 per calendar quarter—you probably won't have to pay UC taxes. In most states, you must pay state UC taxes for employees if you're paying federal UC taxes, also called FUTA taxes. However, some states have more strict requirements. Contact your state labor department for the exact payroll amounts.

b. State Income Tax Withholding

All states except Alaska, Florida, Nevada, South Dakota, Texas, Washington and Wyoming have income taxation. New Hampshire and Tennessee impose income taxes on dividend and interest income only. If you do business in a state that imposes state income taxes, you must withhold the applicable tax from your employees' paychecks and pay it to the state taxing authority. No state income tax withholding is required for workers who qualify as independent contractors.

It's easy to determine whether you need to withhold state income taxes for a worker: If you are withholding federal income taxes, then you must withhold state income taxes as well. Each state has its own income tax withholding forms and procedures. Contact your state tax department for information.

c. State Disability Insurance

Five states have state disability insurance programs to provide employees with coverage for injuries or illnesses that are not related to work. Injuries that are job-related are covered by workers' compensation. (See Section E. below.) The states with disability insurance are California, Hawaii, New Jersey, New York and Rhode Island. Puerto Rico also has a disability insurance program.

In these states, employees contribute to disability insurance in amounts their employers withhold from their paychecks. Employers must also make contributions in Hawaii, New Jersey, New York and Puerto Rico.

Except in New York, the disability insurance coverage requirements are the same as for UC insurance. If you pay UC for a worker, you must withhold and pay disability insurance premiums as well. You need not provide disability for independent contractors.

C. Tax Reporting for Independent Contractors

If you hire an independent contractor, you don't have to worry about withholding and paying state or federal payroll taxes or filling out lots of government forms. This is one reason independent contractors generally prefer hiring other independent contractors rather than employees.

However, if you pay an unincorporated independent contractor $600 or more during the year for business-related services, you must:

- file IRS Form 1099-MISC telling the IRS how much you paid the worker, and
- obtain the independent contractor's taxpayer identification number.

The IRS imposes these requirements because it is concerned that many independent contractors avoid paying taxes by failing to report all their income. To help prevent this, the IRS wants to find out how much you pay independent contractors you hire and make sure it has their correct tax ID numbers.

The filing and ID requirements apply to all independent contractors you hire who are sole proprietors or partners in partnerships. This covers the vast majority of independent contractors. However, these requirements don't apply to corporations, probably because large businesses have a strong legislative lobby. The IRS has attempted to change the law to include corporations, but so far it hasn't succeeded.

This means that if you hire an incorporated independent contractor, you don't have to file anything with the IRS.

Example: Bob, a self-employed fabric designer, pays $5,000 to Yvonne, a CPA, to perform accounting services. Yvonne has formed her own one-person corporation called Yvonne's Accounting Services, Inc. Bob pays the corporation, not Yvonne personally. Since Bob is paying a corporation, he need not report the payment on Form 1099-MISC or obtain Yvonne's tax ID number.

This is one of the main advantages of hiring incorporated independent contractors, because the IRS uses Form 1099 as a lead to find people and companies to audit.

However, it's wise to make sure you have the corporation's full legal name and obtain its federal employer identification number. Without this information, you may not be able to prove to the IRS that the payee was incorporated. An easy way to do this is to have the independent contractor fill out IRS Form W-9, Request for Taxpayer Identification Number, and keep it in your files. This simple form merely requires the corporation to provide its name, address and EIN.

When in Doubt, File a Form 1099

The IRS may impose a $50 fine if you fail to file a Form 1099 when required. But that's the least of your worries. If you don't file a Form 1099 and the IRS later audits you and determines you misclassified the worker, you'll be subject to severe penalties.

If you're not sure whether you must file a Form 1099-MISC for a worker, go ahead and file one anyway. You lose nothing by doing so and will save yourself the severe consequences of not filing if you were legally required to do so.

For a detailed discussion of the consequences of not filing a 1099 form, see *Hiring Independent Contractors: The Employer's Legal Guide*, by Stephen Fishman (Nolo).

There are two exceptions to the rule that you don't have to file 1099 forms for payments to corporations. You must report all payments of $600 or more you make to a doctor or lawyer who is incorporated. However, this is necessary only where the payments are for your business. You need not report payments you make to incorporated doctors or lawyers for personal services—for example, if you hire a doctor to treat your bronchitis or hire a lawyer to write your will.

1. $600 Threshold for Independent Contractor Income Reporting

You need to obtain an unincorporated independent contractor's taxpayer ID number and file a 1099 form with the IRS only if you pay the independent contractor $600 or more during a year for business-related services. It makes no difference whether the sum was one payment for a single job or the total of many small payments for multiple jobs.

> *Example:* Andre, a 3-D mixed media artist, hires Thomas, a self-employed programmer, to help create a computer program. Andre classifies Thomas as an independent contractor and pays him $2,000 during the year. Thomas is a sole proprietor. Since Andre paid Thomas more than $599 for business-related services, Andre must obtain Thomas's taxpayer ID number and file Form 1099 with the IRS reporting the payment.

In calculating whether the payments made to an independent contractor total $600 or more during a year, you must include payments for parts or materials the independent contractor used in performing the services. For example, if you hire a painter to paint your home office, the cost of the paint would be included in the tally.

However, not all payments you make to independent contractors are counted towards the $600 threshold.

a. Payments for Merchandise

You don't need to tell the IRS about payments that were solely for merchandise or inventory. This includes raw materials and supplies that will become a part of the craft goods you intend to sell.

> *Example:* Betty pays $5,000 to purchase leather pieces from Joe's Leather, a sole proprietorship he owns. Betty intends to resell the leather as pouches. The payment need not be counted toward the $600 threshold because Betty is purchasing merchandise from Joe, not services.

b. Payments for Personal Services

You need only count payments you make to independent contractors for services they perform in the course of your trade or business. A trade or business is an activity carried out for gain or profit. You don't count payments for services that are not related to your business, including payments you make to independent contractors for personal or household services or repairs. Running your home is not a profit-making activity.

2. Obtaining Taxpayer ID

Some independent contractors work in the underground economy—that is, they're paid in cash and never pay any taxes or file tax returns. The IRS may not even know they exist. The IRS wants you to help track these people down by supplying the taxpayer ID numbers from all independent contractors who meet the requirements explained above.

If an independent contractor won't give you his or her number, or the IRS informs you that the number the independent contractor gave you is incorrect, the IRS assumes the person isn't going to voluntarily pay taxes. So the IRS requires you to withhold taxes from the compensation you pay the independent contractor and remit them to the IRS. This is called backup withholding. If you fail to backup withhold, the IRS will impose an assessment against you equal to 30% of what you paid the independent contractor.

a. Avoiding Backup Withholding

Backup withholding can be a bookkeeping burden for you. Fortunately, it's usually easy to avoid. Have the independent contractor fill out and sign IRS Form W-9, Request for Taxpayer Identification Number. Retain the Form W-9 in your files; you don't have to file it with the IRS. This simple form merely requires the independent contractor to list his or her name and address and taxpayer ID number. Partnerships and sole proprietors with employees must have a federal employer identification number (EIN), which they obtain from the IRS. In the case of sole proprietors without employees, the taxpayer ID number is the independent contractor's Social Security number.

If the independent contractor doesn't already have an EIN but promises to obtain one, you don't have to backup withhold for 60 days after he or she applies for one. Have the independent contractor fill out and sign the W-9 form, stating "Applied For" in the space where the ID number is supposed to be listed. If you don't receive the independent contractor's ID number within 60 days, you'll have to start backup withholding.

b. Backup Withholding Procedure

If you are unable to obtain an independent contractor's taxpayer ID number or the IRS informs you that the number the independent contractor gave you is incorrect, you'll have to do backup withholding. You must begin doing so after you pay an independent contractor $600 or more during the year. You need not backup withhold on payments totaling less than $600.

To backup withhold, deposit with your bank 30% of the independent contractor's compensation every quarter. You must make these deposits separately from the payroll tax deposits you make for employees. You report the amounts withheld on IRS Form 945, Annual Return of Withheld Federal Income Tax. This is an annual return you must file by January 31 of the following year. See the instructions to Form 945 for details. You can obtain a copy of the form by calling the IRS at 800-TAX-FORM, by contacting your local IRS office or by downloading it from the IRS website (www.irs.gov).

3. Filling Out Your Form 1099

One 1099-MISC form must be filed for each independent contractor to whom you paid $600 or more during the year. You must obtain original 1099 forms from the IRS (the form cannot be photocopied, because it contains several pressure-sensitive copies). Each 1099 form contains three parts and can be used for three different workers. All your 1099 forms must be submitted together along with one copy of Form 1096, which is a transmittal form—the IRS equivalent of a cover letter. You must also obtain an original Form 1096 from the IRS; submitting a photocopy is not permitted. Obtain these forms by calling the IRS at 800-TAX-FORM or by contacting your local IRS office.

4. Clothing Producers and Other Workers Treated as Statutory Employees

Special rules apply for workers who make or sew buttons, quilts, gloves, bedspreads, clothing, needlecraft products or similar products. Under these rules, your workers will be considered statutory employees (that is, the government *says* they are employees by law) if the following requirements are satisfied:

- your crafts business produces quilts, gloves, bedspreads, clothing, needlecraft products or similar products
- the worker performs services away from your place of business—usually in his or her home or workshop, or in another person's home
- the worker performs this work only on goods or materials that you furnish
- the work is performed according to your specifications; generally, such specifications are simple and consist of patterns or samples, and
- the worker is required to return the processed material to you or a person designated by you.

If the work meets all these requirements, you must pay half the employer's share of FICA and withhold FICA taxes from the worker's pay and send it to the IRS, just as for any other employee. However, no FICA tax is imposed if you pay the worker less than $100 during a calendar year.

Example: Rosa sews quilts at home. She works for various quilt makers, including Upscale Quilts, Inc. Upscale provides Rosa with all the fabric and supplies she must sew. The only equipment Rosa provides is a needle. Upscale gives Rosa a sample of each quilt and a pattern. When Rosa finishes each batch of quilts, she returns it to Upscale. Rosa is a statutory employee.

You also must complete a Form W-2, Wage and Tax Statement, for each of your statutory employees. (If you were allowed to treat them as independent contractors, you would instead complete Form 1099-MISC, the form used to report independent contractors' income to the IRS.) The W-2 will show how much Social Security and Medicare tax was withheld from the worker's pay.

You can avoid having a worker classified as a statutory employee if the worker does not:

- Perform services personally for you. Sign a written agreement with the worker stating that the worker has the right to subcontract or delegate the work out to others. This way, you make clear that the worker doesn't have to do the work personally.
- Make a substantial investment in your equipment or work facilities. Encourage the worker to invest in outside facilities, such as her own workspace.
- Have a continuing relationship with your crafts business. A continuing relationship means working for the hiring firm on a regular or recurring basis. Avoid a continuing relationship with the worker by assigning single projects, not ongoing tasks.

D. Firing Workers

A crucial distinction between independent contractors and employees concerns how long you must keep them around. You do not have an unrestricted right to fire an independent contractor as you do with most employees.

1. You Can't Fire an Independent Contractor

Strictly speaking, you can't fire an independent contractor. If the contractor fails to perform the services —that is, breaches the agreement—you can terminate your arrangement. But if the contractor has performed and you terminate your agreement without a legal reason, the independent contractor can sue you. If

he wins, he can get an order requiring you to pay a substantial amount of money in damages. In short, your right to legally terminate an independent contractor's services is limited to situations where the independent contractor breaks the terms of your written or oral agreement.

Example: Julie owns Lucky Handbags and hires Morty, an independent designer, to create her website. She agrees to pay Morty half his fee at the beginning and the other half when he completes the website. Morty is almost done with his work when Julie decides to hire Frankie, her new boyfriend, to create the website. She tells Morty to stop working—that is, terminates her agreement and refuses to pay Morty the second installment. Morty can sue Julie for the remaining payments and any other financial damages that are a consequence of her action.

2. You Can Fire At-Will Employees

Most employees are considered "at will," which means just about what it sounds like: At-will employees are free to quit at any time, for any reason; and you are free to fire them at any time and for any reason— unless your reason for firing is illegal. We cover these illegal reasons to fire, including discrimination, bad faith and public policy violations, below.

Generally, however, you may fire an at-will employee for even the most idiosyncratic reasons—for example, you simply want to hire someone else as a replacement. You are also free to change the terms of employment—job duties, compensation or hours, for example—for any reason that isn't illegal. Your workers can agree to these changes and continue working or reject the changes and quit. In other words, the employment relationship is voluntary. You cannot force your employees to stay forever, and they cannot require you to employ them indefinitely.

You cannot arbitrarily fire an employee if it is forbidden by:

- **An employment contract.** Whether written, oral or implied, an employment contract can limit your right to fire the employee. For these employees, the language or nature of the contract usually spells out the terms of employment, including when and for what reasons the employees can be fired.

- **State or federal laws.** You're prohibited from firing, disciplining or demoting an employee in bad faith, in violation of public policy or for a discriminatory or retaliatory reason.

a. Employment Contracts

Employees who have entered into employment contracts with their employers are often not subject to the at-will doctrine. If, because of one of the contract provisions, the employer can't fire at will, or has promised the employee a job for a set period of time, that contract trumps the at-will rules. These employment contracts often spell out the length and terms of the worker's employment and specify how and when the employment can end. Sometimes these contracts require a valid business reason ("good cause") for termination. Other contracts might spell out in detail the types of employee misconduct or business troubles that would allow either party to end the contract.

Not all employment contracts limit an employer's right to fire at will, however. Some contracts expressly reserve the employer's right to fire, while setting forth other agreed-upon terms of the employment relationship (pay, position, job duties and hours, for example). We explain how and when you might use either a contract limiting your right to fire or a contract preserving your at-will rights in the sections that follow.

To write an employment contract that preserves your right to fire at will, you must:

- include explicit language stating that employment is at will
- exclude any restrictions, however indirect, on your right to fire, and
- get your employee to sign the agreement (and sign it yourself). Let's look at these requirements in more detail.

What's an Implied Contract?

If you convey to your employee, through some combination of oral statements, written policies and conduct, that the employee will be fired only for cause, the employee may be able to convince a judge or jury that you should be held to your words and actions. An implied employment contract is a legal hybrid. It is an enforceable agreement that has not been reduced to a formal contract or explicitly stated orally, but instead is implied from a combination of oral statements, written statements and conduct. To prove an implied contract, an employee will have to show that you led him to believe he would not be fired without a good reason. The employee doesn't have to prove that you wrote or said those words, however. Instead, the employee must show that your statements, personnel policies and actions towards the employee all led him to believe (as would any reasonable employee in his position) that his job was secure. You may be swimming in implied contract waters if you have:

- given the employee regular promotions, raises and positive performance reviews
- assured the worker that her employment was secure or would continue as long as she performed well
- promised, explicitly or implicitly, that the employee's position would be permanent
- employed the worker for a lengthy period before firing her, or
- adopted policies that place limits on your right to fire workers at will.

You can avoid creating an implied employment contract by stating that employment is at will. In your written employment policies, including your employee handbook or personnel manual, state clearly that employment at your company is at will and explain what this means. Also: Ask employees to sign an at-will agreement. Don't make promises of continued employment. Don't refer to employees as "permanent."

b. State and Federal Laws

You violate state or federal laws when your fire, demote or discipline an employee:

- in violation of public policy
- in bad faith
- for a discriminatory reason, or
- for a retaliatory reason.

Violations of public policy. You violate public policy when you fire or discipline an employee for reasons most people would find morally or ethically wrong. States have different rules about what constitutes public policy. The federal government and some states have laws explicitly prohibiting employers from firing or punishing employees for doing certain things, like reporting a health and safety violation or taking family medical leave. Some states allow employees to file public policy lawsuits even when no statute spells out exactly what the employer can and cannot do. A good rule for employers is to consult an attorney whenever you are considering firing, demoting or disciplining an employee who has recently exercised a civic right, refused to engage in questionable activity or blown the whistle on workplace problems.

Bad faith. Employers have a duty to treat their employees fairly and in good faith. What this duty amounts to, as a practical matter, varies from state to state. Simply firing or disciplining a worker is not enough to breach this duty—an employer who treats employees honestly and with respect, even those employees who must be disciplined or fired, runs no risk. However, an employer who treats an employee in a particularly callous way or fires an employee for a malevolent reason—particularly if the firing was intended to deprive the employee of benefits to which she would otherwise be entitled—may be successfully sued for violating this basic principle. Not every state allows employees to sue an employer for violating the duty of good faith and fair dealing. And some states allow only employees who have an employment contract to bring these claims. Because of these variations between states' laws, you may want to consult with a lawyer if you are concerned about good faith and fair dealing claims—the duty might not even apply to you.

Discrimination. Perhaps the most common complaint employees take to court is that they were fired or disciplined for discriminatory reasons. These claims can be tough to combat. They are intensely personal and upsetting for all involved, which increases the danger that emotions, rather than reason, will hold sway. And there are strong legal prohibitions against discriminating in the workplace. Even when you are sure that you fired or disciplined a worker for a valid, nondiscriminatory reason, there is always the chance that an administrative agency, judge or jury will disagree. Your first line of defense is to familiarize yourself with the laws that might be invoked against you so you can stay out of trouble in the first place, as summarized below.

State discrimination laws also prohibit discrimination in employment. For more information, along with the agencies responsible for enforcing antidiscrimination laws in each state, check Nolo's Legal Research Center (www.nolo.com). You can research municipal antidiscrimination laws at the headquarters of your community government, such as your city hall or county courthouse.

- **The Civil Rights Act.** The federal Civil Rights Act (also known as Title VII, 42 U.S.C. § 2000 and following) applies to all companies with 15 or more employees. Under Title VII, employers may not intentionally use race, skin color, gender, religion or national origin as the basis for workplace decisions, including promotion, pay, discipline and termination. Title VII does not apply to federal government employees or independent contractors.

- **Sexual Harassment.** Title VII, discussed above, also bans sex discrimination and prohibits sexual harassment. Sexual harassment is any unwelcome sexual advance or conduct on the job that creates an intimidating, hostile or offensive work environment. More simply put, sexual harassment is any offensive conduct related to an employee's gender that a reasonable woman or man should not have to endure at work.

- **Pregnancy Discrimination.** The Pregnancy Discrimination Act, or PDA (42 U.S.C. § 2076), prohibits employers from discriminating against an employee because of her pregnancy, childbirth or related medical condition. This means you must treat pregnant workers the same as your other workers, and you may not fire or demote an employee because she is pregnant.

- **Age Discrimination.** The Age Discrimination in Employment Act, or ADEA (29 U.S.C. § 621 to § 634), makes it illegal for employers to discriminate against workers on the basis of age. The ADEA applies to private employers with more than 20 employees. However, the ADEA protects only those workers age 40 or older. Many states also prohibit age discrimination; some of these laws protect younger workers as well or offer wider protections.

- **Retaliation.** Most antidiscrimination laws prohibit employers from retaliating against employees for filing a complaint of discrimination or for cooperating in an investigation of a discrimination complaint. Many state laws contain a similar ban. Juries are particularly sympathetic toward employees who've been retaliated against and routinely award them the highest damages awards.

- **Disability.** The Americans with Disabilities Act, or ADA (42 U.S.C. § 12102 and following), is a federal law that prohibits discrimination against people with physical or mental disabilities. The ADA covers companies with 15 or more employees and applies broadly to private employers. However, the ADA does not apply to state governments. The ADA prohibits employers from terminating a worker because of his disability or because the worker is unable to perform her job without a reasonable accommodation.

For additional information on the ADA, contact the following resources:

- U.S. Equal Employment Opportunity Commission ADA Helpline at 800-669-4000

- U.S. Department of Justice ADA Information Line at 800-514-0301. The U.S. government's website on disabilities is at www.disability.gov
- Job Accommodation Network (JAN), 918 Chestnut Ridge Road, Suite 1, West Virginia University, P. O. Box 6080, Morgantown, WV 26506-6080; 800-232-9675 or 800-526-7234
- Computer Bulletin Board at 800-342-5526.

E. Workers' Compensation

Before the first workers' compensation laws were adopted about 80 years ago, an employee injured on the job had only one recourse: sue the employer in court for negligence—a difficult, time-consuming and expensive process. The workers' compensation laws changed this by establishing a no-fault system. Injured employees give up their rights to sue in court. In return, employees are entitled to receive compensation without having to prove that the employer caused the injury. In exchange for paying for workers' compensation insurance, employers are spared from having to defend lawsuits by injured employees and paying out damages.

Each state has its own workers' compensation system that is designed to provide replacement income and medical expenses for employees who suffer work-related injuries or illnesses. Benefits may also extend to the survivors of workers who are killed on the job. To pay for this, employers in all but three states—New Jersey, South Carolina and Texas, where workers' compensation is optional—are required to pay for workers' compensation insurance for their employees, through either a state fund or a private insurance company. Employees do not pay for workers' compensation insurance.

1. Independent Contractors Are Excluded

You generally need not provide workers' compensation for a worker who qualifies as an independent contractor under your state workers' compensation law. This can result in substantial savings. However, unlike employees, who are covered by workers' compensation, independent contractors can sue you for work-related injuries.

a. Injured Independent Contractors' Rights to Sue You

An employee who is injured on the job can file a workers' compensation claim and collect benefits from your workers' compensation insurer, but cannot sue you in court unless you intended to cause the injury—for example, you beat the employee up. Workers' compensation benefits are set by state law and are usually modest. Employees can obtain reimbursement for medical and rehabilitation expenses and lost income, but can't collect benefits for pain and suffering or mental anguish caused by a work injury.

Your workers' compensation premiums will likely go up if many employees file workers' compensation claims. Still, the premiums will almost certainly be cheaper than defending employee lawsuits.

But an independent contractor who is not covered by workers' compensation can sue you for damages for personal injuries if your negligence—that is, carelessness or failure to take proper safety precautions—caused or contributed to the injury. You will also be held responsible for the negligence of your employees.

b. The Need for Liability Insurance

No matter how small your business, if you hire independent contractors, it is vital that you obtain general liability insurance to protect yourself against personal injury claims by people who are not your employees. A general liability insurer will defend you in court if an independent contractor, a customer or any other nonemployee claims you caused or helped cause an injury. The insurer will also pay out damages or settlements, up to the policy limits. Such insurance can be cheaper and easier to obtain than workers' compensation coverage for employees, so you can still save on insurance premiums by hiring independent contractors rather than employees.

If you don't have general liability insurance already, contact an insurance broker or agent to obtain a policy.

c. Requiring Independent Contractors to Obtain Their Own Coverage

Many hiring firms require workers classified as independent contractors to obtain workers' compensation coverage for themselves. Such coverage is available in most states, even if an independent contractor is running a one-person business.

If you don't do this, your own workers' compensation insurer might require you to cover the independent contractor and pay additional premiums. This is because the independent contractor may claim to be an employee and claim workers' compensation benefits from your insurer if he or she is injured on the job. Your workers' compensation insurer will audit your payroll and other employment records at least once a year to make sure you're paying the proper premiums.

If you require an independent contractor to be insured, obtain a certificate of insurance from the worker. A certificate of insurance is issued by the workers' compensation insurer and is written proof that the independent contractor has a workers' compensation policy. Keep it in your files, and make it available to your workers' compensation insurer when you're audited.

Even if an independent contractor has his or her own workers' compensation insurance, you'll still need to have liability insurance. That's because the independent contractor can sue you in court if he or she is injured due to your negligence. Since you're not the worker's employer, the workers' compensation provisions barring lawsuits by injured employees won't apply to you. Injured independent contractors or their workers' compensation insurers may file these lawsuits.

d. Providing Coverage for Independent Contractor Employees

It may seem unfair, but in all states except Alabama, California, Delaware, Iowa, Maine, Rhode Island and West Virginia, you can be required to provide workers' compensation benefits for an independent contractor's employees. Under state laws that define statutory employees, an independent contractor's uninsured employees are considered to be your employees for workers' compensation purposes if:

- the independent contractor fails to obtain workers' compensation insurance for them, and
- the independent contractor's employees perform work that is part of your regular business—that is, work customarily carried out in your business and other similar businesses.

The purpose of these laws is to prevent employers from avoiding paying for workers' compensation insurance by subcontracting work out to uninsured independent contractors.

Example: Diamond Flower Jewelry receives a large order from a catalog company. In order to fulfill the order, Diamond Flower hires Tom, a subcontractor, to create the jewelry. Tom is an independent crafts worker with his own shop. Tom hires 10 workers to do the work for him. They are all Tom's employees. Tom fails to provide his employees with workers' compensation coverage.

Alice, one of Tom's employees, is injured on the job. Since Tom has no workers' compensation insurance, Alice can file a workers' compensation claim against Diamond Flower, even though she was not Diamond's employee. This is because Alice is Diamond Flower's employee under the state law, and making jewelry is clearly a part of Diamond's regular business.

Because of these statutory employee rules, it's very important for you to require any independent contractor who uses employees to perform services for you to provide them with workers' compensation insurance. Ask to see an insurance certificate establishing that an independent contractor's employees are covered by workers' compensation insurance. In many states, you can also call the state workers' compensation agency to determine if an independent contractor has coverage for his or her employees.

If your own workers' compensation insurer audits your company and discovers that you have hired an independent contractor whose employees do not have workers' compensation coverage, it will likely classify that worker as your own employee for workers' compensation purposes and require you to pay an additional workers' compensation premium.

If you are required to provide workers' compensation benefits to an independent contractor's employees, you are entitled to seek reimbursement for the cost from the independent contractor. But if the independent contractor has no money or can't be located, this legal right will be useless.

2. Determining Who Must Be Covered

Having employees doesn't automatically mean having to buy workers' compensation insurance. Most states exclude certain types of workers from workers' compensation coverage. Nevertheless, most of these exclusions will not apply for crafts workers. Some states also don't require coverage unless you have a minimum number of employees. (See sidebar, "Exclusions for Minimal Numbers of Employees," below.)

Generally, the primary determination a crafts business owner must make is whether the workers should be classified as employees or independent contractors under your state's workers' compensation law. If they're employees, you'll have to provide coverage; if they're independent contractors, you won't. States use different tests to classify workers for workers' compensation purposes.

Exclusions for Minimal Numbers of Employees

The workers' compensation laws of several states exclude employers having fewer than a designated number of employees. In other words, if you have fewer than this minimum number of employees, you don't need to obtain workers' compensation insurance.

State Requirements for Workers' Compensation Coverage	
State	Minimum # of Employees
Alabama	five or more
Arkansas	three or more
Florida	four or more (one or more for construction trades)
Mississippi	five or more
New Mexico	three or more
North Carolina	three or more
Tennessee	five or more
Virginia	three or more

If a crafts worker qualifies as an employee, you must provide workers' compensation coverage. Each state has its own workers' compensation law, with its own definition of who is an employee. However, these state laws follow one of three patterns.

- Most states classify workers for workers' compensation purposes using the common law right of control test. (See subsection a.)
- Other states use a relative nature of the work test, either alone or in conjunction with the common law test. (See subsection b.)
- A few states use different classification schemes. (See subsection c.)

 Most state workers' compensation agencies and state courts interpret their workers' compensation laws to require coverage. This is because the workers' compensation laws are designed to help injured workers, and it's considered beneficial for society as a whole to have as many workers as possible covered. If there is any uncertainty as to how a worker should be classified for workers' compensation purposes, state workers' compensation agencies and courts tend to find that the worker is an employee who should be covered.

a. Common Law States

A majority of state workers' compensation statutes define an employee as one who works for, and

under the control of, another person for hire. To determine whether an employment relationship exists, these statutes ask who has the right to control the details of the work. This is the same common law test used by the IRS and many other government agencies. (See Section A, above.) The list of factors used to measure control varies somewhat from state to state. But the goal is always the same: to determine whether the hiring firm has the right to direct and control the worker in the way he or she works, both as to the final results and as to the details of when, where and how the work is to be done.

b. Relative Nature of the Work Test

Most states now use the common law test discussed above. However, there is a growing trend to use a test that makes it more difficult to establish that a worker is an independent contractor rather than an employee: the relative nature of the work test. This test is based on the simple notion that the cost of industrial accidents should be borne by consumers as a part of the cost of a product or service. If a worker's services are a regular part of the cost of producing your crafts or running your gallery, and the worker is not conducting an independent business, this test dictates that you should provide workers' compensation insurance for the worker.

On the other hand, you don't need to provide workers' compensation if a worker is running an independent business and the worker's services are not a normal, everyday part of your crafts business operations—the cost of which you regularly pass along to your customers.

To determine whether a worker is an employee or independent contractor under the relative nature of the work test, ask two questions:

- Is the worker running an independent business?, and
- Are the workers' services a regular part of the cost of your product or service?

If the answer to both questions is "yes," the worker is an employee for workers' compensation purposes.

Many states use the relative nature of the work test in conjunction with the common law control test. If a worker's status is unclear under the common law test, these states use the second test. Other states use only the relative nature of the work test.

c. Other Tests

A few states have somewhat different tests for determining who qualifies as an employee for workers' compensation purposes. The tests used in Michigan, Minnesota, Oregon, Washington and Wisconsin define who is an employee much more clearly than the common law or relative nature of the work tests. If you're doing business in one of these states, consider yourself fortunate. California is another story, however. California uses at least two tests—the common law test (see subsection a, above) and a second economic reality test. If you pass the common law test, the California Workers' Compensation Appeal Board and courts will use the broader economic reality test to try to find employee status for the workers involved.

3. Consequences of Misclassifying Workers

You are subject to harsh penalties if you misclassify an employee as an independent contractor for workers' compensation purposes and don't provide that employee with workers' compensation insurance. Most state workers' compensation agencies maintain a special fund to pay benefits to injured employees whose employers failed to insure them. You will be required to reimburse this fund or pay penalties used to replenish it.

In addition, most states allow the injured worker to sue you for personal injuries. These states stack the odds against you by not allowing you to raise legal defenses you might otherwise have. For example, in an ordinary lawsuit you might be able to claim that the injury was caused by the employee's own carelessness—but not when dealing with an uninsured, misclassified employee. You will also be subject to fines imposed by your state workers' compensation agency for your failure to insure. These fines vary widely, ranging from $250 to $5,000 per employee. In some cases, the fine is based on the amount of workers' compensation premiums that should have been paid. The workers' compensation agency may

also obtain an injunction—a legal order—preventing you from doing business in the state until you obtain workers' compensation insurance.

If you are doing business as a sole proprietor or partnership, you will be personally liable for these damages and fines. And don't count on hiding behind the corporate shield. In some states, shareholders of an uninsured corporation may be personally liable for injuries sustained by the corporation's employees. For example, in California, any shareholder of an illegally uninsured corporation who holds 15% or more of the corporate stock, or at least a 15% interest in the corporation, may be held personally liable for the resulting damages and fines.

Finally, in almost all states, failure to provide employees with workers' compensation insurance is a crime—a misdemeanor or even a felony. An uninsured employer may be criminally prosecuted and fined and, in rare cases, imprisoned.

4. Obtaining Coverage

Some states allow an employer to self-insure—a process that typically requires the business to maintain a hefty cash reserve earmarked for workers' compensation claims. This isn't practical for most small crafts businesses. You'll probably need to buy insurance, either through a state fund or from a private insurance carrier.

If private insurance is an option in your state, discuss it with an insurance agent or broker who handles the basic insurance for your business. Often you save money on premiums by coordinating workers' compensation coverage with property damage and public liability insurance. A good agent or broker may be able to explain the mechanics of a state fund where that's an option or is required.

For more information on state workers' compensation programs and rules, check the Office of Workers Compensation Programs (OWCP) at the Department of Labor website (www.dol.gov/esa/owcp_org.htm). For a listing of each state's workers' compensation office and related rules, see the clickable map of workers' compensation links at www2.myflorida.com/les/wc/

otherlinks.html. For a discussion of other ways employers can reduce workers' compensation costs, see *Compensation Control: The Secrets of Reducing Workers' Compensation Costs*, by Edward J. Priz (Oasis Press).

F. Works Made for Hire: When You Pay Someone to Create Works

As explained in the Sister Hummel case at the beginning of this chapter, the copyright in an artwork is sometimes owned by the person who paid for it rather than by the artist. When this occurs, the resulting work is called a work made for hire (or simply, a "work for hire"). The basis for this principle is that a business that authorizes and pays for a work should own the rights to the work. This issue is relevant for your crafts business because there are instances in which you may pay a worker to create a copyrightable work and the worker—not you—will own the right to reproduce it. (In Section G, below, we discuss employee ownership of design patents.)

In general, the rules for works made for hire are as follows:

- You own the copyright in any work created by an employee in the course of employment.
- You may—depending on the circumstances—own the copyright in a commissioned work created by an independent contractor for your business (see Section F2, below).

If a work was in fact made for hire, the person paying for the work (the hiring party) is considered to be the copyright owner and is named as the creator (or "author") on an application for copyright registration. The work-for-hire status of a work also affects the length of copyright protection and termination rights. Works made for hire created after 1977 are protected for a period of 95 years from first publication or 120 years from creation, whichever is shorter. Therefore, a work made for hire created in 2002 but not published until 2003 would be protected until 2098 (95 years from the date of publication).

 For a discussion of copyright principles, including what constitutes "publication," see Chapter 8.

1. Works Created by Employees

Every copyrightable work created by an employee within the scope of his or her employment is automatically a work made for hire. The term "scope of employment" does not refer to whether the work was created during business hours or at home; it refers to whether the work is within the "scope" or range of activities expected from the employee. As one court stated, the question is whether it is the kind of work the employee was employed to perform.

If a work is created by an employee within the scope of employment, there are no other requirements and no need for a written agreement—it is a work for hire. It is for this reason that, when sorting out ownership issues, courts first look at whether an employer-employee relationship exists as opposed to an independent contractor relationship.

2. Determining Employee or Independent Contractor Status

How can you tell whether an employer-employee relationship exists? There is no bright-line test—you'll need to weigh a variety of factors similar to those in the common law test discussed in Section A3, above. Of the factors below, the top three should be given the most weight.

- **The provision of employee benefits.** If vacation or health benefits are granted to the artist, this weighs in favor of an employer-employee relationship.
- **The tax treatment of the artist.** If the hiring party pays payroll and employment taxes for the artist, this weighs strongly in favor of an employer-employee relationship. *This is often the determinative factor.*
- **The hiring party's right to control the manner and means by which the work is accomplished.** If the hiring party exercises control, this weighs in favor of an employer-employee relationship.
- **The skill required in the particular occupation.** If the work to be performed requires a unique skill—sculpting, for example—this weighs against an employer-employee relationship.

- **Whether the employer or the artist supplies the instrumentalities and tools of the trade.** If the artist supplies his own tools, this weighs against an employer-employee relationship.
- **Where the work is done.** If the hiring party determines the location of the work, this weighs in favor of an employer-employee relationship.
- **The length of time for which the artist is employed.** The longer the period of work, the more it weighs in favor of an employer-employee relationship.
- **Whether the hiring party has the right to assign additional work projects to the artist.** If the hiring party can assign additional tasks—including tasks that do not result in copyrightable works—this weighs in favor of an employer-employee relationship.
- **The extent of the artist's discretion over when and how long to work.** If the hiring party controls the working times—particularly if it is a regular work week—this weighs in favor of an employer-employee relationship.
- **The method of payment.** If the payment is per job—not per day or week—this weighs against an employer-employee relationship.
- **The artist's role in hiring and paying assistants.** If the artist cannot hire and pay assistants, this weighs in favor of an employer-employee relationship.
- **Whether the work is part of the regular business of the hiring party.** If the hiring party does not regularly perform this type of work—for example, creating photography—this weighs against an employer-employee relationship.
- **Whether the artist is in business.** If the artist has a business, this weighs against an employer-employee relationship.

If the factors above, analyzed as a whole, weigh in favor of an employer-employee relationship, the employer owns any copyrightable works created in the course of employment. If the factors weigh in favor of an independent contractor relationship, the hiring party will own the work only if certain conditions are met, as discussed in Section F3, below.

For more information on the law regarding independent contractors, see *Hiring Independent Contractors: The Employer's Legal Guide,* by Stephen Fishman (Nolo).

3. Independent Contractor Works Made for Hire

As you will realize after reading this section, it's quite unusual for a crafts work created by an independent contractor to qualify as a work made for hire. That doesn't mean the person paying for the work can't acquire copyright ownership—I'll discuss that in Section F4, below—but the method of acquiring ownership is different from the work made for hire method.

That said, a copyrighted work created by an independent contractor (unlike a work created by an employee) is not automatically classified as a work made for hire. For an independent contractor's work to qualify as a work made for hire, three requirements must be met:

- the work must be specially ordered or commissioned—for example, the hiring party must request that the work be created; it cannot already be in existence
- the work must fall within a group of specially enumerated categories (outlined below), and
- a written agreement must be signed by both parties indicating it is a work made for hire.

A work-for-hire agreement should be signed before the independent contractor commences work. However, at least one court has held that the agreement can be executed after the work is completed, provided that at the time the work was created, the parties intended to enter into such an agreement. However, the facts of the case must clearly show the parties' intent.

Example: A magazine paid an artist by check for drawings done over a seven-year period. On the back of each check was a statement that indicated the drawings were works made for hire.

A court of appeals ruled that the artist's signature of the checks for the entire period demonstrated that he was aware of and accepted the arrangement. (*Playboy Enterprises, Inc. v. Dumas,* 53 F.3d 549 (2d Cir. 1995).)

a. Work-Made-for-Hire Categories

The work of an independent contractor crafts artist will be a work made for hire only if it falls within one of several enumerated categories. Many work-made-for-hire categories are inapplicable to artists—for example, a translation, atlas or test or answer material for a test. Below are those categories that may have some relation to crafts works:

- a contribution to a collective work—for example, creating a pewter chess set for a book featuring many chess sets
- a part of a motion picture or other audiovisual work—for example, creating a tapestry for the set of a television show
- a supplementary work—a work prepared for publication as a supplement to a work by another artist for the purpose of introducing, concluding, illustrating, explaining, revising, commenting upon or assisting in the use of the other work—for example, a publisher is producing a book featuring famous quilts and asks you to diagram a pattern for one of them, and
- an instructional text used in teaching—for example, a book demonstrating how to create crochet works, provided that it is designed for use in day-to-day teaching activity. If it is not intended as part of a regular teaching program, it will not qualify.

Any work created by an independent contractor that does not fall within one of the above categories cannot be a work made for hire. (As you can see, most crafts work will not qualify.) This is so even if the parties have signed a written agreement stating that the work is a work made for hire.

Example: A fiber artist is commissioned to create a work for a school auditorium. The artist signs an agreement entitled "Work Made For Hire." The artist (not the school) owns the copyright in the fiber work because these textile and fiber works are not included among the enumerated categories of works by independent contractors that can be works made for hire.

b. Work-Made-for-Hire Agreement

Below is a simple work-for-hire agreement. Remember, it is always necessary to use this agreement with an independent contractor—for example, if you pay an artist to create a design for your jewelry. Strictly speaking, it is not necessary to use this agreement when a work is to be created by an employee. The employer automatically owns an employee's work created within the course of employment, regardless of whether there is a written agreement. However, employers often prefer to use written agreements to make it clear to employees that the employer owns copyright.

You'll find additional copies of the following Work-Made-for-Hire Agreement in Appendix B and on the CD-ROM at the back of this book.

c. Explanation of Work-Made-for-Hire Agreement

In the "Services" section, insert the work that the contractor is supposed to perform, for example, "Create a series of Gothic fabric designs." Insert the amount to be paid to contractor in the "Payment" section.

The section titled "Works Made for Hire—Assignment of Intellectual Property Rights" establishes that the work is made for hire. However, if the work does not meet the requirements of copyright law, a backup provision is added that converts the arrangement to an assignment. This type of provision is commonly used by businesses seeking to make sure that ownership rights have been acquired.

The "Warranty" provision provides an assurance that the Contractor owns the work and that the work is not an infringement. This is necessary to provide an assurance that the work is not taken from another source.

This agreement includes some miscellaneous provisions ("Entire Agreement," "No Joint Venture" and so on). For a detailed explanation of these provisions, see Chapter 9, Section B24.

4. Acquiring Ownership of Works by Assignment

As explained in Section F3, above, it is unlikely that you will acquire initial copyright ownership of a crafts work created by an independent contractor under work-made-for-hire principles. If you would like to get the copyright transferred to you, you can do so by executing an assignment agreement or by inserting an assignment provision in your independent contractor agreement. You cannot do this with an oral agreement. An assignment must be in writing.

In Chapter 8, I explain that an assignment is a transaction in which a copyright is permanently transferred. Assuming you execute the assignment prior to the performance by the independent contractor, the payment to the independent contractor is sufficient compensation for the copyright. Sometimes, in return for the transfer, the independent contractor might also either get a lump sum or a continuing payment known as a royalty. Two examples of assignments are provided in Chapter 8, Section Q and in Appendix B. The second example, the artwork assignment, can be used with an independent contractor crafts artist.

G. When Workers Create Patentable Innovations

If you pay someone to create a design that's patentable, the rules are a little different than they are for copyrights. (See Chapter 7 for an explanation of the difference between copyrights and patents.)

- You will automatically own any patentable rights in a design if it was created by an employee (not an independent contractor) who was hired to design (see Section G1).

- You can alternately gain ownership of patentable rights in a design if the worker (whether employee or independent contractor) signs a written agreement transferring the rights to you (see Section G2).

An employer may also obtain more limited rights, known as shop rights, to employees' designs in certain specific circumstances.

1. Employed to Design

If you hire someone to create designs, or if designing is one of the worker's job functions, you will own the patent rights to any designs created by the worker during the course of the employment. Despite this principle—known as the "hired to invent" rule—most businesses prefer to use a written agreement (as described in Section G2, below), because it is easier to enforce.

The rules discussed here are for design patents —the type of patent most likely to apply to crafts works. However, the same rules would apply for utility patents, which are for functional, not ornamental innovations. For an explanation of the distinction between utility and design patents, see Chapter 7.

Work-Made-for-Hire-Agreement

This Work Made for Hire Agreement (the "Agreement") is made between _____

_____ ("Company"), and

_____ ("Contractor").

Services. In consideration of the payments provided in this Agreement, Contractor agrees to perform the following services: _____

_____

_____

Payment. Company agrees to pay Contractor as follows: _____

_____

Works Made for Hire—Assignment of Intellectual Property Rights. Contractor agrees that, for consideration that is acknowledged, any works of authorship commissioned pursuant to this Agreement (the "Works") shall be considered works made for hire as that term is defined under U.S. copyright law. To the extent that any such Work created for Company by Contractor is not a work made for hire belonging to Company, Contractor hereby assigns and transfers to Company all rights Contractor has or may acquire to all such Works. Contractor agrees to sign and deliver to Company, either during or subsequent to the term of this Agreement, such other documents as Company considers desirable to evidence the assignment of copyright.

Contractor Warranties. Contractor warrants that the Work does not infringe any intellectual property rights or violate any laws and that the Work is original to Contractor.

General Provisions.

Entire Agreement. This is the entire agreement between the parties. It replaces and supersedes any and all oral agreements between the parties, as well as any prior writings. Modifications and amendments to this agreement, including any exhibit or appendix hereto, shall be enforceable only if they are in writing and are signed by authorized representatives of both parties.

Successors and Assignees. This agreement binds and benefits the heirs, successors and assignees of the parties.

Notices. Any notice or communication required or permitted to be given under this Agreement shall be sufficiently given when received by certified mail, or sent by facsimile transmission or overnight courier.

Governing Law. This agreement will be governed by the laws of the State of _____.

Waiver. If one party waives any term or provision of this agreement at any time, that waiver will only be effective for the specific instance and specific purpose for which the waiver was given. If either party fails to exercise or delays exercising any of its rights or remedies under this agreement, that party retains the right to enforce that term or provision at a later time.

Severability. If a court finds any provision of this agreement invalid or unenforceable, the remainder of this agreement will be interpreted so as best to carry out the parties' intent.

Attachments and Exhibits. The parties agree and acknowledge that all attachments, exhibits and schedules referred to in this agreement are incorporated in this agreement by reference.

No Agency. Nothing contained herein will be construed as creating any agency, partnership, joint venture or other form of joint enterprise between the parties.

☐ **Attorney Fees and Expenses.** The prevailing party shall have the right to collect from the other party its reasonable costs and necessary disbursements and attorney fees incurred in enforcing this Agreement.

☐ **Jurisdiction.** The parties consent to the exclusive jurisdiction and venue of the federal and state courts located in _____ [county], _____ [state], in any action arising out of or relating to this agreement. The parties waive any other venue to which either party might be entitled by domicile or otherwise.

☐ **Arbitration.** Any controversy or claim arising out of or relating to this agreement shall be settled by arbitration in _____ [county], _____ [state], in accordance with the rules of the American Arbitration Association, and judgment upon the award rendered by the arbitrator(s) may be entered in any court having jurisdiction. The prevailing party shall have the right to collect from the other party its reasonable costs and attorney's fees incurred in enforcing this agreement.

Signatures

Each party represents and warrants that on this date they are duly authorized to bind their respective principals by their signatures below.

COMPANY:

_____

Signature

_____

Typed or Printed Name

_____

Title

_____

Date

CONTRACTOR:

_____

Signature

_____

Typed or Printed Name

_____

Title

_____

Date

Work-Made-for-Hire Agreement (Page 2)

2. Assignment Agreements

You can assure ownership of any patentable designs by requiring employees or independent contractors to assign these rights to you. When these arrangements are used with employees, they are sometimes called "pre-invention" agreements, because the worker is agreeing to assign patent rights before the design is actually created. The following clause can be used for an employee:

> **Assignment of Innovations.** Employee agrees that any design, invention, process, system or patentable creation (Innovation) conceived, originated, discovered or developed in whole or in part by Employee: (1) as a result of any work performed by Employee with Company's equipment, supplies, facilities, trade secret information or other Company resources; or (2) on Company's time shall be the sole and exclusive property of Company, provided that the Innovation either relates to Company's business or anticipated research. Employee agrees to sign and deliver to Company (either during or subsequent to his employment) such documents as Company considers desirable to evidence: (1) the assignment to Company of all rights of Employee, if any, in any such Innovation; and (2) Company's ownership of such Innovations. And in the event Company is unable to secure Employee's signature on any necessary document, Employee appoints Company (and each of its duly authorized officers and agents) as his agent and attorney-in-fact, to act for and in his behalf and to execute and file any such document. Employee agrees to promptly disclose in writing to Company all such designs or discoveries made or learned by Employee during the period of employment that are related to Company's business, that result from tasks assigned to Employee by Company or from the use of facilities owned or otherwise acquired by Company.

For an example of a patent assignment that can be used for independent contractors, see the Artist Assignment provided in Chapter 8.

Limitations on Pre-Invention Assignments

Five states (California, Illinois, Minnesota, North Carolina and Washington) have laws that limit pre-invention assignments to employers. These laws prevent an employer from claiming ownership of a patentable creation if the creation:

- is created with the employee's resources
- does not result from work performed for an employer, and
- does not relate to the employer's business.

For example, if you are employed as a crafts worker and you invent a new method of book binding at home with your own resources, then your employer cannot claim ownership of your book binding invention in these five states. The California statute also requires employers to inform employees about the law. This is usually done by adding a statement to the employment agreement, as follows:

> Employee assigns to Company all right, title and interest Employee may have or acquire in and to all such Innovations created by Employee. Innovations that qualify fully under the provisions of California Labor Code § 2870 et seq. shall not be subject to this provision.

3. Shop Rights

Even though you may not acquire ownership of a patent or trade secret created by an employee or independent contractor, you may acquire a limited right to use these innovations, known as a shop right. With a shop right, the worker retains ownership of the patent or trade secret, but the employer has a right to use it without paying the worker.

A shop right can only arise if the worker uses the employer's resources (materials, supplies, time) to create an innovation. (Other circumstances may be relevant, but use of employer resources is the most important criterion.)

H. When Workers Learn Business Secrets

Does your crafts business have valuable information that you expose to workers but that you'd like to keep under wraps from competitors? It could be your customer list, a unique method for affixing beads to metal or a secret formula used to create a fabric dye. This confidential information is a form of property whose value could drop to zero if other companies got their hands on it. In legal terms, these are your business's *trade secrets,* and you want to prevent your employees or independent contractors from disclosing these secrets to the public.

Who owns employee-created trade secrets? If an employee creates a trade secret for your business, the rules regarding ownership of that secret are the same as for design patents—that is, you will own it if the employee was hired to create such secrets, or the employee signed an agreement assigning such secrets. See Section G, above.

1. Nondisclosure Agreements

When it comes to trade secrets, the primary concern for most crafts businesses is that an employee or independent contractor will walk away with this valuable information. To protect the confidentiality of such information, use a nondisclosure agreement (or NDA). In a nondisclosure agreement, one or both parties agree to keep certain information specified in the agreement confidential. A person who reveals or misuses your protected information after signing a nondisclosure agreement can land in serious legal trouble. You can seek a court order barring further disclosure or misuse of your information, and you can also sue for financial damages.

It is not essential to use an NDA with employees. State laws prohibit employees from improper disclosure of your trade secrets, even without a written agreement. But using an NDA does give you additional benefits if you have to sue an employee who has disclosed or misused your trade secrets. These benefits can include larger financial damages, payment of lawyer fees, a guarantee about where the dispute will be resolved (your headquarters state, for example) and what mechanism will be used to resolve it (arbitration vs. lawsuit).

Keep in mind that nondisclosure agreements won't protect just *any* business information; the information must qualify as a trade secret. To qualify as a trade secret and be protected by an NDA, your business information must meet three criteria:

- the information can't be generally known or readily ascertainable
- the information must provide economic value or a competitive advantage, and
- the information must be treated with secrecy— that is, you must take reasonable steps to protect it.

The minimum safeguards you should take to protect your trade secrets include keeping your secrets out of sight when not in use, marking documents containing secrets as confidential and, of course, using NDAs.

Don't leave secrets within easy view. If you leave your secrets exposed so that someone—for example, the janitor who cleans your shop—can see them, you will have a difficult time protecting them even with an NDA.

Asking employees (or contractors) to sign a restrictive agreement such as an NDA (or the noncompete or nonsolicitation agreements discussed in Section H2) may seem burdensome or out of character. But the American Society of Industrial Security estimates that U.S. businesses lose at least $24 billion a year because of stolen trade secrets, most of it from the transfer of secrets by employees. Using a nondisclosure agreement may prove to be the most effective method of protecting your crafts business and its confidential information.

An example of a basic NDA is provided below.

You'll find additional copies of the Nondisclosure Agreement in Appendix B and on the CD-ROM at the back of this book.

Nondisclosure Agreement

This Nondisclosure Agreement (the "Agreement") is made between _____ _____ (the "Disclosing Party") and _____ (the "Receiving Party"). The Parties agree to the following terms and conditions. Receiving Party acknowledges that the following information constitutes confidential trade secret information ("Confidential Information") belonging to Disclosing Party: _____ _____.

In consideration of Disclosing Party's disclosure of its Confidential Information to Recipient, Receiving Party agrees that it will not disclose Disclosing Party's Confidential Information to any third party or make or permit to be made copies or other reproductions of Disclosing Party's Confidential Information.

This Agreement does not apply to any information which:

   (a) was in Receiving Party's possession or was known to Receiving Party, without an obligation to keep it confidential, before such information was disclosed to Receiving Party by Disclosing Party

   (b) is or becomes public knowledge through a source other than Receiving Party and through no fault of Receiving Party

   (c) is or becomes lawfully available to Receiving Party from a source other than Disclosing Party, or

   (d) is disclosed by Receiving Party with Disclosing Party's prior written approval.

This Agreement and Receiving Party's duty to hold Disclosing Party's trade secrets in confidence will continue until the Confidential Information is no longer a trade secret or until Disclosing Party sends Receiving Party written notice releasing Receiving Party from this Agreement, whichever occurs first.

If any legal action arises relating to this Agreement, the prevailing party will be entitled to recover all court costs, expenses and reasonable attorney fees.

This is the entire agreement between the parties regarding the subject matter. It supersedes all prior agreements or understandings between them. All additions or modifications to this Agreement must be made in writing and must be signed by both parties to be effective.

This Agreement is made under, and will be interpreted according to, the laws of the State of _____.

If a court finds any provision of this Agreement invalid or unenforceable as applied to any circumstance, the remainder of this Agreement will be interpreted so as best to effect the intent of the parties.

Dated: _____

DISCLOSING PARTY

_____
Name of Business

_____
Signature

_____
Printed Name and Title

_____
Address

RECEIVING PARTY

_____
Name of Business

_____
Signature

_____
Printed Name and Title

_____
Address

Nondisclosure Agreement

2. Noncompetes and Nonsolicitation: When an NDA Is Not Enough

A noncompetition agreement (also known as a "noncompete" or "covenant not to compete") is a contract in which someone agrees not to compete with you for a certain period of time. Noncompetition and nondisclosure agreements both have the same goal: to prevent a competitor from using valuable business information. The difference is that a nondisclosure prohibits disclosure to a competitor, while a non-compete prohibits even working for a competitor or starting a competing business. In other words, the noncompete is broader and can be more heavy-handed in its effect—so heavy-handed, in fact, that some states refuse to enforce (or limit enforcement of) noncompetes signed by employees.

States with restrictions include Alabama, California, Colorado, Florida, Louisiana, Montana, Nevada, North Dakota, Oklahoma, Oregon, South Dakota and Texas. In general, you should consult with an attorney before entering into a noncompete agreement, because non-compete agreements are a potential minefield. Many courts are averse to enforcing them, and employees dislike being asked to sign them. In addition, there's a growing body of public information that helps employees break noncompete agreements (see, for example, www.breakyournoncompete.com).

I recommend you avoid using noncompetes, except perhaps for a key employee—someone with an intimate knowledge of your crafts business and clients —that is, an employee who realistically could hurt your business by competing with it.

A nonsolicitation agreement prohibits a former employee from soliciting your customers or employees for a period of time. Most states will generally enforce nonsolicitation agreements that don't:

- unfairly restrict an employee's ability to earn a living, or
- unfairly limit a competitor's ability to hire workers or solicit customers through legitimate means.

Customer Lists as Trade Secrets

For many crafts artists, their primary trade secret is customer information. But trade secret law may not protect your customer list. If a dispute over a customer list ends up in court, a judge generally considers the following elements when deciding whether or not the list qualifies as a trade secret:

- Is the information in the list ascertainable by other means? For example, can someone using a search engine or email directory create a similar customer list? A list that's readily ascertainable can't be protected.
- Does the list include more than names and email addresses? For example, if your customer list includes purchasing information or special needs for online customers, it's more likely to be protected, because this information adds value.
- Did it take a lot of time or effort or did you create a special system for assembling your list? A customer list that requires more effort is more likely to be protected under an NDA.
- Is your customer list long-standing or exclusive? If you can prove that a customer list is special to your business and has been used for a long time, the list is more likely to be protected.

Chapter

6

Trademarks and Trade Dress

For decades, three companies in the Black Hills of South Dakota have manufactured and sold gold jewelry featuring three-color gold in a grape and leaf design under the trademark "Black Hills Gold Jewelry." One day, a company from North Dakota began advertising its "Black Hills Gold Jewelry" (also with a gold grape and leaf design) in South Dakota newspapers. The company's ads included images of the Black Hills, such as pictures of Mount Rushmore. The South Dakota companies were unhappy with this northern invasion—after all, they had exclusively identified their product as being *the* "Black Hills Gold Jewelry" and had built a substantial customer base. They sued to enforce their rights in the trademark.

Under trademark law, a company can prevent a competitor from using a similar trademark if it is likely to confuse consumers as to the origin of goods. But the three companies in South Dakota had a few hurdles to overcome. In typical trademark spats, one company, not three, claims exclusive rights to a mark. And under trademark law, a mark that simply describes the geographic origins—for example, informs consumers that the jewelry is from the Black Hills—is harder to protect, because it is considered a "weak" trademark (this topic is discussed in more detail in Section A3, below).

A federal court sorted through these issues and ultimately determined that the designation "Black Hills Gold Jewelry" should only be used by jewelry manufacturers located in the Black Hills. The court ruled that consumers who saw "Black Hills Gold Jewelry" were likely to believe they were buying a product produced in the Black Hills of South Dakota, and, on that basis, the North Dakota company was deceiving consumers by using the trademark. (*Black Hills Jewelry Manufacturing Co v. Gold Rush, Inc.*, 633 F.2d 746 (8th Cir. 1980).)

This ruling highlights a basic trademark principle: If consumers have developed an association between a product and its name or designation, it's wrong to allow competitors to trade off that association by using a similar name.

Chances are your business will never be involved in a trademark problem. Few crafts businesses run into conflicts with competitors regarding the name of their products or services. But in the event that you are choosing a name for your crafts products, gallery or crafts services, or you are concerned about someone using your trademark, this chapter will provide helpful advice, including:

- trademark basics—the essentials you'll need to know regarding trademark principles and protections (see Section A)
- using your own name as a trademark—the rules for using your family name for your crafts business (see Section A6)
- staying out of trademark trouble—when you can or cannot use a trademark, and how to gauge the odds that you'll face a dispute (see Section B)
- trade dress—when you can claim that your crafts style or appearance of your goods is protected as a trademark (see Section C)
- trademark searching—how to determine if someone else is using a similar trademark (see Section D), and
- federal registration—how to federally register your trademark online (see Section E).

For more detailed trademark information, including how to search and register trademarks, consult *Trademark: Legal Care for Your Business & Product Name,* by Stephen Elias (Nolo).

A. Trademark Basics

Trademarks are big business—just ask companies like Coca-Cola, McDonald's and Nike, whose existence and value is tied directly to their marks. Few people are aware that this whole trademark business was invented thousands of years ago by crafts artisans, eager to distinguish their works. Greek and Roman potters imprinted ceramic marks on their works, medieval paper makers invented watermarks to distinguish their papers, printers and furniture makers created unique marks identifying their crafts and gold and silver smiths used hallmarks—a series of markings stamped on gold and silver products—to signify the quality and maker of the product.

Trademarks can serve you in the same way as they did our crafts ancestors. You can claim exclusive trademark rights to any word, symbol or device that identifies and distinguishes your crafts products or services. (When a trademark is used to identify services, for example, FedEx for delivery services, it's sometimes referred to as a service mark. Both trademarks and service marks are referred to as trademarks throughout this chapter.)

The most popular types of trademarks are product names, for example, "Wilburton Pottery" or "One-of-A-Kind Weaver." However, there are other types of trademarks, including slogans, logos, domain names and trade dress. A distinctive combination of elements may serve as a trademark (see Section C, below.) There are also two offshoots of trademarks: collective marks that identify an organization, and certification marks that certify that a product or service has a certain quality, meets a certain standard or is from a certain geographic location (see Section A8, below).

Figure 6-1: Crown and initials logo used by Kiss My Ring Jewelry

1. First User Gets Rights

If you are the first crafts company to use a trademark in commerce, that is, the first to advertise or sell products or services under the mark, you acquire trademark rights and can stop others from using an identical or similar mark.

Example: A Spanish company was the first to use the trademark MAJORICA (on a ribbon or crest design) for its manufactured pearl jewelry. A second company later sought to use MAJORCA for its pearl jewelry (also in a crest design). A federal court prohibited the second user, because MAJORCA was phonetically and visually indistinguishable from MAJORICA and was likely to confuse consumers. (*Industria Espanola De Perlas Imitacion v. National Silver,* 459 F.2d 1049 (CCPA 1972).)

However, simply being the first user of a mark may not get you all the protection you need. There are a lot of other qualifications that determine whether you can assert trademark rights, for example, the geographical extent of your use, whether the mark is weak or strong or whether you have abandoned your right to use the mark. Subsequent sections will elaborate on these issues.

In order to stop a competitor, you will need to file a lawsuit and obtain a court order. The government will not enforce your trademark rights for you. You will also realize after reading this chapter that many rules and decisions regarding trademarks seem arbitrary or are based on money and not fairness. This is often the case in trademark disputes where big companies use trademark law to bully smaller competitors. Companies such as Mattel (owner of the Barbie trademark) and Toys R Us became trademark powerhouses by vigilantly asserting their trademark rights against all potential infringers.

2. Goods and Services: The Net of Trademark Protection

As explained, crafts artists are the source of (or culprits behind) the modern trademark. One important feature of the early crafts marks—for example, ceramic marks and paper watermarks—was that they had the power to identify only a certain class of goods. For example, a hallmark for silver and gold products might have significance on a silver bowl, but it would have no meaning on the bottom of an earthenware bowl. The class of goods for the mark was limited to the type produced by the maker.

This rule is still a cornerstone of trademark law. You can only stop others from using a similar mark on goods or services with which the mark is used, intended to be used or likely to be used.

Figure 6-2: ACC Trademark

ACC (see Figure 6-2) is a trademark for the American Craft Council, an organization that provides services including crafts shows, exhibitions, resources and marketing services for crafts business. If another company wanted to use ACC as a trademark for cardiology and education services (American College of Cardiology), sports services (Atlantic Coast Conference), insurance services (the Accident Compensation Corporation) or a musical group (Angel Corpus Christi), the American Craft Council would have difficulty stopping these uses because the American Craft Council is not using, intending to use, or likely to use ACC for these other services. That is, crafts, cardiology, insurance, basketball and music are not competitive or related services or goods. They are not offered through the same channels of distribution or in the same retail outlets. However, if another company were to offer crafts shows and used the ACC trademark or logo, that use might confuse consumers as to their source. The American Craft Council could stop this competitive use. With rare exceptions—see Section B2, below—noncompeting uses of a similar trademark cannot be prohibited.

Creating a trademark doesn't create rights. Trademark rights do not arise because you create a trademark—for example, design a logo or coin a slogan. Trademark rights only occur if you use the trademark in commerce. You can reserve trademark rights—see Section E, below—but these rights will not vest unless you eventually use the mark in commerce.

3. Weak and Strong Trademarks

Trademark protection is based around a "strength" classification system. Strong trademarks are distinctive, and you can immediately stop others from using one similar to yours. Weak trademarks are not distinctive. You cannot federally register a weak trademark, and you can't stop others from using a similar weak trademark—unless you pump up the mark with consumer awareness or "secondary meaning" (discussed below).

One way of reviewing trademark strength is to determine whether the mark is readily distinguishable from other marks. When we use the term "distinguishable" or "distinctive" we mean, would a consumer associate the mark with a product or service? Would the consumer associate it with a certain quality, image or source? For example, when seeing the "People's Pottery" trademark in a store, many consumers are aware that the retailer sells made-in-America crafts products. In other words, the retailer has distinguished itself from others. Generally, a mark is strong if it is:

- born strong (so unique or clever that it is classified as "inherently distinctive"—"Splendor in the Glass" for glassware is a good example), or

- made strong (it becomes distinctive through sales and advertising, as did the "People's Pottery" mark).

Marks that are born strong are immediately memorable. They may be coined terms (made-up words), such as "Brillig & Slithy Toves Stoneware." Or they may be arbitrary words—that is, words whose meanings are not associated with the goods—for example, "Yellow Telephone" or "Modern Nymph" for jewelry. Strong marks may also be suggestive of some quality of the goods, for example, "Bella Bella" (describing the beauty of) handcrafted furniture, "StoryPeople" for wooden sculptures or "Tribal Trills" for stoneware whistles.

Weak marks are made strong by companies investing money in advertising. For example, the Rosen Group is a weak mark (most surnames are weak marks—see Section A6, below) that has been made strong because it has been heavily advertised and promoted to crafts businesses.

As a general rule, the more that the mark describes the goods (for example, Beads n Things), the weaker or less distinguishable the mark. Why? Because the mark describes the product, it doesn't distinguish it. Only advertising and sales (secondary meaning) will strengthen a weak mark and make it distinguishable. Unfortunately, this classification system is not an exact science—there are no foolproof tests for determining if a mark is strong. A decision is usually made by a judge or trademark examiner who weighs the various factors described in the following sections. In reviewing decisions by judges or trademark examiners, you may well disagree with the reasoning as to whether a mark is distinctive. Many trademark decisions are simply subjective determinations, much like a referee's call at a football game. This is an accepted fact of life in trademark law.

4. Trademark Registration

Trademark rights can be acquired without filing a federal or state trademark registration. The South Dakota companies in the "Black Hills Gold Jewelry" example, above, did not have federal registrations, yet they were able to stop a competitor from using a similar mark. Without a registration, you have what is known as common law trademark rights. You can assert these common law rights over any subsequent users who sell similar goods within your geographic market. However, if that user operates outside your business's geographic area, your common law rights are worthless. For most crafts artists, this is not an issue and federal registration is not a necessity.

Federal registration will, nevertheless, strengthen and broaden your trademark rights, including:

- **Right to use the ® symbol.** Only the owner of a federally registered mark may use the symbol ® in conjunction with goods or services.
- **Constructive notice of date of first use.** The filing date of your trademark application gives you nationwide priority as of that date.
- **Statutory damages and attorney fees.** The owner of a registered mark may, under some circum-

stances, recover lost profits, damages and costs in a federal court trademark infringement lawsuit.

- **Criminal penalties and damages.** Certain criminal penalties as well as treble damages may be assessed in a lawsuit for counterfeiting a registered trademark. Counterfeiting is an extreme form of trademark infringement in which an identical trademark is used on goods or services. For example, putting a fake Tiffany's trademark on competing jewelry would be considered counterfeiting.
- **Right to stop importation of infringing marks.** The owner of a registered mark can deposit a copy of the registration with U.S. Customs in order to stop the importation of goods bearing an infringing mark.
- **Incontestability.** After five years of continuous use, a federally registered mark can, with some exceptions, become immune from challenge.
- **Basis for foreign applications.** A federal registration may serve as the basis for filing a trademark application in certain foreign countries.

If these benefits are important to your crafts business, and if you believe your trademark adds substantial value to your business, you should proceed with federal registration as described in Section E, below. (Federal registration will be helpful in a legal dispute, for example, if a chain store copies your product *and* your trademarked name.) Federal trademark registration takes time (over a year to accomplish) and money ($325 at the time this book was published). The United States Patent and Trademark Office (USPTO) administers federal registrations. The USPTO can be accessed on the Internet (www.uspto.gov).

You may not need state trademark registration. Because state trademark registration only protects you within one state, I do not recommend it. Chances are, you will be selling your crafts products across state lines. However, if you are interested in pursuing state registration, it is usually done by the Secretary of State in your state. For an index of all state and federal trademark law websites, see the *All About Trademarks Website* (www.ggmark.com).

Symbols Indicating a Trademark

Typically, the symbols ®, TM or SM are used along with trademarks—as in The Crafts Report® or Cape Cod Crafters of New England™. The symbol ® indicates that a trademark has been registered at the USPTO. It is illegal to use the ® symbol if the trademark in question has no USPTO registration. There is no legal requirement that the ® be used, but the failure to use it may limit the amount of damages that the trademark owner can recover in an infringement lawsuit. If the trademark hasn't been registered, the TM symbol can be used. Similarly, the SM symbol can be used for service marks that have not been registered. The TM and SM have no legal significance other than to indicate the fact that the owner is claiming trademark rights.

5. No Trademark Protection

There are some situations in which no trademark protection is available or possible. In these situations, the intended trademark cannot be registered, and the owner has no right to stop others using a similar mark.

- **Nonuse.** If you stop using a trademark in commerce and indicate an intention not to resume use, the mark is no longer protectible, and anyone can use it.
- **Generic terms.** If you attempt to use the name of the goods—for example, you use the term "Leather" or "Jewelry" as the sole name for your leather or jewelry goods—the name will not be protected by itself, because it is a generic term. You can, however, use these terms in conjunction with other terms—for example, Zen Woodwork or Genius Jewelry.
- **Weak marks that have not achieved secondary meaning.** As explained in Section A3, above, a weak (or descriptive) mark cannot be protected without proof of consumer awareness.
- **Functional features.** A functional element of your crafts or its packaging is not protectible as a trademark (see Section C, below).

6. Using Your Surname as Your Crafts Trademark

Many crafts artists use their first name, last name or both as a trademark, for example, "Wedemeyer Original Works" or "Perie Brown Creations." Others use a variation on the name, for example, "Ellie Mac Design" (owned by Elenora Macnish) or "Lucyland" for a line of hand-milled soap. Using your own name makes sense. After all, crafts are a highly personalized occupation requiring unique skills, and historically crafts goods are known by the name of the creator, for example "Johnson Brothers" crockery. There are some advantages to using your own name:

- You have less chance of infringing on someone else's trademark, unless, coincidentally, another crafts artist has an identical or similar name.
- You won't have to file a fictitious business statement (sometimes known as a *dba*) with your local county clerk when you create your business.
- You may have an easier time preserving your rights to a domain name.

But there may be some downsides to choosing a personal name as your trademark. In the case of common names, you may be surprised to find that someone else has preempted your field. For example, anyone with the family name Hummel will have a difficult time obtaining a trademark for figurines. More important, you may be surprised to learn that it's often difficult to register trademarks that use a family name, because the USPTO often considers family names to be weak trademarks (see Section A3, above). In the event you wish to register or assert rights to a family name, here are the rules:

- **Primarily a surname (weak).** A family name that is perceived primarily as a person's name is descriptive (weak) and can't be registered. The owners cannot stop others from using a similar mark without proof of secondary meaning (see Section A3, above). This is also true if the surname is used with other generic terms (for example, "Steinberg Gourds" or "O'Neill Glass Art"), or is used with initials. If the additional wording is more than a generic term, or if it creates a play on words—for example, Boyd Wright's "Wright Made Products," the mark may be strong and registrable.

- **Not primarily a surname (may be weak or strong)**. Some family names have a dictionary meaning, for example, Nathan Lefthand operates "Lefthand Studio." In these cases, the mark is not automatically presumed to be weak. You will have an easier time registering or protecting it.
- **Multiple surnames.** Generally, when a surname is combined with another surname (such as "Bernard & Sokoloff Art Glass"), it is not presumed to be weak, and you will have an easier time registering or protecting it.
- **Surnames combined with a design.** If the design is not particularly distinctive (for example, simple geometric shapes), the mark is considered weak. This is not the case if the design has some unique or distinctive features.

7. Relationship of Domain Names and Trademarks

As you are probably aware, a domain name is an address for a website. Domain names consist of a top level such as com, gov, org or net, and a second level, the name preceding the dot in ".com."

In Chapter 4, Section C, information is provided on registering and protecting a domain name. One factor to consider in choosing your trademark is whether the corresponding domain name is available. Bear in mind that registration of a domain name does not grant trademark rights. Therefore, when choosing a trademark, it is wise to review the availability of the trademark as a domain name. This can be done for free at www.nsi.com or at many other sites on the Internet, located by typing "domain name" into any search engine.

Trademark owners often vie for the same domain name. For example, the Arrow glass design company and the Arrow shirt company may both want the domain arrow.com. Although the term "Arrow" can function as a trademark for both companies since they have separate goods, there can be only one

arrow.com. The first company to register the domain name acquires it. If a trademark owner wants to acquire rights from a legitimate domain name owner, the only solution is to negotiate to buy the rights.

Trade Names and Trade Marks: There's a Difference

A trade name is the name of a business. It is not necessarily a trademark, but it can serve as one if it is used to advertise or sell a product or service. For example, not many consumers are aware of the Minnesota Mining and Manufacturing Company (a trade name), but most consumers are aware of its trademarked products such as Scotch Tape and Post-its. Your trade name (usually the name under which you register your business) will not become a trademark unless you use it in connection with the sale of your goods by putting that name on the tag of your products and advertising your products under that name.

---

8. Collective Marks and Certification Marks

Trademark law has two stepchildren: collective marks that signify membership in an organization, and certification marks that attest to a certain quality or standard. Collective and certification marks share some qualities and standards with trademarks, but they also have rules of their own.

a. Collective Marks

A collective mark signifies membership in an organization. For example, the collective mark "Crochet Guild of America" signifies membership in this crafts organization. A collective mark can also function as a trademark or service mark, signifying that a product or service originates from an organization. If you are a member of a group or organization (for example, "The Maine Crafts Guild"), you probably want to limit use of the name to members of the guild. You don't want nonmembers to use the name (that would undermine the group's standards), and you don't want another club to use the same name. In order to protect your group's right to the mark, you should federally register your group name as a collective mark.

The collective mark is owned by the organization (not by any particular member). The Maine Crafts Guild collective mark could be used to sell member products (selected crafts works) or offer services (knitting lessons). In other words, a collective mark can be used in two ways: to signify membership or as a trademark. To federally register your organization's collective mark, use the form included on the CD-ROM at the back of the book or visit the USPTO website (www.uspto.gov). Go to the home page, click Trademarks (on the left side of the page), click "File for a Trademark" (under Registration) and click "Apply for a New Mark" (under PrinTeas).

b. Certification Marks

A certification mark attests to some standard, quality or origin of goods. For example, if you create ceramic lamps, you probably want to include the UL certification mark on your works indicating that Underwriters Laboratory has certified the safety of the product. As a purchaser of crafts supplies, you may seek a certain quality or standard, for example, 100% Cotton. Or perhaps you might want a certification that indicates the cotton was produced by an organic farm in California, for example, the CCOF certification mark (California Certified Organic Farmers).

A crafts organization or a group of suppliers can organize to certify some standard, for example, that jewelry is manufactured in the Black Hills of South Dakota, by applying to the federal government for a certification mark. To federally register your certification mark, use the form included on the CD-ROM at the back of the book or visit the USPTO website (www.uspto.gov). Go to the home page, click Trademarks (on the left side of the page), click "File for a Trademark" (under Registration) and click "Apply for a New Mark" (under PrinTeas).

B. Staying out of Trouble

You've probably read about companies that have been told to stop using names, logos or other marks because a competitor believes the mark infringes on theirs. If you receive a warning like this (known as a "cease and desist" letter), consult with an attorney (see Chapter 11 for information on finding an attorney). Below is information that will help you avoid trademark troubles and, in the event you do run into a problem, will help you evaluate your position.

1. Infringement

Trademark infringement occurs when one company uses another company's trademark (or a substantially similar mark) in a manner that is likely to confuse consumers into believing that there is some connection, affiliation or sponsorship between the two companies. Usually this occurs when a trademark is used on similar goods.

Example 1: PLAY-DOH is the trademark for one of the most popular crafts products for children, a modeling compound that comes in various colors. (In the two- to seven-year-old age group, one in every two children currently owns a PLAY-DOH product.) In the mid 1990s, a competitor, Rose Art Industries, began selling a modeling compound for children known as FUNDOUGH. A federal court determined that consumers were likely to be confused by the simultaneous use of FUNDOUGH and PLAY-DOH and prohibited Rose Art from using that trademark for its modeling compounds. (*Kenner Parker Toys v. Rose Art Industries*, 963 F.2d 350 (CAFC 1992).)

Example 2: "Artcarved" and "Art Crest," both used as trademarks for jewelry, were found not likely to infringe each other. A federal court determined that the two words were sufficiently different in pronunciation and meaning not to be confused by consumers. (*J. R. Wood and Sons v. Reese Jewelry*, 278 F.2d 157 (2d Cir. 1960).)

When determining likelihood of confusion, courts use several factors derived from a 1961 case, *Polaroid Corp. v. Polarad Elecs. Corp.* 287 F.2d 492 (2d Cir.), *cert denied,* 368 U.S. 820 (1961). These factors, sometimes known as the "Polaroid factors," may vary slightly as federal courts apply them throughout the country. The factors are intended as a guide, and not all of the factors, as listed below, may be particularly helpful in any given case. The term "senior user" refers to the first user of the trademark; "junior user" signifies the later user.

- **Strength of the senior user's mark.** The stronger or more distinctive the senior user's mark, the more likely the confusion.
- **Similarity of the marks.** The less similarity between the two marks, the less likely the confusion.
- **Similarity of the products or services.** The more that the senior and junior user's goods or services are related, the more likely the confusion.
- **Likelihood that the senior user will bridge the gap.** The higher the probability that the senior user will expand into the junior user's product area, the more likely there will be confusion.
- **The junior user's intent in adopting the mark.** If the junior user adopted the mark in bad faith, confusion is more likely.
- **Evidence of actual confusion.** Proof of consumer confusion is not required, but is powerful evidence of infringement.
- **Sophistication of the buyers.** The more sophisticated the purchaser, the less likely the confusion.
- **Quality of the junior user's products or services.** In some cases, the lesser the quality of the junior user's goods, the more likely the confusion.

2. Trademark Dilution

Trademark rules prohibit someone from commercially using an existing trademark if the use is likely to cause customer confusion (see above). However, sometimes even if there's little likelihood of customer confusion, a company with a famous trademark can stop another company who commercially uses its famous trademark in a manner that blurs the two companies in the customers' minds. This is referred to as trademark dilution and occurs when the integrity of a famous trademark is "muddied" by an unwanted or insulting commercial association.

Example: Joshua designs a wooden holder for toilet paper rolls and names it Rolls Royce. Consumers are not likely to think that the Rolls Royce auto company produced the holder, but the auto company could stop Joshua from using the name by claiming that the association with toilet paper rolls dilutes its classy and famous trademark.

The alteration of a trademark in a comparative advertisement has also been found to be a dilution. In a television advertisement, an equipment manufacturer animated the John Deere "deer" logo and appeared to make it run from the competition. The competitor was found liable for trademark dilution. (*Deere & Company v. MTD Prods. Inc.,* 34 USPQ 1706 (S.D. NY 1995).) Based on this ruling, it would be unwise to modify another company's trademark unless it can be justified under free speech or rules regarding the "parody" of a trademark.

3. When You Need Permission to Use a Trademark

The answer to whether a given use is legally okay will usually depend on a number of factual issues, and can sometimes be tricky to figure out. Keep in mind, however, that even if you're legally entitled to use a trademark, that doesn't mean that the trademark owner will always be agreeable. If you're forced into court to prove that your use is allowed by law, in a sense you've already lost the battle. You'll need to carefully weigh the benefits of using the trademark if you suspect the owner will fight you with legal action.

- **Informational uses.** Informational (or "editorial") uses of a trademark do not require permission from the owner. These are uses that inform, educate or express opinions protected under the First Amendment of the United States Constitution (protecting freedom of speech and of the press). For example, permission is not required to use the Shell gasoline logo at your website when discussing the various ways that sea shells have been used in American crafts and art.

- **Comparative advertising.** It's permissible to use a trademark when making accurate comparative product statements in advertisements. However, since comparative advertisements tend to raise the hackles of trademark owners, an attorney knowledgeable in trademark or business law should review the advertisement.

- **Commercial uses.** Commercial uses of a trademark in your advertising, promotion or marketing require permission (except for cases of comparative advertising; see above). For example, don't wear a T-shirt that says "Chanel" in a print advertisement for your jewelry.

- **Using trademarks in crafts products.** Proceed with caution if you're using trademarks as part of your crafts art—for example, producing a fabric with a repeating image of the American Express card or producing earrings that feature the Apple computer logo. You may be able to argue that your use is informational (see above) and is protected by the First Amendment. However, this argument may be a loser if it looks like you're trading off the success of a trademark rather than commenting upon it. For example, a company that sold trading cards of collectible cars was prohibited from reproducing Chrysler trademarks and trade dress, because Chrysler licensed similar collectible products. (*Chrysler Corp. v. Newfield Publications Inc.*, 880 F. Supp. 504 (E.D. MI 1995).) Be aware that making a First Amendment argument means that you've already triggered a company's ire, and you will have to deal with the consequences. This isn't to discourage you from speaking out against corporate branding, just to alert you to the potential morass that awaits if you do.

- **Parodies.** A trademark parody occurs when a trademark is imitated in a manner that pokes fun at the mark, for example, by selling caps printed with the words, "Mutant of Omaha."

Bear in mind that offensive parodies are the ones most likely to trigger lawsuits. For example, lawsuits were filed over lewd photos of the Pillsbury Doughboy and of nude Barbie dolls and imagery entitled "Malted Barbie" and "The Barbie Enchiladas." Although the artist in the case involving Barbie dolls (see below) eventually won his claim, it required substantial legal effort and expense. (*Mattel Inc. v. Walking Mountain Productions, Inc.* 2001 U.S. App. LEXIS 2610; (9th Cir. 2002).) Weigh the legal consequences carefully before proceeding. A trademark parody is less likely to run into problems if it doesn't compete with the trademarked goods and services and doesn't confuse consumers—that is, they get the joke and do not believe the parody product comes from the same source as the trademarked goods. Also keep in mind that all humorous uses are not parodies. To avoid trouble, the use should specifically poke fun at the trademark.

4. Trademark Disclaimers

A disclaimer is a statement intended to minimize confusion in consumer's minds or deflect liability. A disclaimer is only effective if it is prominently placed, permanently affixed, can be read and understood and really minimizes confusion. A disclaimer, by itself, will not provide a shield against litigation. However, when properly done, a disclaimer can minimize confusion and prevent dilution.

Example: "Fur Rendezvous" is the trademark for a winter festival held in Anchorage, Alaska. The trademark is owned by the Greater Anchorage corporation. Vernon Nowell, a private citizen with no affiliation to the festival, created and sold lapel pins with the words "Fur Rendezvous." When Greater Anchorage objected to Nowell selling the pins, he consulted his attorney and developed a disclaimer, glued to the back of the pins, which states: "This pin, and V.L. Nowell, have no connection whatever with, nor has the pin been approved by, Anchorage Fur Rendezvous,

Inc., or Greater Anchorage, Inc." In addition, the disclaimer explained that "Fur Rendezvous is a registered trademark of Greater Anchorage, Inc." When Nowell sold the pins, he handed out fliers explaining the history of the festival and the pin and explicitly stating that "This pin has no connection with nor has it been approved by Anchorage Fur Rendezvous, Inc. or Greater Anchorage, Inc." A federal court permitted Nowell to sell the pins as long as the disclaimers were included. (*Greater Anchorage, Inc., v. Nowell*, 1992 U.S. App. LEXIS 22906 (9th Circuit 1992).)

C. Trade Dress

In 2000, the Supreme Court handed down a ruling that sent a chill through the hearts of crafts makers. The case, brought by Samara Brothers, a clothing company that manufactures a line of children's one-piece outfits appliquéd with hearts, flowers and fruit, claimed that Wal-Mart copied Samara's designs and sold the knock-offs at a lower price than offered by Samara.

Samara sued Wal-Mart, arguing that Wal-Mart had violated trade dress law. Trade dress is part of trademark law, and, like a trademark, it protects those aspects of a product that distinguish it from competing goods. Trade dress protects the appearance of a product or packaging but not its functional aspects. For example, in Samara's case, trade dress protection would extend only to the appearance of the hearts, flowers and fruit, not to the functioning aspects or shape of the clothing. Trade dress does not require any form of government registration and does not require much originality.

Initially it appeared as if Samara was the victor when Wal-Mart was ordered to pay Samara $1.6 million for copying the product design. But the Supreme Court overruled that judgment, holding Samara's designs could not be protected under trade dress law unless Samara could prove that the designs were used to identify the source of the product (Samara) rather than the product itself.

In other words, in order for trade dress to apply, a customer seeing the arrangement of appliques of hearts, flowers and fruit on children's clothing would have to think of Samara as the source in the same way that a customer who sees the Nike logo on products associates those products with Nike. In the Wal-Mart case there was no evidence that customers associated the designs strictly with Samara.

The result of this Supreme Court decision is that your crafts product design will only be protected under trade dress law if you can demonstrate that its appearance serves to identify you as the source. In general, extensively exploited crafts items, for example, the Cabbage Patch Kids or Hummel figurines, are more likely to acquire the standard of customer association required by the Supreme Court.

Why does trade dress protection hinge on whether customers associate specific designs with the creators of those designs? The rationale is to prevent customer confusion in the marketplace. In other words, it's unfair for a customer to believe she is buying a polychromed wood sculpture from Wendell Castle when it is actually a knockoff made in Korea.

This customer association is known as secondary meaning, and there is no bright-line test for determining it. You can demonstrate secondary meaning by a showing of high sales volume, extensive advertising, a long period of use, unsolicited publicity such as newspaper articles or television shows and customer surveys and other proof that customers associate the appearance with you. For example, one company proved secondary meaning in its lawn furniture designs with evidence of $1.2 million spent advertising the product line, gross sales of approximately $5 million and testimony by customers stating they associated the design with the company.

The Supreme Court's ruling is a depressing shift in the law for crafts makers, making it easier for catalog companies and chain stores to knock off an item and sell it. However, the ruling emphasizes the importance of shoring up your rights under trade dress and trademark principles.

Since trade dress protection for your craft design is difficult to get, you should consider two alternatives, including:

- **Copyright.** Copyright protection allows you to stop anyone who creates an identical or substantially similar version of your crafts product. (For more information, read Chapter 8.)
- **Design and utility patent.** Design patent protection allows you to stop anyone who makes, uses or manufactures the ornamental design of your crafts product. (For more information, read Chapter 7.)

To protect any rights you may have to trade dress protection, keep track of all publicity, advertising and sales for your crafts products. These are the elements that demonstrate customer associations. Finally, keep track of any complaints by your customers who were confused by the knockoffs and thought they originated with you.

The trade dress rules we have discussed apply to product designs. You are more likely to qualify for trade dress for product packaging, product names and product logos, for which the rules are different. For that reason, your packaging, name and logo should be as distinctive as possible, and you should attempt to incorporate your trademark (your name or logo) into the work. If a competitor copies any of these elements, you will have better odds of stopping the theft.

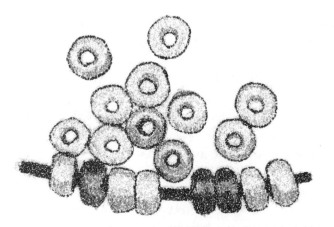

D. Trademark Searching

The purpose of a trademark search is to determine if a similar name or mark is being used on similar goods or services. The person performing the search must delve into collections of trademarks (known as trademark databases) and search through business directories and news articles describing names of products or services. With the advent of Internet access, a competent search can be performed online. Professional search firms perform these tasks and prepare written reports for a fee of several hundred dollars.

A trademark search should locate substantially similar variations on the mark. For example, if a crafts artist selling bird cages intends to use the name Bird Man for his products, he would need to search for that name as well as soundalikes ("Byrd"), plurals ("Bird Men"), gender variations ("Bird Women" or "Bird Boy") and perhaps foreign translations. The search would have to be broad enough to find substantially similar terms for bird cages and for related product services and goods such as bird food. Even though these are not the products or services for which the mark is intended, these categories are considered "related goods or services" and may result in potential conflicts.

If a search determines that the desired mark or a substantially similar mark is already in use, it's time to rethink your choice of mark. Frustrating though this is, it's better than closing your eyes to the competition and hoping for the best. Failure to search— or to act on what you discovered in a search—can have expensive consequences. If you rush to market, blind to the fact that a similar trademark is already being used by a competitor, the competitor may obtain a court order preventing your use of the trademark, and you may also have to pay monetary damages and attorney fees.

The most economical method of searching is to start with a preliminary search on the Internet. If the preliminary search turns up similar marks, you can then narrow your choices before proceeding to a professional search report.

- **Stage One: Preliminary search.** A preliminary search should begin with a review of the USPTO Trademark database followed by a more extensive search of fee-based online trademark databases. Following this, a search should be made for unregistered (or common law) marks by reviewing Internet news databases, domain name sources and trade directories.

- **Stage Two: Professional search.** If the preliminary search does not turn up any similar marks (referred to as "potential conflicts"), you can, if you wish, hire a professional search firm to prepare a complete report of any similar federal, state, common law or, if desired, international trademarks. Since these searches are expensive (often $300-$400), I would suggest bypassing this professional search unless you are either entering into a licensing agreement or distribution agreement (see Chapter 9) in which you must promise your trademark does not infringe, or your crafts products are becoming successful and you need the peace of mind that comes with knowing you are not infringing any existing marks. Two companies that perform

professional searches are Thomson & Thomson (www.thomson-thomson.com) and Trademark Research Corporation, (www.cch-trc.com).

The USPTO database offers a free and simple screening system, with some limitations. The USPTO database does not include trademark applications filed during the last two to four months, nor does it contain any information on state, foreign or common law trademarks or inactive applications and registrations.

1. The USPTO Trademark Database

To use the USPTO trademark database, go to the website (www.uspto.gov) and click "Search Trademarks." You'll have four search options:

- **New user form search** uses words or combinations of words as search terms. This is the easiest place to start your search (see Figure 6-3).

- **Structured form search** uses the Boolean search system of connectors such as "and" and "or."

- **Free form search** uses Boolean identifiers and 30 different fields to search. For example, a search can be made of "Owner Name" or "International Class."

UNITED STATES PATENT AND TRADEMARK OFFICE

Trademark Electronic Search System (TESS)

TESS was last updated on Tue Jun 18 04:31:25 EDT 2002

| PTO HOME | TRADEMARK | TESS HOME | STRUCTURED | FREE FORM | BROWSE DICT | BOTTOM | HELP |

View Search History:

WARNING: AFTER SEARCHING THE USPTO DATABASE, EVEN IF **YOU** THINK THE RESULTS ARE "O.K.," DO **NOT** ASSUME THAT YOUR MARK CAN BE REGISTERED AT THE USPTO. AFTER YOU FILE AN APPLICATION, THE USPTO MUST DO ITS OWN SEARCH AND OTHER REVIEW, AND MIGHT REFUSE TO REGISTER YOUR MARK.

- ⦿ Plural and Singular ○ Singular
- ⦿ Both   ○ Live   ○ Dead

Search Term: Bird Man

Field: Combined Word Mark (BI,TI,MP,TL)

Result Must Contain: All Search Terms (AND)

[Submit Query]   [Clear Query]

[Logout] *Please logout when you are done to release system resources allocated for you.*

Figure 6-3: New User Search Form

The USPTO trademark website provides extensive help online. Since it is free and there are no time limitations on its use, companies can search endlessly for trademarks, soundalikes and other potentially confusing variations.

2. Fee-Based Online Trademark Databases

Below is a list of fee-based trademark databases. These databases are more extensive and expensive than the USPTO. Charges may accrue on an hourly, daily or monthly basis. Some services charge a subscription fee with additional searching fees. Some services charge additional fees for providing trademark images or downloading or printing database information.

- Saegis (www.thomson-thomson.com)
- Dialog (www.dialog.com)
- Micropatent (www.micropatent.com)
- Westlaw (www.westlaw.com)
- LEXIS/NEXIS (www.lexis-nexis.com)
- Corporate Intelligence (www.trademarks.com)
- Trademark Register (www.trademarkregister.com).

3. Internet Searching

Online business and product directories can provide information about unregistered marks. For example, the Thomas Register of American Manufacturers (www.thomasregister.com) includes over 124,000 brand names in 60,000 product categories.

The fact that a company is using a name as its trade or business name does not necessarily mean that it is being used as a trademark. Further research may be necessary.

Another method for locating unregistered marks is to search an online trade publication. For example, many crafts and gallery trademarks can be found by reviewing *The Crafts Report Magazine* (www.craftsreport.com) or *Niche Magazine* (www.nichemag.com).

4. Analyzing Results

When reviewing your results, you won't need to be concerned about "dead" marks (usually indicated in the right column of your search results). As the name suggests, dead marks are completely out of circulation. In fact, they are no longer registered with the USPTO. (See Figure 6-4.) Dead marks were most often forsaken by their owners, after which their trademark protection expired. (See Figure 6-5.)

If you find an identical or nearly identical mark to the one you had in mind being used on similar or related goods, your answer is pretty clear: Don't use your intended mark. Trademark searching becomes more complicated when the search uncovers marks that are similar but *not* identical being used on similar goods or services. For example, a gallery wants to go by the name Blue Moon Gallery. A trademark search indicates several registered trademarks using "Blue" for galleries and retail outlets (for example, Blue Sky, Blue Ridge, Blue Heron, Blue Ribbon and Blue and Green Apple). There are also several companies using "Moon" (such as Moon So Bright and Winter Moon).

In a situation like this, the gallery needs to consider two issues:

1. Is "Blue Moon Gallery" likely to confuse consumers of the other retail services using the words "Blue" or "Moon"?
2. Are any of the retail services using the trademarks with "Blue" or "Moon" aggressive trademark owners who are likely to hassle the Blue Moon owners?

A trademark attorney might determine that consumers were unlikely to be confused by various galleries named Blue Sky, Blue Ridge, Blue Heron, Blue Ribbon and Blue and Green Apple. Consumers of gallery services are usually fairly sophisticated and could discern the difference between the names. But whether a trademark is likely to confuse people is not a science. Attorneys and judges always analyze these issues on a case-by-case basis, so there are few hard and fast rules. If unsure of how to proceed, consult with a trademark attorney.

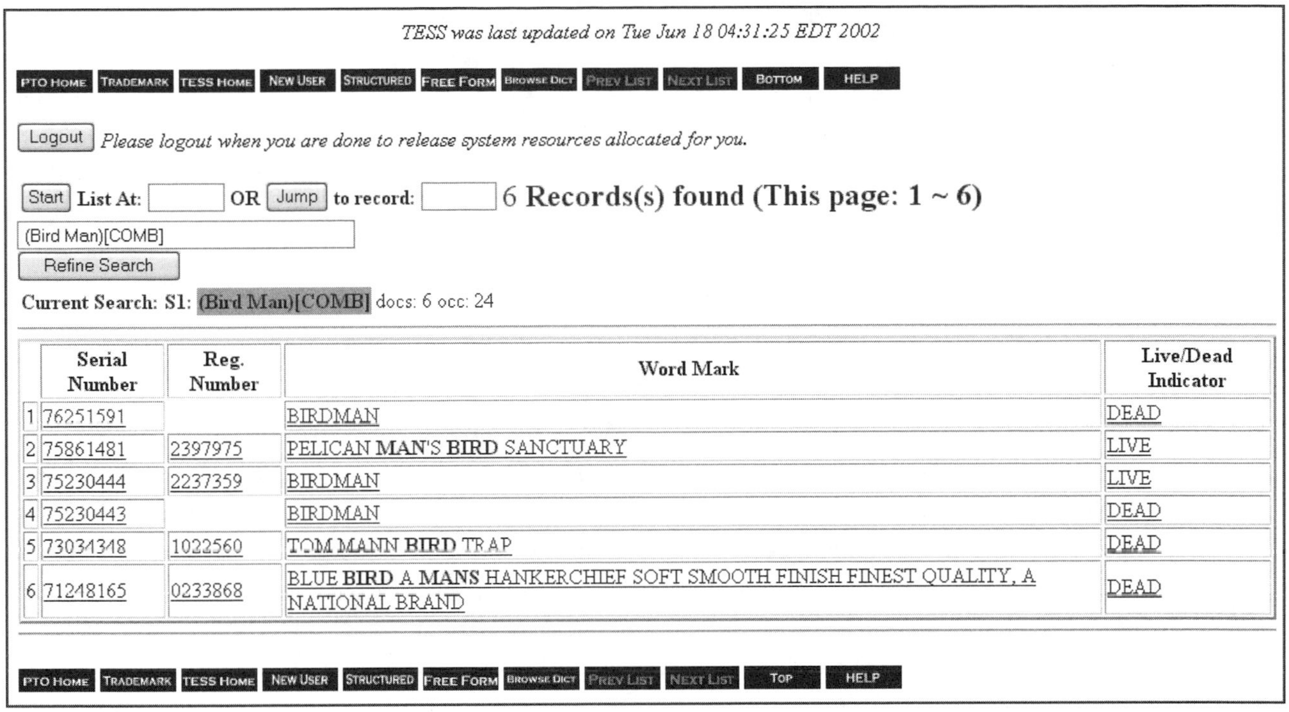

TESS was last updated on Tue Jun 18 04:31:25 EDT 2002

PTO HOME | TRADEMARK | TESS HOME | NEW USER | STRUCTURED | FREE FORM | BROWSE DICT | PREV LIST | NEXT LIST | BOTTOM | HELP

Logout *Please logout when you are done to release system resources allocated for you.*

Start List At: [ ] OR Jump to record: [ ] **6 Records(s) found (This page: 1 ~ 6)**

(Bird Man)[COMB]

Refine Search

Current Search: S1: (Bird Man)[COMB] docs: 6 occ: 24

	Serial Number	Reg. Number	Word Mark	Live/Dead Indicator
1	76251591		BIRDMAN	DEAD
2	75861481	2397975	PELICAN MAN'S BIRD SANCTUARY	LIVE
3	75230444	2237359	BIRDMAN	LIVE
4	75230443		BIRDMAN	DEAD
5	73031348	1022560	TOM MANN BIRD TRAP	DEAD
6	71248165	0233868	BLUE BIRD A MANS HANKERCHIEF SOFT SMOOTH FINISH FINEST QUALITY, A NATIONAL BRAND	DEAD

PTO HOME | TRADEMARK | TESS HOME | NEW USER | STRUCTURED | FREE FORM | BROWSE DICT | PREV LIST | NEXT LIST | TOP | HELP

Figure 6-4: Dead Marks

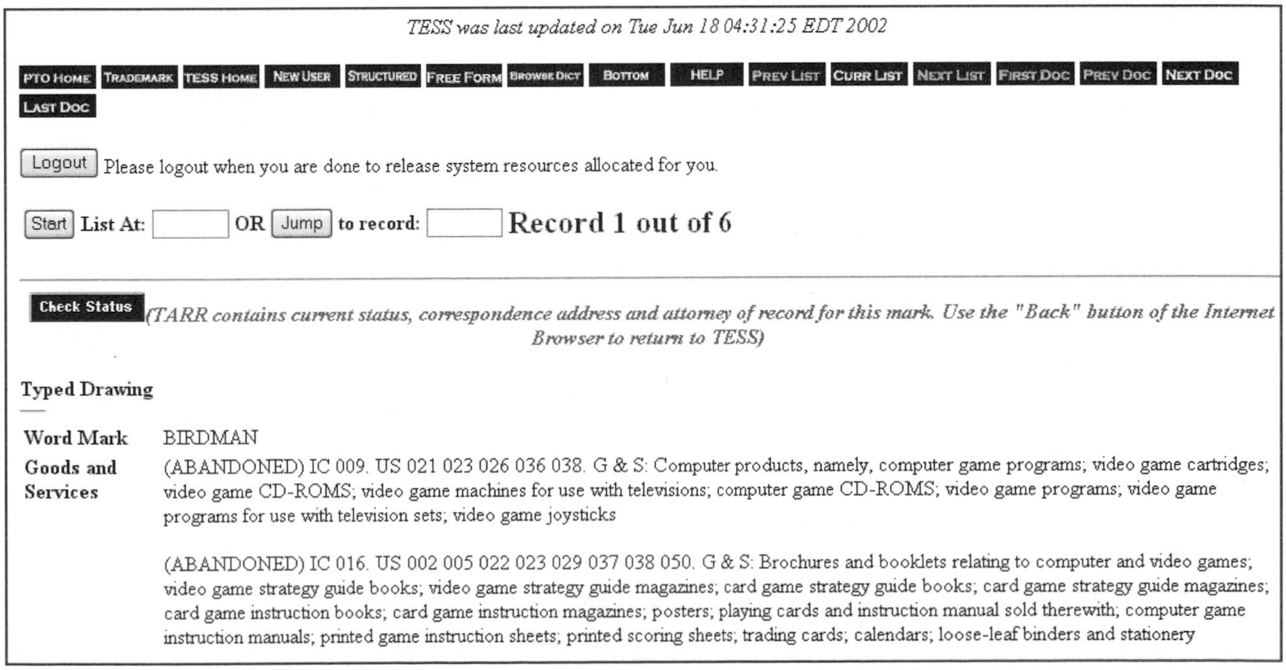

TESS was last updated on Tue Jun 18 04:31:25 EDT 2002

PTO HOME | TRADEMARK | TESS HOME | NEW USER | STRUCTURED | FREE FORM | BROWSE DICT | BOTTOM | HELP | PREV LIST | CURR LIST | NEXT LIST | FIRST DOC | PREV DOC | NEXT DOC

LAST DOC

Logout *Please logout when you are done to release system resources allocated for you.*

Start List At: [ ] OR Jump to record: [ ] **Record 1 out of 6**

Check Status *(TARR contains current status, correspondence address and attorney of record for this mark. Use the "Back" button of the Internet Browser to return to TESS)*

Typed Drawing

Word Mark   BIRDMAN

Goods and Services   (ABANDONED) IC 009. US 021 023 026 036 038. G & S: Computer products, namely, computer game programs; video game cartridges; video game CD-ROMS; video game machines for use with televisions; computer game CD-ROMS; video game programs; video game programs for use with television sets; video game joysticks

(ABANDONED) IC 016. US 002 005 022 023 029 037 038 050. G & S: Brochures and booklets relating to computer and video games; video game strategy guide books; video game strategy guide magazines; card game strategy guide books; card game strategy guide magazines; card game instruction books; card game instruction magazines; posters; playing cards and instruction manual sold therewith; computer game instruction manuals; printed game instruction sheets; printed scoring sheets; trading cards; calendars; loose-leaf binders and stationery

Figure 6-5: Abandoned Marks

E. The Federal Registration Process

Below is an explanation for how to prepare and file a federal trademark application. Before you begin your federal application, you'll need to figure out what theory it's based on. Most federal trademark applications are based on either "use in commerce" or an applicant's intention to use the trademark (referred to as an "intent-to-use" or ITU application).

1. The Trademark Application Process

The process for both "in use" and "intent-to-use" application involves three steps:

- **Preparation and filing of application.** A trademark application consists of a completed application form, a drawing of the mark, the filing fee and a specimen of the mark. You can either mail the materials to the USPTO or file the application electronically and pay by credit card.
- **Examination by the USPTO.** Upon receipt, the trademark application is given a number and assigned to a USPTO examining attorney. If there is an error or inconsistency in the application, or if the examining attorney believes that registration is inappropriate, the attorney will contact the applicant to discuss the objection. The applicant can respond to the objections or can abandon the application. The examining attorney will either approve the mark for publication or reject it. If it is rejected, the applicant may challenge the rejection.
- **Publication in the Official Gazette**. Once the examining attorney approves the mark, it is published in the Official Gazette. The public is given thirty days to object to the registration. If no one objects, a trademark registration will be issued (or in the case of an ITU application, the mark will be allowed pending use in commerce.) If there is an objection from the public, the matter will be resolved through a proceeding at the USPTO.

The total time for an application to be processed may range from a year to several years, depending on the basis for filing and the legal issues that may arise in the course of examining the application. The registration expires ten years from the date of registration. You have certain obligations to maintain your trademark registration—for example, you must file a Section 8 Declaration of Continued Use between the fifth and sixth anniversary of the registration. Information about these maintenance requirements can be obtained at the USPTO website or by reviewing *Trademark: Legal Care for Your Business & Product Name,* by Stephen Elias (Nolo).

Attorneys at the USPTO use the *Trademark Examiners Manual of Procedure (TMEP)* as guidance for substantive and procedural trademark issues. If a trademark owner has questions regarding the application process, the TMEP is the most reliable source for assistance. The TMEP is available online (www.uspto.gov/web/offices/tac/tmep).

2. Preparing the Federal Trademark Application: The TEAS System

The preferred method of preparing the federal trademark application is to use the online Trademark Electronic Application System (TEAS) located at the PTO's website (www.uspto.gov/teas/index.html). TEAS is an interactive system in which the user is asked a series of questions. If a question is not answered or an essential element is not completed, the applicant is asked to correct the error. The application can be printed out and mailed (using the PrinTEAS system), or it can be sent electronically (using the e-TEAS system). The system is remarkably easy to use, and there's a low probability of error in preparing the form.

In recent years, the USPTO has discouraged federal applications prepared by methods other than the TEAS system. There have been rumors that, sometime in the future, use of the TEAS system will be mandatory for trademark applicants. However, there is still no requirement that the "official" TEAS form be used. Applicants can create their own application forms by typing the necessary information onto a sheet of paper. If you're doing this, the application form should be doubled-spaced on 8½ x 11-inch paper with a 1½-inch margin on the left and top of the page.

It is also permissible to complete forms prepared for publications, for example, forms photocopied from the publication *Basic Facts About Trademarks*, available from the U.S. Department of Commerce, Patent & Trademark Office, Washington, DC 20231. I have not included blank applications for trademarks or service marks in this book since I highly recommend using the TEAS system. I have included applications for certification and collective marks (see Section A8, above) because these cannot be completed online. An example of a completed trademark application is provided at the end of this chapter. Below, I have highlighted some issues that may arise when completing the TEAS application.

a. Basis for Application

On the trademark application, you will be asked the basis for your application. If you have already used the mark in connection with the sale of crafts goods or services, then you would check "Yes" under "Use in Commerce." As for dates of use, you will need to provide the date (or your best guess as to the dates) you first sold goods or services using the trademark, anywhere. You will also need to provide the date when you first sold your work or services outside your state (for example, through an Internet sale or during travel to a crafts fair). If you have not yet used the mark but have a bona fide intention to use the mark, check "Yes" under "Intent to Use."

b. Identification of the Class of Goods or Services

You will need to identify your class of goods. The USPTO uses the International Schedule of Classes of Goods and Services to group related goods. This helps them make appropriate comparisons of the mark. For example, glassware, porcelain and earthenware are in Class 21. You can register your work in many classes, but each class registration costs $325 (check current fees at the USPTO website).

To identify the class for your goods, search the USPTO's goods and services manual online. Go to the home page, click "Trademarks" (on the left side of the page), then look under the heading "Trademark Manuals" and click "Acceptable Identification of Goods and Services Manual." On the page titled "Acceptable Identification of Goods and Services Manual" (see Figure 6-6), click "Search" and type in the crafts product that you sell (see Figure 6-7). The class number is indicated after the letter G (for Goods) or S (for Services). For example, in Figure 6-8, flower baskets, plant baskets and picnic baskets are all in Class 21. Two sources for guidance in identifying goods are the *Trademark Examiners Manual of Procedure* (*TMEP*) and the *U.S. Patent and Trademark Office Acceptable Identification of Goods and Services Manual*, which lists appropriate choices of identification of goods and services in alphabetical order and by class. Both of these guides can be obtained in book form, on CD-ROM or online at the USPTO website. The International Schedule of Classes and Goods is provided at the end of this chapter.

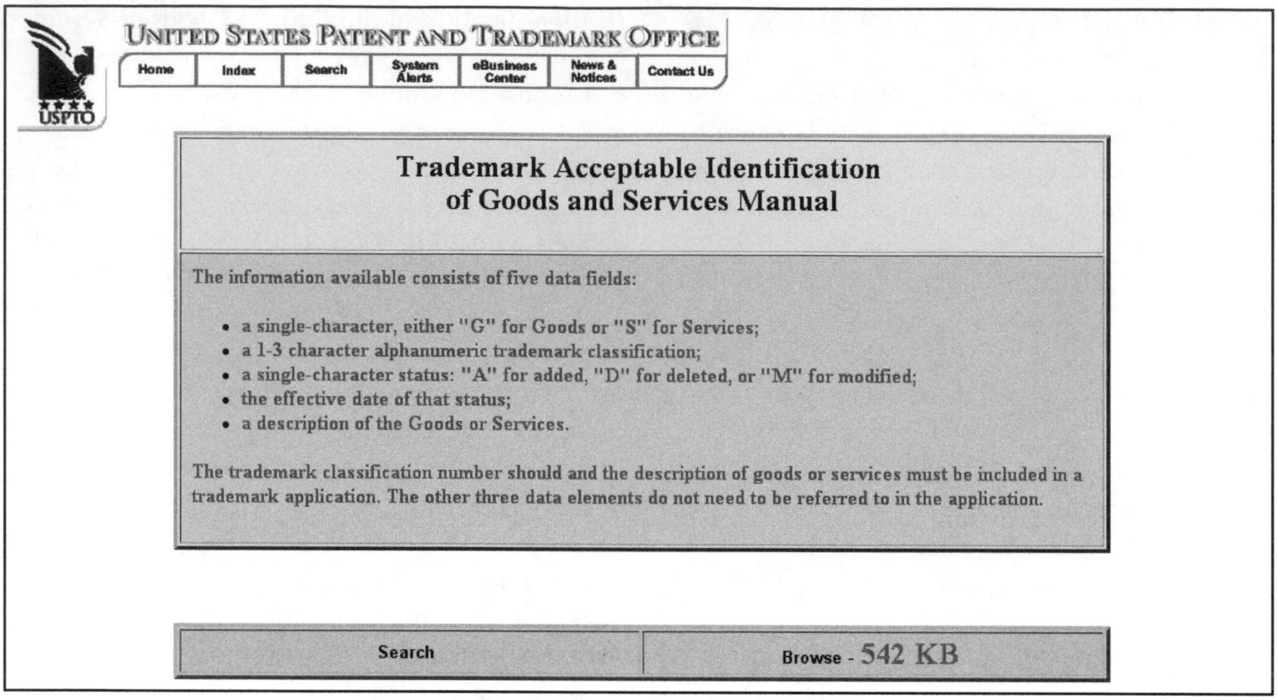

UNITED STATES PATENT AND TRADEMARK OFFICE

| Home | Index | Search | System Alerts | eBusiness Center | News & Notices | Contact Us |

Trademark Acceptable Identification of Goods and Services Manual

The information available consists of five data fields:

- a single-character, either "G" for Goods or "S" for Services;
- a 1-3 character alphanumeric trademark classification;
- a single-character status: "A" for added, "D" for deleted, or "M" for modified;
- the effective date of that status;
- a description of the Goods or Services.

The trademark classification number should and the description of goods or services must be included in a trademark application. The other three data elements do not need to be referred to in the application.

| Search | Browse - 542 KB |

Figure 6-6: Acceptable Identification of Goods and Services Manual

UNITED STATES PATENT AND TRADEMARK OFFICE

| Home | Index | Search | System Alerts | eBusiness Center | News & Notices | Contact Us |

Search the Trademark Acceptable Identification of Goods and Services Manual

This is a searchable index of current identification codes for trademark Goods and Services. *Deleted identification codes are not included in this index; they may be viewed in the browsable list.*

Please enter any word that will identify goods or services.

Search For [baskets]   [SEARCH] [RESET]

Return a maximum of [250 ▼] results.

Help on Boolean Search Operators:

- AND (e.g., *tennis and table*)

  The search results will include only those IDs which contain both words.

- OR (e.g., *tennis or table*)

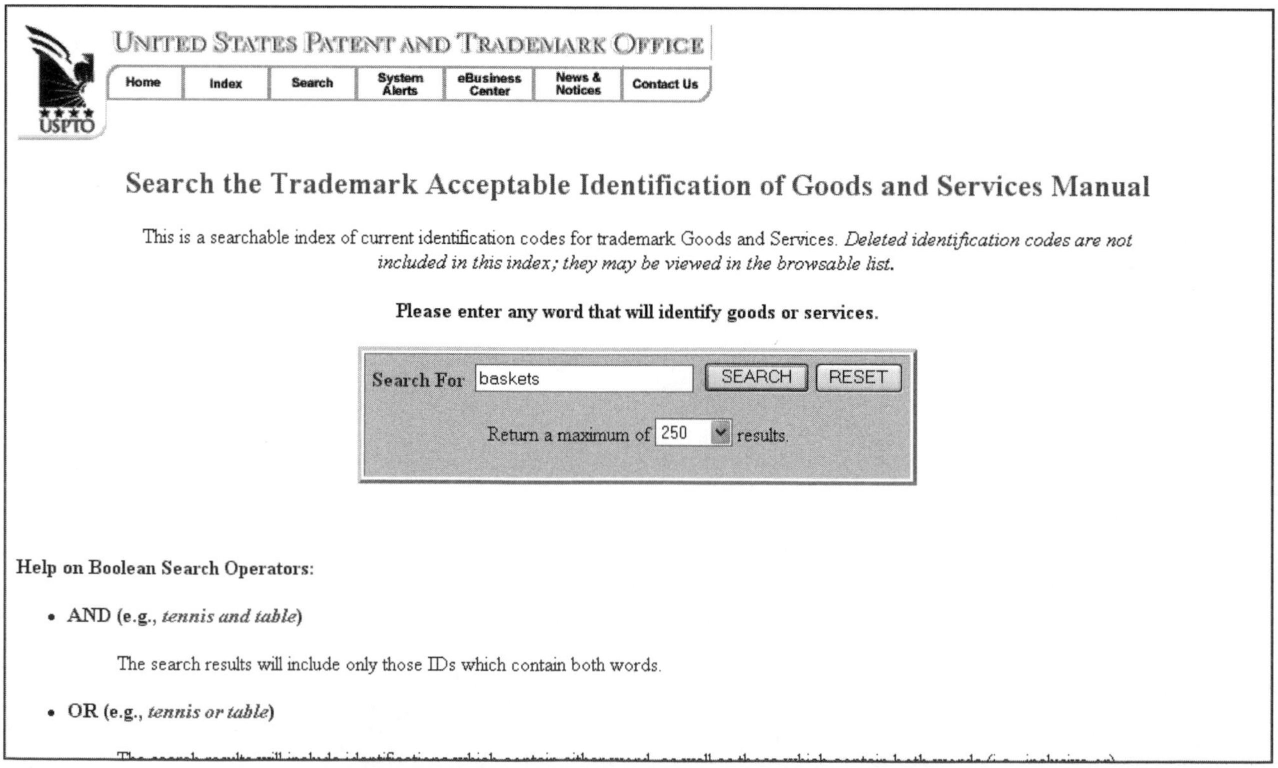

Figure 6-7: Search the Acceptable Identification of Goods and Services Manual

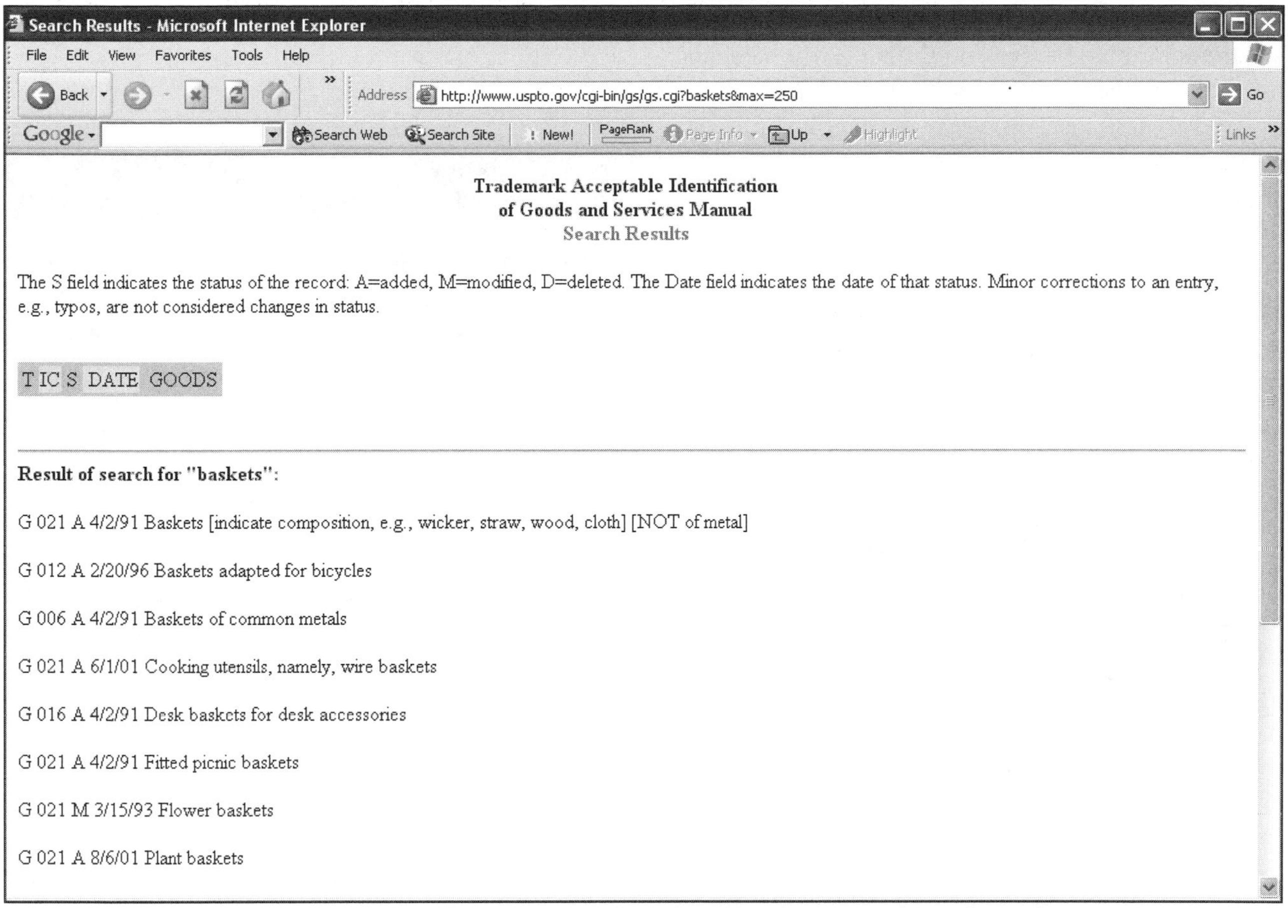

Figure 6-8: Acceptable Identification of Goods and Services Manual Search Results

c. Description of the Goods or Services

Along with the class for the goods, you will need to provide a description of the goods or services. This description is different from the listing of the International Class. For example, if you are selling key rings (International Class 6, "non precious metal goods"), the listing should state "key rings," not "non precious metal goods."

The description should be precise. If your description is too broad, the USPTO's trademark examining attorney will negotiate an appropriate description with you. (According to a USPTO survey, the applicant's identification of goods and services was questioned in more than fifty percent of trademark applications.)

Again, two sources for guidance in identifying goods are the *Trademark Examiners Manual of Procedure (TMEP)* and the *USPTO Acceptable Identification of Goods and Services Manual,* both available online.

When using the TEAS system, choosing the proper description is simplified because the TEAS system is electronically linked to the USPTO *Acceptable Identification of Goods and Services Manual.* An applicant can type in a word related to the goods and examine sample descriptions and lists of goods and services.

d. Identification of the Mark

If the mark is a word or group of words, identification of the mark is straightforward. The mark may be identified simply as "Just Jules" or "Hooky Wooky Hats." But if the mark is a stylized presentation of the word, a graphic symbol, a logo, a design or any of the other devices permitted under trademark law, a statement must be provided that clearly identifies the mark. If you're using the TEAS system, type in the word mark or, in the case of a stylized mark, attach a graphic file (either JPG or GIF format) containing a black and white rendition of the mark. Insert a written description in the appropriate box.

For the broadest protection for a word mark, register it free of any lettering style. This will give you the ability to use the trademark in various fonts, rather than being restricted to your original presentation of the mark.

e. Information About the Applicant

The applicant—your crafts business—can be an individual, a partnership, a corporation, an association such as a union, social club or cooperative or a joint ownership by some combination of any these forms. If you are acting on behalf of a partnership, include the names and citizenship of the general partners and the domicile of the partnership. If you are representing a corporation, include the name under which the business or group is incorporated and the state or foreign nation under which it is organized.

Your own citizenship is required as well as a mailing address. If you are doing business under a fictitious name, that information should be provided, especially if it is included on any specimen furnished with the application. If the mark is owned jointly by two entities, that should be stated as well. Supplying this information online using TEAS is facilitated by typing the appropriate information into the form. Drop-down menus and online help screens are available to guide you.

f. Declaration

You are required to provide a declaration, a sworn statement or other verification that the facts in the trademark application are true. You, or an officer of your corporation or association, should sign the declaration. The TEAS application provides an all-purpose declaration that can be used for both ITU applications and for trademarks that are in use.

Disclaimers

Many trademarks include words or phrases that, by themselves, cannot be protected under trademark law. For example, no person can claim an exclusive right to the word "pottery" or "basket." To allow one person an exclusive right to use such terms would decimate the English language. Therefore, the trademark office usually requires a disclaimer as to certain portions of trademarks. For example, if an applicant wanted to register the mark Lucky Jewelry, the applicant would be required to disclaim "jewelry." This means that apart from the use as a part of the trademark, the applicant claims no exclusive right to use the word "jewelry."

---

g. Specimen

If your application is based on actual use of your mark in commerce, you'll need to enclose a specimen —that is, an actual example of the trademark being used on your goods or in your offer of services. In the case of ITU applications, the specimen must be filed later, together with a document entitled "Amendment to Allege Use." An actual specimen, rather than a facsimile, is preferred. If you're using the PrinTEAS form to apply, enclose a traditional specimen, as described in this section. If you're filing electronically with e-TEAS, you'll see that the USPTO provides a means for attaching a digital photograph of the specimen. Since crafts works are goods, a label, tag or container for the goods is considered to be an acceptable specimen of use for a trademark. A letterhead or business card is unacceptable as a trademark specimen because it doesn't follow the goods through the stream of commerce.

PTO Form 1478 (Rev 9/98)
OMB Control #0651-0009 (Exp. 08/31/2004)

Trademark/Service Mark Application

* To the Commissioner for Trademarks *

<DOCUMENT INFORMATION>
<TRADEMARK/SERVICEMARK APPLICATION>
<VERSION 1.22>

<APPLICANT INFORMATION>
<NAME>   Andrea Stim
<STREET>   950 Parker Street
<CITY>   Berkeley
<STATE>   CA
<COUNTRY>   USA
<ZIP/POSTAL CODE>   94710
<TELEPHONE NUMBER>   510-704-1976
<FAX NUMBER>   510-548-5902
<E-MAIL ADDRESS>   richs@nolo.com
<AUTHORIZE E-MAIL COMMUNICATION>   Yes

<APPLICANT ENTITY INFORMATION>
<INDIVIDUAL: COUNTRY OF CITIZENSHIP>   USA

<TRADEMARK/SERVICEMARK INFORMATION>

<MARK>   hooky wooky

<TYPED FORM>   Yes
~ Applicant requests registration of the above-identified trademark/service mark in the United States Patent and Trademark Office on the Principal Register established by the Act of July 5, 1946 (15 U.S.C. §1051 et seq., as amended). ~

<BASIS FOR FILING AND GOODS/SERVICES INFORMATION>
<USE IN COMMERCE: SECTION 1(a)>   Yes
~ Applicant is using or is using through a related company the mark in commerce on or in connection with the below-identified goods/services. (15 U.S.C. §1051(a), as amended.). Applicant attaches one SPECIMEN for each class showing the mark as used in commerce on or in connection with any item in the class of listed goods and/or services. ~
<SPECIMEN DESCRIPTION>   tags affixed to crocheted hats and clothing
<INTERNATIONAL CLASS NUMBER>   025
<LISTING OF GOODS AND/OR SERVICES>   crocheted hats and clothing
<FIRST USE ANYWHERE DATE>   11/01/2001
<FIRST USE IN COMMERCE DATE>   11/01/2001

<FEE INFORMATION>
<TOTAL FEES PAID>   325

<NUMBER OF CLASSES PAID>   1
<NUMBER OF CLASSES>   1

<LAW OFFICE INFORMATION>
~ The USPTO is authorized to communicate with the applicant at the below e-mail address ~
<E-MAIL ADDRESS FOR CORRESPONDENCE>   richs@nolo.com

<SIGNATURE AND OTHER INFORMATION>
~ **PTO-Application Declaration**: The undersigned, being hereby warned that willful false statements and the like so made are punishable by fine or imprisonment, or both, under 18 U.S.C. §1001, and that such willful false statements may jeopardize the validity of the application or any resulting registration, declares that he/she is properly authorized to execute this application on behalf of the applicant; he/she believes the applicant to be the owner of the trademark/service mark sought to be registered, or, if the application is being filed under 15 U.S.C. §1051(b), he/she believes applicant to be entitled to use such mark in commerce; to the best of his/her knowledge and belief no other person, firm, corporation, or association has the right to use the mark in commerce, either in the identical form thereof or in such near resemblance thereto as to be likely, when used on or in connection with the goods/services of such other person, to cause confusion, or to cause mistake, or to deceive; and that all statements made of his/her own knowledge are true; and that all statements made on information and belief are believed to be true. ~

<SIGNATURE>_____   * please sign here*

<DATE>   _____
<NAME>   Andrea Stim

The information collected on this form allows the PTO to determine whether a mark may be registered on the Principal or Supplemental register, and provides notice of an applicant's claim of ownership of the mark. Responses to the request for information are required to obtain the benefit of a registration on the Principal or Supplemental register. 15 U.S.C. §§1051 et seq. and 37 C.F.R. Part 2. All information collected will be made public. Gathering and providing the information will require an estimated 12 or 18 minutes (depending if the application is based on an intent to use the mark in commerce, use of the mark in commerce, or a foreign application or registration). Please direct comments on the time needed to complete this form, and/or suggestions for reducing this burden to the Chief Information Officer, U.S. Patent and Trademark Office, U.S. Department of Commerce, Washington D.C. 20231. Please note that the PTO may not conduct or sponsor a collection of information using a form that does not display a valid OMB control number.

Drawing Page
Date/Time Stamp: Monday, 06-24-2002 16:11:53 EDT

Applicant:
Andrea Stim
950 Parker Street
Berkeley , CA 94710
USA

Date of First Use Anywhere: 11/01/2001
Date of First Use In Commerce: 11/01/2001

Goods and Services:
crocheted hats and clothing

Mark:

HOOKY WOOKY

International Schedule of Classes of Goods and Services

Goods

1. Chemical products used in industry, science, photography, agriculture, horticulture, forestry; artificial and synthetic resins; plastics in the form of powders, liquids or pastes, for industrial use; manures (natural and artificial); fire extinguishing compositions; tempering substances and chemical preparations for soldering; chemical substances for preserving foodstuffs; tanning substances; adhesive substances used in industry.

2. Paints, varnishes, lacquers; preservatives against rust and against deterioration of wood; colouring matters, dyestuffs; mordants; natural resins; metals in foil and powder form for painters and decorators.

3. Bleaching preparations and other substances for laundry use; cleaning, polishing, scouring and abrasive preparations; soaps; perfumery, essential oils, cosmetics, hair lotions; dentifrices.

4. Industrial oils and greases (other than oils and fats and essential oils); lubricants; dust laying and absorbing compositions; fuels (including motor spirit) and illuminants; candles, tapers, night lights and wicks.

5. Pharmaceutical, veterinary and sanitary substances; infants' and invalids' foods; plasters, material for bandaging; material for stopping teeth, dental wax, disinfectants; preparations for killing weeds and destroying vermin.

6. Unwrought and partly wrought common metals and their alloys; anchors, anvils, bells, rolled and cast building materials; rails and other metallic materials for railway tracks; chains (except driving chains for vehicles); cables and wires (nonelectric); locksmiths' work; metallic pipes and tubes; safes and cash boxes; steel balls; horseshoes; nails and screws; other goods in nonprecious metal not included in other classes; ores.

7. Machines and machine tools; motors (except for land vehicles); machine couplings and belting (except for land vehicles); large size agricultural implements; incubators.

8. Hand tools and instruments; cutlery, forks and spoons; side arms.

9. Scientific, nautical, surveying and electrical apparatus and instruments (including wireless), photographic, cinematographic, optical, weighing, measuring, signalling, checking (supervision), life-saving and teaching apparatus and instruments; coin or counterfreed apparatus; talking machines; cash registers; calculating machines; fire extinguishing apparatus.

10. Surgical, medical, dental and veterinary instruments and apparatus (including artificial limbs, eyes and teeth).

11. Installations for lighting, heating, steam generating, cooking, refrigerating, drying, ventilating, water supply and sanitary purposes.

12. Vehicles; apparatus for locomotion by land, air or water.

13. Firearms; ammunition and projectiles; explosive substances; fireworks.

14. Precious metals and their alloys and goods in precious metals or coated therewith (except cutlery, forks and spoons); jewelry, precious stones, horological and other chronometric instruments.

15. Musical instruments (other than talking machines and wireless apparatus).

16. Paper and paper articles, cardboard and cardboard articles; printed matter, newspaper and periodicals, books; bookbinding material; photographs; stationery, adhesive materials (stationery); artists' materials; paint brushes; typewriters and office requisites (other than furniture); instructional and teaching material (other than apparatus); playing cards; printers' type and cliches (stereotype).

International Schedule of Classes of Goods and Services (continued)

17. Gutta percha, india rubber, balata and substitutes, articles made from these substances and not included in other classes; plastics in the form of sheets, blocks and rods, being for use in manufacture; materials for packing, stopping or insulating; asbestos, mica and their products; hose pipes (nonmetallic).

18. Leather and imitations of leather, and articles made from these materials and not included in other classes; skins, hides; trunks and travelling bags; umbrellas, parasols and walking sticks; whips, harness and saddlery.

19. Building materials, natural and artificial stone, cement, lime, mortar, plaster and gravel; pipes of earthenware or cement; roadmaking materials; asphalt, pitch and bitumen; portable buildings; stone monuments; chimney pots.

20. Furniture, mirrors, picture frames; articles (not included in other classes) of wood, cork, reeds, cane, wicker, horn, bone, ivory, whalebone, shell, amber, mother-of-pearl, meerschaum, celluloid, substitutes for all these materials, or of plastics.

21. Small domestic utensils and containers (not of precious metals, or coated therewith); combs and sponges; brushes (other than paint brushes); brushmaking materials; instruments and material for cleaning purposes, steel wool; unworked or semi-worked glass (excluding glass used in building); glassware, procelain and earthenware, not included in other classes.

22. Ropes, string, nets, tents, awnings, tarpaulins, sails, sacks; padding and stuffing materials (hair, kapok, feathers, seaweed, etc.); raw fibrous textile materials.

23. Yarns, threads.

24. Tissues (piece goods); bed and table covers; textile articles not included in other classes.

25. Clothing, including boots, shoes and slippers.

26. Lace and embroidery, ribands and braid; buttons, press buttons, hooks and eyes, pins and needles; artificial flowers.

27. Carpets, rugs, mats and matting; linoleums and other materials for covering existing floors; wall hangings (nontextile).

28. Games and playthings; gymnastic and sporting articles (except clothing); ornaments and decorations for Christmas trees.

29. Meats, fish, poultry and game; meat extracts; preserved, dried and cooked fruits and vegetables; jellies, jams; eggs, milk and other dairy products; edible oils and fats; preserves, pickles.

30. Coffee, tea, cocoa, sugar, rice, tapioca, sago, coffee substitutes; flour, and preparations made from cereals; bread, biscuits, cakes, pastry and confectionery, ices; honey, treacle; yeast, baking powder; salt, mustard, pepper, vinegar, sauces, spices; ice.

31. Agricultural, horticultural and forestry products and grains not included in other classes; living animals; fresh fruits and vegetables; seeds; live plants and flowers; foodstuffs for animals, malt.

32. Beer, ale and porter; mineral and aerated waters and other nonalcoholic drinks; syrups and other preparations for making beverages.

33. Wines, spirits and liqueurs.

34. Tobacco, raw or manufactured; smokers' articles; matches.

Services

35. Advertising and business.

36. Insurance and financial.

37. Construction and repair.

38. Communication.

39. Transportation and storage.

40. Material treatment.

41. Education and entertainment.

42. Miscellaneous.

Chapter

7

Design Patents

*I*n 1997, Alan Philipson and his son, Andre, patented a design for a decorative bead shaped like a woman's breasts (see Figure 7-1). The Philipsons sold the patent to a New Orleans company, Superior Merchandise, and the design quickly became the best-selling bead in the company's line—especially popular during Mardi Gras, when celebrants on floats throw thousands of beads to parade watchers.

Figure 7-1: Decorative Bead

Superior later sued a competitor, M.G.I. Wholesale, who had begun selling a similar bead. In defense, M.G.I. argued that the U.S. Patent and Trademark Office (USPTO) made a mistake granting the design patent to the Philipsons. The human anatomy can't be appropriated by one designer, said M.G.I.'s attorneys, and anyway, the design was obvious. (This standard, known as nonobviousness, is discussed in Section C3, below.)

The judge didn't buy M.G.I.'s argument. The Philipsons were not claiming rights in the human anatomy, said the judge, they were only claiming rights for their anatomical design on beads. There was no evidence of a previous bead with a similar design, and if it was obvious, the judge asked, why was M.G.I. copying the Philipsons' design? The judge upheld the patent and declared M.G.I. an infringer. (*Superior Merchandise v. M.G.I. Wholesale,* 52 U.S.P.Q.2D 1935 (E.D. La. 1999).)

Whether or not you believe that beads shaped like breasts are worth creating—or copying—this case graphically illustrates the power of a design patent. Of the four types of legal protection for crafts works—copyright, design patent, trade secret and trademark—the design patent is probably the most potent. (It's been described as a "copyright with teeth.")

Although design patents offer broad legal rights, they haven't been widely accepted among crafts designers because of the time, expense and legal hurdles involved in the registration process. The application, drawings and filing fees can cost $165 to $1,500, depending on whether you use a patent attorney. In addition, your design must be new and not obvious to others in the crafts field. Finally, you must file your application within one year of any publication or offer for sale.

Despite the work involved, a design patent may be worth the time and expense—for example, if you have a new design that is a best seller or if you feel certain a specific design will be copied by competitors.

In this chapter we'll explain:

- how you get a design patent (see Section A)
- how you can use a design patent to protect your rights (see Section B)
- what qualifies for a design patent, and how to make sure your design hasn't already "been done" (see Section C)
- the differences between a design patent and copyright protection (see Section D)
- how to prepare and file a design patent application (see Section E), and
- how to let the world know your work is patented (see Section F).

⚠️ **Design patents (and legal protections like copyrights, trade secrets and trademarks) are weapons, not shields.** In order to use them, you must sue or threaten to sue anyone who trespasses on your rights.

A. How to Get a Design Patent

As you'll see from the illustrations in this chapter, design patent law protects a wide variety of crafts designs—virtually any new ornamentation that's intended for a useful object such as a table, hat, ring, belt buckle and so on. You are eligible for a design patent if your design is new and isn't obvious to those in your crafts field. (An example of an obvious design would be a birdhouse in the shape of a standard, A-frame house.) You must file your application within a year of its publication or first offer for sale. If your application is approved by the USPTO, you'll become the proud owner of a design patent. These standards are explained in more detail in Section C, below.

If you don't want to do it all yourself, you'll have to pay between $750 and $1,500 for:

- an attorney to draft the application
- a patent drafts person to create the drawings, and
- the filing fee (currently $165).

It is possible to save money and prepare and file your own design patent—see Section E, below, for instructions. Unless you pay for expedited (speedy) processing of your application, a design patent takes 12 to 24 months to obtain, and you cannot use it to stop others from copying until the patent has been granted. (The USPTO has indicated that it will place design patents on a faster track than utility patents, which can take two to three years.) Design patents automatically expire 14 years after they're issued and cannot be renewed.

As the creator of the design patent, you will have the right to apply for the patent. The only exceptions are if you signed away your rights to someone else or you were employed to create the design. (For historical reasons, the USPTO often refers to the designer as the inventor and to the design as the invention.) If someone contributed to a new, non-obvious element of your design (see Section C, below), they would be a co-inventor, and you should reach an agreement as to your ownership of the patent.

 For an example of co-inventor agreements, see my book *License Your Invention* (Nolo).

If you're employed to create designs, your employer may own rights in any potential design patents. Ownership depends on the contents of your employment agreement, employment manual policies, whether you used your employer's time and resources to create the design and state laws regarding employee ownership rights. For more on employer ownership of rights, see Chapter 5.

B. What Good a Design Patent Does You

You can do two things with a design patent:

- stop others who create substantially similar designs (see subsection 1), and
- license, sell or otherwise exploit your design (see subsection 2).

1. How to Stop Design Thieves

For over a century, crafts artists have used design patent laws to stop infringements. In one of the earliest reported cases, a jeweler in 1881 was awarded financial damages when a competitor copied his patented design featuring a bird on a twig with a diamond-studded leaf. (*Wood v. Dolby,* 7 F. 475 (1881).)

For 14 years from the date your design patent is granted, you can stop anyone from making, using or selling your design or a substantially similar design on similar crafts goods. In order to stop an infringer, you must file a lawsuit in federal court. You'll have to show the court that an ordinary observer would be deceived into thinking that your item and the infringing item are the same. For example, the court in the ornamental bead case found that the beads were substantially similar even though they were not identical. Superior Merchandise sold a single flat-backed bead; its competitor sold a back-to-back (and anatomically impossible) bead.

A design patent is interpreted through patent drawings that you file as part of your design patent application. These drawings define your rights and show the USPTO how the world will see your unique design. The design patent only protects what is disclosed in the drawings, so if you later change the design substantially, you can't protect it unless you apply for a new patent.

2. How to Exploit Your Patented Design

Besides chasing infringers, you can earn money by exploiting your design—for example, another company might pay you to license your design for a salt and pepper shaker. In this case, you would retain the patent and the company would acquire a limited right to use the design and would pay out periodic royalties. (Licensing is discussed in Chapter 9.) You can also sell all rights ("assign") to the patent to a company in return for a lump sum or royalties.

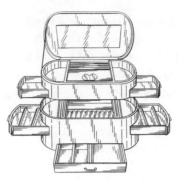

Figure 7-2: Oval Jewelry Box

C. What Qualifies for a Design Patent

In order to qualify for a design patent, you must create a new, original, ornamental and nonobvious design. In addition, the design cannot have been published, sold or offered for sale more than one year before filing your application. Below is a summary of these elements.

Figure 7-3: Jewelry Box

1. What Makes a Design Ornamental

A design patent is granted for the way something looks, not the way it works. As one judge stated, the design must be created for the purpose of "ornamenting" a functional object. Consider the design patent granted for the oval jewelry box in Figure 7-2. The patent only protects the appearance—the shape and proportions—of the box, not the way in which the box functions. The same is true for the jewelry box in Figure 7-3, the clock design in Figure 7-4, the glass-top coffee table in Figure 7-5, the combined high chair and rocking horse in Figure 7-6 and the candle in Figure 7-7. The designers acquire rights to prevent others from copying the form of these objects, not their function.

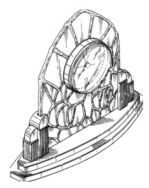

Figure 7-4: Clock

Some crafts artists may find the term "ornamentation" puzzling, since it normally applies to superficial imagery. Under patent law, however, the meaning is broader. Ornamentation refers to the inseparable visual appearance of the functional object—for example, the shape and proportions of the jewelry box in Figure 7-3, the shape and patterns of the

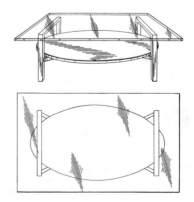

Figure 7-5: Glass-top Coffee Table

glass bottle in Figure 7-8 or the patterns, inlay and overall appearance of the double dresser with mirror in Figure 7-9.

This inseparable design has to create a unique appearance. Unlike copyright law, minimalism is not frowned upon. For example, the bowl with handles in Figure 7-10 and the glass in Figure 7-11 are minimal designs that were both granted design patents.

If a design is purely functional, it won't be considered ornamental (and a design patent won't be granted). Generally, if there are several ways to achieve the same function with different designs, the USPTO will find the design to be ornamental.

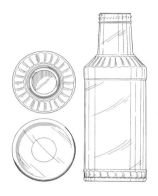

Figure 7-8: Glass Bottle

Figure 7-9: Double Dresser With Mirror

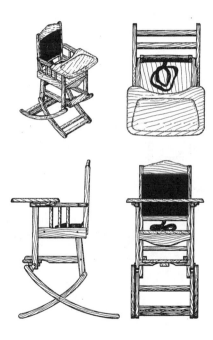

Figure 7-6: Combined High Chair and Rocking Horse

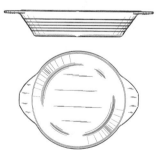

Figure 7-10: Bowl With Handles

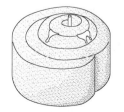

Figure 7-7: Candle

Figure 7-11: Glass

Example: Apparently, there is no shortage of design ideas when it comes to creating shower caddies. There's the nautical approach (Figure 7-12), the feline angle (Figure 7-13), the fan style (Figure 7-14), the basic wire design (Figure 7-15), a variation on the basic design (Figure 7-16), the metal basket (Figure 7-17) the jazzy wire fashion (Figure 7-18), full frontal (Figure 7-19), industrial (Figure 7-20) and tubular (Figure 7-21). (And these are only a fraction of the design patents for shower caddies.) The wide variety of designs demonstrates that the function of these devices—to hold shower supplies such as soap and shampoo—is not limited by any one specific form.

Figure 7-16: Variation on Basic Shower Caddy

Figure 7-17: Metal Basket Shower Caddy

Figure 7-12: Nautical Shower Caddy

Figure 7-13: Kitty Shower Caddy

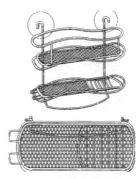

Figure 7-18: Jazzy Wire Shower Caddy

Figure 7-19: Full Frontal Shower Caddy

Figure 7-14: Fan Shower Caddy

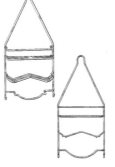

Figure 7-15: Basic Wire Shower Caddy

Figure 7-20: Industrial Shower Caddy

Figure 7-21: Tubular Shower Caddy

To be ornamental, the design should be visible during normal intended use or at some other commercially important time—for example, if the design is visible at the time of sale or in an advertisement.

Example: The design of a waterbed mattress is not visible during normal use (see Figure 7-22), because it's hidden under the sheets and blankets. However, the unusual design is visible in advertisements and at the time of purchase. It's eligible for a design patent. (*Larson v. Classic Corp.*, 683 F. Supp. 1202 (N.D. Ill. 1988).)

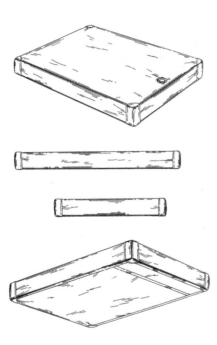

Figure 7-22: Waterbed Mattress

What's a useful article? Design patents only protect useful articles. Paintings, silk screens, sculpture, books, photographs or two-dimensional surface ornamentation that is separable from the object (such as decals) are not considered "useful articles". These types of designs are more likely to be protected under copyright law (see Chapter 8).

2. What Makes a Design New and Original

In order to be new, your design must differ in some way from all previous designs. The USPTO refers to existing designs as *prior art*. Prior art consists of previously issued patents and other published materials (see sidebar, "What is Prior Art?," below). If your design differs visually in some way from the prior art, you have made it over this hurdle.

Example: Walter E. Durling obtained a design patent for a sectional sofa with a corner table and end tables (see Figure 7-23). A competitor with a similar design claimed that Durling was not entitled to a design patent because prior art existed—a sectional manufactured by another company—and therefore that the patent should be declared invalid. The federal court of appeals disagreed. The court acknowledged that the prior art "had the same basic design concept," but said that the two designs created different visual impressions. Therefore, Durling's design was new, original and patent-worthy. (*Durling v. Spectrum Furniture Co. Inc.*, 101 F.3d 100 (Fed. Cir. 1996).)

Figure 7-23: Durling Design Sectional Sofa With a Corner Table and End Tables

One way of finding out whether someone else had your great design idea first is to conduct a search for prior art using the Internet (see subsection 2a, below). An Internet search has its limitations, though. It is not considered to be as thorough as searching at the USPTO, where you (or a professional searcher that you hire) can unearth all of the existing design patents in your classification (for example, tables, candle-holders and so on.).

Considering the costs of a professional search at the USPTO, I would say that a basic Internet search combined with your own knowledge of the field is probably sufficient and cost-effective. That's because the cost of a search conducted by a patent professional will exceed, by several hundred dollars, the cost of your design patent application. The downside is that if prior art exists that you have not uncovered, the USPTO will reject your application. In that case, however, you will only be out the $165 filing fee and not the $300-$500 for a search fee.

After you submit your application, a patent examiner will make a prior art search to verify that your design is novel.

⚠ Prior art may be lurking in the shadows. If the patent is granted and prior art is later discovered that shows your design is not new, your patent can be invalidated.

In addition to being new, your design must be original. The USPTO guidelines state:

Clearly a design that simulates a well-known or naturally occurring object or person is not original as required by the statute. Furthermore, subject matter that could be considered offensive to any race, religion, sex, ethnic group or nationality is not proper subject matter for a design patent application. (35 U.S.C. § 171 and 37 CFR § 1.3.)

These guidelines may seem at odds with the bead case discussed at the beginning of this chapter. In that case, a common anatomical shape was used, and it may have been offensive to members of the female sex and to members of some religious groups. Keep in mind that the standard for originality is often interpreted quite loosely and on a case-by-case basis. Although the USPTO and courts have, in the past, invalidated design patents that resembled human babies (*In re Smith,* 77 F.2d 514 (CCPA 1935)), it is rare that originality is a stumbling block to obtaining a design patent.

What Is Prior Art?

Prior art includes:

- any design used on a functional object in public use or on sale in the U.S. for more than one year before the filing date of the design patent application
- anything that was publicly known or used by others in this country before the date the design was created
- anything that was made or built in this country by another person before the date your design was created
- any work that was the subject of a prior design patent, issued more than one year before the filing date of your design patent or any time before the date you created the design, or
- any work whose publication occurred more than one year before the filing date of your design patent or any time before the date you created the design.

---

a. Searching for Prior Art

To search for prior art using the Internet, or to view images and text for the design patents mentioned in this article, go to the USPTO website (www.uspto.gov). You will get the best results searching via the patent classification system—a method of classifying designs by subject matter, described below.

A less effective, but sometimes useful, method is to use the "Search Patents" feature on the USPTO home page. Type in the design patent number if you have it (all design patent numbers start with the letter "D"), or use the Quick Search feature. In Quick Search you set two criteria. In one box, type a term that will help identify similar design patents (for example, "quilt" or "denim") and in the second search box, type in the letter "D" and set the drop-down menu for "Patent Number" (to let the search engine know you are only seeking design patents). Again, this shortcut approach is not as effective as the method described below. But it may get you started or help you quickly locate the classification for your crafts.

💡 **To see images of any patent, open the patent onscreen.** This is usually accomplished by clicking the patent number, then clicking "Images" (it's boxed near the top of the page). If the drawing doesn't appear after you click, you may need to download free software known as a "TIFF-viewer." One place to get it is AlternaTIFF (www.alternatiff.com).

b. Finding the Right Class and Subclass for Your Design

To accomplish a search using the USPTO classification system, follow the seven steps detailed below. Remember, this search is an essential element of demonstrating that your design is novel and nonobvious.

💡 **Bypass these steps for finding the class/subclass if you know of a patented design that is similar to yours.** You can locate that patent using the search methods described in Section 2a, above—for example, searching by name of design, inventor or company that owns the patent. Once you find the patent, you can see how the USPTO categorized it.

1. **Locate the Patent Classification home page.** Start at the USPTO home page (www.uspto.gov) (Figure 7-24). Click the drop-down menu next to "Select a Search Collection" and choose "Manual of Patent Classification." This will take you to the Patent Classification Home Page (Figure 7-25).

2. **Select Index to Classification.** Click the drop-down menu next to "Look In" and choose "Index to Classification."

3. **Type in a keyword.** To locate the class for your design, type in a broad keyword that might describe

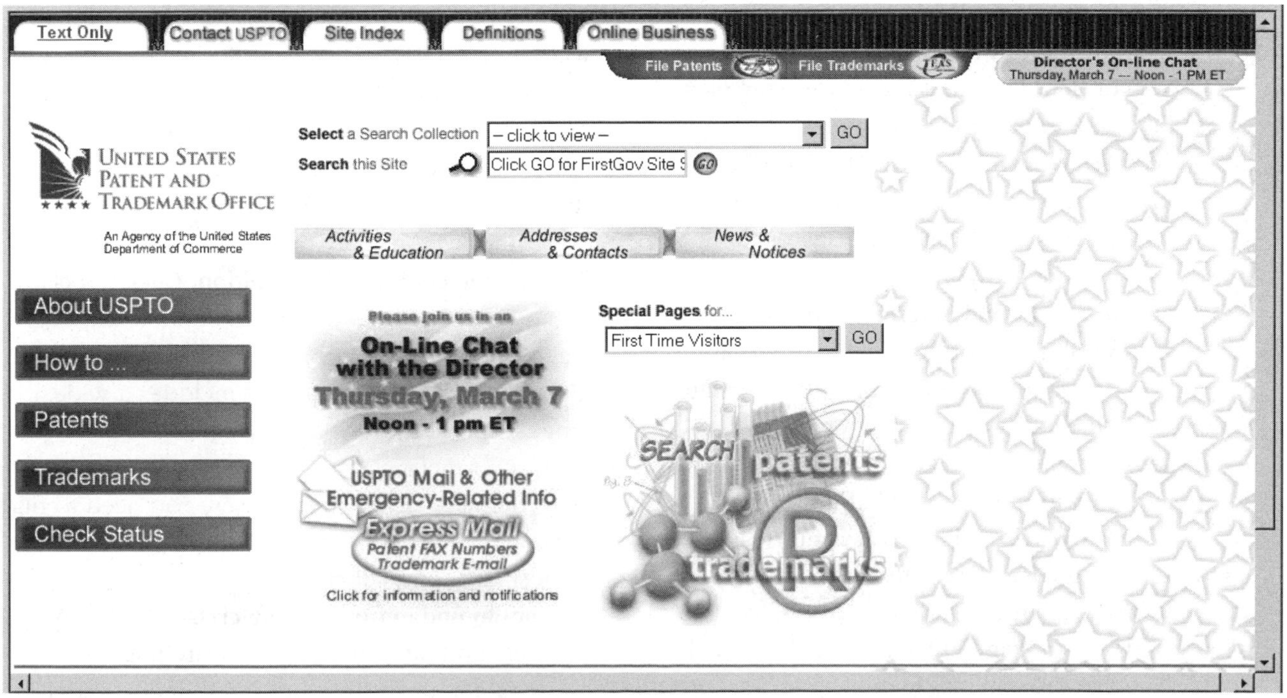

Figure 7-24: USPTO Home Page

Figure 7-25: Patent Classification Home Page

your class of crafts goods. For example, "jewelry" or "pottery" will work as keywords. You can type in more than one word at a time—for example, "glass bead"—but you must also select the appropriate drop-down menu choice: "Any Word" (which will find any class that contains either word) or "All Words" (which will only find classes that contain every word in your list).

4. Examine your results and determine your class. Your search will take you to an alphabetically organized class/subclass index page that contains your search term. If you type in "jewelry," for example, you would be taken to a list of patent items starting with the letter "J." (Finding your search term on a particular result page is simple—use the "Find on This Page" feature in your Internet browser. In Internet Explorer, click "Edit," then "Find on this Page.") Under Jewelry, you'll find a list of jewelry items, such as bracelets, finger rings and lockets (Figure 7-26).

Many of these have classifications that begin with the letter "D." These are design classifications for jewelry. Since D11 appears quite often, that is probably a major class for jewelry items. Keep in mind that you are only looking for classes that start with the letter "D," so you can avoid any that don't (they're for utility patents).

5. Examine the class and its definition. Click the class number to see how the class is defined and to make sure it's suitable for your crafts. For example, if we click D11, we see that it includes a wide range of possible subclasses (Figure 7-27).

6. Find your subclass. Once you get to the page that lists your class and its subclasses, you need to find the correct subclass. Review the list until you find an accurate class/subclass.

7. Attempt to find more than one class/subclass. We recommend that you continue searching and checking the results of your initial index search for more than one class/subclass.

```
        Hand tools for ....................  81 /  7
    Working ...............................  125 / 30.01
        Holders for while grinding ........  451 / 389
Jewelry ....................................  63
    Adhesive jewelry ......................  63 / DIG 1
    Box, design ...........................  D09 / 414+
        Dresser type ......................  D03 / 903*
    Bracelets .............................  63 / 3+
    Chain .................................  D11 / 13
    Clip,clamp,clasp ......................  D11 / 86+
    Design ................................  D11 / 1+
    Earrings ..............................  63 / 12+
    Finger rings ..........................  63 / 15+
    Functional fasteners ..................  D11 / 200+
    Garment attached vase .................  D11 / 143+
    Gem setting ...........................  63 / 26+
    Illumination combined .................  362 / 104
    Lockets ...............................  63 / 18+
    Making ................................  29 / 896.4+
        Finger-ring forming and sizing .....  29 / 8
        Gem and jewel setting in metal .....  29 / 10
    Ornamental pins .......................  63 / 20
    Perfumed jewelry ......................  63 / DIG 2
    Plastic jewelry .......................  63 / DIG 3
    Setting ...............................  63 / 20
        Design ............................  D11 / 9
    Tie clasp or tack .....................  63 / 20
        Design ............................  D11 / 202+
    Trays .................................  206 / 566
    Watch and chain attachments ...........  63 / 21+
```

Figure 7-26: USPTO Listing of Jewelry

```
 237    ... Frame perimeter having bilateral symmetry
 238    . Simulative (34)
 239    .. Animate
 240    ... Humanoid
 241    .. Plant life
 1      JEWELRY (1)
 2      . Combined
 3      . Encircling, i.e., necklace, bracelet, etc. (2)
 4      .. Bangle or armlet type
 5      ... Overlapping ends
 6      .. Major design element disposed on continuous strand
 7      ... Pendant having singular suspension point (3)
 8      .... Plural pendant
 9      ... Asymmetrical along longitudinal axis
 10     .... And laterally
 11     .. Strung
 12     .. Interlocked (4)
 13     ... Wire type, i.e., chain (5)
 14     ... Simulative
 15     ... Arcuate surface pattern in plan (6)
 16     .... With gem or stone
 17     .... Circular or oval
 18     .... Sinuous
 19     .. Longitudinally expanding type (7)
 20     ... Continuous filament or coil
 21     ... Arcuate pattern in plan
 22     .... Circular or oval
 23     .... Sinuous
 24     ... Triangular pattern in plan
 25     ... Quadrilateral pattern in plan
 26     .. Finger ring or mounting (8)
 27     ... Open or having disconnected ends
 28     ... Having axial shift
```

Figure 7-27: USPTO Listing of Subclasses

c. Use the Class/Subclass to Find Prior Art

Once you've categorized your design by potential class/subclass, you're ready to locate relevant prior art by plunging into the vast databases of existing and expired U.S. design patents.

Follow these steps to complete your class/subclass searching.

1. **Start at the patent searching home page.** Click "Search Patents" on the USPTO home page. Choose "Quick Search" under "Patent Grants" (on the left side of the Web page).

2. **Search for patents by class/subclass.** On the Quick Search page, set the Select Years drop-down menu to "All Years." Type in the class/subclass you want to search, and set the drop-down menu for "Current US Classification." (See Figure 7-28.)

3. Read and save relevant patents. Copy or download the information from the Web page and save the patent on your computer. A sample patent from our search is shown in Figure 7-29.

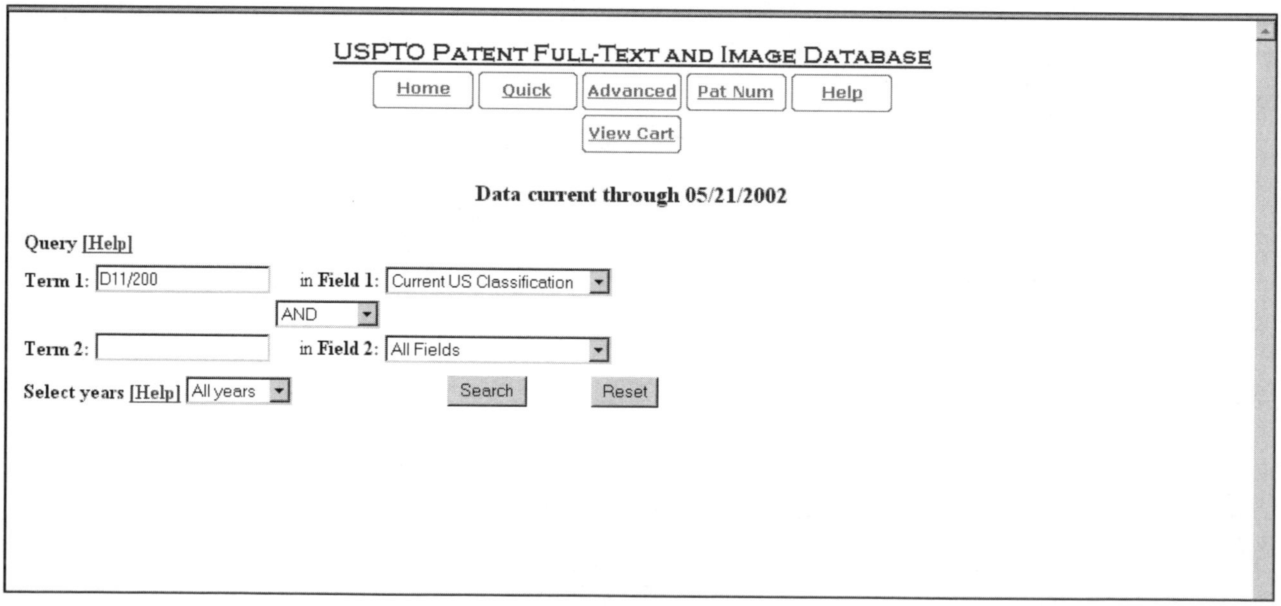

Figure 7-28: USPTO Quick Search Page

United States Patent [19]

Boruszewski

[11] **Patent Number:** **Des. 408,324**

[45] **Date of Patent:** **∗∗Apr. 20, 1999**

[54] **TIE CLIP**

[76] Inventor: **Thomas E. Boruszewski**, 5825 Laramie Way, San Diego, Calif. 92120

[∗∗] Term: **14 Years**

[21] Appl. No.: **29/084,121**

[22] Filed: **Feb. 24, 1998**

[51] **LOC (6) Cl.** **02-07**

[52] **U.S. Cl.** **D11/202**; D11/200-205; D11/228; D11/215; D11/74

[58] **Field of Search** 24/711.2, 711.3, 24/27, 49.1, 53, 54, 56, 66.2, 14.5, 66.4, 533; D8/370; 2/145; D27/183

[56] **References Cited**

U.S. PATENT DOCUMENTS

15,622	12/1884	Preble	D8/382
D. 273,720	5/1984	Romberger	D11/202
D. 321,470	11/1991	Gerrard	D8/370
2,151,164	3/1939	Silverman	D11/203
3,529,327	9/1970	Missakian	24/56

Primary Examiner—Ralf Seifert
Attorney, Agent, or Firm—Frank G. Morkunas

[57] **CLAIM**

I claim the ornamental design for the tie clip, as shown and described.

DESCRIPTION

FIG. 1 is a perspective view of a tip clip illustrating my new design;
FIG. 2 is a front elevation view of the tie clip illustrating my new design;
FIG. 3 is a bottom plan view of the tie clip illustrating my new design;
FIG. 4 is a top plan view of the tie clip illustrating my new design;
FIG. 5 is a side elevation view of the right-side of the tie clip illustrating my new design;
FIG. 6 is a rear elevation view of the tie clip illustrating my new design; and,
FIG. 7 is a side elevation view of the left-side of the tie clip illustrating my new design.

1 Claim, 1 Drawing Sheet

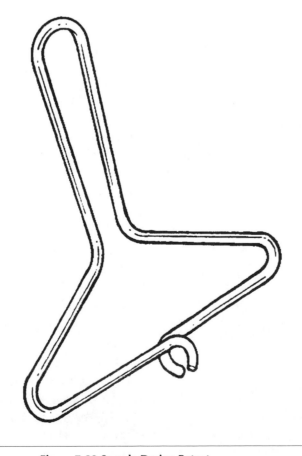

Figure 7-29 Sample Design Patent

3. What Makes a Design Nonobvious

In order to qualify for a design patent, your design must not be considered obvious by others in your crafts field. The concept of nonobviousness was summed up by Albert Szent-Gyorny as the ability "to see what everybody has seen and think what nobody has thought." Nonobviousness does not require great originality or craftsmanship; it only requires the ability to visualize things a little differently. For example, you can demonstrate nonobviousness by:

- the use of a familiar form in an unfamiliar medium—such as the use of a floral pattern as a candle holder (Figure 7-30)

Figure 7-30: Floral Pattern Candle Holder

- a slight change that produces a striking visual effect—such as alternating the position of hearts on a wedding ring (Figure 7-31)

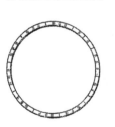

Figure 7-31: Wedding Ring

- the omission of a visual element commonly associated with similar designs—such as the waterbed design in Figure 7-22, which is distinguishable by the absence of visible seams on the top and sides of the mattress, or

- a juxtaposition of elements that creates an unexpected visual statement—such as embedding a poker chip in the bottom of a shot glass (Figure 7-32).

Figure 7-32: Shot Glass With Poker Chip

Indicators that help prove your design meets the "nonobvious" test include:

- it has enjoyed commercial success
- it has a visual appearance that's unexpected
- others have copied the design
- the design has been praised by others in the field
- others have tried but failed to achieve the same result, or
- you created a design that others said could not be done.

It is possible for a design to be novel but to be obvious as well. For example, a court determined that a design for an alcohol server that was shaped like an intravenous dispenser ("Combined Stand and Container for Storing Liquids" in Figure 7-33) was novel—no such design had been used for serving alcohol—but it was obvious and therefore not patentable. (*Neo-Art, Inc. v. Hawkeye Distilled Products, Co*, 654 F. Supp. 90 (C.D. Cal. 1987) *aff'd* 12 U.S.P.Q. 1572 (CAFC 1989).)

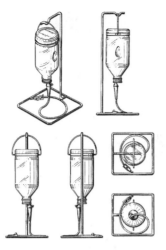

Figure 7-33: Combined Stand and Container for Storing Liquids

The difference between novelty and nonobviousness is that novelty is analyzed by asking whether someone has previously made a similar design, while nonobviousness is analyzed by asking whether your peers would have previously considered making the design. In practical terms, though, the two standards often overlap. For this reason, the lack of any prior art becomes important in demonstrating both nonobviousness and novelty.

4. Beware the One-Year Deadline

You cannot get a design patent if you wait more than a year after the design was publicly available to file your patent application. Another way to put this is that after one year following a sale, offer for sale, public or commercial use or public knowledge about your design, that design will no longer be considered novel by the USPTO. If the USPTO is unaware of the public sale or use and issues a design patent, the patent will be declared invalid if it can later be shown that the design was publicly shown or sold. Therefore, the clock starts ticking once you post your design on your website, show your design at a crafts show or print postcards with the design.

If you miss the one-year cutoff date, you can no longer seek patent protection for your design. However, you may still be able to protect it under other legal principles such as copyright (see Chapter 8) or perhaps trade dress laws (see Chapter 6).

D. Comparing Design Patents and Copyright

Copyrights and design patents both do the same thing—protect your visual imagery—but they do it in different ways, and they sometimes do it for different subject matter. A design patent protects the visual appearance of a useful object—for example, the shape, proportion and patterns that distinguish one doorknob from another. Copyright covers a broader palette and protects any original artistic expression—whether architecture, photography, music, writing or dance. These two legal protections overlap when functional objects—for example, bronze bells, table tiles, clay pots or candles—embody a distinctive or pleasing visual appearance.

The good news is that you don't have to choose one protection over the other. If your work qualifies for both copyright and design patent protection, you can—if it's worth the effort—claim both simultaneously. For example, the designers of the quilt design in Figure 7-34 or the puppet in Figure 7-35 have obtained both types of protection. The table below highlights the similarities and differences between the two forms of legal protection.

Figure 7-34: Quilt Design

Copyright vs. Design Patent

	Copyright	Design Patent
What types of crafts are hardest to protect?	**Minimal works are harder to protect than ornate ones.** The less ornate the design for your crafts work, the harder it is to obtain copyright protection. That's because the design must be conceptually separable from the object. For example, the glass in Figure 7-36 could probably acquire copyright protection; the glass in Figure 7-11 would have a very hard time. (Both designs acquired protection under design patent law.)	**Less "useful" crafts are harder to protect.** Design patents protect ornamentation on useful articles—and the USPTO has a limited view of what's "useful." For example, paintings, silk screens, sculpture, books, photographs or two-dimensional surface ornamentation that is separable from the object (such as decals) are not "useful articles." In other words, any craft that is "art for art's sake" cannot get a design patent. (All of these examples could be protected under copyright law.)
What's the cost?	**Copyright protection is free.** However, if you choose to fortify your protection and register (recommended), the application fee is $30.	**Total costs, including the application fee, will come to $165 to $1,500 depending on whether you use an attorney.**
How long does it take to obtain?	**It's automatic.** You get copyright once you create the work. If you choose to register, the process can take up to 12 months.	**One to two years.** You have to register to obtain a design patent, and the examination process can take up to 24 months.
How long does it last?	**Life of the artist plus 70 years.**	**14 years from the date the patent is issued.**
How effective is it for stopping infringers?	**Copyright infringement is the harder to prove.** It's not enough that two works are substantially similar; you have to prove that the infringer had access to your work and copied it. The infringer can claim certain defenses—for example, the fair use doctrine, which allows limited copying for purposes of commentary.	**Design patent infringement is the easier to prove.** Design patent infringement is easier to prove than copyright infringement; you only have to prove the works are substantially similar. You don't have to prove that the infringer saw and copied your work.
Which should you choose?	**Copyright chooses you.** If your work qualifies for copyright, you obtain copyright protection automatically. To determine if your work qualifies, review Chapter 8. You can fortify your rights by registering with the U.S. Copyright Office.	**Choose design patent if:** (1) you don't qualify for copyright protection and you are concerned that someone will copy your work and deprive you of significant sales, or (2) you qualify for copyright but believe that the work will be one of your leading sellers and at high risk for copying.

Figure 7-35: Frankenstein Puppet

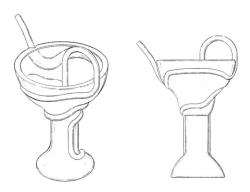

Figure 7-36: Margarita Glass

The combined use of copyright and design patent protection is most effective in crafts works where the design can exist in another medium—for example, the design on a quilt could also be transferred to paper or fabric. A toy or a puppet may lend itself to animation or reproduction on merchandise. In that case, design patent law can effectively halt the copying of the craft, and copyright law can stop its being copied in other mediums.

Example: Consider the Frankenstein-style puppet in Figure 7-35. Imagine that, without permission of the designers, a movie studio creates an animated series based upon the puppet. The studio also sells copycat puppets, as well as merchandise containing the puppet's image.

Under patent and copyright law, the designers can stop the movie studio from making, selling or using substantially similar puppets. Under copyright law, they can stop the studio from making the animated series and related merchandise.

Are There Other Types of Protection?

In unusual cases, crafts works may qualify for protection other than copyrights or design patents. Below is a summary of additional types of legal protection.

Utility patents. Utility patents protect the way something works—for example, a novel clasp you created for a necklace or a unique mounting system to display glassware. Utility patents are granted for machines, processes, devices or other useful objects. They are fairly expensive ($5,000 to $10,000) and last for approximately 17-18 years. For more information, visit the Nolo website (www.nolo.com) and click on "Patents and Trade Secrets," or visit the USPTO website (www.uspto.gov).

Trade secrets. A trade secret is any confidential information with economic value that gives a business an advantage over its competitors—for example, a method or process for affixing color to glass. Trade secrets are protected under state and federal laws and through the use of nondisclosure agreements. For more information on trade secrets, read Chapter 5.

Trademarks. A trademark is any word, symbol, design, device, logo or slogan that identifies and distinguishes one product or service from another, like the unique name you use to identify your craft products. For more information on trademarks, read Chapter 6.

Trade dress. Trade dress is a subcategory of trademark law that applies to the packaging or total appearance of a product or service. As a result of a recent Supreme Court ruling, trade dress is less favorable as a source of protection for crafts. For more information on trade dress, see Chapter 6.

E. Preparing a Design Patent Application

With the exception of the glass-top coffee table in Figure 7-5, every design patent application shown in this chapter was prepared by a patent attorney. Patent attorneys and patent agents—professionals who have been licensed to practice before the USPTO—provide security when filing a design patent application. They can analyze your design and properly advise you on whether pursuing a design patent is worthwhile. If so, the attorney or agent can prepare the application. If there is a problem at the USPTO—for example, an examiner challenges your application—the attorney or agent can respond and keep the application on track.

That said, if you're a self-starter with a do-it-yourself mindset, you can, with a bit of work, prepare your own design patent application and save approximately $500 to $1,000.

Below, I present basic instructions for preparing a design patent application. However, providing extensive details for this application is beyond the scope of this book. If you would like more information, read David Pressman's *Patent It Yourself* (Nolo), or read and download the design patent information provided at the USPTO website (www.uspto.gov).

The design patent application consists of:

- the "specification"—a short written document
- drawing(s) showing the appearance of your design
- the Design Patent Application Transmittal—a cover sheet that accompanies your application
- the Declaration—an oath provided by the designer
- the Fee Application Transmittal Form, and
- a fee ($165)

1. The Specification

The specification is quite simple to prepare. I've provided a sample one for a pin design (Figure 7-36) created by my sister.

Figure 37: Earring Design (Front and Back View)

The elements of the specification are fairly straightforward. Here's a quick breakdown of how to approach them:

- **Preamble**—one or two boilerplate sentences announcing that you're seeking a design patent.
- **Specification**—the place to introduce your design by name. A basic title such as "glass bowl," "puppet" or "steel table" will work best.
- **Cross References to Related Applications**—here, you indicate if you have filed a previous design patent application to which this one is related.
- **Statement Regarding Federally Sponsored R & D**—indicate here if the design was prepared under a government grant or as part of government research.
- **Description of the Figure(s) of the Drawings**—describe the view presented in each of the drawing sheets.
- **Feature Description**—provide a short description of your design, for example, "My candle is characterized by a pinwheel effect that gradually slopes outward."

Box Design
Commissioner for Patents
Washington, D.C. 20231

PREAMBLE:

The petitioner(s) request that Letters Patent be granted to petitioners for the new and original design set forth in the following specification.

SPECIFICATION

Petitioners have invented a new, original and ornamental design entitled "PIN" of which the following is a specification. Reference is made to the accompanying drawings, which are a part of the specification, the Figures of which are described as follows:

CROSS REFERENCES TO RELATED APPLICATIONS: None

STATEMENT REGARDING FED SPONSORED R & D: None

D. DESCRIPTION OF THE FIGURE(S) OF THE DRAWINGS:

Fig. 1 is a front view of my new PIN

Fig. 2 is a rear view of the PIN

E. FEATURE DESCRIPTION: My PIN is characterized by a rectangular sheet of metal loosely framed by wire wrapping.

CLAIM: I Claim: The ornamental design for PIN as shown and described.

Express Mail Label #

Date of Deposit _____

Sheet 1 of 1

Figure 1

Front View

Figure 2

Rear View

You can also note your claim to copyright protection. Some patent attorneys have begun mentioning the work's copyright in the design patent application. The purpose of this statement is to alert the public that although it is okay to copy the drawings for purposes of design patent law, it is not permitted to copy the drawings for other, nonpatent-related purposes. If you want to provide such a statement, include the following language after your feature description: "A portion of the disclosure of this patent document contains material to which a claim for copyright is made. The copyright owner has no objection to the facsimile reproduction by anyone of the patent document or the patent disclosure as it appears in the Patent and Trademark Office patent file or records, but reserves all other copyright rights whatsoever."

2. Drawings

As you can see from the drawings in this chapter, design patent drawings are technical and stylized. Each element—for example, the stippling (use of dots), the linear shading (use of lines) and the distinctive patterns (for indicating colors)—has a special meaning. You are allowed to provide informal drawings with your application, such as rough sketches or photographs, but your application will not be examined until you provide formal drawings similar to those shown in this chapter. For that reason, and to avoid delays, I recommend that you provide formal drawings. (The only reason to furnish informal drawings is that you are in a hurry to obtain an early filing date but you haven't had time to draft the drawings.)

With a little drawing skill or computer graphics knowledge, you can prepare formal drawings for your design patent application. In their book *How to Make Patent Drawings Yourself* (Nolo), David Pressman and Jack Lo explain how to prepare these drawings using computer software or pen and ink. One chapter is devoted solely to design patent drawing rules. If you prefer to have a professional draft your drawings, you can accomplish this relatively inexpensively (around $80 per drawing sheet; a sheet may contain one or two figures). You can probably find a suitable patent drafts person by typing "patent drawing" in your Internet search engine. Or, a good list of drafts people is provided at the Pipers website (www.piperpat.co.nz/resource/drawings.html).

Designs are commonly depicted in different views or figures—for example, top views, side views or disassembled views. You should present as many views as are necessary to demonstrate your design. Each view provides another way of "seeing" the design. Each view is given a discrete figure number (abbreviated as "Fig" in patent law).

3. The Design Patent Application Transmittal

You must submit a cover sheet with your design patent application. The USPTO has prepared one that we recommend you use. A sample is shown below. To obtain this form, go to the USPTO home page (www.uspto.gov) and click "Patents" on the left side of the screen. Click "Forms," then follow the instructions to download Form SB0018. You must have a copy of Adobe Acrobat on your computer to download this PDF form. Save the form to your computer. That way, you can use it again without connecting to the Internet.

The cover sheet is a "fillable" PDF form, which means that if you have a current version of Adobe Acrobat, you can enter (but not save) information onto the form. If you don't have the technology to fill in the form on your computer, print out a copy of the form and fill in the blanks using a typewriter or pen.

- **First Named Inventor.** At the top of the form, there's a box for supplying the First Named Inventor. Fill in the name of one of the designers.
- **Title.** In this section, provide your design title as indicated in your specification.
- **Express Mail Label Number.** Copy this number from the Express Mail label (the bottom page). You don't have to use U.S. Express Mail. If you wish, or if you're not in the United States, you can mail your design patent application by regular mail or by an overnight express service such as Federal Express. However, any document

PTO/SB/18 (08-00)
Approved for use through 10/31/2002. OMB 0651-0032
U.S. Patent and Trademark Office; U.S. DEPARTMENT OF COMMERCE
Under the Paperwork Reduction Act of 1995, no persons are required to respond to a collection of Information unless it displays a valid OMB control number.

DESIGN PATENT APPLICATION TRANSMITTAL	Attorney Docket No.	
	First Named Inventor	
	Title	
(Only for new nonprovisional applications under 37 CFR 1.53(b))	Express Mail Label No.	

ADDRESS TO:
Assistant Commissioner for Patents
Box Design
Washington, DC 20231

DESIGN V. UTILITY: *A "design patent" protects an article's ornamental appearance (e.g., the way an article looks) (35 U.S.C. 171), while a "utility patent" protects the way an article is used and works (35 U.S.C. 101). The ornamental appearance of an article includes its shape/configuration or surface ornamentation upon the article, or both. Both a design and a utility patent may be obtained on an article if invention resides both in its ornamental appearance and its utility. For more information see MPEP 1502.01.*

APPLICATION ELEMENTS
See MPEP chapter 1500 concerning design patent application contents.

1. ☐ Fee Transmittal Form *(e.g., PTO/SB/17)*
    (Submit an original, and a duplicate for fee processing)

2. ☐ Applicant claims small entity status.
    See 37 CFR 1.27.

3. ☐ Specification   *[Total Pages* ☐ *]*
    (preferred arrangement set forth below, MPEP 1503.01)
    - Preamble
    - Cross References to Related Applications
    - Statement Regarding Fed sponsored R & D
    - Description of the figure(s) of the drawings
    - Feature description
    - Claim (only one (1) claim permitted, MPEP 1503.03)

4. ☐ Drawing(s) *(37 CFR 1.152)* *[Total Sheets* ☐ *]*

5. Oath or Declaration   *[Total Pages* ☐ *]*

    a. ☐ Newly executed (original or copy)

    b. ☐ Copy from a prior application (37 CFR 1.63 (d))
        (for continuation/divisional with Box 16 completed)

        i. ☐ **DELETION OF INVENTOR(S)**
            Signed statement attached deleting
            inventor(s) named in the prior application, see
            37 CFR 1.63(d)(2) and 1.33(b)

6. ☐ Application Data Sheet. See 37 CFR 1.76

ACCOMPANYING APPLICATION PARTS

7. ☐ Assignment Papers (cover sheet & document(s))

8. ☐ 37 CFR 3.73(b) Statement   ☐ Power of
    (when there is an assignee)   Attorney

9. ☐ English Translation Document *(if applicable)*

10. ☐ Information Disclosure   ☐ Copies of IDS
    Statement (IDS)/PTO-1449   Citations

11. ☐ Preliminary Amendment

12. ☐ Return Receipt Postcard (MPEP 503)
    (Should be specifically itemized)

13. ☐ Certified Copy of Priority Document(s)
    (if foreign priority is claimed)

14. ☐ Request for Expedited Examination of
    a Design Application (37 CFR 1.155)
    (NOTE: Substitute "Box Expedited Design" for
    "Box Design" in the address indicated above.)

15. ☐ Other: ....
    ....

16. If a CONTINUING APPLICATION, *check appropriate box, and supply the requisite information below and in a preliminary amendment, or in an Application Data Sheet under 37 CFR 1.76:*

☐ Continuation   ☐ Divisional   ☐ Continuation-in-part (CIP)   of prior application No.: _____

Prior application information: Examiner _____   Group Art Unit: _____

For CONTINUATION or DIVISIONAL APPS only: The entire disclosure of the prior application, from which an oath or declaration is supplied under Box 5b, is considered a part of the disclosure of the accompanying continuation or divisional application and is hereby incorporated by reference. The incorporation <u>can only</u> be relied upon when a portion has been inadvertently omitted from the submitted application parts.

17. CORRESPONDENCE ADDRESS

☐ Customer Number or Bar Code Label   *(Insert Customer No. or Attach bar code label here)*   or ☐ Correspondence address below

Name	
Address	
City	State	Zip Code
Country	Telephone	Fax

Name (Print/Type)	Registration No. (Attorney/Agent)	
Signature		Date

that you send by Express Mail that includes the Express Mail Number on the cover letter will be considered received on the day you mail it. (37 C.F.R. § 1.10.)

- **Application Elements.** Check the "Fee Transmittal Form" box and check "Applicant claims small entity status." (You have small entity status if you are an independent designer, or if the company that owns the design is a nonprofit, or a for-profit company with 500 or fewer employees.) Check the "Specification" box and indicate how many pages you're sending in the box to the right. Check the "Drawings" box and indicate the number of drawing sheets in the box to the right.
- **Oath or Declaration.** Check the "Newly executed" box. You will include a separate declaration.
- **Application Data Sheet.** Do not check this box. (An Application Data Sheet is a voluntary submission that includes additional information about you and your design—there's no need to bother with it.)
- **Accompanying Application Parts.** With the exception of the "Return Receipt Postcard," these choices will probably be inapplicable to you.
- **Correspondence Address.** Provide an address where the USPTO can send correspondence regarding your design. If you have a USPTO Customer Number (many law firms and corporations do), mark the box and provide the number, or use a bar code sticker. Otherwise, mark the box "Correspndence address below" and write the name of the individual or company that should receive mail from the USPTO. If you fail to include something in your package, the PTO's Office of Preliminary Examination will send you a letter telling you what to do and what fees you will be charged for the error. Supply what is needed, following the instructions in the letter.

4. Declaration

The declaration, Form SB/01, is a two-page form that can be downloaded from the USPTO website. Check

the box "Declaration Submitted With Initial Filing" and provide the title of your design. On page 2, list the designers and their addresses. Sign the declaration where it is marked "Inventor's Signature."

5. Fee Transmittal

The Fee Transmittal, Form SB/17, is a one-page form that can be downloaded from the USPTO website. Indicate your method of payment. Your choices are:

- **Check or Money Order.** If you pay by check or money order, mark this box and include a check payable to Commissioner for Patents.
- **Deposit Account Number.** Disregard this box unless you maintain a deposit account at the USPTO.
- **Payment by Credit Card.** If you want to pay by credit card, check this box and download and complete an additional form (Form 2038: Credit Card Payment Form and Instructions). You cannot fill out Form 2038 on your computer; you'll need to print it and complete it by hand or typewriter. In the box titled "Description of Request and Payment Information" (in the section called Request and Payment Information), write Design Patent Application Fee. Leave the rest of this section blank. The remainder of Form 2038 is easy to complete—instructions are provided when you download the form.

In the box marked "Fee Calculation," write the fee (currently $165) in the box next to "Design filing fee." At the bottom of the form, provide your name, your telephone number and the date. Sign the form on the indicated line.

6. Return Postcard

It's important to include a return postcard with your application (and every document that you send to the USPTO). Once you get it back, tape it into your file. The postcard will be a permanent record that your application was received. (Your U.S. Express Mail tracking information and cancelled check also provide useful evidence of receipt—tape these into your file as well.)

Write your mailing address on the front of the postcard. On the back, write:

Design patent application of [*your name or names*] for [*title of design*] consisting of [*number of*] _____ pages of specification, [*number of*] _____ drawing sheets and filing fee of $_____ received today: [*date*].

7. Mailing

Assemble your completed cover sheet, specification, drawing sheets, return postcard and check or Form 2038 if paying by credit card. Address your package to:

Box Design
Commissioner for Patents
Washington, DC 20231

Enclose your materials and take the Express Mail to the Post Office. Don't deposit the envelope in a regular or even an Express Mail mailbox, since you won't immediately receive the Express Mail receipt. Instead, take the Express Mail directly to the Post Office and ask the clerk to date-stamp the sender's copy of the Express Mail receipt with her rubber stamp.

Speeding Your Design Patent Application

If you're in a hurry, are especially concerned that your design will be stolen or can afford the hefty fee, you can pay a "Rocket Docket" fee to have your design patent application expedited. Currently, this adds $900 to the regular $165 fee. Unfortunately, the USPTO doesn't make clear exactly how much time you'll save. For information on the Rocket Docket procedure, its benefits and current fees, check the USPTO website.

If Problems Arise With Your Application

In a perfect world, your design application will sail through the examination process and you will, within 18 to 24 months, receive a notice that it's been approved. However, things don't always go this smoothly. An examiner may object to your application for any of the reasons expressed in Section C, above, or due to technical errors with your application. It's beyond the scope of this book to advise you how to respond to examiner notices. If you run into a problem and want to handle it on your own, I would suggest reading David Pressman's *Patent It Yourself* (Nolo). Although the book primarily deals with utility patents, it provides a lot of helpful information on design patents and offers a thorough explanation of the USPTO examination process—including suggestions on responding to examiner objections.

F. Marking the Design Patent Number

Once you acquire a design patent, it's essential that you mark your crafts work with your design patent number. (You'll receive this number when the USPTO grants your patent.) Any placement is suitable, provided that the number can be located by an ordinary user. For example you can place the number on the back of an earring.

Failure to include the notice could cost you money if you later sue an infringer—even if you win. For example, in a case in which the Nike shoe company sued Wal-Mart, a court ruled that Nike could not collect a portion of Wal-Mart's profits or collect statutory damages (damages fixed by law) if it was proven that Nike had failed to mark the design patent number on one of its shoe designs. *(Nike Inc. v. Wal-Mart Stores,* 138 F.3d 1437 (E.D. Va. 1998).)

Patent Numbers of Design Figures Shown in Chapter 7

Figure Number	Patent Number	Figure Number	Patent Number
1	D398879	17	D434257
2	D418298	18	D428745
3	D433326	19	D407249
4	D384895	20	D392135
5	D450487	21	D417990
6	D288868	22	D270693
7	D426326	23	D339243
8	D452655	29	D408324
9	D374570	30	D410756
10	D456673	31	D70209
11	D454278	32	D448241
12	D371830	33	D260432
13	D372304	34	D449485
14	D417991	35	D411596
15	D394771	36	D453093
16	D396585		

Copyright

*I*n 1995, Lisa Graves sued Pottery Barn, claiming that the company had stolen her copyrighted design for Bird's Nest napkin rings (see Figure 8-1). Pottery Barn's lawyer denied the company's made-in-India napkin rings were copies. He also argued that Graves' work was not entitled to copyright, claiming her design was based on real-life bird's nests. After all, he contended, no one can claim legal rights to something created in nature.

As Lisa's attorney, I contacted an ornithologist, Kimball Garrett, at the Natural History Museum of Los Angeles County. Mr. Garrett examined Lisa's napkin ring and stated that the design was not similar to any existing bird's nest, and that without a bottom, the design could never function as a nest anyway. In other words, Lisa had created something artistic, not copied something from nature. Soon after, Pottery Barn settled, paid Lisa for lost sales and stopped selling copies of her napkin ring.

Lisa Graves' battle with Pottery Barn illustrates that it's not enough to claim you have a copyright; you must be able to enforce your rights by filing a lawsuit and proving that your work meets copyright standards.

In the last decade, many crafts workers have had to take a crash course in copyright law. For example, makers of quilt patterns recently found themselves in a Napster-like controversy as their work was widely circulated online without permission. Chat rooms exploded with debates on the subject. Was it really wrong, some quilt makers asked, to take designs without permission? Wasn't sharing part of the crafts tradition?

Copyright disputes also became more prevalent as chain stores and catalog companies stepped up their manufacture of crafts knock-offs. These companies brazenly copied works, knowing that crafts artists can't afford to fight long legal battles. When crafts workers do challenge the big retailers—as in the case of jeweler Paul Morelli (discussed in Section D1, below)—the results are sometimes disappointing.

I've devoted this chapter to copyright basics, including:

- the automatic copyright covering all original works (Section A)

Figure 8-1: Bird's Nest Napkin Ring

- how copyright protects you, and how long it lasts (Sections B and C)
- what types of creative work do and don't qualify for copyright protection (Sections D and E)
- why to register your copyright with the U.S. Copyright Office (Section F)
- how to register with the U.S. Copyright Office (Sections G through L)
- circumstances under which you can use someone else's copyrighted work (Sections M through P)
- how to sell or assign your copyright (Section Q)
- what rights a purchaser of your crafts gets (Section R)
- what infringement is (Section S)
- how to prevent destruction of your work (Section T), and
- how to acquire a personal release (Section U)

 This chapter focuses on copyright ownership, registration and avoiding typical copyright problems. I discuss how to respond to a copyright rip-off in Chapter 11 and works made for hire—a copyright principle affecting ownership of employee-created works—in Chapter 5.

A. Getting Copyright Protection Without Registering

You don't have to file an application and register with the U.S. Copyright Office to get copyright. You get it once you create the work. In other words, once you finish a bracelet, wood sculpture or glass candelabra—you get the copyright! That said, I recommend registering, particularly for those crafts works that are more likely to inspire copies. Registration provides advantages and creates helpful presumptions (see Section F, below).

There are two occasions when you don't get this automatic copyright after creating a work:

- the work is not copyrightable (discussed in Section D, below), and
- someone hired you to create the work, and it was "work made for hire" (see Chapter 5, Section F).

B. How a Copyright Protects You

You can do two things with your copyright:

- chase after people who rip your work off, and
- earn money by licensing or selling your rights.

If someone uses your copyrighted work without your permission—or, in legal terms, infringes your copyright—you can go after them, make them stop and perhaps collect a financial payment for the damage they've done. You can take these actions against anyone who, without your permission, copies your work, displays your work, makes photos of it, broadcasts it on television or makes variations or miniatures of it.

You can also make money by giving your rights to someone else, either temporarily (a license) or permanently (an assignment). For example, the artists who created Cabbage Patch Dolls have earned millions from licensing their creation. In return for letting a company "use" their copyrighted designs, they earn a royalty based upon each doll sold. I discuss assignments in Section Q, below and licensing in Chapter 9.

C. How Long Your Copyright Lasts

Copyright protection begins once a work is created and generally lasts for the life of the artist plus 70 years (for works created by a single author). Works

made for hire (see Chapter 5) are protected for 120 years from their date of creation or 95 years from their first publication, whichever is longer. The same duration of copyright will apply regardless of whether the work is registered.

D. What Type of Work Qualifies for Copyright

Start with the assumption that your original crafts work is protected under copyright law. As a general rule, if you didn't copy it from someplace else and it has some artistic expression, you can claim copyright. However, some crafts works—particularly functional and minimal works—may not come under copyright's blanket of protection. In these cases, you may find that the Copyright Office or a potential infringer will challenge your rights. Generally, claiming copyright becomes more difficult if:

- your designs are minimal and use common shapes (see subsection 1, below), or
- it's difficult to separate the art from the function in your work (see subsection 2, below).

⚠ **When in doubt, register with the Copyright Office.** Don't conclude, based on the information in this section, that you can't get a copyright. Let the Copyright Office be the judge. Regardless of your opinion about your work's functionality or minimalism, attempt to register it. (Your judgment may be more critical than that of the Copyright Office.) Getting a registration doesn't guarantee you can stop others—your copyright can still be challenged in a court battle—but it creates a presumption of validity that's tough to beat.

1. Problems Protecting Minimal Designs and Common Shapes

If your crafts work is minimal—that is, you avoid artistic statements in favor of pure craftsmanship—or if your work uses common geometric or natural shapes, you may have difficulty claiming copyright protection. Every copyrighted work must demonstrate originality. It can be difficult to spot that original touch when the art is understated or drawn from common shapes.

Since copyright protects originality, not craftsmanship, even the most beautifully stitched leather goods or stunning glassware may not qualify for protection. In short, the more ornate work is more likely to acquire copyright.

Consider the dilemma faced by Paul Morelli, a jewelry maker whose works are offered in upscale stores like Neiman Marcus and Bergdorf Goodman. In 1987, he created a jewelry line called "Sprinkled Diamond." The first piece was a heart-shaped pendant with a zigzag pattern of inlaid diamonds flush to the surface.

Within a few years, Tiffany & Co.—after reviewing slides of Morelli's work—began selling a similar line of jewelry. Unfortunately, Morelli was not able to register his work with the Copyright Office, normally a prerequisite for filing a lawsuit. The Copyright Office claimed Morelli's minimalist designs lacked sufficient originality. In other words, because they were primarily basic geometric shapes, they lacked the creativity necessary to qualify for copyright. Morelli sued Tiffany & Co. anyway, under a rarely used law that permits an artist to file a lawsuit without a registration.

In his lawsuit, Morelli argued that the Copyright Office had erred. At the trial, a Justice Department attorney, John Fargo, explained why the government rejected Morelli's work:

"Common shapes—a heart, the square shape of a pillow earring, a circular shape of a ring or a bracelet —those are not copyrightable by themselves. They're geometric shapes that are free for all to use. The problem with minimalist work is it doesn't leave a lot in the way of expression."

Morelli's expert witnesses testified that his designs were the result of great creativity and were innovative, but it was not enough to overcome the jury's belief that the jewelry lacked copyrightable expression. The result was a major win for Tiffany & Co., which was able to continue selling its $30-million-a-year *Etoile* line.

2. Separating Art From Function

Copyright law won't protect a functional object like a lamp or a shoe. These "useful articles" may be protected under patent law. Their names and appearance can sometimes also be protected under trademark law. But copyright only protects expressions of ideas, not useful objects.

This doesn't mean you can't get a copyright for your elephant-shaped cup or your flower-patterned casserole cozies. You can always claim copyright protection for the arty aspects of your work—the elephant shape and your original flower pattern— but not for the functional features.

> *Example:* Daniel creates a whimsical hand-painted jewelry box. Daniel can stop others from copying his whimsical design on any other media —for example, on toy chests, puzzles, pot holders or websites. But he cannot claim copyright in the functional aspects of the jewelry box—the way it closes, the system of storage or the hinge mechanism on the back.

Sometimes, it's difficult to conceive of the art separate from the function—that is, the art and function seem to merge so completely that one cannot exist without the other. When that happens, it's hard to get copyright, because the design is considered necessary to the function.

Judges or the Copyright Office examiners often resolve this issue by asking the question, "Can this crafts work be created in many alternate ways and still function?" If there are many alternate designs, than the design is not crucial to the function.

Consider the bird's nest napkin rings in Figure 8-1. There are many ways to make napkin rings other than with a bird's nest design. In fact, there are many alternative types of bird's nest designs that can be used to create napkin rings. (In preparation for her case, Lisa Graves demonstrated several other ways a wire napkin ring could be created.) Since there were so many alternative ways to express a napkin ring with a bird's nest motif, the function (holding napkins) and the design (the unique wire and solder design) were not inseparable. In short, Lisa Graves could not stop Pottery Barn from creating a bird's nest napkin ring, but she could stop them from making a napkin ring with the same shape, same number of windings and similar use of solder.

Below are more real-life cases that grappled with these same issues.

Example 1: The KOOSH ball is a sphere-shaped object with floppy, wiggly, elastic filaments radiating from a core. The Copyright Office denied copyright registration for the KOOSH ball because the ball's function could not be separated from any artistic expression. (*OddzOn Prods. v. Oman,* 924 F.2d 346 (D.C. Cir. 1991).) (Despite the lack of copyright protection, the KOOSH ball is protected under patent and trademark laws.)

Example 2: Jewelry designer Barry Kieselstein-Cord sued a company that copied his belt-buckle designs. (*Kieselstein-Cord v. Accessories by Pearl, Inc.,* 632 F.2d 989 (2d Cir. 1980).) At first, the court held that the belt buckles were not copyrightable because it was not possible to physically separate the sculptural work (the jewelry design) from the functional object (the belt buckle). However, a higher court reversed that decision and found that the artistic features of the belt buckle were *conceptually* separable, and Kieselstein-Cord was able to claim copyright protection.

Example 3: In 1995, the manufacturer of stylized chrome motorcycle parts attempted to register some of the company products (for example, kickstand mount, speedometer visor) as sculptural works. The Copyright Office refused to register these items, claiming that their function could not be separated from their claimed aesthetic worthiness. A court upheld this decision, agreeing that the sculptural or artistic aspects were not conceptually separable. (*Custom Chrome Inc. v. Ringer,* 35 U.S.P.Q.2d 1714 (D. D.C. 1995).)

Why were the results different in the belt buckle and motorcycle cases? The stylish beauty of the motorcycle parts was inseparable from their function. Alternatively, there may not have been suitable alternatives for expressing the kickstand mount or visor.

As you can see, the function/art issue is similar to the minimalism issue in Section D1, above. Again, the more ornate the design, the *more likely* it is that the Copyright Office or courts will see how the design is separate from the function.

Clothing Designs—Can't Get No Respect

Clothing designs are one of the few groups of works that do not qualify for copyright protection. This explains the endless clothing design knockoffs found in retail stores. The Copyright Office has steadfastly maintained that the art cannot be separated from the function in clothing designs. It's not as if clothing designers haven't tried. One costume designer attempted to sneak her work through the Copyright Office by claiming it was soft sculpture. Other designers have petitioned Congress for a new type of legal protection. There are some workarounds. You can protect unique artwork featured on clothing, and you can protect arrangements of fabric—for example, quilt designs used on clothing. You can also copyright the pattern used to make clothing. But try as you might, you will not be able to protect the actual design of the clothing.

E. How to Obtain the Copyright in a Photograph of Your Crafts Work

Photographs or slides of your crafts products consist of two copyrights—the copyright in the photograph (owned by the photographer) and your copyright in the underlying crafts product. If you took the picture, then you own both copyrights. If not, the photographer must give you permission to reproduce the image. Usually, this isn't an issue since the photographer grants you—either explicitly or implicitly—carte blanche to use the photographs. Most crafts workers don't bother with the issue, and photographers rarely haggle over it.

But if you're concerned about your right to use photographs and want to guarantee a broad range of uses for the photos—for example, to be able to reproduce them on your website, on postcards or in a crafts magazine—have the photographer assign all rights in the photographs to you. You don't need a full-blown agreement—although I provide an assignment agreement in Section Q, below. Instead, you can just include the statement, "Photographer assigns all copyright in the photographs to [*your name*]" on the photographer's invoice and ask the photographer to sign it. Sometimes a photographer may be willing to assign copyright but wishes to retain the right to reproduce copies for a portfolio. That's okay. Just write out your understanding.

The dual copyrights in a photograph of crafts also work in your favor. Since you control the reproduction of your copyrighted crafts design, the photographer would need your permission to reproduce photos of your crafts. In other words, you could halt the photographer's unauthorized use of photos of your copyrighted work.

F. Do You Need to Register With the Copyright Office?

Although you do not need a copyright registration to claim copyright, I recommend that you apply for one. From a practical point of view, having a copyright registration sometimes speeds up resolution of copyright disputes. It lets the other side know you're serious, it frightens some pirates and, because of the potential for an award of attorney fees and statutory damages discussed below, it may help you attract a lawyer to take your case. Here's a summary of some registration benefits:

- If you register your artwork within five years of publication, you are presumed to be the owner of the artwork and to have a valid copyright.
- If you register your artwork prior to an infringement, or within three months of its publication, you may be entitled to special payments

known as "statutory damages" and to attorney fees from the person you sued.
- You can only file a copyright infringement lawsuit if you've registered your artwork first.

The filing fee for registration is currently $30, and the registration process takes approximately six months. It's possible to expedite the registration for an added fee, in which case it can be acquired within five working days. Expediting a copyright registration is not for convenience; it is only allowed in urgent cases (see sidebar, "Expediting Copyright Registrations," below).

The U.S. Copyright Office

You can find the U.S. Copyright Office on the Web (www.copyright.gov; see Figure 8-2), or you can write to the Copyright Office, Library of Congress, Washington, DC 20559-6000. (I recommend getting what you need through the Internet rather than by mail.) You can download copyright application forms or copyright circulars (special publications that explain copyright laws and rules in plain language) by visiting the Copyright Office website or calling the Copyright Office's Fax on Demand service at 202-707-2600. You can call also obtain copyright information and applications by calling 202-707-9100.

G. How "Publication" of Your Artwork Affects Its Registration

Whether a crafts work is "published" or "unpublished" affects the copyright registration process. Publication:
- can trigger deadlines for obtaining registration benefits (see Section F, above)
- is relevant for completing the application form, and
- affects how many copies you must deposit with the Copyright Office.

The word "publication" has a broader meaning than you might expect in the copyright world. A work is considered to be published under copyright law if you sell, distribute or offer to sell or distribute copies of your artwork to the public. Artwork displayed in a competition is not a publication, but when you display it for sale at a trade show, that's considered to be a publication.

⚠️ **Posting artwork on a website may—or may not— be a publication.** Neither the courts nor the Copyright Office has issued any definitive rulings on this. Take a conservative approach and consider website uses—particularly if you're offering the items for sale—as constituting publication.

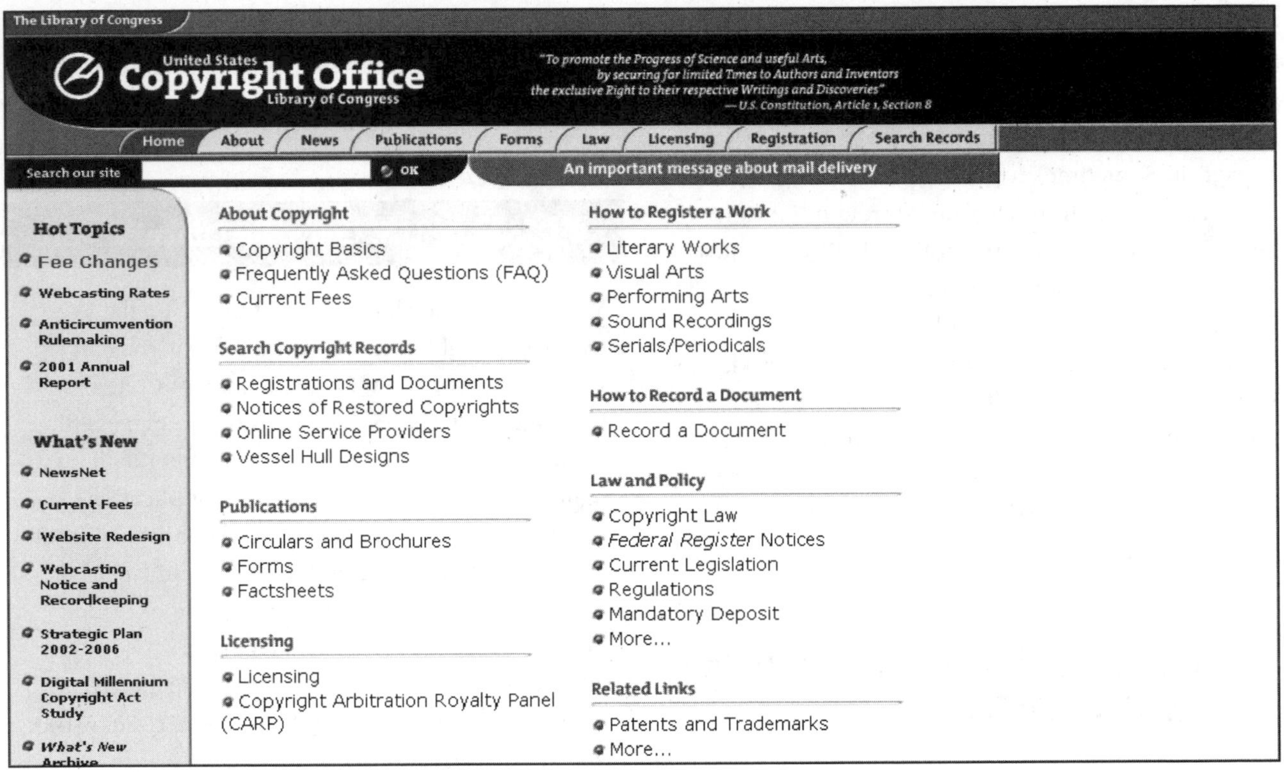

Figure 8-2: U.S. Copyright Office Website

Publication Examples	
Publication of Artwork	**Not a Publication of Artwork**
Reproducing image of pottery in a magazine	Displaying pottery in a museum
Reproducing jewelry image on promotional postcards	Public slide show of jewelry
Making copies of a promotional video that contains glasswork	Broadcasting glasswork on television (except for offers for sale)
Signing a contract to allow copies of your wood carving to be reproduced on merchandise	Making copies of wood carvings but not distributing them to the public
Offering downloads of wind chime images from a website	Limited distributions of wind chimes for a limited purpose—for example, sending a few copies to magazine editors as a demonstration of your talent

H. Choosing Whether to Register Your Works in Groups

You don't necessarily have to register each of your works one by one. To save time and money, it's possible to register a group or collection of your crafts works—depending on whether the conditions described in subsections 1 and 2, below, have been met. The registration requirements and process will depend on whether the works are unpublished or published.

There is, however, one drawback to registering a group of works. If several of the items in your group registration are infringed, you may recover less money than if each work had been registered separately.

Unsure of whether to register separately or in groups? Register your most popular works individually, and register the rest in collections.

1. Registering a Group of Unpublished Crafts Works

A group of unpublished works may be registered as a collection if all of the following conditions are met:

- you've organized the images of the works that you want copyrighted into an orderly collection (for example, each image is glued to a page within a bound book or loose-leaf volume)
- the collection has a single title identifying it as a whole (for example, "Hannah's Summer 2002 Crochet Collection"), and
- one person has created all of the works in the collection or has contributed to all of the works (for example, one artist does a series of collaborations with different artists).

2. Registering a Group of Published Works

You can register a published work that contains various works—such as a published book of your crafts works, a bound collection of postcards of your work or a poster containing several of your crafts items. For example, a crafts artist who creates a collection of sculptured chess pieces, a playing board

and an ornate box to hold the pieces can claim a single copyright in the set. In order to register a published work containing many works, one person must have created all of the works.

I. Preparing the Form VA Copyright Application

Use Form VA for registering your crafts works, whether you register them individually or in groups. In addition to the $30 filing fee, you will need to furnish copies of your work: two copies if it is published and one copy if it is unpublished. The formats that are acceptable for deposit are provided in a Copyright Office document called Circular 40, "Copyright Registration for Works of the Visual Arts." (You can see an example of a completed copyright registration below.)

Copies of Form VA as well as Circular 40 are included on the CD-ROM at the back of this book. (Form VA and Circular 40 are also available at the Copyright Office website.)

You probably won't need much help completing Form VA. The instructions that accompany Form VA (and can also be found in Circular 40) are straightforward and easy to follow. Don't knowingly make any false or fraudulent statements on your application —these can only cause problems down the road if you sue someone. (See 17 U.S.C. § 506(e).)

The Adobe Acrobat version of Form VA is considered "fillable," meaning that you can type information directly into the form visible on your screen. Although you can print the completed form, you can't save the data. So once you turn off the computer or close the program, you'll lose any information you typed into the form.

After you've completed Form VA, print the two pages of the form onto one sheet of paper. Print head to head (top of page 2 is directly behind the top of page 1) using both sides of a single sheet. You must use either an inkjet or laser printer (lasers are preferable). Forms printed by a dot matrix printer will not be accepted by the Copyright Office.

CERTIFICATE OF REGISTRATION

UNITED STATES COPYRIGHT OFFICE

THE LIBRARY OF CONGRESS

OFFICIAL SEAL

This Certificate issued under the seal of the Copyright Office in accordance with title 17, United States Code, attests that registration has been made for the work identified below. The information on this certificate has been made a part of the Copyright Office records.

Marybeth Peters

REGISTER OF COPYRIGHTS
United States of America

FORM VA
UNITED STATES COPYRIGHT OFFICE

REGISTRATION NUMBER

VA 683-009

EFFE

JUN 1 9 1995
Month   Day   Year

DO NOT WRITE ABOVE THIS LINE. IF YOU NEED MORE SPACE, USE A SEPARATE CONTINUATION SHEET.

1

TITLE OF THIS WORK ▼

Bird's Nest Napkin Ring

NATURE OF THIS WORK ▼ See instructions

3-Dimensional Sculpture

PREVIOUS OR ALTERNATIVE TITLES ▼

PUBLICATION AS A CONTRIBUTION If this work was published as a contribution to a periodical, serial, or collection, give information about the collective work in which the contribution appeared.   **Title of Collective Work ▼**

If published in a periodical or serial give: Volume ▼   Number ▼   Issue Date ▼   On Pages ▼

2

a NAME OF AUTHOR ▼

Lisa Graves

DATES OF BIRTH AND DEATH
Year Born ▼   Year Died ▼
1961

Was this contribution to the work a "work made for hire"?
☐ Yes
☒ No

AUTHOR'S NATIONALITY OR DOMICILE
Name of Country
OR { Citizen of ▶ USA
Domiciled in ▶

WAS THIS AUTHOR'S CONTRIBUTION TO THE WORK
Anonymous?   ☐ Yes ☒ No
Pseudonymous? ☐ Yes ☒ No

If the answer to either of these questions is "Yes," see detailed instructions

NATURE OF AUTHORSHIP Briefly describe nature of the material created by this author in which copyright is claimed. ▼

3-Dimensional Sculpture

NOTE
Under the law, the "author" of a "work made for hire" is

b NAME OF AUTHOR ▼

DATES OF BIRTH AND DEATH
Year Born ▼   Year Died ▼

Was this contribution to the work a "work made for hire"?
☐ Yes
☐ No

AUTHOR'S NATIONALITY OR DOMICILE
Name of Country
OR { Citizen of ▶
Domiciled in ▶

WAS THIS AUTHOR'S CONTRIBUTION TO THE WORK
Anonymous?   ☐ Yes ☐ No
Pseudonymous? ☐ Yes ☐ No

If the answer to either of these questions is "Yes," see detailed instructions

NATURE OF AUTHORSHIP Briefly describe nature of the material created by this author in which copyright is claimed. ▼

NAME OF AUTHOR ▼

DATES OF BIRTH AND DEATH
Year Born ▼   Year Died ▼

Was this contribution to the work a "work made for hire"?
☐ Yes
☐ No

AUTHOR'S NATIONALITY OR DOMICILE
Name of Country
OR { Citizen of ▶
Domiciled in ▶

WAS THIS AUTHOR'S CONTRIBUTION TO THE WORK
Anonymous?   ☐ Yes ☐ No
Pseudonymous? ☐ Yes ☐ No

If the answer to either of these questions is "Yes," see detailed instructions

NATURE OF AUTHORSHIP Briefly describe nature of the material created by this author in which copyright is claimed. ▼

3

a YEAR IN WHICH CREATION OF THIS WORK WAS COMPLETED This information must be given in all cases.
1991 ◀ Year

b DATE AND NATION OF FIRST PUBLICATION OF THIS PARTICULAR WORK Complete this information ONLY if this work has been published.
Month ▶ August Day ▶ 1 Year ▶ 1991   ◀ Nation

4

COPYRIGHT CLAIMANT(S) Name and address must be given even if the claimant is the same as the author given in space 2.▼

Lisa Graves dba ASIL
874 41st Street
Oakland CA 94608

See instructions before completing this space

APPLICATION RECEIVED
JUN. 19, 1995
ONE DEPOSIT RECEIVED
JUN. 19, 1995
TWO DEPOSITS RECEIVED

REMITTANCE NUMBER AND DATE

DO NOT WRITE HERE OFFICE USE ONLY

TRANSFER If the claimant(s) named here in space 4 are different from the author(s) named in space 2, give a brief statement of how the claimant(s) obtained ownership of the copyright.▼

MORE ON BACK ▶ • Complete all applicable spaces (numbers 5-9) on the reverse side of this page
• See detailed instructions   • Sign the form at line 8

DO NOT WRITE HERE

Page 1 of _____ pages

Form VA Copyright Application (front)

EXAMINED BY

CHECKED BY

☐ CORRESPONDENCE
   Yes

FORM VA

FOR
COPYRIGHT
OFFICE
USE
ONLY

DO NOT WRITE ABOVE THIS LINE. IF YOU NEED MORE SPACE, USE A SEPARATE CONTINUATION SHEET.

PREVIOUS REGISTRATION Has registration for this work, or for an earlier version of this work, already been made in the Copyright Office?

☐ Yes ■ No If your answer is "Yes," why is another registration being sought? (Check appropriate box) ▼

☐ This is the first published edition of a work previously registered in unpublished form.

☐ This is the first application submitted by this author as copyright claimant.

☐ This is a changed version of the work, as shown by space 6 on this application.

If your answer is "Yes," give: **Previous Registration Number** ▼   **Year of Registration** ▼

5

DERIVATIVE WORK OR COMPILATION Complete both space 6a & 6b for a derivative work; complete only 6b for a compilation.

a. Preexisting Material Identify any preexisting work or works that this work is based on or incorporates. ▼

b. Material Added to This Work Give a brief, general statement of the material that has been added to this work and in which copyright is claimed. ▼

6

See instructions
before completing
this space

DEPOSIT ACCOUNT If the registration fee is to be charged to a Deposit Account established in the Copyright Office, give name and number of Account.

Name ▼   **Account Number** ▼

7

CORRESPONDENCE Give name and address to which correspondence about this application should be sent.   Name/Address/Apt/City/State/Zip ▼

Richard W. Stim, Esq.
1282 47th Avenue
San Francisco CA 94122-1130

Area Code & Telephone Number ▶   415-681-4907

Be sure to
give your
daytime phone
◀ number

CERTIFICATION* I, the undersigned, hereby certify that I am the

Check only one ▼

☐ author

☐ other copyright claimant

☐ owner of exclusive right(s)

■ authorized agent of_____Lisa Graves_____
Name of author or other copyright claimant, or owner of exclusive right(s) ▲

8

of the work identified in this application and that the statements made
by me in this application are correct to the best of my knowledge.

Typed or printed name and date ▼ If this application gives a date of publication in space 3, do not sign and submit it before that date.

_____Richard Stim_____   date ▶ 6-12-1995

Handwritten signature (X) ▼
Richard W. Stim

MAIL CERTIFICATE TO

Certificate will be mailed in window envelope

Name ▼
Richard W. Stim, Esq.

Number/Street/Apartment Number ▼
1282 47th Avenue

City/State/ZIP ▼
San Francisco CA 94122-1130

9

YOU MUST
• Complete all necessary spaces
• Sign your application in space 8
SEND ALL 3 ELEMENTS
IN THE SAME PACKAGE
1. Application form
2. Non-refundable $10 filing fee
   in check or money order
   payable to Register of Copyrights
3. Deposit material
MAIL TO:
Register of Copyrights
Library of Congress
Washington, D.C. 20559

* 17 U.S.C. § 506(e) Any person who knowingly makes a false representation of a material fact in the application for copyright registration provided for by section 409, or in any written statement filed in connection with the application, shall be fined not more than $2,500.

June 1989—100,000   ☆U.S. GOVERNMENT PRINTING OFFICE: 1989—241-428/80.024

Form VA Copyright Application (back)

Space 1: Title and Nature of the Work

Space 1 requires that you provide the title and alternate or previous title of your work. The Copyright Office requires the title in order to index the work in its records. Nondescriptive titles such as "Work Without a Title" can be used. If you're registering a group of works, use a title that indicates it's a collection—for example, "Twelve Summer Bowls." The alternate or previous title refers to any additional title under which someone searching for the registration might look.

Space 1: Nature of Work

Space 1 of Form VA also requires information about the "nature of the work." Provide a brief description—for example, needlework, mosaic, jewelry design, fabric design or three-dimensional sculpture.

Space 1: Publication as a Contribution

If your crafts work was first published as part of a serial publication or as part of a collective work—for example, your decorated pillowcase designs first appeared in *Rosie Magazine*—present the required information about the magazine.

Space 2: The Author

Copyright law refers to you—the person who created the work—as "author." Provide your name, unless you wish to be anonymous or pseudonymous. Also provide your date of birth and nationality. Repeat this procedure in subsequent spaces for anyone who co-authored your crafts. A co-author is someone who, at the time the work was created, made a copyrightable contribution

> *Example:* While sitting in your booth at a trade show, your five-year-old son adorns the top of one your intricately carved wooden jewelry boxes with an image of a dragon. At first you're angry ... but then a buyer from a chain store sees it and orders 100. The design—combining your intricate woodwork and his dragon image—is a work of co-authorship.

Space 2: Works Made for Hire

If you created this work by yourself, and you were neither commissioned to make it nor working for a crafts business at the time, check "no" under the question, "Was this contribution to the work a work made for hire?" Otherwise, read Chapter 5, Section F before checking either box.

Space 2: Nature of Authorship

Provide a brief description of your work, for example, Three-Dimensional Sculpture or Jewelry Design.

Space 3: Creation and Publication

In Space 3, provide information about the dates of creation and first publication of the work. Your work was created on the day you completed it—the date you stood back and said, "I'm done." To determine when your work was published, see Section G, above. Give the full date (that is, month, day and year) when the work was published. If you're unsure, it's okay to write "approximately" (for example, approximately June 4, 2002).

Space 4: The Copyright Claimant

In Space 4, provide information about the person claiming copyright—probably you or your crafts business. Use your or your business's full legal name and address.

Space 4: Transfer

If the person named as copyright claimant is not the same as the person in Space 2 (the "author"), explain how the transfer from author to claimant occurred. For example if you created the work but then transferred the rights in it to your corporation, you would write, "by written contract" or "by written assignment." (Don't attach the transfer documents. These should be recorded separately or at a later date with the Copyright Office.) The procedure for recording such documents is described in Circular 12, issued by the Copyright Office.

 Circular 12 is available on the CD-ROM at the back of this book.

Space 5: Previous Registration

Here, you must indicate any previous copyright registrations for this work or for earlier versions of the work. The Copyright Office is only concerned with whether this work or a previous version has been *registered*, not whether it's gained any other copyright protection. If it hasn't been registered, check the NO box.

Space 5: Basis for Seeking New Registration

If you checked the YES box earlier in Space 5, then check the box that best describes why you're seeking a new registration—for example, if this is a changed version of the work, or if this is the first application submitted by you as copyright claimant.

Space 5: Previous Registration Number and Year of Registration

If this work was previously registered, indicate the registration—the number listed on the upper right-hand corner of the registration beginning with the letters VA, for example, VA-13-800.

Space 6: Derivative Work or Compilation

In Space 6, you must determine whether the work you're registering is a derivative work or a compilation.

A derivative work is a modification of a previous work (regardless of whether the previous work was registered). For example, if you had carved a wood block design, then created a second design adding additional flora, the second design would be a derivative.

A compilation is a collection of material—for example, a book titled "The Crafts Report's 100 Greatest Crafts Artists"—in which someone assembled, selected or organized the preexisting materials without transforming them. The author of a compilation seeks to protect the collection, not the individual works. A collection of your crafts works is *not* a compilation, since you're seeking to protect all of the individual works, not the manner in which they are arranged or selected.

If you're registering a derivative work, complete 6a and 6b. If you are registering a compilation, complete 6b.

Example: Jenna is registering her hand-carved "J-bird." It's a variation of a work she created last year, entitled Jenna's Bird. Jenna would complete Space 6 as follows:

6a (preexisting material): previous sculpture, Jenna's Bird.

6b (material added): changed proportions of head and body, changed size and color of plumage.

Space 7: Deposit Accounts and Correspondence

If you have a deposit account—an account for applicants registering works on a regular basis—complete this section. (It's usually not worth obtaining a deposit account unless you are registering hundreds of works.) Otherwise, skip this portion of Space 7 and provide your correspondence information so the examiner can contact you if any questions arise.

Space 8: Certification

Check the Author box if you're filling out the form and if you are the person (or one of the persons) named in Space 2 of the application. In some circumstances, you may also prepare the application if you're someone other than the crafts artist. For example, the crafts artist may be deceased, and you've been granted legal power to prepare the registration on behalf of the artist's family.

Check Other Copyright Claimant if you're filling out the application and you're the copyright claimant in Space 4 (that is, you obtained you copyright ownership by purchasing or licensing it from the creator).

Check Owner of Exclusive Rights if you're filling out the application and you own a limited right, for example, the exclusive right to reproduce the work for a period of years, but you're not the author or the copyright claimant.

Check Authorized Agent if you're filling out the form as the authorized representative of the author, claimant or owner of exclusive rights.

Space 8: Signature

After you check the appropriate box in Space 8, type or print your name and date and sign it where marked. Bear in mind that by signing the application, you will be certifying to the Copyright Office that the information contained in the application is correct to the best of your knowledge. A "false representation of a material fact" in a copyright application may result in a fine of up to $2,500.

Space 9: Mailing Information

Space 9 of the copyright application becomes the mailing label when the certified registration is mailed back to you. That is, after the application has been processed, it will be mailed back in a window envelope, and Space 9 (Mailing Information) will be your own address, showing through.

The Fee

A filing fee is required along with the application and deposit material. The fee is currently $30 per application, but check the Copyright Office for current fee information before sending your application. You can pay by personal check, cashier's check or money order, but don't send cash. If your checking account has insufficient funds, the Copyright Office will not proceed with registration or will revoke the registration if it has already been issued.

J. Including Copies of Your Work With the Registration Application

You must include copies or images of your work with your application. As a general rule, one copy is deposited for unpublished works; two for published. If your crafts work is three-dimensional, like most crafts, send two-dimensional "identifying material" such as photographs of your works. The photographs should clearly and accurately represent the work. If you've ever sent in jury photos of a work, you've already got a good idea of how to achieve this.

K. Sending Your Registration Application

Normally, U.S. mail would be a fine way to send your application, though you have the choice of using other mailing services as well. However, as a result of anthrax scares, all mail service to the Copyright Office was halted for several months, starting on October 17, 2001. First-class mail started arriving again on March 4, 2002, but only in small amounts. As a result of irradiation procedures, processing applications is expected to take nine months or longer.

If you are concerned about this delay or that mail will be lost, you might want to send your parcel by U.S. Express mail or some other overnight courier. This does not guarantee faster processing, but it does guarantee proof of receipt.

If you must have your application dealt with quickly after it reaches the Copyright Office, review the sidebar, "Expediting Copyright Applications," below.

Expediting Copyright Applications

For an expedited handling fee of $580 (on top of the $30 filing fee), the Copyright Office will process an application within five working days. You cannot choose this service for mere reasons of convenience; it is only allowed in urgent cases. You can request it using the form "Request for Special Handling," included in Copyright Circular 10. As an alternative to using this form, you can prepare a cover letter answering the following questions:

- Why is there an urgent need for special handling? (for example, upcoming litigation, a pending customs matter, a looming contractual or publishing deadline, or other reasons you specify).
- If you're requesting the rapid action in order to go forward with litigation: (a) Is the litigation actual (the suit will definitely be filed) or prospective (the suit *may* be filed)?; (b) Are you the plaintiff (the person claiming infringement) or defendant (the person accused of infringement) in the action?; (c) What are the names of the parties, and what is the name of the court where the action is pending or expected?

You must certify that the statements in the letter are correct to the best of your knowledge, and you must provide a mailing address and phone number for contact. The letter and the envelope should be addressed to Special Handling, Library of Congress, Dept. 100, Washington, DC 20540. Money orders or cashiers checks are recommended for the fee. A personal check will be accepted, but if the check bounces, the registration will be revoked. Expedited registrations can be sent by Federal Express or other overnight courier. It is wise to include a prepaid return envelope (for example, FedEx, Express Mail and so on) for overnight mailing of the Certificate of Registration back to you.

L. Posting a Copyright Notice on Your Work

Because of the automatic copyright on creative works, you don't have to wait until your work is registered to place your copyright notice on your work. Although not required for works published after March 1, 1989, it's still advisable to place the familiar copyright notice (for example, Copyright © 2001 Art Jones) on each published copy of your crafts work. This tells anyone who sees the work that the copyright is being claimed, who is claiming it and when the work was first published. This notice prevents an infringer from later claiming that the infringement was accidental, and may provide additional benefits when you seek damages from an infringer. You can place the notice on the back of a work provided that it's visible from that angle. For example, if you can take a painting off the wall and read the information on the back or if you can lift up a vase and find the notice on the bottom, it's okay.

M. Getting Permission to Use Someone Else's Work

So far, my discussion has focused on your copyrights—what you get by creating and, if you choose to, registering a work. In this section, I'll shift course a bit. I'll discuss what to do when you want to use someone else's copyrighted work in conjunction with your own—for example, you'd like to reproduce someone's photographs on your pillowcases. (In Chapter 9, I discuss a related topic—how to license someone else's work to use on your own.)

The consequences of failing to get permission can be quite expensive. In 1980, photographer Art Rogers took a photograph of a friend's eight puppies. Seven years later, artist Jeff Koons, without Rogers' permission, used the photograph as the basis of a series of wood sculptures. Rogers sued over the unauthorized use of his photo, and Rogers later was awarded several hundred thousand dollars in damages along with an order prohibiting Koons from making or selling any more of the sculptures.

If Koons had asked Rogers for permission before starting the sculptures, Rogers could have refused, or he could have asked for a payment, perhaps a percentage based upon the revenue from the statues. In either case, Koons would have saved over a half million dollars in damages and attorney fees.

This isn't to say that if you use something without permission you will suffer the same result as Jeff Koons. The risk of a lawsuit depends not just upon your particular use, but upon other factors such as the likelihood that the use will be spotted, whether you are a "worthy" target for litigation and whether the other side is inclined to sue.

But even if you don't get sued, there's always a potential risk when you fail to ask for permission to use someone else's work. You may not have to pay damages, but you may have to destroy inventory, molds or accompanying promotional material. The more successful your crafts business becomes, the more likely that a copyright owner will learn of your use and take action.

What does it take to acquire permission? The first step is to determine whether you can use the work without asking for permission. Permission is not always necessary, because copyright law does not protect all materials. For example, works published before 1923 in the United States are in the public domain and free to use. However, a work is not in the public domain simply because it has been posted on the Internet (a popular fallacy) or because it doesn't sport a copyright notice (another fallacy).

The second step in getting permission is to identify the owner of the work you want to use. Often, you can locate the rights owner just by looking at the copyright notice on the work. Sometimes, more detailed research is required, for example, searching the records of the Copyright Office.

The third step in getting permission is to identify the rights you need. Identifying the rights can be as simple as stating your intended use—for example, that you'd like to reproduce a photograph on post-

cards. Generally, you will need to consider three common rights variables:

- exclusivity
- term, and
- territory.

Most permission requests are nonexclusive, meaning that others can use the material in the same way as you. An exclusive permission agreement means you are the only person who has the right to use the work as described in the agreement.

The length of time for which the use is allowed is often referred to as the "term." If there is no established limitation on the use, you are allowed to use the material for as long as you want or until the copyright owner revokes the permission. Your rights under a permission agreement may be limited to a certain geographic region, referred to as the "territory."

Once you identify the owner and the rights needed, it's time to contact the owner and ask for permission. The primary issue that arises when seeking permission is whether payment is necessary. Sometimes the owner of the work will not require payment if the amount being used is quite small or if the owner is eager for exposure. Sometimes, an owner may agree to suspend payment until your crafts project becomes profitable, or the owner may condition payment on other factors.

Finally, you need to formalize the arrangement. Oral permission agreements are legally enforceable. Moreover, even if you have no explicit oral agreement, you may still have a right to use a work if permission can be implied from the way the parties have behaved.

Example: Lou, a jeweler, asks for permission to reproduce Tom's photo within ten pendants. Tom responds that he will grant permission for $100. After receiving the payment, Tom sends the photographs to Lou. A permission agreement may be implied from Tom's conduct.

That said, relying on an oral or implied agreement is often a mistake. You and the rights owner may have misunderstood each other or remembered the terms of your agreement differently. For that reason, written agreements are preferable. These need not be formal or in legalese. A simple statement of permission signed by the person granting permission is usually suitable.

It's also possible for you to hire an artist or other creative person to create a work for you.

- If the creative person qualifies as your employee, you will automatically own all rights to the work created on your behalf, and no permission will be required.

- If the person creating the work is not an employee, he or she is an independent contractor, and your ownership of the contractor's work is not automatic.

To guarantee your ownership of an independent contractor's work, you should use either a work-made-for-hire agreement (see Chapter 5, Section F) or an assignment agreement (see Section Q, below).

In summary, a conservative approach to using material created by others will best protect your crafts business. Unless you are certain that the material is in the public domain or that your use is legally excusable, I advise you to seek permission. If you are not sure, you'll have to either make your own risk analysis or obtain the advice of an attorney knowledgeable in copyright or media law.

As a general rule, it is wise to operate under the assumption that all materials are protected by copyright law unless conclusive information indicates otherwise.

 You may need other permissions. Permission is sometimes needed to reproduce a trademark or to use a real person's image. A trademark is any word, symbol or device that identifies and distinguishes a product or service. Permission is generally needed if your use is commercial and is likely to confuse consumers or to tarnish the trademark's reputation (see Chapter 6). Your use of an individual's image or name may require permission if you are implying a commercial connection between the individual and your product. For example, you will need permission to include a celebrity's image on a belt buckle or in an advertisement. A sample model release is included in Section U, below.

N. When It's Fair for You to Use Pieces of Others' Works

Under a legal doctrine known as "fair use," there are times when you have the right to discuss, criticize or poke fun at copyrighted works without seeking permission from the copyright owner. In general, fair use permits you to copy small portions of a work for "transformative" purposes such as parody, scholarship or commentary. For example, a political cartoonist can freely copy an image of a copyrighted character for purposes of making an editorial cartoon.

The difficulty of applying fair use is that the standard is often subjective. That is, you can't guarantee that your use is a fair use until a judge says so at the end of a lawsuit—and at that point you may be bankrupt from legal fees. On the flip side, the problem with suing people over their "unfair" use of your work is that you can't know in advance whether you'll win and thus whether the legal fees will be worth it.

The upshot is this: Tread carefully in the realm of fair use. For a more detailed discussion of fair use, consult Stephen Fishman's *The Copyright Handbook* (Nolo) or check out a website devoted to fair use (http://fairuse.stanford.edu).

O. How the First Sale Doctrine Protects Certain Uses of Others' Works

The first sale doctrine permits the owner of a copy of a copyrighted work to resell, destroy or loan this copy. You can utilize the first sale doctrine for your own benefit. For example, if you're a frame maker, you can purchase copyrighted posters and resell them in your custom-made frames. Similarly, if you are a cabinetmaker, you can apply copyrighted postcards to the outside of a bureau. But beware—as with fair use, the rules are sometimes confusing (see sidebar, "To Frame or to Mount?," below).

To Frame or to Mount?

As with many areas of copyright law, there is some confusion as to the boundaries of the first sale doctrine. Two cases involving the framing of artwork seem to have arrived at different results. In one case, a company purchased a book of prints by the painter Patrick Nagel, cut out the individual images and mounted them in frames for resale. The Ninth Circuit Court of Appeals in California held that this practice was an infringement and was *not* permitted under the first sale doctrine. (*Mirage Editions, Inc. v. Albuquerque A.R.T. Co.*, 856 F.2d 1341 (1988); and see *Greenwich Workshop Inc. v. Timber Creations, Inc.*, 932 F. Supp. 1210 (C.D. Cal. 1996).)

In a different case, however, a company purchased note cards and mounted them on tiles. (*Lee v. Deck the Walls, Inc.*, 925 F. Supp. 576 (N.D. Ill. 1996); and see *C.M. Paula Co. v. Logan*, 355 F. Supp. 189 (D.C. Texas 1973).) A federal court in Illinois determined that this practice was *not* an infringement and was permitted under the first sale doctrine. Under these rulings, a person in California cannot mount individual images from an art book, while a person in Illinois *can* mount individual note cards.

Should it matter whether the object that is mounted is from an art book or from a note card? Perhaps: In the California case, the justices felt that removing individual images from a bound collection altered the works. In other words, Nagel's estate did not intend for the works to be separated from the collection. Therefore, this framed use was considered a derivative work. In the Illinois case, the judge did not believe that mounting an individual note card, already separate, created a derivative work, since the image was not altered or modified.

P. Free Use of Works in the Public Domain

Permission is not needed to reproduce artwork that is in the public domain: that is, anything that was published in the United States before 1923, or any copyrighted work that was published before 1964 and whose copyright was not renewed.

Determining whether a work is in the public domain requires research. The Copyright Office does not maintain a list of public domain works. Private companies can perform searches and furnish public domain reports, but this gets expensive. If you're interested in pursuing public domain works, I'd recommend you review the only authoritative text on the subject, *The Public Domain: How to Find & Use Copyright-Free Writings, Music, Art & More*, by Stephen Fishman (Nolo).

Q. When to Use Copyright Assignments

Let's say you create a portrait of a client using colored puka shells. The client loves it and wants to own all rights to the work—including the right to reproduce the image. The client makes you an offer you can't refuse, and you sell the copyright. This permanent transfer of copyright ownership is known as an "assignment." You're still the author of the work, but you're not the owner.

A work-made-for-hire agreement is different, because the person paying for the work is considered the owner *and* author of the work. For example, when the Disney Company employs animators who create a cartoon, the Disney Company is the author and owner of the cartoon.

An assignment is a transaction in which a copyright is permanently transferred. In return for the transfer, the copyright owner might get a lump sum or a continuing payment known as a "royalty." An assignment differs from a license agreement (discussed in Chapter 9), because under the terms of a license, the artist retains the copyright and grants only a temporary, conditional right to use the work. An assignment may also provide a method by which the rights are assigned back to the artist in the event of a certain condition—for example, if the person who purchased the copyright (the "assignee") stops selling the work.

An assignment may not last for the full term of copyright protection. The heirs of the author may reclaim rights 35 years from the date of the assignment. For example, an artist who assigned rights to you in 2003 can reclaim the rights in 2038. Since many works do not have a useful economic life of more than 35 years, this recapture right is often not important.

An assignment must be in writing. Notarization is not required. If there are multiple owners of the copyright, for example, the work was created by two artists, the signatures of all owners must be obtained for the assignment. Assignments can be recorded with the Copyright Office. There is no legal requirement that an assignment be recorded, but doing so provides public notice of the transfer and may provide advantages in the event of a dispute over ownership or infringement. For information regarding recording assignments, read Circular 10, "Recordations of Transfers and Other Documents."

Circular 10 is included on the CD-ROM at the back of this book.

1. Basic Copyright Assignment

Below are two copyright assignments that can be used for any type of completed artwork. The Basic Copyright Assignment is intended for a simple purchase of artwork rights for a lump sum—for example, you want to buy the copyright in an existing photograph. The Artwork Assignment Agreement is intended if you hire an artist to create a work and you wish to own all rights or, vice versa, someone is hiring you. This differs from the Commission Agreement in Chapter 5 because, in that case, the artist makes a crafts work for client but retains copyright.

a. Assignment

You'll find copies of the Basic Copyright Assignment in Appendix B and on the CD-ROM at the back of this book.

b. Explanation for Basic Copyright Assignment

In the first two blanks of the first paragraph, insert the artist's name and the title of the work. In the next blank space, either describe the work or enter "See Attachment A" and attach a copy of the work to the assignment. If you attach a copy, be sure to label it "Attachment A."

In the next paragraph, insert the amount of the payment and the name of the assignee. The artist (or artists) must sign the agreement.

2. Artwork Assignment Agreement

The Artwork Assignment Agreement provides for assignment of a copyright in artwork, but can be modified to cover photography or crafts. The assignment includes optional provisions for payment of expenses and for dispute resolution.

a. Artwork Assignment

You'll find copies of the Artwork Assignment Agreement in Appendix B and on the CD-ROM at the back of this book.

b. Explanation for Artwork Assignment Agreement

Since the artist is assigning all rights in the performance, the "Grant" section is as broad as possible, and the artist will not retain any rights to the artwork.

The "Services" section should be used if the artist has been hired to perform a specific job. If the artwork has already been completed and this provision is not needed, strike it or enter "N/A" for "not applicable."

The "Warranty" section is an assurance that the artist owns the rights being granted and a promise not to sue the company for legal claims such as

Copyright Assignment

I, _____ ("Artist"),

am owner of the work entitled _____

(the "Work") and described as follows: _____

_____ .

In consideration of $_____ and other valuable consideration, paid by _____

_____ ("Assignee"), I assign to Assignee and Assignee's

heirs and assigns, all my right title and interest in the copyright to the Work and all renewals and extensions of

the copyright that may be secured under the laws of the United States of America and any other countries, as

such may now or later be in effect. I agree to cooperate with Assignee and to execute and deliver all papers as

may be necessary to vest all rights to the Work.

Signature(s) of Artist(s):

_____

_____

_____

Artwork Assignment Agreement

This Artwork Assignment Agreement (the "Agreement") is made between _____
_____ ("Company"), and
_____("Artist").

Services

Artist agrees to perform the following services: _____
_____ and create the following artwork (the "Art") entitled:

_____ .

The Art shall be completed by the following date: _____.

During the process, Artist shall keep the Company informed of work in progress and shall furnish test prints of the Art prior to completion.

Payment

Company agrees to pay Artist as follows:

$_____ for performance of the art services and acquisition of the rights provided below.

Rights

Artist assigns to the Company all copyright to the Art and agrees to cooperate in the preparation of any documents necessary to demonstrate this assignment of rights. Artist retains the right to display the work as part of Artist's portfolio and to reproduce the artwork in connection with the promotion of Artist's services.

Expenses

Company agrees to reimburse Artist for all reasonable production expenses including halftones, stats, photography, disks, illustrations or related costs. These expenses shall be itemized on invoices, and in no event shall any expense exceed $50 without approval from the Company.

Credit

Credit for Artist shall be included on reproductions of the Art as follows:_____
_____ .

Artist Warranties

Artist is the owner of all rights to the Art and warrants that the Art does not infringe any intellectual property rights or violate any laws.

General Provisions

Entire Agreement. This is the entire agreement between the parties. It replaces and supersedes any and all oral agreements between the parties, as well as any prior writings. Modifications and amendments to this Agreement, including any exhibit or appendix hereto, shall be enforceable only if they are in writing and are signed by authorized representatives of both parties.

Successors and Assignees. This agreement binds and benefits the heirs, successors and assignees of the parties.

Notices. Any notice or communication required or permitted to be given under this Agreement shall be sufficiently given when received by certified mail, or sent by facsimile transmission or overnight courier.

Governing Law. This Agreement will be governed by the laws of the State of _____.

Waiver. If one party waives any term or provision of this agreement at any time, that waiver will only be effective for the specific instance and specific purpose for which the waiver was given. If either party fails to exercise or delays exercising any of its rights or remedies under this agreement, that party retains the right to enforce that term or provision at a later time.

Severability. If a court finds any provision of this Agreement invalid or unenforceable, the remainder of this Agreement will be interpreted so as best to carry out the parties' intent.

Attachments and Exhibits. The parties agree and acknowledge that all attachments, exhibits and schedules referred to in this Agreement are incorporated in this Agreement by reference.

No Agency. Nothing contained herein will be construed as creating any agency, partnership, joint venture or other form of joint enterprise between the parties.

☐ **Attorney Fees and Expenses.** The prevailing party shall have the right to collect from the other party its reasonable costs and necessary disbursements and attorney fees incurred in enforcing this Agreement.

☐ **Jurisdiction.** The parties consent to the exclusive jurisdiction and venue of the federal and state courts located in _____ [county], _____ [state], in any action arising out of or relating to this Agreement. The parties waive any other venue to which either party might be entitled by domicile or otherwise.

☐ **Arbitration.** Any controversy or claim arising out of or relating to this Agreement shall be settled by arbitration in _____ [county], _____ [state], in accordance with the rules of the American Arbitration Association, and judgment upon the award rendered by the arbitrator(s) may be entered in any court having jurisdiction. The prevailing party shall have the right to collect from the other party its reasonable costs and attorney's fees incurred in enforcing this agreement.

Signatures

Each party represents and warrants that on this date they are duly authorized to bind their respective principals by their signatures below.

COMPANY   ARTIST(S)

_____   _____
Date   Date

_____
Name of Business

_____   _____
Authorized Signature   Signature

_____   _____
Printed Name and Title   Printed Name

_____   _____
Address   Address

copyright infringement. If you wish, you may include an arbitration or mediation section (see Chapter 11 for details).

It is unusual that the artist would be a minor, but in that event, the artist and the artist's parent or guardian should sign a consent that states something to the effect of: "I am the parent or guardian of the minor named above. I have the legal right to consent to and do consent to the terms and conditions of this agreement."

R. What Rights the Purchaser of a Crafts Work Acquires

By buying a work, you don't gain rights in it. An artist who sells a piece of work still controls the right to make copies of the work, along with many of the other rights protected by copyright.

Example: Del purchases Eloise's handmade fabric. If Del wants to reproduce and sell the design as a computer screensaver, he must first get Eloise's permission.

Still, copyright law has limits, and the copyright owner cannot prevent the purchaser from selling, lending or renting the artwork, all activities permitted under the first sale doctrine, discussed above. The first sale doctrine also gives a purchaser the right to destroy a purchased work—although certain fine art crafts works such as sculptures and limited edition prints and photographs are exempt from this rule (see Section T, below).

S. Infringement of Copyright

Any unauthorized use of a copyrighted work that violates the copyright owner's exclusive rights in the work constitutes an infringement, for example:

- making unauthorized copies of a jewelry design
- reproducing a fabric design without permission on paper products, or
- creating a sculpture based on a photograph.

Once you suspect infringement, you may file a lawsuit against the infringer for damages in a federal court, provided that the copyright has been registered with the U.S. Copyright Office. An expedited registration process is available for those who have not previously registered and need to get into court right away (see Section F, above). But the fact that the infringement began before the registration occurred will diminish the rights and remedies available in court, unless the work was first published less than three months previously.

Whether or not a work will be found to have infringed an earlier copyrighted work depends largely on three factors:

- Was the first work the subject of a proper copyright? This factor is satisfied if the first work was independently created, shows enough creativity and is fixed in a tangible medium (see Section D, above).
- Did the infringer copy the work? In the absence of an admission that copying occurred, this factor depends on (1) whether the author of the second work had access to the earlier work, and (2) whether there is a substantial similarity between the two works. The stronger the similarity, the greater the chance that a court will find that infringement occurred.
- Is there any reason to excuse the infringement? (See defenses below.)

One of the requirements of proving infringement is that the infringer had access to your work. Sometimes this can be proven by the fact that the similarity between the two works is so close that the infringer *must* have seen your work. For example, in a 1997 case, makers of Beanie Babies sued a company marketing a pig bean bag known as "Preston the Pig." Preston was nearly identical to the Beanie Baby known as "Squealor." Access was presumed. (*Ty Inc. v. GMA Accessories Inc.* 132 F.3d 1167 (7th Cir. 1997).)

Some courts use a three-step approach in deciding whether there's a substantial similarity between the two works (important for proving the second factor, above). First, they identify the aspects of the two works that are subject to copyright protection. That is, they first filter out the unprotectible aspects of a work as discussed in Section D, above.

Then the court makes an objective comparison of these aspects to see how alike they are. If they are similar enough to warrant a suspicion of infringement, the courts then make a subjective determination as to whether the works are substantially similar enough to justify a finding of infringement.

In the event someone infringes your copyright, you can file a lawsuit in federal court asking the court to:

- issue orders (restraining orders and injunctions) to prevent further violations
- award money damages if appropriate, and
- in some circumstances, award attorney fees.

Whether the lawsuit will be effective and whether damages will be awarded depends on whether the alleged infringer can raise one or more legal defenses to the charge. Common legal defenses to copyright infringement are:

- too much time has elapsed between the infringing act and the lawsuit (the statute of limitations defense)
- the infringement is allowed under the fair use defense
- the infringement was innocent (the infringer had no reason to know the work was protected by copyright)
- the infringing work was independently created (that is, it wasn't copied from the original), or
- the copyright owner authorized the use in a license.

For advice on how to respond to a copyright infringement, including how to find an attorney to deal with the problem, read Chapter 11.

T. Preventing the Destruction of Crafts Works

Certain types of crafts works receive *more* rights than are normally granted under copyright law. The federal government has created a statute—the federal Visual Artists Rights Act (VARA)—that grants rights affecting reselling and destruction of artworks. Only some crafts works receive protection under VARA—paintings, drawings, prints, photographs or sculptures in a single copy or limited edition of 200 copies or fewer (that are signed and consecutively numbered).

What happens if your wood sculpture is reproduced in a museum booklet or in a magazine review? Does that mass production remove the work from VARA status? No, you can still claim VARA rights as to the original.

1. When Crafts Become Fine Art: Preservation

The VARA statute protects you, as the creator of a work of visual art, from "intentional distortion, mutilation or other modification of that work which would be prejudicial to your honor or reputation." This is the most powerful right granted under the VARA provisions. For example, if a collector buys a limited edition silkscreen from you (fewer than 200 prints were made), the collector cannot destroy it without your permission. If the work is destroyed, you can sue under VARA and recover damages, provided you can prove that your reputation was damaged.

The rule regarding destruction does not apply if:

- the work was created prior to enactment of the VARA provisions on December 1, 1990
- you specifically waive the rights in a written statement, or
- the destruction or modification results from the passage of time or because of the materials used to construct the work. For example, certain works such as ice sculptures and sand sculptures by their nature self-destruct, and the owner would have no obligation to affirmatively prevent such destruction.

2. Length and Transferability of VARA Protection

Although copyright protection normally lasts for the life of the artist plus 70 years, the rights granted under VARA last only for the life of the artist. Once the artist dies, VARA protection no longer exists, and the work can be destroyed without seeking consent.

Examples of What's Protected and Not Protected by VARA	
Protected by VARA	**Not Protected by VARA**
A limited edition of 18 copies of a silkscreen, numbered and signed by the artist.	A silkscreen image reprinted on 1,000 posters.
A one-of-a kind sculpture of Noah's ark.	Miniature replicas of Noah's ark sold by a mail-order company.

3. No VARA Rights If Work Is Made for Hire

Under certain circumstances, the person who employs an artist or commissions an artwork acquires copyright ownership. (This "work-made-for-hire" principle is discussed in Chapter 5.) If artwork is created as work made for hire, there are no VARA rights. That is, although normal copyright law applies to the work, neither the artist nor the person commissioning the work can claim rights under VARA.

U. Model Releases

In this section we provide and discuss personal release agreements that permit the use of a person's name and image. These rights overlap with copyright —they are actually a separate area of law known as right of publicity—and we include them in this chapter because you may be taking photographs of people for, or using model images in, your copyrighted work. (Note: Personal releases are often referred to as model releases, although the term "model" can be used for anyone, not just professional models.) There are two classes of personal releases: blanket releases and limited releases.

A blanket release permits any use of the photographic image of the person signing the release and is suitable if the company or photographer needs an unlimited right to use the image. If you want all rights to the person's image for all purposes, use a blanket release. If the model is only consenting to a specific use—for example, in your crafts advertisement—then use a limited release that specifies the particular ways the image and name may be used. If a use

exceeds what's permitted under the limited release, the person can sue for breach of the agreement. For example, a model who had signed a release limiting use of her image for a museum brochure sued when the photo appeared on a Miami transit card.

1. Get It in Writing

Although oral releases are generally valid, you should always try to get a release in writing. This way, the model can't claim he or she never agreed to the release. In addition, the terms of an oral release can be hard to remember and even harder to prove in court if a dispute arises.

2. Make It Clear

When a release is sought for a specific purpose, do not hide or misrepresent facts to get the signature. A fraudulently obtained release is invalid. For example, a model was told that his image would be used by an insurance company and signed a blanket release based upon that statement. However, a viaticals company that pays cash for life insurance policies owned by AIDS victims used the photo. A Florida court permitted the model to sue.

3. Keep It Simple

Release agreements usually do not include many of the legal provisions found in other agreements in this book. Instead, releases are often "stripped down" in order to not trigger lengthy discussion or negotiation. So keep your release short and simple (see sidebar, "Honey, I Shrunk the Release," below).

Honey, I Shrunk the Release

You may find it easier to obtain a signed release if you shrink the release information to the size of a 3x5 or 5x7 card. Photographers have found that photo subjects find the smaller documents less intimidating. Some photographers reduce the material to a font size that fits on the back of a business card. However, if you make the contract so tiny that it's difficult to read, a court will be less likely to enforce it.

4. Get It Signed ASAP

It is sometimes difficult to track down a subject after a photo has been created. Also, there is less incentive for the subject to sign the release at a later date. Therefore, most photographers obtain releases prior to or directly after a photo session or when the model is paid.

5. Unlimited Personal Release Agreement

The Unlimited Personal Release Agreement shown below is a blanket release agreement. It permits you to use the model's image and name in all forms of media throughout the world, forever.

You'll find copies of the Unlimited Personal Release form in Appendix B and on the CD-ROM at the back of this book.

6. Limited Personal Release Agreement

The Limited Personal Release Agreement, shown below, allows you to use the model's name or image only for the purposes specified in the agreement.

You'll find copies of the Limited Personal Release Agreement in Appendix B and on the CD-ROM at the back of this book.

7. Explanation for Limited and Unlimited Personal Releases

The "Grant" paragraph establishes the rights granted by the person. In the unlimited agreement, a "blanket" grant is used. This grant is broad and intended to encompass all potential uses whether informational, commercial or other.

In the limited agreement, the uses must be listed—for example, "for use on a postcard advertising the crafts business." This release also has limitations regarding territory and term. Insert the appropriate geographic region and term—for example, North America with a two-year term.

The release is the person's promise not to sue the company for legal claims such as libel and invasion of privacy.

If the person is a minor, the parent or guardian should sign where it is marked Parent/Guardian Consent.

Since issues about release authenticity often crop up many years after a photo was made, a witness should sign the agreement to verify the person's signature or the signature of the parent. The witness should be an adult. An employee or assistant is suitable.

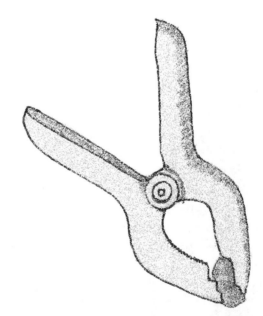

Unlimited Personal Release Agreement

Grant. For consideration which I acknowledge, I irrevocably grant to _____
_____ ("Company")
and Company's assigns, licensees and successors the right to use my image and name in all forms and media, including composite or modified representations, for all purposes, including advertising, trade or any commercial purpose throughout the world and in perpetuity. I waive the right to inspect or approve versions of my image used for publication or the written copy that may be used in connection with the images.

Release. I release Company and Company's assigns, licensees and successors from any claims that may arise regarding the use of my image, including any claims of defamation, invasion of privacy or infringement of moral rights, rights of publicity or copyright. Company is permitted, although not obligated, to include my name as a credit in connection with the image.

Company is not obligated to utilize any of the rights granted in this agreement.

I have read and understood this agreement, and I am over the age of 18. This agreement expresses the complete understanding of the parties.

_____   _____
Signature   Witness Signature

_____
Name

_____
Address

_____

_____
Date

[Include if the person is under 18]

Parent/Guardian Consent. I am the parent or guardian of the minor named above. I have the legal right to consent to and do consent to the terms and conditions of this model release.

_____   _____
Parent/Guardian Signature   Witness Signature

_____
Parent/Guardian Name

_____
Parent/Guardian Address

_____

_____
Date

Limited Personal Release Agreement *[For Specific Uses Only]*

Grant. For consideration which I acknowledge, I grant to _____ ("Company") and Company's assigns, licensees and successors, the right to use my image for the following purposes:

_____

in the following territory _____ for a period of _____ year(s) (the "Term").

I grant the right to use my name and image for the purposes listed above in all forms and media, including composite or modified representations, and waive the right to inspect or approve versions of my image used for publication or the written copy that may be used in connection with the images.

[Select if appropriate]

☐ **Payment.** For the rights granted during the Term, Company shall pay $_____ upon execution of this release.

☐ **Renewal.** Company may renew this agreement under the same terms and conditions for _____ year(s), provided that Licensee makes payment of $_____ at the time of renewal.

Release. I release Company and Company's assigns, licensees and successors from any claims that may arise regarding the use of my image, including any claims of defamation, invasion of privacy or infringement of moral rights, rights of publicity or copyright. Company is permitted, although not obligated, to include my name as a credit in connection with the image.

Company is not obligated to utilize any of the rights granted in this Agreement.

I have read and understood this agreement, and I am over the age of 18. This Agreement expresses the complete understanding of the parties.

_____   _____
Signature   Witness Signature

_____
Name

_____
Address

_____

_____
Date

[Include if the person is under 18]

Parent/Guardian Consent. I am the parent or guardian of the minor named above. I have the legal right to consent to and do consent to the terms and conditions of this model release.

_____   _____
Parent/Guardian Signature   Witness Signature

_____
Parent/Guardian Name

_____
Parent/Guardian Address

_____

_____
Date

Chapter

9

Licensing

7extile designer Rebecca Yaffe (www.
rebeccayaffe.com) creates colorful hand-dyed
and hand-painted fabrics using materials
such as silk charmeuse and silk crepe. For eight and
a half years, she sold clothing made from her fabrics.
In 1999, however, she changed her strategy, stopped
making clothes and sold just the fabrics. Suddenly,
Yaffe found herself thrust into a new market, with
different customers, different competitors and
different trade shows. "I ended up with two types of
new customers: small manufacturers such as clothing
designers and lamp designers, and small fabric
stores."

Yaffe also ended up with a third type of customer—
licensees—companies who wanted to use her designs
on their own products. The first licensee to approach
her was a small decorative paper company. "They
looked at my fabric and saw it translated into decorative paper. They said, 'We want you to design paper
for us for a 5% royalty.'" Yaffe spent an intense week
preparing designs. The company eventually manufactured 20 different versions of her paper.

Later, a subsidiary of a large fabric company asked
for the right to license 16 of Yaffe's designs. This time,
Yaffe received an advance payment (to be deducted
from future royalties). These two forays into licensing
have proven positive, and Yaffe is crossing her fingers
in hopes that bigger licensing deals will come her
way. She has partnered with an experienced textile
businessman who is investigating other licensing
possibilities.

The path to royalty payments is not always so easy.
A licensor like Rebecca Yaffe must negotiate the
license agreement, determine financial terms, examine
and approve the licensed products and develop
personal radar to separate the trustworthy licensees
from the troublesome ones. But the rewards can make
it all worthwhile—for example, years after creating a
design, Yaffe still earns royalty payments. "I recently
had a cool experience in Seattle. I was in a store and
my papers were hanging there. Two and a half years
later and those designs are still making money."

In this chapter I help you grapple with the legal
and business issues of licensing, provide explanations
for all the key provisions of typical license agreements

and provide examples of two agreements—a long
form license agreement and an abbreviated one.

The Artist Is the Licensor; the Manufacturer Is the Licensee

When you license your work, you are the licensor.
The person or company who manufactures your
work is the licensee. In addition to the traditional
crafts artist/manufacturer arrangement, a crafts artist
can also license from another crafts artist. I explain
how that might happen in Section A5, below.

Finding licensing opportunities is beyond the
scope of this chapter. Crafts artists often locate
licensing opportunities by talking to artists in similar
lines, checking classified ads in trade magazines or
exhibiting their work at trade shows (see Chapter 3).
You may also wish to use the services of a licensing rep
(see Chapter 10).

A. Crafts Licensing Overview

When you license your crafts work or design to be
manufactured, the agreement is usually referred to as
a "merchandise license." You may find it crass to
refer to your art as merchandise, but lawyers use this
terminology to distinguish your arrangement from
other licensing arrangements such as invention or
trademark licenses. Merchandise refers to any common
consumer product that has some utility or function,
for example, a T-shirt, ceramic cup or handbag, or
jewelry.

Deciding whether to pursue a licensing opportunity
requires weighing its potential benefits against other
business issues. Is the licensed merchandise the type
you would normally make and sell? Will the licensed
merchandise cut into your existing sales or make current clients unhappy? Will the license provide you with
new opportunities or freedom from manufacturing
and selling? Once you have considered these issues,
you'll be much better prepared to field an offer.

1. How Much Will You Get?

You benefit from licensing because you retain legal ownership of the work—for example, you keep your copyright or design patent—but someone else makes and sells it or something using its image. In return for granting the license, you receive a percentage—known as a royalty—of the profits. In addition, you may receive an advance payment secured by future royalties.

> *Example:* National Jewelers licenses a design from Sarah and pays Sarah an advance of $5,000 against a royalty of 5%. National produces and sells $200,000 worth of the licensed jewelry. Sarah earns $10,000 in royalties, but National deducts $5,000 as compensation for the advance. (In Section B9, below, I'll provide more details on royalties and advances.)

In addition to paying royalties, the licensee must meet obligations set forth in the license agreement governing quality control, timely payments and continuing to offer the merchandise for sale. If the licensee fails to perform according to these obligations, the licensor can terminate the agreement. Termination should not be taken lightly, since it can cause great expense for both parties, including the loss of income for the licensor and the loss of a substantial investment for the licensee.

Royalty rates for merchandise licensing vary depending on the merchandise involved. Below are some royalty estimates:

- greeting cards and gift wrap—2% to 5%
- household items such as cups, sheets, towels—3% to 8%
- fabrics, apparel (T-shirts, caps and so on), decals—2% to 10%
- posters and prints—10% or more.

These royalties are commonly a percentage of net sales—usually the total or "gross" income received, less quantity discounts and customer returns. Some companies, however, may deduct more sums from the income before paying royalties. This makes the allowable deductions virtually as important as the royalty rate in determining how much money ultimately comes your way. For example, a royalty rate of 2% of net sales (as defined above) with no deductions may earn you more than you'd get from a 5% royalty rate from which marketing, shipping, commissions and related expenses are deducted. I'll explain the intricacies of net sales, gross sales and deductions in Section B9, below.

Always Check Out the Licensee

The suggestions we provide about license agreements will help protect your interests—but keep in mind that every agreement is only as solid as the parties who sign it. Make an effort to learn about the licensee. Ask for names of other designers from whom the company has licensed works, and talk to them about their experiences with the company. Find out the company's record regarding payments, credits and other issues that matter to you. Use the Internet to research any articles about the company—for example, check business websites to see if the company has been rated badly or has been the subject of lawsuits. (For information on checking a business's status and rating, see Chapter 3, Section A.)

---

2. You Are Licensing Legal Rights

Under a license agreement, you retain ownership of the legal rights to your crafts but, for a limited time, you "rent" these rights to someone else. That person or company then manufactures and sells the work. The right that you license may be a copyright, design patent, trademark or even trade secret used to create your work. If you have no legal rights, a licensee does not have to obtain your permission or pay you to use the work. In other words, you will have difficulty licensing your work if there are no legal rights to protect in it. For more information on your legal rights, review Chapters 6 to 8.

3. Do You Need an Attorney?

If you're a savvy, confident businessperson capable of reading contracts, you can probably negotiate your own license agreement. Many licensors use an attorney for their first license but proceed on their own with subsequent agreements. Whether you need to use an attorney usually depends on the following factors:

- **The parties.** If the licensee is a large corporation represented by attorneys, you'll probably need the assistance of an attorney.
- **The quality of the license agreement.** You'll have less need for an attorney if the other side provides an easy-to-understand agreement.
- **The work being licensed.** If a company wants to license your best-selling or signature work, you may want to invest in an attorney's help to give that work the extra protection it deserves.
- **Your comfort level.** If legal agreements just make you nervous, you might as well secure some backup and retain a knowledgeable licensing attorney.

For more information on hiring attorneys, review Chapter 11. Even if you use an attorney, you'll save money and increase your licensing awareness by reading this chapter. That way, you won't have to pay the attorney to educate you about the common concepts I describe here.

4. Who Furnishes the License Agreement?

Generally, the licensee drafts, prepares and presents you with the merchandise license agreement. Before it does so, however, the two of you should work out the financial terms—for example, the royalty rate, rights being transferred, length of time the agreement will last and other similar issues. To help you prepare this information, I have included a Merchandise License Worksheet in Section C, below. Use it to keep track of the essential terms of your agreement. Sometimes these terms are included on an exhibit that's attached to the agreement. (Our model agreement includes such an exhibit.)

Prior to signing, but after the terms are agreed upon and the license is furnished, one or both parties may need to ask for changes to the agreement. For example, the licensor may want to modify provisions about sublicensing or dispute resolution. Be prepared to make modifications, to cut and paste provisions or to restructure and reorder the agreement. These types of changes are common.

5. When Crafts Workers Are Licensees

Lori Sandstedt's artfully embellished handbags and colorful bracelets (www.lorimarsha.com) have proven a commercial and critical success (two of her handbag designs were selected as finalists for the 2002 Niche Awards). Sandstedt has no shortage of creative ideas, but when she met a like-minded artist who painted images on tiles, she wondered: What if she could incorporate the other artist's work onto her handbags? Discussions about the project left Sandstedt with many questions. "I wondered what was the right amount to pay for a royalty, and I was also unsure whether royalties were paid on net sales or a percentage of the wholesale price. Do I pay per image used? What if I used more than one image on a handbag? And where can I find a license agreement?"

You'll find the answers to most of Lori Sandstedt's questions in this chapter. In general, if you're licensing someone else's work, you'll need to start by asking:

- How much will it cost per item to manufacture the work?
- How much will it cost to ship it?
- How much commission must you pay to distributors or agents?
- How long will it take you to get the product to market?
- What's your net profit from each item?

Once you know these numbers, you can get a rough idea what offer to make to a potential licensor. Bear in mind that many other variables may play into your offer, such as the fame of the artist or the economics of mass production.

Underlying Lori Sandstedt's questions is another, more philosophical issue: How can a crafts business earn a profit from someone else's work and still maintain integrity and credibility? The key to negotiating any license agreement—whether with a large company or a local artist—is your ability to justify your position and to understand the other party's point of view. To accomplish this, you must do a thorough economic analysis, and you must be flexible in your discussions.

Creativity and flexibility help when negotiating. If you run into an impasse over terms, consider a system that rewards increasing sales—for example, a sliding royalty scale that rises as sales targets are reached. If one party is nervous about the deal, try making the period short—say, one year—with a renewal if sales targets are reached.

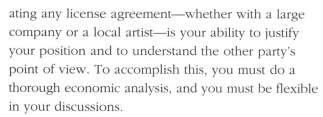

Little People, Big Bucks

How much can a crafts artist earn from licensing? Consider the story of Georgia crafts artist Xavier Roberts. In the 1970s, Roberts created his soft-sculpture "babies" known as "Little People" and dressed them in old clothes found at local yard sales. A year later, Roberts and five college friends created Original Appalachian Artworks and began offering the creations as Cabbage Patch Kids. One unique feature of the Cabbage Patch Kids was that a purchaser "adopted" each creation (adoption papers were included with each sale).

The dolls became popular throughout the southeastern United States. In 1983, representatives of the Coleco toy company entered into a license agreement with Original Appalachian Artworks to manufacture and sell the dolls.

In the two decades since the Coleco deal, Roberts's crafts have generated over $3.2 billion (selling over 90 million dolls). For Appalachian Artworks, licensing has proven to be a successful strategy. When Coleco's license terminated in 1990, Appalachian was able to license to another toy company, Hasbro. Later, in 1995, it licensed to Mattel. In addition, Appalachian Artworks has entered into other license agreements with other companies. For example, it has licensed the right to make Cabbage Patch Kids videos, recordings and other merchandise.

B. Analyzing a License Agreement

In this section I'll analyze the provisions of a standard merchandise license agreement. I'll assume that you, the crafts worker, are the licensor. So when I refer to "you" I am speaking about the person who owns the design and is licensing it to a manufacturer. When I refer to the licensee, I'm referring to the company who will manufacture the design. (Though it's also possible that you may license another crafts worker's work.)

The licensee may furnish a pre-prepared merchandise license agreement. In that case you will need to read and review it, comparing its provisions to the model agreement in this book. Unfortunately, there are no rules for the ordering and placement of provisions in a license agreement. Many agreements seem haphazardly organized. In order to analyze an agreement, be prepared to spend several hours, and follow these steps:

- Make a photocopy of the agreement.
- Locate the major provisions (as discussed below) and, in the margin, label them according to the titles—for example, "grant of rights" or "arbitration." That way, you can find them quickly when making comparisons.
- Compare each provision with the language suggested in this chapter.
- Underline everything in the licensee's version that you don't like or don't understand.
- Prepare a chart listing each provision and your concerns.
- Convert the chart into a response letter detailing your requested changes.

Below I explain the provisions in the long-form merchandise license agreement.

Licenses Compared With Assignments

If you see the word "assign" in the proposed license agreement, watch out. An assignment means that a craft artist is selling legal rights in a work to someone else—for example, if you were to sell your copyright in a fabric design. This is far different from the "rental" arrangement I've been describing. If you assign all your rights in a work, then that's it—you can't reproduce and sell that work any longer. There may be an occasion where an assignment makes sense—for example, sometimes you can assign all rights for the term of the license and they will be assigned back to you after it's over, or you may receive a large sum of money for an assignment. Nevertheless, if the licensee seems to be angling for an assignment, have an attorney review the draft agreement to guarantee that you're not permanently giving up all rights. Alternatives to licensing are discussed elsewhere in this book including assignments (Chapter 8) and work-made-for-hire-agreements (Chapter 5).

A last reminder before you review the agreement. You are the licensor. The manufacturer is the licensee.

The full text of the long and short form merchandise agreements is provided in Appendix B and on the CD-ROM at the back of the book.

1. Introductory Paragraph

The introductory paragraph should identify the people or companies entering into the agreement, known as the "parties." The introductory paragraph may also include the parties' business structure (corporation, sole proprietorship and so on) and business address. Insert that information, if desired, following the name of each party—for example, "Artco Manufacturing, a California corporation located at 434 W. Oakdale Avenue, Los Angeles, California."

Instead of Licensee and Licensor, the agreement can be drafted to use the names of the parties throughout the agreement or terms such as "Artist" for the licensor and "Manufacturer" for the licensee. But once you've chosen to use certain terminology such as this, make sure to use it consistently throughout the agreement.

Sample:

Introduction

This License Agreement (the "Agreement") is made between _____ (referred to as "Licensor") and _____ (referred to as "Licensee").

 The parties agree as follows:

"Whereas" Provisions

In some license agreements, the introductory information is referred to as the "Whereas" provisions. For example, the agreement might read: "Whereas DTK Decorating Company (the licensee) desires to acquire rights." The use of the term "whereas" has no particular legal significance, and I have abandoned it in our model agreements.

---

2. The Work

Your crafts work (the design or crafts work) is referred to as the "Work." Any appropriate term can be substituted instead of "work"—for example, "the Design" or "the Jewelry"—as long as this terminology is used consistently within the agreement. If more than one work is being licensed from the licensor, each work can be identified separately, such as Work #1, Work #2 and so on. You don't need to go into great detail yet—it's customary to do this in the first attachment to the agreement, "Exhibit A." There, you'll describe each work, or, if possible, reference a separate photocopy of the artwork or text that will also be attached to the agreement. (Exhibit A is further described in Section B27, below.)

The Work. The Work refers to the work described in Exhibit A. Licensor is the owner of all rights to the Work, and Licensee shall not claim any right to use the Work except under the terms of this Agreement.

3. The Licensed Product

A licensed product is any merchandise that incorporates the work. If the definition of the product is too narrow, the licensee may be precluded from certain markets. For example, if the licensed product is described as "T-shirts," other shirts like tank tops could not be sold. Similarly, the term "ceramic cups" precludes the sale of plastic cups. If, however, you want to keep the range of potential merchandise narrow, be sure to define your licensed product very specifically. For instance, instead of "upper body apparel," define your licensed product only as "T-shirts." The definitions should be inserted in Exhibit A.

Sample:

Licensed Products. Licensed Products are defined as the Licensee's products incorporating the Work specifically described in Exhibit A (the "Licensed Products").

4. The Grant of Rights

The grant of rights (also known as the "grant") officially permits use of the work, describes the legal rights being licensed and establishes whether the rights are exclusive or nonexclusive. In a merchandise license agreement, the grant must include the following rights:

- **The right to reproduce.** This refers to the right to make copies of the work or merchandise. This is similar to the grant of rights for a regular license agreement that gives the right to make copies on various media such as print or film. This right is essential for the merchandise agreement. Without it, the licensee won't even get to square one. The right to reproduce is not unlimited. The agreement specifically limits it to the use of the material on "Licensed Products." In other words, the artwork can only be used

on specific products as defined in the attached exhibit.

- **The right to distribute copies.** This refers to the right to sell or give away the work.

Reproduction and distribution are closely related and every merchandise license agreement requires both rights. Other rights, however, are optional. Below, I discuss what optional rights may be granted, and the difference between exclusive and nonexclusive rights.

a. Optional Rights

The following rights may be included in a merchandise agreement:

- **The right to adapt or create derivatives.** This refers to the right to modify the work—for example, to alter a design so that only a portion is used. The result of the modification is referred to as a derivative work. If the licensee plans to create a derivative work, the grant of rights must reflect that permission has been granted to modify the original work. The language in the model agreement allows you to own any modifications or contributions the licensee makes to the work. If this language is not included, you and the licensee may become co-authors of any jointly created derivative work—a result you may not desire (for more on co-authorship, see Chapter 8).

- **The right to display publicly.** This refers to the right to publicly exhibit or display a licensed product. Even without acquiring this right in the agreement, the licensee can, under copyright law, display the artwork (as it is included on the merchandise) in connection with advertisements.

b. Exclusive vs. Nonexclusive Rights

Every merchandise license agreement is either exclusive or nonexclusive. Exclusive means that only the licensee will have the rights granted in the agreement —no one else can be given those same rights for as long as the agreement lasts. Nonexclusive means that the owner of the crafts can give the same rights to someone else—for example, two different companies could license your pottery designs. The primary reason a licensee wants exclusive rights is to prevent a competitor from using the same material.

An exclusive license is usually more expensive than a nonexclusive license, but not always. For example, the fee for an exclusive license to use an image on auto seat covers may be the same as a nonexclusive license simply because the seat cover market is limited and there are few manufacturers. However, an exclusive license for T-shirts or calendars may be two or three times the cost of a nonexclusive license.

Sample:

Grant of Rights

Licensor grants to Licensee:

[select one]

☐ an exclusive license

☐ a nonexclusive license

to reproduce and distribute the Work in the Licensed Products.

Licensor grants to Licensee:

[select if appropriate]

☐ the right to modify the Work to incorporate it in the Licensed Products provided that Licensee agrees to assign to Licensor its rights, if any, in any derivative works resulting from Licensee's modification of the Work. Licensee agrees to execute any documents required to evidence this assignment of rights and to waive any moral rights and rights of attribution provided in 17 U.S.C. § 106A of the Copyright Act.

☐ the right to publicly display the Work as incorporated in or on the Licensed Products.

5. Sublicenses

A sublicense allows the licensee to turn around and license its rights to another company. For example, a licensee may want to grant rights to other companies in the United States or in foreign countries, where the licensee is not prepared to play an active role itself. The only problem with sublicensing is that a new company—one with which you had no chance to meet and negotiate—suddenly has the right to make your design. In addition, you may be apprehensive about having your work sublicensed, especially if it's going somewhere where it would be expensive for you to enforce your legal rights. (You can also limit foreign sublicensing by restricting the territory covered by the agreement to a particular country. See Section B7, below.)

The safest route is to give the licensee a very limited right to sublicense rights abroad—one conditioned on you giving your consent to the deal. That way, you can review each sublicense agreement to determine its relative advantages and disadvantages. If you are experienced at selling in foreign markets and can handle foreign licensing yourself, then you will probably want to prohibit foreign sublicensing and retain those rights. The model agreement provides three choices regarding sublicensing. You can either:

- not permit sublicensing
- permit sublicensing only with your written consent, or
- permit sublicensing with your written consent, while stating that your consent cannot be unreasonably withheld. This is the preferred option for most licensees, because it means that you can only withhold consent for a valid business reason.

Sample:

Sublicense

[Select one]

☐ **Consent required.** Licensee may sublicense the rights granted pursuant to this Agreement provided Licensee obtains Licensor's prior written consent to such sublicense, and Licensor receives such revenue or royalty payment as provided in the Payment section below. Any sublicense granted in violation of this provision shall be void.

☐ **Consent to sublicense not unreasonably withheld.** Licensee may sublicense the rights granted pursuant to this Agreement provided Licensee obtains Licensor's prior written consent to such sublicense, and Licensor receives such revenue or royalty payment as provided in the Payment section below. Licensor's consent to any sublicense shall not be unreasonably withheld. Any sublicense granted in violation of this provision shall be void.

☐ **No sublicensing permitted.** Licensee may not sublicense the rights granted under this Agreement.

6. Reservation of Rights

Ordinary contract law says that if you do not grant a specific right, you have retained (also known as "reserved") that right. Although it is makes no legal difference whether you state this fact in your agreement, most licensors prefer to include this statement.

Sample:

Reservation of Rights: Assignment of Good Will. Licensor reserves all rights other than those being conveyed or granted in this Agreement.

7. Territory

You can geographically limit where the licensee can exercise rights, by defining a "territory" in your agreement. If the territory is to be the entire world, insert the word "worldwide" into this section. If the territory is to be a specific region or country, insert that information. As a general rule, restrict the territory to regions where the licensee has previously sold goods with success. If in doubt, simply limit the agreement to North America (the United States and Canada).

Sample:

Territory. The rights granted to Licensee are limited to _____ (the "Territory").

8. Term

By including a Term provision in your agreement, you can limit how long the merchandise license lasts. As a general rule, the licensee wants permission for as long as possible in order to properly develop and exploit the work. You, as the licensor, are likely to prefer a shorter period. That way, if you're not happy with the licensor's performance or you want out for some other reason, you'll have less time to wait before the agreement comes to a natural ending point—for example, one year instead of two or three years.

The date that an agreement commences is usually referred to as the effective date. If the agreement has a fixed date of termination, say in ten years, you would start counting the ten years at the effective date.

Our model agreement prohibits a term that is longer than U.S. copyright or design patent protection would last. This makes sense, because once these legal rights expire, the licensee should not have to pay to use the licensed work while the rest of the world can use it for free.

Even if no time limit is expressed, U.S. copyright law allows you, under some circumstances, to terminate the merchandise license after 35 years. This is true even if the agreement contains a statement that the license is "forever" or "in perpetuity."

Sample:

Term. The "Effective Date" of this Agreement is defined as the date when the Agreement commences and is established by the latest signature date.

☐ **Specified term with renewal rights.** This Agreement shall commence upon the Effective Date and shall extend for a period of _____ years (the "Initial Term"). Following the Initial Term, Licensee may renew this Agreement under the same terms and conditions for _____ consecutive _____ periods (the "Renewal Terms"), provided that Licensee provides written notice of its intention to renew this Agreement within thirty (30) days before the expiration of the current term. In no event shall the Term extend beyond the period of United States copyright protection for the Work and design patent protection, if applicable.

9. Payments

Under your license agreement, you will be paid a royalty, that is, a continuing payment based upon a percentage of the income from the licensed product. In other words, if the merchandise sells well, you'll receive more money. In some cases, a licensee must make payments in advance of royalties (known as "advances") or must pay fixed or "guaranteed minimum annual royalty" payments (see below) regardless of sales. In other words, money and time may be spent even if the licensed product is not successful. Below are definitions of some royalty terms you might need to use.

- **Gross sales** refers to the total amount billed to customers. **Net sales** are usually defined as the licensee's gross sales minus certain deductions. In other words, the licensee calculates the total amount billed to customers and deducts certain items before paying the royalty. It is generally acceptable to deduct from gross sales any amounts paid for taxes, credits, returns and discounts made at the time of sale. It is also common to deduct shipping (the cost of getting the products to the buyer).

- An **advance against royalties** is an up-front payment to you, usually made at the time the license agreement is signed. An advance is almost always credited or "recouped" against future royalties, unless the agreement provides otherwise. It's as if the licensee is saying, "I expect you will earn at least $1,000 in royalties, so I am going to advance you that sum at the time I sign the agreement." When you start earning royalties, the licensee keeps the first $1,000 to repay the advance. If the licensor doesn't earn the $1,000 in royalties, the licensee takes a loss. You don't have to return the advance unless you breach the agreement.

- A **percentage of net sales** (the licensed product royalty) is the most common form of licensing payment. Net sales royalty payments are computed by multiplying the royalty rate against net sales. For example, a royalty rate of 5% multiplied by net sales of $1,000 equals a net sales royalty of $50. Estimates of merchandise royalties are provided in Section A1, above.

- A **per unit royalty** is tied to the number of units sold or manufactured, not to the total money earned by sales. For example, under a per unit royalty you might receive $.50 for each licensed product sold or manufactured. The licensee cannot choose both per unit and net sales royalties. If the licensee intends to license your work for a free distribution, for example, giving out hundreds of the products at a promotion, check the "manufactured" box. If the licensee will be offering your work for sale (not for free), check the "sold" box. Generally, net sales royalties are preferred over per unit royalties because revenue may come from sources such as sublicensing, in which case the total net sales will be easier to track.

- A **guaranteed minimum annual royalty payment** (GMAR) is when the licensee promises that you'll receive a specific payment every year, regardless of how well the merchandise sells during each year. The licensee pays the GMAR at the beginning of the year. At the end of that year, if the earned royalties exceed the GMAR, you're paid the difference. If the GMAR exceeds the earned royalties, the licensee takes a loss. To avoid taking the loss, a licensee may insist that the agreement contain a clause stating that this difference will be carried forward and deducted against the next year's royalties. Also don't be surprised if the licensee wants to limit the initial term of the agreement. Otherwise, the licensee risks being locked into paying GMARs when the merchandise is not selling at all.

- On rare occasions, a licensee may pay you a **one-time license fee** at the time of signing the agreement. This fee differs from an advance, because it is not deducted from royalties. The licensee may arrange to make the payment when the licensed product is first distributed. That way, if the licensed product is not produced, the licensee does not have to pay.

- If the license agreement permits **sublicensing**, keep the provision for sublicensing revenue in the agreement. (See the section of the Agreement entitled "Sublicensing.")

Sample:

Payments. All royalties ("Royalties") provided for under this Agreement shall accrue when the respective Licensed Products are sold, shipped, distributed, billed or paid for, whichever occurs first.

Net Sales. Net Sales are defined as Licensee's gross sales (that is, the gross invoice amount billed customers) less quantity discounts or rebates and returns actually credited. A quantity discount or rebate is a discount made at the time of shipment. No deductions shall be made for cash or other discounts, commissions, manufacturing costs or uncollectible accounts, or for fees or expenses of any kind that the Licensee may incur in connection with the Royalty payments.

Fees

[Select one or more provisions]

☐ **Advance Against Royalties.** As a nonrefundable advance against Royalties (the "Advance"), Licensee agrees to pay to Licensor upon execution of this Agreement the sum of $_____.

☐ **Licensed Product Royalty.** Licensee agrees to pay a Royalty of ___% percent of all Net Sales revenue of the Licensed Products ("Licensed Product Royalty").

☐ **Per Unit Royalty.** Licensee agrees to pay a Royalty of $_____ for each unit of the Licensed Product that is: *[select one]*
　☐ manufactured.
　☐ sold.

☐ **Guaranteed Minimum Annual Royalty Payment.** In addition to any other advances or fees, Licensee shall pay an annual guaranteed royalty (the "GMAR") as follows: $_____. The GMAR shall be paid to Licensor annually on _____. The GMAR is an advance against royalties for the twelve-month period commencing upon payment. Royalty payments based on Net Sales made during any year of this Agreement shall be credited against the GMAR due for the year in which such Net Sales were made. In the event that annual royalties exceed the GMAR, Licensee shall pay the difference to Licensor. Any annual royalty payments in excess of the GMAR shall not be carried forward from previous years or applied against the GMAR.

☐ **License Fee.** As a nonrefundable, nonrecoupable fee for executing this license, Licensee agrees to pay to Licensor upon execution of this Agreement the sum of $_____.

☐ **Sublicensing Revenues.** In the event of any sublicense of the rights granted pursuant to this Agreement, Licensee shall pay to Licensor _____% of all sublicensing revenues.

Payments and Statements to Licensor. Within thirty (30) days after the end of each calendar quarter (the "Royalty Period"), an accurate statement of Net Sales of Licensed Products along with any royalty payments or sublicensing revenues due to Licensor shall be provided to Licensor, regardless of whether any Licensed Products were sold during the Royalty Period. All payments shall be paid in United States currency drawn on a United States bank. The acceptance by Licensor of any of the statements furnished or royalties paid shall not preclude Licensor questioning the correctness at any time of any payments or statements.

10. Audits

In case one day you suspect that the licensee has failed to properly pay royalties, you'll want the right to perform an audit to detect and quantify the shortfall. The Audit provision describes when you (or your representative) can access licensee records. If the audit uncovers an error of a certain magnitude—usually a sum between $500 and $2,000—the licensee will have to not only compensate you for the shortfall, but pay for the audit, as well. Insert an amount in the blank space. If the audited sum is lower than this amount, you are the one who will have to pay for the audit.

Sample:

Audit. Licensee shall keep accurate books of accounts and records covering all transactions relating to the license granted in this Agreement, and Licensor or its duly authorized representatives shall have the right, upon five days' prior written notice and during normal business hours, to inspect and audit Licensee's records relating to the Work licensed under this Agreement. Licensor shall bear the cost of such inspection and audit, unless the results indicate an underpayment greater than $_____ for any six-month (6-month) period. In that case, Licensee shall promptly reimburse Licensor for all costs of the audit along with the amount due with interest on such sums. Interest shall accrue from the date the payment was originally due, and the interest rate shall be 1.5% per month, or the maximum rate permitted by law, whichever is less. All books of account and records shall be made available in the United States and kept available for at least two years after the termination of this Agreement.

Late Payment. Time is of the essence with respect to all payments to be made by Licensee under this Agreement. If Licensee is late in any payment provided for in this Agreement, Licensee shall pay interest on the payment from the date due until paid at a rate of 1.5% per month, or the maximum rate permitted by law, whichever is less.

11. Warranties and Indemnity

Warranties are contractual promises that you and the licensor will make, as explained further in subsection a, below. If you break one of these promises, you will—under the indemnity provision—have to pay for any costs that result. (The same will be true for the licensor.) In this way, warranties and indemnity work together. Indemnities are discussed in more detail in subsection b, below.

A merchandise license can also be written without including warranties or indemnity provisions. They are recommended, but not essential for the agreement.

a. Warranties

In some agreements, warranties are labeled as "covenants" or "representations." Regardless of the title, they are essentially the same things—promises made between the parties. For example, you might promise that you own the rights in the crafts product and that the crafts work doesn't infringe third-party rights. (Third parties are people who are not part of the agreement.) In case you feel uncomfortable making this kind of assurance, the model agreement provides a more palatable warranty, stating that you have "no knowledge as to any third-party claims." In other words, you recognize the remote possibility that the crafts work may infringe someone's copyright, but you—after performing a reasonable investigation—don't have any knowledge that it does.

You should ask that the licensee provide a warranty that sales and marketing of the licensed product will conform to applicable laws. A sample provision is included in the model merchandise agreement.

If an agreement includes a warranty but not an indemnity provision, the parties can still sue for "breach of warranty." However, you would have to go to court to for a decision on whether the breaching party must pay the costs or attorney fees associated with the breach.

Sample:

Licensor Warranties. Licensor warrants that it has the power and authority to enter into this Agreement and has no knowledge as to any third-party claims regarding the proprietary rights in the Work that would interfere with the rights granted under this Agreement.

Licensee Warranties. Licensee warrants that it will use its best commercial efforts to market the Licensed Products and that their sale and marketing shall be in conformance with all applicable laws and regulations, including but not limited to all intellectual property laws.

b. Indemnity

Indemnity is recommended, but is not essential for the agreement. A licensor who provides indemnity is agreeing to pay for the licensee's damages in certain situations. For example, if you indemnify the licensee against infringement, you will have to pay damages (and legal fees) if the licensee is sued by a company claiming that your work is a copy of its work. In this way, indemnity acts like a powerful shield. The licensee can deflect a lawsuit and make you pay for the damages and legal fees. Indemnity provisions are also sometimes referred to as "hold harmless" provisions, because the language for an indemnity provision often states that the "Licensor shall hold the Licensee harmless from any losses, and so on".

If possible, you should avoid indemnity, as it means taking on a legal obligation to pay someone else's legal costs. If a licensee is insistent, however, you may have to agree to this provision. But hold firm on insisting that the amount not be larger than any amounts you have received under the agreement.

In some cases, you may insist on establishing an indemnity fund. With such a fund, if indemnity is triggered, the licensee stops paying you royalties and places these payments into the fund. This deprives you of ongoing royalty payments but prevents you from having to pay out any additional money for indemnity. You may also request that the licensee provide you with indemnification as well. Indemnification would protect you from any third-party claims arising from illegal licensee business practices or from any additions or modifications that the licensee makes to your design.

Sample:

Indemnification by Licensor

[Select one if appropriate]

☐ **Licensor indemnification without limitations.** Licensor shall indemnify Licensee and hold Licensee harmless from any damages and liabilities (including reasonable attorney fees and costs) arising from any breach of Licensor's warranties as defined in Licensor's Warranties, above.

☐ **Licensor indemnification limited to amounts paid.** Licensor shall indemnify Licensee and hold Licensee harmless from any damages and liabilities (including reasonable attorney fees and costs) arising from any breach of Licensor's warranties as defined in Licensor's Warranties, above. Licensor's maximum liability under this provision shall in no event exceed the total amount earned by Licensor under this Agreement.

☐ **Licensor indemnification with limitations.** Licensor shall indemnify Licensee and hold Licensee harmless from any damages and liabilities (including reasonable attorney fees and costs) arising from any breach of Licensor's warranties as defined in Licensor's Warranties, above, provided:

(a) such claim, if sustained, would prevent Licensee from marketing the Licensed Products or the Work

(b) such claim arises solely out of the Work as disclosed to the Licensee, and not out of any change in the Work made by Licensee or a vendor

(c) Licensee gives Licensor prompt written notice of any such claim

(d) such indemnity shall only be applicable in the event of a final decision by a court of competent jurisdiction from which no right to appeal exists and

(e) the maximum amount due from Licensor to Licensee under this paragraph shall not exceed the amounts due to Licensor under the Payment section from the date that Licensor notifies Licensee of the existence of such a claim.

Indemnification by Licensee. Licensee shall indemnify Licensor and hold Licensor harmless from any damages and liabilities (including reasonable attorney fees and costs):

(a) arising from any breach of Licensee's warranties and representation as defined in the Licensee Warranties, above

(b) arising out of any alleged defects or failures to perform of the Licensed Products or any product liability claims or use of the Licensed Products, and

(c) arising out of advertising, distribution or marketing of the Licensed Products.

12. Intellectual Property Rights

If you have not filed a copyright registration or a design patent covering your work and do not plan to, the licensee may register for protection under this provision. For information about copyright registration, consult the Copyright Office website at www.copyright.gov. It is common for the licensee to deduct the reasonable costs of registration from future royalties.

Sample:

Intellectual Property Registration. Licensor may, but is not obligated to, seek in its own name and at its own expense appropriate copyright registrations or design patent registrations for the Work, if applicable. Licensor makes no warranty with respect to the validity of any copyright or design patent that may be granted. Licensor grants to Licensee the right to apply for registration of the Work or Licensed Products provided that such registrations shall be applied for in the name of Licensor and licensed to Licensee during the Term and according to the conditions of this Agreement. Licensee shall have the right to deduct its reasonable out-of-pocket expenses for the preparation and filing of any such registrations from future royalties due to Licensor under this Agreement. Licensee shall obtain Licensor's prior written consent before incurring expenses for any foreign copyright or design patent applications.

Compliance With Intellectual Property Laws. The license granted in this Agreement is conditioned on Licensee's compliance with the provisions of the intellectual property laws of the United States and any foreign country in the Territory. All copies of the Licensed Product as well as all promotional material shall bear appropriate proprietary notices.

13. Credits

The Credit provision allows you to advise the licensee of any credit you want to appear on the merchandise. For instance, if I wanted to be credited for a photograph I was licensing, I would insert the following desired credit line:

© 2002 Rich Stim

The licensee's failure to include the credit could provide a basis for termination. The Credit section also provides the licensee with the right to use the licensor's name and trademark in advertising for the merchandised product. If you are an established crafts artist, the licensee will have a strong motivation to use your name (and maybe your image) in advertising and promotional materials.

Sample:

Licensor Credits. Licensee shall identify Licensor as the owner of rights to the Work and shall include the following notice on all copies of the Licensed Products: "[copyright] _____. All rights reserved." Licensee may, with Licensor's consent, use Licensor's name, image or trademark in advertising or promotional materials associated with the sale of the Licensed Products.

14. Infringement by Third Parties

Imitation may be a form of flattery, but it's also a form of infringement. Unethical competitors often create imitations of successful licensed products. If you do not have the money to fight an infringer, this provision allows the licensee to sue or settle with infringers. It provides for funding of a lawsuit and for determining how to divide any money that is recovered from the infringer. The provision in our model agreement establishes a 50/50 division of any award money after payment of attorney fees.

Sample:

Infringement by Third Parties. In the event that either party learns of imitations or infringements of the Work or Licensed Products, that party shall notify the other in writing of the infringements or imitations. Licensor shall have the right to commence lawsuits against third persons arising from infringement of the Work or Licensed Products. In the event that Licensor does not commence a lawsuit against an alleged infringer within sixty (60) days of notification by Licensee, Licensee may commence a lawsuit against the third party. Before filing suit, Licensee shall obtain the written consent of Licensor to do so, and such consent shall not be unreasonably withheld. Licensor will cooperate fully and in good faith with Licensee for the purpose of securing and preserving Licensee's rights to the Work. Any recovery (including, but not limited to, a judgment, settlement or license agreement included as resolution of an infringement dispute) shall be divided equally between the parties after deduction and payment of reasonable attorney fees to the party bringing the lawsuit.

15. Exploitation

When it comes to licensing your work, exploitation is a good thing. You want to be sure that the licensee won't simply sit on your work, which would prevent you from earning the royalties you're anticipating. If your agreement is an exclusive one, inaction by the licensee would be doubly frustrating, since you would be unable to license the product to anyone else. The exploitation provision addresses these concerns by setting a date by which the licensee must release the licensed product. Sometimes the release date is set to coincide with a specific trade show or a seasonal catalog. If the licensee fails to meet this date, you can claim that there has been a "material breach," which is a basis for termination of the license agreement.

Sample:

Exploitation Date. Licensee agrees to manufacture, distribute and sell the Licensed Products in commercially reasonable quantities during the term of this Agreement and to commence such manufacture, distribution and sale by _____ [*date*]. This is a material provision of this Agreement.

16. Approval of Samples and Quality Control

This provision gives you the right to look at and approve samples and prototypes of the artwork before it goes into full production. The provision gives the licensee an incentive to reproduce your work properly—and it prevents nasty surprises. If

you have the clout and bargaining power, you may expand this provision to give you a right to inspect the manufacturing facilities and to reject any subcontracting manufacturing if their standards are insufficient.

Sample:

Approval of Samples and Quality Control. Licensee shall submit a reasonable number of preproduction designs, prototypes, and camera-ready artwork prior to production, as well as pre-production samples of the Licensed Product to Licensor, to assure that the product meets Licensor's quality standards. In the event that Licensor fails to object in writing within ten (10) business days after the date of receipt of any such materials, such materials shall be deemed to be acceptable. At least once during each calendar year, Licensee shall submit two (2) production samples of each Licensed Product for review. Licensee shall pay all costs for delivery of these approval materials. The quality standards applied by Licensor shall be no more rigorous than the quality standards applied by Licensor to similar products.

17. Licensor Copies and Right to Purchase

You will probably want some free copies of the licensed product, for yourself and your close friends and relatives. This provision allows you and the licensee to specify how many you'll receive. The number you agree upon will probably depend on the value of the product and the size of the market—obviously, the licensee doesn't want you to undercut his profits by playing Santa Claus. If you think your generosity will exceed the number of free copies, you can negotiate for the right to purchase more product at the wholesale cost.

Sample:

Licensor Copies and Right to Purchase. Licensee shall provide Licensor with _____ copies of each Licensed Product. Licensor has the right to purchase from Licensee, at Licensee's manufacturing cost, at least _____ copies of any Licensed Product, and such payments shall be deducted from Royalties due to Licensor.

18. Confidentiality

Though it may seem obvious that your discussions are confidential, you'd be surprised at how easy it is for you—or the other party—to forget this and disclose confidential information provided by one party. When you're deep in a conversation with your friend, hairdresser or mechanic, it may seem so natural to say, "This company I'm dealing with is planning to expand into the fabric business." You've now revealed potentially important facts about the condition of the other party's business. Confidential information includes any information that gives a business an advantage and is maintained in confidence.

The Confidentiality clause below reminds each party to preserve the other's confidential information —and allows each to sue for breach of contract if the other slips up.

Sample:

Confidentiality. The parties acknowledge that each may have access to confidential information that relates to each other's business (the "Information"). The parties agree to protect the confidentiality of the Information and maintain it with the strictest confidence, and no party shall disclose such information to third parties without the prior written consent of the other.

19. Insurance

Those patterned mugs may look innocent now, sitting on the shelf. But you should never underestimate the capacity of consumers to use products in a way that injures them—and then blame someone else for it. If a consumer is injured using the licensed product and claims it's defective, you and the licensee can be sued under a legal theory called "product liability."

For these reasons, you want to make sure that the licensee, as the one who'll be selling the merchandise, acquires product liability insurance. The first benefit of such insurance is that the insurance company—not you or the licensee—will have to defend the claim. That's a significant benefit, because legal fees can add up quickly, even in a case that you ultimately win. In addition, by requiring that the licensee name you in the policy, you will be shielded from paying damages in the event that a customer wins a product injury claim. The minimum amount of coverage inserted for the policy should be $1,000,000.

⚠ **Product liability insurance doesn't usually cover trademark, patent or copyright lawsuits.** The licensee needs a separate business policy for protection against infringement claims.

Sample:

Insurance. Licensee shall, throughout the Term, obtain and maintain, at its own expense, standard product liability insurance coverage, naming Licensor as an additional named insured. Such policy shall provide protection against any claims, demands and causes of action arising out of any alleged defects or failure to perform of the Licensed Products or any use of the Licensed Products. The amount of coverage shall be a minimum of $_____, with no deductible amount for each single occurrence for bodily injury or property damage. The policy shall provide for notice to the Licensor from the insurer by registered or certified mail in the event of any modification or termination of insurance. The provisions of this section shall survive termination for _____ years.

20. Termination

Even without a termination provision, either party can terminate a merchandise license agreement if the other party commits a "material breach." A material breach means a substantial abuse of the agreement— for example, if the licensee uses the crafts work for purposes not described in the agreement.

Most licensors will insist upon a written termination provision and will seek some or all of the rights listed in our model agreement, including the right to terminate as to a specific portion of the territory if it is not exploited.

Sample:

Licensor's Right to Terminate. Licensor shall have the right to terminate this Agreement for the following reasons:

[Select one or more provisions]

☐ **Failure to make timely payment.** Licensee fails to pay Royalties when due or fails to accurately report Net Sales, as defined in the Payment section of this Agreement, and such failure is not cured within thirty (30) days after written notice from the Licensor.

☐ **Failure to introduce product.** Licensee fails to introduce the product to market by the date set in the Exploitation section of this Agreement or to offer the Licensed Products in commercially reasonable quantities during any subsequent year.

☐ **Assignment or sublicensing.** Licensee assigns or sublicenses in violation of this Agreement.

☐ **Failure to maintain insurance.** Licensee fails to maintain or obtain product liability insurance as required by the provisions of this Agreement.

☐ **Failure to submit samples.** Licensee fails to provide Licensor with preproduction samples for approval.

☐ **Termination as to unexploited portion of territory.** Licensor shall have the right to terminate the grant of license under this Agreement with respect to any country or region included in the Territory in which Licensee fails to offer the Licensed Products for sale or distribution or to secure a sublicense agreement for the marketing, distribution and sale of the product within two (2) years of the Effective Date.

21. Effect of Termination

If the licensee breaches the agreement for any of the reasons provided under "Licensor's Right to Terminate"—for example, the licensee stops paying you royalties—the licensee should not be permitted to continue profiting from your art by selling off inventory. If the agreement has expired or ended amicably, however, it's reasonable to permit the licensee to sell off the remaining inventory during a fixed time period, say six months. Naturally, the licensee must also pay royalties and provide an accounting for these products.

Sample:

Effect of Termination. Upon termination of this Agreement ("Termination"), all Royalty obligations as established in the Payments section shall immediately become due. After the Termination of this license, all rights granted to Licensee under this Agreement shall terminate and revert to Licensor, and Licensee will refrain from further manufacturing, copying, marketing, distribution or use of any Licensed Product or other product that incorporates the Work. Within thirty (30) days after Termination, Licensee shall deliver to Licensor a statement indicating the number and description of the Licensed Products that it had on hand or is in the process of manufacturing as of the Termination date.

Sell-Off Period. Licensee may dispose of the Licensed Products covered by this Agreement for a period of ninety (90) days after Termination or expiration, except that Licensee shall have no such right in the event this agreement is terminated according to the Licensor's Right to Terminate, above. At the end of the post-Termination sale period, Licensee shall furnish a royalty payment and statement as required under the Payment section. Upon termination, Licensee shall deliver to Licensor all original artwork and camera-ready reproductions used in the manufacture of the Licensed Products. Licensor shall bear the costs of shipping for the artwork and reproductions.

22. Dispute Resolution

To avoid the high costs associated with formal court trials, many contracts now commit the parties to trying alternative methods of resolving their disputes first. Your two main choices are arbitration and mediation.

With arbitration, the parties hire one or more arbitrators—experts at resolving disputes—to evaluate the dispute and make a determination. Even if neither party is entirely happy with the arbitrator's decision, they have to live with it—that's why it's often called "binding arbitration." With mediation, a neutral evaluator helps the parties settle their dispute themselves. That is, the mediator offers advice so that the parties can reach a solution together, but doesn't interject his or her own solution. Mediation and arbitration are referred to as alternative dispute resolution or ADR.

The model agreement includes two alternative dispute resolution provisions. The second is only for arbitration. The first provides for mediation first, then for arbitration if mediation fails. (For a discussion of the pros and cons of arbitration, see Chapter 11.)

Sample:

Dispute Resolution

[Select one if appropriate]

☐ **Mediation and Arbitration.** The parties agree that every dispute or difference between them arising under this Agreement shall be settled first by a meeting of the parties attempting to confer and resolve the dispute in a good faith manner. If the parties cannot resolve their dispute after conferring, any Party may require the other Party to submit the matter to nonbinding mediation, utilizing the services of an impartial professional mediator approved by all parties. If the parties cannot come to an agreement following mediation, the parties agree to submit the matter to binding arbitration at a location mutually agreeable to the parties. The arbitration shall be conducted on a confidential basis pursuant to the Commercial Arbitration Rules of the American Arbitration Association. Any decision or award as a result of any such arbitration proceeding shall include an assessment of costs, expenses and reasonable attorney's fees and shall include a written record of the proceedings and a written determination of the arbitrators. An arbitrator experienced in _____ law shall conduct any such arbitration. An award of arbitration shall be final and binding on the parties and may be confirmed in a court of competent jurisdiction.

☐ **Arbitration.** If a dispute arises under or relating to this Agreement, the parties agree to submit such dispute to binding arbitration in the state of _____ or another location mutually agreeable to the parties. The arbitration shall be conducted on a confidential basis pursuant to the Commercial Arbitration Rules of the American Arbitration Association. Any decision or award as a result of any such arbitration proceeding shall be in writing and shall provide an explanation for all conclusions of law and fact and shall include an assessment of costs, expenses and reasonable attorney fees. An arbitrator experienced in licensing law shall conduct any such arbitration. An award of arbitration may be confirmed in a court of competent jurisdiction.

23. No Special Damages

If either party breaches the agreement, state laws provide that the nonbreaching party can recover the amount of the loss directly resulting from the breach. For example, if the licensee fails to accurately pay royalties, you can sue to recover the unpaid amount, along with attorney fees if the agreement provides for such fees (see Section C22, above). However, under some state laws, claims may be made for additional damages—for example, special or punitive damages that are awarded to punish the breaching party. These are sometimes double or triple the amount of damage that the nonbreaching party actually suffered. If you and the other party agree that you don't want to expose each other to this level of risk, you can insert a No Special Damages provision into your agreement. This provision prevents either party from claiming any damages other than those actually suffered directly from the breach.

Sample:

No Special Damages. Licensor shall not be liable to Licensee for any incidental, consequential, punitive or special damages.

24. Miscellaneous Provisions

Many agreements contain provisions entitled "Miscellaneous" or "General." These provisions actually have little in common with one another except for the fact that they don't fit anywhere else in the agreement. They're contract orphans and for that reason are usually dumped at the end of the agreement. Lawyers often refer to these provisions as "boilerplate." Don't be misled by the fact that boilerplate is buried at the back of the agreement. You'll be turning straight to that page if you're in the middle of a dispute with the licensee and need to know the procedures for resolving the dispute and how a court will enforce the agreement.

Even though the Miscellaneous and General provisions are important, they are not mandatory. In other words, if you and the licensee agree to leave them out, you can do so without affecting the validity of the remaining agreement. Below is a summary of common boilerplate provisions.

a. Entire Agreement

The Entire Agreement provision (sometimes referred to as the "Integration" provision) establishes that the agreement is the final version and that any further modification must be in writing. It prevents parties from later claiming, "But you told me such-and-such."

Sample:

Entire Agreement. This is the entire agreement between the parties. It replaces and supersedes any and all oral agreements between the parties, as well as any prior writings. Modifications and amendments to this Agreement, including any exhibit or appendix hereto, shall be enforceable only if they are in writing and are signed by authorized representatives of both parties.

b. Successors and Assigns

In the event the agreement is assigned, or another company succeeds one of the parties—for example, a company buys the licensee—this provision assures that the acquiring party is bound by the Agreement.

Sample:

Successors and Assignees:
This Agreement binds and benefits the heirs, successors and assignees of the parties.

c. Notices

The Notices provision tells each party how to alert the other one if a dispute arises. If a party fails to follow these notice procedures, he or she won't get very far toward resolving the dispute until proper notification has been provided.

Sample:

Notices. Any notice or communication required or permitted to be given under this Agreement shall be sufficiently given when received by certified mail, or sent by facsimile transmission or overnight courier.

d. Governing Law

Every state has its own laws regarding contract interpretation. Though you might assume that the laws of the state in which you're currently sitting will govern your license agreement, that's not necessarily so. Parties in disputes over past contracts have been known to look around for states with laws that work to their advantage and argue that the other state's law applies. You can avoid this shopping around game by inserting a simple provision—sometimes called a "Choice of Law" provision—stating which state's law will govern any lawsuit. Does it matter which state is chosen? Some states have a reputation for being better for certain kinds of disputes, but, generally, the differences between states' laws are not great enough to make this a major negotiating issue.

Sample:

Governing Law. This Agreement will be governed by the laws of the State of _____.

e. Waiver

A Waiver provision permits the parties to forego or give up claim to a portion of the agreement without establishing a precedent for themselves. In other words, you don't have to enforce every part of the agreement every time you possibly could in order to keep it alive. For example, if you accept late royalty payments for two months (thereby waiving the portion of the contract that requires timely royalty payments), the Waiver provision says that you haven't established a precedent allowing late royalty payments.

Sample:

Waiver. The failure to exercise any right provided in this Agreement shall not be a waiver of prior or subsequent rights.

f. Severability

This provision (sometimes referred to as the "Invalidity" provision) permits a court to sever (or take out) a portion of the agreement that's no longer good while keeping the rest of the agreement intact. Otherwise, if one portion of the agreement becomes invalid, a court may rule that the whole agreement has been dragged down into invalidity along with it.

Sample:

Severability. If a court finds any provision of this Agreement invalid or unenforceable, the remainder of this Agreement will be interpreted so as best to carry out the parties' intent.

g. Attachments

The Attachment provision guarantees that any attachments (documents sometimes referred to as "exhibits," which are attached to the agreement) will be included as part of the agreement.

Sample:

Attachments and Exhibits. The parties agree and acknowledge that all attachments, exhibits and schedules referred to in this Agreement are incorporated in this Agreement by reference.

h. No Agency

The relationship between you and the licensee is defined by the agreement. But to an outsider, it may appear that you have a different relationship, such as a partnership or joint venture. It's possible that an unscrupulous licensee will try to capitalize on this appearance and make a third-party deal. If that deal goes bad, you could find the third party coming to you to put matters right. In order to avoid liability for such a situation, most agreements include a provision disclaiming any relationship other than licensee/licensor.

Sample:

No Agency. Nothing contained herein will be construed as creating any agency, partnership, joint venture or other form of joint enterprise between the parties.

i. Attorney Fees

The Attorney Fees provision establishes that the winner of a legal dispute receives payment for legal fees. Without this optional provision, each party has to pay its own attorney fees.

Sample:

Attorney Fees and Expenses. The prevailing party shall have the right to collect from the other party its reasonable costs and necessary disbursements and attorney fees incurred in enforcing this Agreement.

j. Jurisdiction and Venue

In the event of a dispute, the Jurisdiction and Venue provision establishes which state and county the lawsuit or arbitration must be filed and heard in. Of course, each party will prefer going to court in its home county. Therefore, this section is optional and a matter of negotiation. If the section creates too much contention, remove it. In disputes over contracts that contain no reference to jurisdiction, the location is usually determined by whoever files the lawsuit. If a jurisdiction clause is used, it should list the same state as named in the Governing Law section (discussed in subsection d, above).

Sample:

Jurisdiction. The parties consent to the exclusive jurisdiction and venue of the federal and state courts located in _____ [*county*], _____ [*state*], in any action arising out of or relating to this Agreement. The parties waive any other venue to which either party might be entitled by domicile or otherwise.

In Some States, Jurisdiction Clauses Are Invalid

In the past, many courts believed that citizens should not be able to bargain for jurisdiction (sometimes referred to as forum shopping), and these courts would not enforce jurisdiction provisions. Today, only three states—Alabama, Idaho and Montana—refuse to honor jurisdiction provisions in agreements.

25. Assignability

Although you might think of your agreement as being between you and the licensee alone, that's not always the way business works. It is possible that the licensee may, at some point, wish to transfer the rights under your agreement to another company. Normal contract law allows her to do this by "assigning" her rights to a third party—unless you insert a provision to stop or control this.

For example, let's imagine that the licensee has two agreements with you: one to license your earring design and the other to license your bracelet design. The licensee later decides it only wants to concentrate on earrings. It wants to assign its rights in the bracelet design to a company that specializes in bracelet merchandising. You may—or may not—be happy with the change. For example, if the new company has a bad reputation when it comes to paying royalties, you're likely to regard this as a disaster. For this reason, our model agreement provides three choices regarding assignability.

The first option requires that your written consent be given for an assignment. Under this option, you can review the deal and decide, for any reason, that you don't like the assignment and won't have it.

The second choice also requires your written consent, but you must not refuse it without having a valid business reason. A valid business reason usually means an actual and substantial business risk—for example, the new company has a negative financial rating.

The third provision permits a transfer without your consent, so long as the new party is a company purchasing the licensee's business. Some licensees insist on this provision because they want the freedom to sell the whole company (and its license agreements).

Sample:

Assignability

[Select one]

☐ **Assignment requires licensor consent.** Licensee may not assign or transfer its rights or obligations pursuant to this Agreement without the prior written consent of Licensor. Any assignment or transfer in violation of this section shall be void.

☐ **Licensor consent not unreasonably withheld.** Licensee may not assign or transfer its rights or obligations pursuant to this Agreement without the prior written consent of Licensor. Such consent shall not be unreasonably withheld. Any assignment or transfer in violation of this section shall be void.

☐ **Licensor consent not required for assignment to parent or acquiring company.** Licensee may not assign or transfer its rights or obligations pursuant to this Agreement without the prior written consent of Licensor. However, no consent is required for an assignment or transfer that occurs: (a) to an entity in which Licensee owns more than fifty percent of the assets, or (b) as part of a transfer of all or substantially all of the assets of Licensee to any party. Any assignment or transfer in violation of this section shall be void.

26. Signatures

Each party must sign the agreement. If individuals are signing on behalf of a company, then the people who sign must have the authority to do so. Use the rules expressed in Chapter 11 to determine how the agreement should be signed.

Sample:

Signatures. Each party represents and warrants that on this date they are duly authorized to bind their respective principals by their signatures below.

By: _____

Date: _____

Licensor Name: _____

By: _____

Date: _____

Licensee Name/Title: _____

27. Exhibit A

Agreements often have attachments known as "exhibits," which are stapled to the agreement. In license agreements, the exhibit summarizes some of the essential business elements. For example, in the model agreement, Exhibit A includes a description of the work, the licensed product and, if applicable, the sales minimum required to renew the agreement. One important advantage of using an exhibit is that if you are dealing with multiple licensees or if you are licensing more than one item to one licensee, you may be able to keep the body of the agreement the same and only change the exhibit.

Sample:

Exhibit A

The Property _____

Licensed Products _____

Sales Requirements:
$_____ in Gross Sales per year.

28. Right of First Refusal

Some merchandise agreements include a provision known as a right of first refusal. Its purpose is to give the licensee the first shot at licensing any new works from you. For example, if you previously licensed a series of crockpot designs, the licensee will want the first opportunity to license your new designs. If another company makes a better offer than the licensee, this provision gives the licensee a period of time to match the offer.

Sample:

Right of First Refusal
Licensor may identify and develop new works suitable to be used as Licensed Products ("New Works"). Licensee shall have the first right to license such New Works, and the parties shall negotiate in good faith to reach agreement as to the terms and conditions for such license. In the event that the parties fail to reach agree-

ment and Licensor receives an offer from a third party for the New Works, Licensee shall have 30 days to notify Licensor whether Licensee desires to execute a license on similar terms and conditions. In the event that Licensee matches any third-party terms and conditions, Licensor shall enter into a License Agreement with Licensee and terminate negotiations with any third parties.

The full text of the long form merchandise agreement is provided in Appendix B and on the CD-ROM at the back of this book.

C. Licensing Worksheet

I've provided this Merchandise License Worksheet to help you keep track of the elements in your merchandise license agreement. A copy is included in Appendix B and on the CD-ROM at the back of this book.

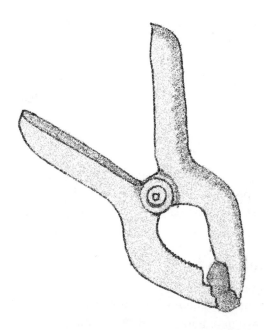

Merchandise License Worksheet

Licensee

Name of Licensee Business _____

Licensee Address _____

_____

Licensee Business Form

☐ sole proprietorship   ☐ general partnership   ☐ limited partnership

☐ corporation   ☐ limited liability company

State of incorporation _____

Name and position of person signing for Licensee _____

Property Definition

Design Patent No. _____

Design Patent Application Serial No. _____

Copyrightable Features _____

_____

Copyright Registration No(s). _____

Trade Secrets _____

_____

Trademarks _____

_____

Trademark Registration No(s). _____

Licensed Products Definition

Industry (Have you limited the license to a particular industry?) _____

Product (Have you limited the license to a particular product or products?) _____

_____

Territory

☐ Worldwide; or

☐ Countries _____

☐ States _____

Merchandise License Worksheet (Page 1)

Rights Granted *(check those rights granted to Licensee)*

- ☐ sell
- ☐ make or manufacture
- ☐ distribute
- ☐ use
- ☐ revise

- ☐ import
- ☐ lease
- ☐ right to improvements
- ☐ derivatives (copyright)
- ☐ copy (copyright)

- ☐ advertise
- ☐ promote
- ☐ other rights _____
- ☐ other rights _____
- ☐ other rights _____

Rights Reserved

- ☐ all rights reserved (except those granted in license)
- ☐ no rights reserved
- ☐ specific rights reserved

Have you signed any other licenses? ☐ Yes   ☐ No   If so, do you need to reserve specific rights?

_____

Term

Have you agreed upon:

- ☐ a fixed term (How long? _____)
- ☐ unlimited term until one party terminates
- ☐ other _____

- ☐ a term limited by design patent length
- ☐ an initial term with renewals (see below)

Renewals

If you have agreed upon an initial term with renewals:

How many renewal periods? _____

How long is each renewal period? _____

What triggers renewal?

- ☐ Licensee must notify of intent to renew
- ☐ Licensor must notify of intent to renew
- ☐ Agreement renews automatically unless Licensee indicates it does not want to renew.

Net Sales Deductions

What is the Licensee permitted to deduct when calculating net sales?

- ☐ quantity discounts
- ☐ promotion and marketing costs
- ☐ credits & returns

- ☐ debts & uncollectibles
- ☐ fees
- ☐ other _____

- ☐ sales commissions
- ☐ freight & shipping

Is there a cap on the total amount of the deductions?   ☐ Yes   ☐ No

If so, how much? _____

Merchandise License Worksheet (Page 2)

Royalty Rates

☐ Licensed Products _____%

☐ Combination Products _____%

☐ Accessory Products _____%

☐ Per Use Royalty _____% or Usage Standard _____

☐ Other Products _____ _____%

☐ Other Products _____ _____%

Do you have any sliding royalty rates?   ☐ Yes   ☐ No

Advances and Lump Sum Payments

☐ Advance $_____   Date Due _____

☐ Lump Sum Payment(s) $_____   Date Due _____

Guaranteed Minimum Annual Royalty (GMAR)

☐ GMAR $_____   Date Due _____

☐ Does the GMAR carry forward credits?

☐ Does the GMAR carry forward deficiencies?

Audit Rights

No. of audits permitted per year _____

No. of days' notice _____

Chapter 10

Sales Representative Agreement

My sister, Barbi Jo (or "BJ" as her friends call her), built her crafts business, Barbini (www.barbini.net), with the help of sales reps. "My business really took a leap when one of my sales reps wrote orders for Nordstrom's East Coast stores," says Barbi Jo. "That really opened the door for my other sales reps to get me into the Nordstroms in their territories." As Barbi Jo's business expanded, so did her use of sales reps. At one time she had no fewer than four regional reps working to sell her jewelry.

Now, 15 years later, she's severed all ties with reps except for a catalog rep. "They were helpful when I started, but I don't have the time—you have to prepare a complete line for the rep and replace it whenever you have a new line—and if the rep is carrying ten other artists, which is pretty common, then you may find you're not getting the attention you expect.

"It gets more complicated if you're doing trade shows," she adds. "Let's say you're at the Philadelphia [BMAC] show and you sell to a New Jersey store. Is your New Jersey rep entitled to a cut? That depends on the arrangement, but usually, yes, the rep expects a cut for every sale in her territory, or at least a cut of the reorders. After a while I found that it wasn't worth the effort.

"Reps can be very valuable," says BJ. "I love my catalog rep. He's great. But when you're choosing your reps, do some research. Don't rely on the rep's promises; reps always promise they're going to do fabulous things with your work. So, get references. For example, find out what other lines they carry, and talk to those artists. Don't ask about money, because most artists won't discuss their sales numbers. Ask about consistency of sales. Does the rep consistently perform well? Do you get along with the rep? And you definitely want a good personality match."

How can an artist find a rep? "They have booths at wholesale crafts shows, or they may approach you directly. They also maintain showrooms, for example, in New York City at 225 Fifth Avenue (The New York Gift Building; www.225-fifth.com) or 41 Madison (The New York Merchandise Mart; www.41madison.com).

Also, if your rep has a showroom, you may be charged a monthly fee to exhibit work there.

"And one other rule," advises BJ. "Never pay the rep until you get paid. If you don't get paid, the rep doesn't get paid."

Barbi Jo raises some important concerns, many of which you'll have to weigh based on your current needs. However, once you've settled on using a particular rep, your best line of defense in case something goes wrong is a written agreement that defines both parties' rights and responsibilities. Many reps use their own agreement. If yours does, compare the provisions in that agreement with the model agreement in this chapter to better understand the commitments you and the rep will be making. All agreements can be modified, so don't be shy about asking for changes. If the rep doesn't have a pre-prepared agreement, use the agreement in this chapter and modify it to meet your needs.

Looking for a rep? In "How to Find and Profit From Using a Sales Rep" (*The Crafts Report*, March, 2000), writer Mary Strope advises:

- talking to artists in similar lines
- checking classified ads in trade magazines
- calling or visiting stores where you would like to sell your work, and
- attending trade shows.

Strope also recommends giving each rep what she calls a Rep Kit. That's a three-ring binder containing your company history, business policies, accounts and "everything the rep needs to know about doing business with you."

The model agreement we provide in Section A, below, covers the many activities that a sales rep might take on in marketing your crafts and increasing your revenues. These include:

- operating showrooms and making sales to the trade or to collectors
- traveling to shops and taking wholesale orders
- brokering licensing deals with manufacturers, and
- helping you earn special order commissions.

The agreement also offers various ways to split revenue and avoid disputes with your sales rep. In Section B, below, I provide a detailed explanation of each provision of the model agreement.

A. Model Sales Representative Agreement

As you'll see below, the model agreement covers a good deal of ground. In fact, it may seem longer or more complex than you envisioned. Simply remove any provisions labeled "optional" that aren't relevant to your situation and you'll end up with a concise agreement.

If you're using the model agreement for comparative purposes, locate a provision in the rep's agreement and find one that's similar in the model agreement—this shouldn't be too difficult, as the subject headings are likely to be the same or similar. Then read my explanation for the model provision in Section B, below, to help you understand what the sales rep is attempting to do differently.

The model agreement is set out in a letter format. Although a letter agreement appears less formal than a traditional contract, it is just as enforceable. If you don't want to use the letter format, simply remove the date and salutation.

 You'll find additional copies of the Model Sales Representative Agreement in Appendix B and on the CD-ROM at the back of this book.

B. Explanation for Sales Representative Agreement

Below, I translate, decode and otherwise advise on how to handle the provisions of the model Sales Representative Agreement.

1. Introductory Paragraph

Insert the date, your name as Artist and the name of the sales representative or the sales representative's company.

2. Appointment

This provision establishes whether your relationship with the sales representative is exclusive or nonexclusive, and establishes in what geographical areas the sales representative will represent your works. Exclusive means that while the agreement is in force, only the sales representative (not you or another sales representative) can represent the works: 1) within the territory you define, and 2) for those sources of revenue set out in the agreement. If the relationship is nonexclusive, then others (including you) could solicit potential deals within the territory and for those purposes.

Choose the type(s) of representation you desire, for example, retail accounts, wholesale accounts and so on, by checking the appropriate box. If you choose licensing rights, specify the type of licensing—for example, licensing for posters, postcards, T-shirts, buttons, caps and whatever else you and the sales rep envision. You can be as broad or as narrow as you want in defining licensing rights, for example: "all forms of merchandise licensing" or "fabrics". Also choose "commissioned works" if your sales representative will represent you for purposes of getting you work on commission, for example, from collectors.

3. Territory

Insert a statement in the Territory section to reflect the regions in which you have granted rights, for example, "New York," "New England" or "the world excluding North America."

If you already have accounts in these territories, you should exclude them from the agreement by checking the optional provision and listing the accounts on Attachment A.

Two other optional provisions are provided to deal with sales made by the Artist, not the rep, within the Territory. You should only choose these optional provisions if your arrangement is exclusive. If your agreement is nonexclusive within the territory, you don't need to account for sales that you make in the territory without the rep's help.

Sales Representative Letter Agreement

Date: _____

Dear: _____

This letter sets forth the terms and conditions of the agreement (the "Agreement") between_____
_____ ("Artist") and _____
_____ ("Sales Representative"). Artist is the owner of all rights in certain
crafts works (referred to as the "Works") and described more fully in Attachment A to this Agreement.

Appointment. Artist agrees to have Sales Representative serve as

    ☐ an exclusive   ☐ a nonexclusive

sales representative for the Works in the Territory to

    ☐ retail accounts   ☐ commissioned works, including: _____

    ☐ wholesale accounts   ☐ licensing rights for the following markets: _____

    ☐ trade (wholesale) sales of crafts work

Territory. Sales Representative will represent Artist in the following territory: _____
_____ (the "Territory").

[Optional]

☐ The accounts and companies listed in Exhibit A are excluded from this Agreement, and Sales Representative
shall not call on these accounts and shall not be entitled to income from such sources.

[Optional (use only if Agreement is exclusive)]

☐ Artist may advertise via ☐ Internet ☐ mail   to accounts in the Territory. In that event, revenues from
such sales shall be accounted for as follows: _____
_____ .

☐ Artist may attend trade shows or meet with accounts or collectors in the Territory. In the event that Artist
obtains a sales order or agreement in the Territory from such solicitations, revenues shall be accounted for
as follows: _____
_____ .

Obligations of Sales Representative; Disclaimer. Sales Representative shall use best efforts to contact and solicit
sales or other sources of revenue, as described above, and present and communicate sales information between
the parties. Nothing in this Agreement shall be interpreted by Artist or Sales Representative as a promise or
guarantee as to the outcome of any solicitation or negotiation by Sales Representative on behalf of Artist or the
Works. Any representations as to the likelihood of success regarding exploitation of the Works are expressions
of opinion only. Sales Representative is free to conduct business other than on Artist's behalf, including business
or agency relationships with other Artists.

[Optional]

☐ **Sales Representative Reimbursement.** Representative shall be reimbursed for the following expenses from any net revenue or net receipts as described in the "Payments" section, below (the "Work Income"). These reimbursements shall be deducted from Work Income before splitting the resulting revenues or receipts, provided that such expenses are solely for the purpose of promoting Artist:

☐ promotional mailings   ☐ paid advertising   ☐ shipping

☐ insurance   ☐ travel   ☐ telephone

Artist's written approval is required for any individual expense over $_____.

In the event that any such costs are incurred for the benefit of other clients of Sales Representative as well as for Artist, the expenses shall be prorated to reflect each client's actual expenses.

☐ Artist shall pay the following fees for showroom exhibit costs: _____

_____.

Obligations of Artist.

Artist will provide Sales Representative with:

☐ _____ samples of the Works, which samples shall remain the property of Artist and shall be returned upon termination of this Agreement or upon thirty (30) days' notice from Artist. Sales Representative shall have the limited right to display, copy and distribute the Works solely in conjunction with promoting the works and fulfilling obligations as set forth under this Agreement.

☐ printed materials as follows: _____

_____.

Artist shall also perform the following duties: _____

_____.

Payments. As compensation for the services provided above, Sales Representative shall receive the following compensation:

[Check and complete appropriate choices]

☐ _____% of net receipts from all sales made by Sales Representative to retail accounts.

☐ _____% of net receipts from all sales made by Sales Representative to wholesale accounts.

☐ _____% of net revenues from any licensing agreements for the Works.

☐ _____% of net revenues from any commissions obtained by Sales Representative.

Artist agrees that all income paid as a result of any sales or agreements solicited or negotiated by Sales Representative for the Works (the "Works Income") shall be paid directly to Artist. Works Income shall include, but not be limited to, advances, guarantees or license fees.

Artist shall issue payments to Sales Representative within ten (10) days of Artist's receipt of any Works Income along with any client accountings as provided by the licensee.

The party responsible for all billings and collections shall be:

☐ Sales Representative

☐ Artist

Each party shall keep accurate books of account and records covering all transactions relating to this Agreement, and either party or its duly authorized representative shall have the right upon five (5) days' prior written notice, and during normal business hours, to inspect and audit the other party's records relating to this Agreement.

Rights. Artist represents and warrants that Artist has the power and authority to enter into this Agreement and is the owner of all proprietary rights, whether they are copyright or otherwise, in the Works.

Advertising.

[Choose one]

☐ Sales Representative can use Artist's name, likeness, trademarks and trade names in Sales Representative's advertising and promotions.

☐ Sales Representative can use Artist's name, likeness, trademarks and trade names in Sales Representative's advertising and promotions, but must obtain Artist's prior approval for every such use.

Assignment. This Agreement shall not be assignable by either party without the written authorization of the nonassigning party.

Termination. This Agreement may be terminated at any time at the discretion of either Artist or Sales Representative, provided that written notice of such termination is furnished to the other party thirty (30) days prior to such termination.

[Optional]

☐ If this Agreement is terminated by Artist, and within _____ (____) months of termination Artist enters into an agreement for assignments, sales or licenses with any client or company for whom Sales Representative had entered into agreements on Artist's behalf during the term of this Agreement, Artist agrees to pay Sales Representative the fees established in this Agreement. This obligation shall survive termination of this Agreement.

No Special Damages. Neither party shall be liable to the other for any incidental, consequential, punitive or special damages.

General Provisions

Entire Agreement. This is the entire agreement between the parties. It replaces and supersedes any and all oral agreements between the parties, as well as any prior writings. Modifications and amendments to this Agreement, including any exhibit or appendix hereto, shall be enforceable only if they are in writing and are signed by authorized representatives of both parties.

Successors and Assignees. This Agreement binds and benefits the heirs, successors and assignees of the parties.

Notices. Any notice or communication required or permitted to be given under this Agreement shall be sufficiently given when received by certified mail, or sent by facsimile transmission or overnight courier.

Governing Law. This Agreement will be governed by the laws of the State of _____.

Waiver. If one party waives any term or provision of this Agreement at any time, that waiver will only be effective for the specific instance and specific purpose for which the waiver was given. If either party fails to exercise or delays exercising any of its rights or remedies under this Agreement, that party retains the right to enforce that term or provision at a later time.

Severability. If a court finds any provision of this Agreement invalid or unenforceable, the remainder of this Agreement will be interpreted so as best to carry out the parties' intent.

Attachments and Exhibits. The parties agree and acknowledge that all attachments, exhibits and schedules referred to in this Agreement are incorporated in this Agreement by reference.

No Agency. Nothing contained herein will be construed as creating any agency, partnership, joint venture or other form of joint enterprise between the parties.

☐ **Attorney Fees and Expenses.** The prevailing party shall have the right to collect from the other party its reasonable costs and necessary disbursements and attorney fees incurred in enforcing this Agreement.

☐ **Jurisdiction.** The parties consent to the exclusive jurisdiction and venue of the federal and state courts located in _____ [county], _____ [state], in any action arising out of or relating to this Agreement. The parties waive any other venue to which either party might be entitled by domicile or otherwise.

☐ **Arbitration.** Any controversy or claim arising out of or relating to this Agreement shall be settled by arbitration in _____ in accordance with the rules of the American Arbitration Association, and judgment upon the award rendered by the arbitrator(s) may be entered in any court having jurisdiction. The prevailing party shall have the right to collect from the other party its reasonable costs and attorney's fees incurred in enforcing this Agreement.

Signatures. Each party represents and warrants that on this date they are duly authorized to bind their respective principals by their signatures below.

SALES REPRESENTATIVE   ARTIST

_____   _____
Signature   Signature

_____   _____
Printed or Typed Name   Printed or Typed Name

_____   _____
Title   Title

_____   _____
Date   Date

Example: Hans has a nonexclusive contract for wholesale accounts with Joanie, his rep, in the southwestern United States. Hans solicits a wholesale account from a New Mexico gallery without Joanie's help. He does not have to account to Joanie for the New Mexico revenue. However, if the arrangement with Joanie were exclusive, Hans would have to account to Joanie, since she has exclusive rights to represent him in the southwest.

If you and the sales rep agree on one of these optional choices, you'll need to figure out a method of accounting for this nonrep income. Depending on your negotiating leverage, you and the rep might agree on:

- no payment to the rep
- full rep commission
- payment of a portion of the rep commission, or
- payment of the rep's commission for sales after the initial order.

4. Obligations of Sales Representative

This section establishes the sales representative's duties, namely evaluating opportunities, representing your work and negotiating deals. The "disclaimer" language is inserted to protect the sales representative from future claims that the sales representative promised or guaranteed that your work could be sold or licensed. This provision also guarantees that the sales representative is free to take on other clients.

5. Sales Representative Reimbursement

If you choose this optional provision, check the boxes indicating which expenses you will pay. If you must pay an exhibit fee to use the rep's showroom, indicate that fee and when it should be paid, for example, "$50 monthly." Insert an appropriate amount, for example, "$200," in the section indicating that your approval is required for expenses.

6. Obligations of Artist

This section establishes the artist's duties as well as the artist's ownership of the artwork samples. In the event that printed materials are required, indicate what materials should be provided. If any additional duties are required of the artist, write this in the blank space.

7. Payments

Under this provision, the sales representative receives a percentage of all "Works Income." This income is paid directly to the Artist, who then reimburses the sales rep within a fixed time period, for example, 30 days.

Rep commissions for sales range from 10-25%, although they are commonly in the 15-20% range. Commissions to licensing reps are typically between 20% and 33%.

The audit statement provides that each party can audit the other's books. That way, you can check to see what the rep has been doing with the accounts and vice versa. Normally, the artist is responsible for all billings and collections. However, if you and the rep have a different arrangement, check the appropriate box.

8. Rights

The rep will not want any surprises—such as someone claiming that you don't own the work or that your work infringes on someone's copyright. For this reason, you should provide a guarantee that you own the artworks and that you have the right to sell and license them. This won't completely prevent surprises, but it will help keep the sales rep free from liability if something unexpected does pop up.

9. Advertising

The rep may want to use your name, trademarks or picture in promotional ads and at the rep's booth at trade shows. Check the second option if you and the rep have agreed to allow you prior approval of any such uses.

10. Assignment

This provision prevents you and the sales rep from transferring contract obligations to someone else. For example, if the rep sold her business to another rep and wanted to transfer your account as part of the sale, your permission would be required.

11. Termination

What happens if you terminate the sales representative agreement but want to continue your business contact with a company with which you had previously made a deal through the sales rep? Under this provision, if you enter into a sales or licensing agreement with such a company within a fixed period of time after termination, you will have to pay the sales rep a fee (three to six months is common). You can also alter the sales representative's fee for post-termination deals. For example, you can agree that the sales representative will get only one half of the fees if any agreement is entered into after three months but before six months. The sales representative may insist that you change the agreement so that the sales

representative is paid if you enter into a contract with anyone that the sales representative solicited. In that case, in order to be sure that the sales representative has solicited the client or company, request that the sales representative furnish you a list of persons who were solicited (and the dates of solicitation and the name of the person contacted). This list can be furnished at the time of termination, or you can request that the sales representative notify you periodically (say, every six months) of all solicitations during that period.

For information about the miscellaneous provisions—Entire Agreement, Relationships, Governing Law, Modification, Waiver, Severability, Arbitration, Attachments—read Chapter 9, Section B24.

12. Attachment A

Write up a description of the works that the sales rep will be handling for you in the Attachment. As an alternative for listing specific works, you can include a statement such as, "All works created prior to and during the term of this Agreement" or "Any new artworks created during the term of this Agreement." Also, if you are excluding some accounts, list them in Attachment A, as well.

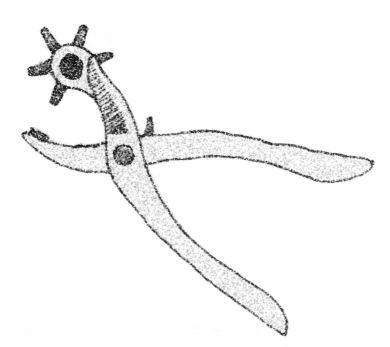

Attachment A

Description of Works:

_____

_____

_____

_____

_____

_____

_____

_____

_____

_____

_____

_____

_____

_____

_____

_____

_____

_____

_____

_____

_____

_____

_____

Excluded Accounts:

_____

_____

_____

_____

_____

Lawyers, Lawsuits and Liability

*I*n September 1999, artist Crispina ffrench (www.crispina.com) was surprised to discover a catalog company selling copies of her "Hood and Pocket Sweater." Every element of Crispina's sweater had been duplicated, including the nine mismatched wool panels, exposed stitching, exposed half-inch hems, six-sided kangaroo pouch and hood with external hem. Adding to the annoyance, the catalog copy trumpeted the fact that the sweaters were "one-of-a-kind" and "imported," as if the foreign origins added to the sweater's cachet. Crispina had achieved considerable attention, including a mention in the *New York Times*, for her hand-made sweaters —produced in her Massachusetts studio using a special process she created to preserve and enhance recycled fabrics.

Crispina and I knew that it would be an uphill battle to protect her clothing designs under principles of copyright (see Chapter 8) or trade dress (see Chapter 6), so we agreed to take a reasonable, non-threatening approach. My letter to the company ended with the hope that the company could "quickly and fairly resolve this matter without litigation."

Within two weeks, the president of the catalog company had written back and thanked me for bringing the matter to the company's attention. He explained that the company had no intention of infringing Crispina's design, and that they had discontinued selling the product. The matter ended quietly. As payment for my services, Crispina provided me with memorable compensation—one of her sweaters!

Most legal altercations don't end this quickly and peacefully. But Crispina's case demonstrates that when you're involved in a legal squabble, you need not assume the worst and start out swinging a big stick. Sometimes disputes can be resolved peacefully and reasonably and sometimes, yes, *sometimes*, people do the right thing. If I had written a typical attorney letter threatening litigation or demanding financial damages, it's possible that the fight would have dragged on much longer than was necessary (and my wife might not have ended up with that fabulous sweater).

In this case, Crispina might have achieved the same result on her own. Unfortunately, that's not true in most infringement battles—a misbehaving company will usually take notice only if a cease and desist demand arrives with a legal letterhead.

When you do need legal help—whether to draft a contract or stop an infringer—you may find it frightening to be thrown into the world of legal fees and legalese. This chapter is designed to remove that fear by:

- helping you find the proper attorney (see Sections A and B) and giving you some confidence when making legal decisions with your attorney
- directing you to low-cost legal services through an arts organization (see Section C)
- offering tips on how to keep your legal fees down (see Section D)
- describing how to evaluate your lawyer's performance (see Section E)
- showing you how to fire an attorney (see Section F)
- using contract provisions to keep future legal hassles within manageable bounds (see Section G)
- explaining how insurance can limit your legal liability (see Section H), and
- clarifying what to do if your work is infringed (see Section I).

A. Hiring Lawyers for Routine Business

If you're like most small business owners, the only time you'll need a lawyer is to take care of some paperwork. For example, you may:

- be forming a business entity such as a corporation, LLC or partnership
- need a contract prepared
- need to review and negotiate a lease
- want to register a trademark, copyright or patent, or
- need to file special tax or business documentation.

You can also choose to handle many of the above matters yourself. See Nolo's online Law Store (www.nolo.com) for helpful books and software. Popular titles include *Incorporate Your Business: A 50-State Legal Guide to Forming a Corporation,* by Anthony Mancuso; *Form Your Own Limited Liability Company,* by Anthony Mancuso; *The Copyright Handbook: How to Protect & Use Written Works,* by Stephen Fishman; and *Patent It Yourself,* by David Pressman.

Lawyers who prepare and review legal documents are referred to as "business" or "transactional" lawyers (versus "litigators," who primarily resolve disputes, as explained in Section B, below). Sometimes a general business lawyer can handle all your transactional work. However, sometimes you'll need a specialist for certain documentation—for example, negotiating a lease may require the help of a real estate lawyer, while filing a trademark registration might best be done with the help of a trademark lawyer.

The right lawyer can be a member of your small business's team—someone who will hear your ideas and confirm that they are legal and do-able as your business grows and progresses. That means that you need to choose carefully. No matter how experienced and well recommended a particular lawyer is, if you feel uncomfortable during your first meeting or two, you may never achieve a good lawyer-client relationship. Trust your instincts, and seek a lawyer whose personality is compatible with your own.

Try to find a lawyer who seems interested in your crafts business and either already knows a lot about your field or seems genuinely eager to learn more about it. Avoid the lawyer who's aloof and doesn't want to get involved in learning the nitty-gritty details of what you do.

Some lawyers are hyper-cautious nitpickers who get unnecessarily bogged down in legal minutiae while a valuable business opportunity slips away. You want a lawyer who blends sound legal advice with a practical approach—someone who figures out a way to do something, not one who offers reasons why it can't be done.

Working with a business attorney is fairly straight-forward—you gather and maintain documents and make decisions based upon your attorney's advice. Below are some tips for saving money with your business attorney:

- **Group together your legal affairs.** You'll save money if you consult with your business lawyer on several matters at one time. For example, in a one-hour conference, you may be able to review the annual updating of your corporate record book, renew your Web hosting agreement and check over a noncompetition agreement you've drafted for new employees to sign.

- **Use flat fees.** When hiring a business attorney, you may be able to obtain a fixed fee for certain transactional work (see Section D, below). Flat fees give your business some predictability; you're not waiting for a billing surprise at the end of the month.

- **Help out.** You or your employees can do a lot of work yourselves. Help gather documents needed for a transaction. Write the first couple of drafts of a contract, then give your lawyer the relatively inexpensive task of reviewing and polishing the document.

- **Avoid spending too much time on contract negotiations.** Lawyer's fees can quickly get out of control if negotiations for contracts drag on too long. Contracts sometimes go through many drafts. As long as you and your attorney are conscientious, you can get away with fewer drafts. Make sure you and the attorney are in agreement as to the goals of the contract negotiation. Tell your lawyer your priorities. Once you have achieved most or all of your goals, be flexible about remaining issues so that you can save time.

- **Use other professionals.** Often, nonlawyer professionals perform some business tasks better and at lower cost than lawyers do. For example, look to management consultants for strategic business planning, real estate brokers or appraisers for valuation of properties, accountants for preparation of financial proposals, insurance agents for advice on insurance protection and CPAs for the preparation of tax returns.

B. Hiring Lawyers for Legal Disputes

When you hire an attorney because you're in the midst of a dispute, you're often looking for a different type of legal animal. You're seeking someone who can defend your turf against others who threaten your livelihood. But don't assume you need the biggest ape in the jungle. Sometimes, a shrewd negotiator or a logical, methodical attorney can be the ideal choice to end a dispute amicably. Below are a few tips for dealing with legal disputes and legal fees:

- **Avoid lawsuits that go on forever.** Beware of litigation! It often costs $10,000 or more, and the main ones who profit are the lawyers. If you're in a dispute, before screaming, "I'll see you in court!," ask your attorney for a realistic assessment of your odds for success and the potential costs. The assessment and underlying reasoning should be in plain English. If a lawyer can't explain your situation clearly to you, he won't be able to explain it clearly to a judge or jury. Also, ask your attorney about alternative dispute resolution methods such as arbitration and mediation (see Section E, below). Finally, keep in mind that some lawyers are greedy, and the longer the dispute drags out, the more the attorney will earn.

- **Be skeptical of an attorney who assures you of a large windfall.** Being legally right about something doesn't necessarily mean being entitled to financial damages. One of the first questions that judges and arbitrators usually ask is whether the complaining party has actually suffered any injury. For example, has an infringing copy of your work deprived you of revenue? Can you prove it? Has a similar trademark reduced your sales? Again, what's the proof? What are the real damages? If you are involved in a contract dispute, be aware that you will rarely obtain a financial windfall. The best that you can usually hope for is for payment of what you would have received if the contract had been performed according to plan.

- **Encourage settlement.** A settlement is a contract signed by both parties, usually executed at the time one party pays the other. A negotiated settlement saves money (litigation costs) and time (you avoid waiting three years for the case to end). Better still, it results in a guaranteed payment (unlike a court judgment that must be collected and enforced). These advantages create an incentive for you to accept less money in a settlement than you would demand in a court case. When deciding whether to accept a settlement, you and your lawyer should consider your likelihood of winning in court and estimate any resulting award of damages if you were to lose.

- **Consider small claims court.** Small claims court judges resolve disputes involving relatively modest amounts of money. (You can sue for between $2,000 and $25,000, depending on your state.) The people or businesses involved normally present their cases to a judge or court commissioner without the help of lawyers. Small claims court rules are designed not to overwhelm the participants with legal or procedural formalities. The judge makes a decision (a judgment) reasonably promptly, often the same day as the hearing. Although procedural rules dealing with when and where to file and serve papers are established by each state's laws and differ in detail, the basic approach to properly preparing and presenting a small claims case is remarkably similar everywhere. For more information, read *Everybody's Guide to Small Claims Court*, by Ralph Warner (Nolo).

C. Finding the Right Lawyer

The novelist Robert Smith-Surtees said there are three sorts of lawyers: able, unable and lamentable. In this section, we'll provide some suggestions for avoiding the latter two.

At least 24 states have organizations that provide legal services and information to the arts community at a reduced rate. To find such an organization near you, check the national directory on the website of the Volunteer Lawyers for the Arts (VLA), the granddaddy of the organizations (www.vlany.org). Click "Resources" on the home page, and then click "National Directory."

These organizations provide low-income artists with free legal advice. Contact the organization nearest you to see if you qualify. For example, the California Lawyers for the Arts (CLA) offers free legal services to artists who earn less than $18,000 per year (or married artists whose joint income is less than $24,000).

If you don't meet the financial requirements for free legal help, groups like the CLA and VLA can save you money through lawyer referral services. Each organization maintains a directory of local attorneys who handle arts-related legal issues. Many offer reduced rates for an initial visit. For example, the CLA will arrange a half-hour consultation with an attorney for $30—a savings of about $70 off a private attorney's normal fee. This initial consultation may be enough to tell you whether or not you should pursue a dispute.

Legal organizations can also save you money on legal fees by offering workshops on topics such as "Copyright Infringement," "Trademark 101" or "Starting and Operating a Nonprofit Corporation." Finally, the mediation and arbitration services provided by these organizations can save you money, as explained in Section E, below.

Although it's not a volunteer legal organization, the Made In the USA Foundation (1925 K Street, N.W., Washington, DC 20006, (202) 822-6060) has filed lawsuits on behalf of crafts artists against stores selling foreign-made knockoffs of U.S. designs (including Wal-Mart, Target and Kohl's).

If you live in an area that does not have a VLA-style group, your best bet for finding the right lawyer is to get recommendations from other crafts artists or organizations. Talk to crafts artists who have actually used a particular lawyer's services. Find out what the person liked about the lawyer, and why. Ask how the legal problem turned out—was the lawyer successful? Ask about the lawyer's legal abilities, communication skills and billing practices. If you have a problem related to copyrights, trade secrets, patents or trademarks, you can ask the American Intellectual Property Law Association (AIPLA); (www.aipla.org) to refer you to an experienced lawyer. A few other sources you can turn to for possible candidates include the director of your state or local chamber of commerce or a law librarian who can identify lawyers in your state who have written books or articles on arts or business law.

Don't fall for attorney advertisements or lists of lawyers provided by a local bar association. Advertisements found in the yellow pages, in newspapers, on television or online say nothing meaningful about a lawyer's skills or manner—just that he could afford to pay for the ad. Similarly, local bar associations often maintain and advertise lawyer referral services. However, a lawyer can usually get on this list simply by volunteering. Very little (if any) screening is done to find out whether the lawyers are any good.

D. Fees and Fee Agreements

You may have heard the joke about the new client who asked the lawyer, "How much do you charge?".

"I charge $200 to answer three questions," replied the lawyer.

"Isn't that a bit steep?"

"Yes," said the lawyer. "What's your third question?".

As the joke indicates, it's important to get a clear understanding about how fees will be computed when you hire a lawyer. And as you bring new tasks to the lawyer, ask specifically about the charges for each. Many lawyers initiate fee discussions, but others forget or are shy about doing so. Bring up the subject yourself. Insist that the ground rules be clearly established. In California, all fee agreements between lawyers and clients must be in writing if the expected fee is $1,000 or more, or is contingent on the outcome of a lawsuit. In any state, it's a good idea to put your fee agreement in writing.

There are four basic ways that lawyers charge. The first is by the hour. In most parts of the United States, you can get competent services for your small business for $175 to $250 an hour.

The cheapest hourly rate isn't necessarily the best deal. A novice who charges only $80 an hour may take three hours to review a contract. A more experienced lawyer who charges $200 an hour may do the same job in half an hour and make better suggestions. Take into account the lawyer's knowledge and reputation and the personal rapport the two of you have—or don't have.

Sometimes a business lawyer quotes a flat fee for a specific job. For example, the lawyer may offer to draw up a distribution agreement for $300, or review and edit your online terms and conditions for $500. You pay the same amount regardless of how much time the lawyer spends.

In some cases, a lawyer may charge a contingent fee. This is a percentage (commonly 33%) of the amount the lawyer obtains for you in a negotiated settlement or through a trial. If the lawyer recovers nothing for you, there's no fee. However, the lawyer does generally expect reimbursement for out-of-pocket expenses, such as filing fees, long-distance phone calls and transcripts of testimony. Contingent fees are common in personal injury lawsuits but relatively unusual in small business cases.

Finally, you may be able to hire a lawyer for a flat annual fee to handle all of your routine legal business. (Such a fee is sometimes called a retainer, although this term can also be used more broadly, as explained in the sidebar, "What Is a Retainer?," below.) You'll usually pay in equal monthly installments. Normally, the lawyer will bill you an additional amount for extraordinary services—such as representing you in a major lawsuit. Obviously, the key to making this arrangement work is to have a written agreement clearly defining what's routine and what's extraordinary.

What Is a Retainer?

A retainer is an advance payment to an attorney. The attorney places the retainer in a bank account (in some states, this must be an interest-bearing account) and deducts money from the account at the end of each month to pay your bill. When the money is depleted, the attorney may ask for a new retainer. If the retainer is not used up at the end of the services, the attorney must return what's left. The amount of the retainer usually depends on the project. For example, retainers for litigation tend to run between $2,000 and $5,000. Some attorneys use the term "retainer" to refer to a monthly fee that the attorney keeps regardless of whether any legal services are performed. In other words, you are paying a monthly fee just to keep the attorney available to you. I recommend against this type of arrangement.

To save yourself money and grief when dealing with an attorney, follow these tips:

- **Keep it short.** If you are paying your attorney on an hourly basis, keep your conversations short—the meter is always running. Avoid making several calls a day. Instead, consolidate your questions and ask them all in one conversation.

- **Get a fee agreement.** Make sure that your fee agreement gives you the right to an itemized statement along with the bill, detailing the work done and time spent. Some state statutes and bar associations require a written fee agreement—for example, California requires that attorneys provide a written agreement when the fee will exceed $1,000.

- **Review billings carefully.** Your lawyer's bill should be clear. Do not accept summary billings such as the single phrase "litigation work" used to explain a block of time for which you are billed a great deal of money.

- **Watch out for hidden expenses.** Find out what expenses you must cover. Watch out if your attorney wants to bill for services such as word processing or administrative services. This means you will be paying the secretary's salary. Also beware of fax and copying charges. Some firms charge clients per page for incoming and outgoing faxes—and the per-page cost can be artificially high.

- **Educate yourself.** In the sidebar, "Do Your Own Legal Research Online," below, you'll find many sources of law on the Web. These sites will help you keep up with specific legal develop ments that your lawyer may have missed. Send pertinent articles to your lawyer—this can dramatically reduce legal research time—and encourage your lawyer to do the same for you.

- **Show that you're an important client.** The single most important thing you can do to tell your lawyer how much you value the relationship is to pay your bills on time. Also, let your lawyer know about plans for expansion and your company's possible future legal needs. And if your business wins an award or otherwise is recognized as being a leader in its field, let your lawyer know about it—everyone feels good when an enterprise they're associated with prospers. Also, let your lawyer know when you recommend her to business colleagues.

E. Evaluating Your Attorney's Services

How do you know if your lawyer is doing a good job? Generally, you can measure a professional's performance (whether it is a doctor, lawyer or dentist) by observing whether the professional:

- provides you with accurate and understandable advice
- permits you to make an informed decision as to how to proceed, and
- works with you to efficiently resolve conflicts and solve problems.

If your attorney is not fulfilling all three of these requirements then there is a problem in the attorney-client relationship. For example, there is generally a problem if:

- your attorney is not returning phone calls within 48 hours
- the bills you're receiving are disproportionate to what the attorney predicted and there is no adequate explanation, or
- you are unable to understand why your attorney is doing certain things or your attorney speaks down to you.

As a general rule, if you leave the lawyer's office confused or unclear as to your course of action, then there is a problem. After all, the primary purpose of an attorney is to counsel you as to your legal options. If you don't understand these options, then the attorney has failed. This doesn't mean that the lawyer will always present a black and white explanation. There are many gray areas in the law. For example, the law regarding business names is often murky. A good attorney will explain this murkiness and evaluate your chances of success if a dispute arises over the use of your intended name.

F. Firing Your Attorney

You can always fire your lawyer. (You're still obligated to pay outstanding bills, though.) But bear in mind that switching attorneys is a nuisance, and you may lose time and money.

How do you fire an attorney? Notify the attorney by letter that you are terminating services and that you request the return of your files. The attorney will probably retain a copy of your files and return the originals to you. Despite your obligation to pay any outstanding bills, the attorney is not allowed to withhold your files until you pay.

If your attorney is representing you to a third party, for example, to a manufacturer, you should also notify the third party that you are no longer working with the attorney and that future correspondence should be sent to you (at least until you retain a new attorney).

The easiest way to switch attorneys is to find a new attorney and have that attorney terminate the old relationship. That is, before terminating one attorney, you would have another attorney prepare to take over any outstanding legal work.

 For more information on how to handle a dispute with your lawyer, see Nolo's eBook *Mad At Your Lawyer,* by Tanya Starnes, available for download on the Nolo website (www.nolo.com).

Keep business and personal bills separate. If you visit your lawyer on a personal legal matter and you also discuss a business problem, ask your lawyer to allocate the time spent and send you separate bills. That helps you at tax time, when you can easily list the business portion as a tax-deductible business expense.

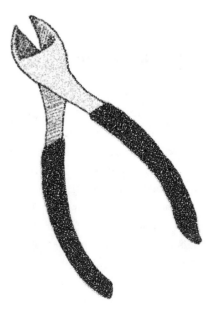

Do Your Own Legal Research Online

The Internet is chock full of valuable information that you can easily ferret out on your own. For starters, Nolo's site (www.nolo.com) offers loads of legal and small business material, as well as legal research links. You might also sample the sites below.

- Findlaw, at www.findlaw.com, is a good place to start any search for legal information, providing a reliable source of links to everything legal.
- Martindale-Hubbell, at www.lawyers.com, contains various helpful features as well as lawyer listings.
- The legal portal, at www.law.com, has separate areas for the public, businesses, lawyers and students.
- The Thomas Legislative Information site, at thomas.loc.gov, contains a wealth of information on bills pending in Congress and laws recently adopted.
- The Court TV Small Business Law Center, at www.courttv.com/legalhelp/business, offers articles on small business law and legal forms.
- Lectric Law Library, at www.lectlaw.com, is a good place to explore a wide range of business law issues. Many business law topics are covered in reasonable depth.
- The Internal Revenue Service, at www.irs.gov, lets you download tax forms, instructions and a wide range of IRS publications.

Look at *Legal Research: How to Find & Understand the Law,* by Stephen Elias & Susan Levinkind (Nolo), a nontechnical book written for the average person. It covers basic legal materials and explains how to use all major legal research tools. It's a helpful resource for framing your research questions—not always an intuitive activity!

G. Using Contract Provisions to Avoid Legal Costs and Hassles

Below is a discussion of four contract provisions usually found at the end of standard business agreements (such as the Merchandise License and Sales Representative agreements discussed elsewhere in this book). These provisions can level the playing field between you and a more well heeled adversary. Ultimately, they can limit how much you spend on lawyers, court costs and damages if you're on the losing end of a dispute. Unfortunately, because these provisions equalize the relationship, one party sometimes rejects them during contract negotiations.

You don't need a contract to use arbitration or mediation. However, if the contract doesn't require one of these alternatives, both parties must agree to the procedure beforehand. If you get into a dispute and only one party wants to use the procedure, that party will be out of luck.

1. Agreeing to Mediation

Many disputes are resolved privately through mediation, an informal procedure in which the parties submit their dispute to an impartial mediator who assists them in reaching a settlement. The settlement decision is not binding, and the parties can disregard the result. That's the key to mediation—nobody is bound by the outcome. Below is sample language you can add to a contract to require mediation of any dispute.

Sample:

Mediation. The Parties agree that every dispute or difference between them arising under this Agreement shall be settled first by a meeting of the Parties attempting to confer and resolve the dispute in a good faith manner. If the Parties cannot resolve their dispute after conferring, any Party may require the other Parties to submit the matter to nonbinding mediation, utilizing the services of an impartial professional mediator approved by all Parties.

2. Agreeing to Arbitration

With arbitration, the parties hire one or more arbitrators—experts at resolving disputes—to evaluate the dispute and to make a determination. Arbitration is often used if the parties fail to reach a settlement during mediation of their dispute. It has both good and not-so-good aspects. Here's an overview of the pros and cons:

- **Arbitration Pros:** Arbitration is usually less expensive and more efficient than litigation. Moreover, the parties can select an arbitrator who has knowledge in the crafts or small business field.

- **Arbitration Cons:** The parties have no right to discovery, that is, the process used during litigation in which the parties must reveal documents and disclose information about their cases. (However, you can include a requirement for discovery in the arbitration provision.) Unlike a court ruling, a binding arbitration ruling is not appealable and can only be set aside by a judge if the arbitrator was biased or the arbitration ruling violated public policy. Arbitrators must be paid, and these fees can run to $10,000 or more. Most participants in arbitration hire attorneys, so you will not avoid paying attorney fees.

Many associations offer private arbitration. The best-known of these is the American Arbitration Association (AAA; www.adr.org). However, if you're in a dispute that needs mediating or arbitrating, first try an arts organization such as the CLA or VLA. (See Section E, above.) For examples of provisions that will guarantee that the arbitration is handled by this type of organization, check the CLA website at www.calawyersforthearts.org/aams.html.

Below is sample contract language requiring the parties to arbitrate any dispute.

Sample:

Arbitration. If a dispute arises under or relating to this Agreement, the Parties agree to submit such dispute to binding arbitration in the state of _____ or another location mutually agreeable to the Parties.

The arbitration shall be conducted on a confidential basis pursuant to the Commercial Arbitration Rules of the American Arbitration Association. Any decision or award as a result of any such arbitration proceeding shall be in writing and shall provide an explanation for all conclusions of law and fact and shall include the assessment of costs, expenses and reasonable attorney fees. An arbitrator experienced in _____ shall conduct any such arbitration. An award of arbitration may be confirmed in a court of competent jurisdiction.

3. Deciding Who Pays Attorney Fees

Many agreements have an "attorney fees and costs" clause. This clause usually provides that if you and the other party end up in a legal battle over the contract, the loser will have to pay the winning (or "prevailing") party's attorney fees plus the costs of preparing the case, including service of process, depositions, court filings and expert witness fees. The clause will apply to disputes that have gone to arbitration, too, since one or both of you may hire lawyers to help you prepare for your case. (Normally, the clause will not apply to lawyers you might hire to help you prepare for mediations.)

An attorney fees clause has the laudable effect of making both of you think twice before initiating arbitration or bringing a lawsuit that you aren't quite sure you can win, since the consequences of losing can be quite expensive.

Below is contract language you can use to require the winner of a dispute to pay attorney fees and costs.

Sample:

Attorney Fees and Expenses. The prevailing party shall have the right to collect from the other party its reasonable costs and necessary disbursements and attorney fees incurred in enforcing this Agreement.

4. Deciding on Jurisdiction

In the event of a dispute, this provision establishes in which state (and county) the lawsuit or arbitration

must be filed. One way to limit your expenses is to guarantee that jurisdiction is in your home county, if possible. That way, you avoid the expense of traveling to a distant location to fight your legal battle. As you can imagine, this section is sometimes a matter of heated discussion. If there is no reference to jurisdiction, the location is usually determined by whoever files a lawsuit. If a jurisdiction clause is used, it should list the same state as the contract provision that describes which state's law governs the agreement (known as the "Governing Law" provision).

Below is contract language you can use to decide in advance where any litigation will take place.

Sample:

Jurisdiction. The parties consent to the exclusive jurisdiction and venue of the federal and state courts located in _____ [county], _____ [state], in any action arising out of or relating to this Agreement. The parties waive any other venue to which either party might be entitled by domicile or otherwise.

 For tips on how an artist can choose a lawyer, save money on legal fees and protect his or her finances, check out the Pauper website (www. thepauper.com).

H. Carrying Adequate Insurance

Like most small business owners, you've probably given some thought to avoiding financial and legal liability. As we explained in Chapter 1, if you organize your business as a corporation or LLC, you'll have taken an important step toward protecting your personal (nonbusiness) assets from someone suing your business and getting a judgment against it. Generally speaking, your home, bank and car will be safe from business creditors and from anyone injured in the course of your business operations.

However, in addition to forming a corporation or LLC, it's an excellent idea to protect yourself from certain legal risks by purchasing insurance. If you are sued, your insurance policy may help pay not

Who Is Authorized to Sign an Agreement?

Someone with the necessary authority must sign an agreement on behalf of each party. To reinforce this, you will note that the sample agreements in this book state that, "Each party has signed this Agreement through its authorized representative." Use the following rules to determine the proper signature form:

- **Sole Proprietorship:** If you are a sole proprietorship, simply sign your own name. If the sole proprietorship has a fictitious business name (sometimes known as a *dba*), insert it above the signature line. For example, if Tom Stein is a sole proprietor doing business as Lucky Guy Glassware, Tom would sign an agreement as follows:

Sole Proprietorship Sample:
Lucky Guy Glassware

By: _____
Tom Stein, sole proprietor

- **Partnership:** When a general or limited partnership enters into an agreement, the only person authorized to sign the agreement is a general partner or someone who has written authority (usually in the form of a partnership resolution) from a general partner. The name of the partnership must be mentioned above the signature line, or the partnership will not be bound (only the person signing the agreement will be bound). For example, say Cindy Barrett is a general partner in Reality Woodworks Partnership. She would sign as follows:

Partnership Sample:
Reality Woodworks Partnership

By: _____
Cindy Barrett, general partner

- **Corporation or LLC:** To bind a corporation or limited liability company (LLC), only a person authorized by the business can sign the agreement. The president or chief executive officer (CEO) usually has such power, but not every executive of a corporation or every member of an LLC has this authority. When in doubt, ask for written proof of the authority. This proof is usually in the form of a corporate resolution or the operating agreement of an LLC. Put the name of the corporation or LLC above the signature line; otherwise, the corporation may not be bound (only the person signing the agreement will be bound). For example, Karen Foley, CEO of Insincere Marketing, should sign as follows:

Corporation or LLC Sample:
Insincere Marketing, Inc., a New York corporation

By: _____
Karen Foley, CEO

If you have doubts about the person's credibility, don't proceed until you are satisfied that the person has full authority to represent the company.

Each party should sign two copies and keep one. This way, both parties have an original signed agreement.

It's also okay to use a faxed signature if both parties accept its authenticity. But if one party later claims a forgery, it may be difficult to prove a signature's authenticity from the fax alone. So if you fax the signed agreement, follow up by mailing or overnighting the signed original.

Although "electronic signatures" are now valid under federal law, we recommend relying on paper agreements and traditional signatures for the time being. Under this law (the Electronic Signatures in Global and International Commerce Act), an electronic contract is an agreement created and "signed" in electronic form—in other words, no paper copies are used. For example, you could write an agreement on your computer and email it to a business associate, who emails it back with an electronic signature indicating acceptance. But secure methods of electronic signatures have not yet been popularized, so stick with paper for now.

only your damages, but also the cost of hiring an attorney to defend you. Most businesses buy insurance to protect them from business catastrophes. Two kinds of insurance are essential:

- **Property insurance** covers damage to the space where you do business and to your computers, furnishings, inventory and supplies. For example, if a fire destroys your studio, the insurance will cover the cost of restoring the studio and replacing your equipment and other tangible assets. Of course, you'll probably have to pay a deductible, and every policy places a cap on the total amount the insurance company will pay.
- **Liability insurance** covers claims and lawsuits by people or businesses that have suffered physical or financial losses because of your business activities. This would include, for example, a claim by a delivery person who trips on a cable in your office, falls and breaks an ankle. As with property insurance, there may be a deductible for you to pay, and there will be a cap on your coverage.

If you have a full-business policy, consider adding an "in-transit" rider. Also known as an "Inland Marine" rider, this covers your inventory when it's in transit. The rider can cover replacement costs or costs arising from damage or theft that occurs while your inventory is away from your studio, for example, being transported to a crafts show.

Your business may find a third kind of insurance helpful:

- **Business interruption insurance** covers losses you incur if you must temporarily curtail or cease operation because of a fire or flood. If your business property is damaged or destroyed, and you have to shut down for two months while your premises are rebuilt and your equipment is replaced, you may lose substantial income and have to pay significant expenses in the interim. These losses and expenses are covered by business interruption insurance.

If you have a website, read your policy carefully. While your liability insurance may cover business legal disputes like defamation or copyright infringement, the policy language may be too narrow to include claims based on your website activities. Traditional policies lump these torts into a category intended for *advertising* activities. Having a website may or may not be treated as advertising under your liability policy.

 Two sources of crafts insurance are Hilb, Rogal and Hamilton Company (800) 523-8336 (www.hrh.com) or RLI Insurance Co. (309) 692-1000 (www.rlicorp.com).

Pay attention to the amount of the deductible. The deductible is the portion of each claim that you're obligated to pay. By having a higher deductible, you can reduce the insurance premium.

I. What to Do If Your Work Is Ripped Off

It's your worst nightmare. A catalog company rips off one of your best-selling items and sells it at a lower price. You know the reality. If you sue, you may end up spending more on attorney fees than you lost from the rip-off—a fact that the company has probably considered. Grrr!!!

Suing a chain store or catalog company may cost anywhere from $5,000 to $100,000 in legal fees. Some infringers know that the cost of fees will exceed any victory in a lawsuit. They tend to take the attitude, "Sue me if you can afford it." In these cases, a lawsuit is a big gamble. However, if you have strong legal protection and a good case, pursuit of a big-time infringer will not be quite as risky, because you will be able to attract an attorney who will take your case on a contingency basis—that is, for a percentage of the judgment.

Unfortunately, there is no foolproof way to prevent someone from ripping off your crafts idea, and there is no guarantee of success in a legal battle. An article in the April 2002 *Fortune Small Business Magazine* highlighted the rash of knockoffs by Target, QVC, Kmart, Wal-Mart and Pottery Barn. In one particularly egregious case, the knockoff maker bought up all the available glass normally used by the glass artist for his picture frames. The more successful a crafts product becomes, the more likely another crafts business, a foreign manufacturer or a catalog company will knock it off. Even though you cannot stop theft, there are laws that you can use to go after these thieves, and there are ways to use your legal rights to deter future thefts. Below, we provide some suggestions for dealing with infringers and thieves.

- **Gather evidence.** The key to prevailing and to ending an infringement dispute quickly is often the evidence that's gathered. Your evidence should present a convincing story of how the work was created and stolen. Keep records of how you created your work in a crafts notebook. If you learn of a rip-off, buy a copy and save the store receipt. If possible, obtain business cards or other contact information from buyers at a show or from anyone who wants to photograph your work. For example, in a case involving Pottery Barn, a client was able to demonstrate that the buyer had seen and taken a copy of the work on the basis of a business card that the buyer left at the artist's booth.

The Foundation for Design Integrity (www.ffdi.org) offers suggestions for relevant evidence at its website. These include documenting your design process, keeping accurate financial records and maintaining an exhibition log.

- **Publicity helps.** Publicity about your business, such as articles about your crafts or awards you've received, will help to demonstrate the legitimacy of your work (a factor for some judges). It can also aid in a trade dress case by demonstrating secondary meaning (see Chapter 6) or in a copyright case by demonstrating

access (see Chapter 8). You can also sometimes use publicity to shame an infringer into settling. For example, when I told one chain store that my client was preparing a press release about the fact that her made-in the-USA works were being knocked off by made-in-India imports, the store settled soon afterwards.

- **Don't say anything till you speak with an attorney.** Never confront an infringer until you have spoken with an attorney. Accusing someone of being a thief, especially if you're wrong, can lead to legal claims against you.

The Happy Prints …

Artist Lisa Graves (see Chapter 8) had created distinctive heart-shaped earrings that were knocked off by Contempo Casuals, the Limited and three other manufacturers (see Figure 8-1). When she created her earrings, she left an incidental thumb mark in the back—a fingerprint. When the infringers copied the work, they simply threw it in a mold and reproduced it with the thumbprint included. As a result, it was difficult for the defendants in the case to claim (as they had) that the earrings were not copied—powerful evidence that helped us settle her case.

- **Remember, not all crafts products qualify for legal protection.** As you may have gathered from Chapters 6, 7 and 8, obtaining copyright, trademark or patent protection is a little like getting a bank loan: some crafts products qualify, and some don't. When a work is not protected, it is considered to be in the public domain, and anyone is free to copy it. Review Chapters 6 through 8 and follow the procedures for registering and protecting copyrights, design patents and trademarks. Registration of copyright, for example, may enable you to claim attorney fees in the event of an infringement.

Taxes

In 1989, Paul Bechtelheimer and his wife Nelda sold their home in Kansas and bought a Pace Arrow motor home outfitted with heat, running water, air conditioning, a refrigerator, a stove, a microwave, a washer, a dryer, two television sets, a couch, a chair and a bed. They hitched a trailer containing their inventory to the motor home and traveled the country, attending over 40 crafts shows a year. At the shows, they sold lamps, figurines and woodcuts, all in a southwestern motif. In 1990 the couple bought a mobile home in Florida, where they stayed for approximately 30 to 50 days a year.

When paying their income taxes, the Bechtelheimers deducted their travel expenses—the costs of traveling to and selling at crafts shows. As explained in Section G, below, the tax law provides that you can deduct travel expenses (including amounts expended for meals and lodging) while away from home in the pursuit of a trade or business (26 USC § 162). However, there's a catch. A taxpayer is not away from home if the home travels with him. After a dispute arose with the IRS, a federal judge ruled the Bechtelheimers were always "at home," even while on the road. Their motor home—not their mobile home in Florida—qualified as their "home" as the term is used in § 162(a)(2) of the tax code. One important factor was that the couple used the Florida mobile home as their studio to work on and store their crafts. Even when they were in Florida, they lived and slept in the motor home. The deduction was void, and the couple was required to pay the government back taxes. (*In re Bechtelheimer,* 239 B.R. 616 (M.D. Fla.1999).)

As the Bechtelheimer case demonstrates, an honest error in judgment can result in an unexpected tax burden. This chapter will provide information and resources to help you avoid such problems. Although tax laws are complex and sometimes unpredictable, by following the basic rules in this chapter, you can maximize your tax benefits with the minimum risk.

It's possible for you to handle all of your tax issues and IRS forms—many crafts people manage all things taxable. Others hire tax professionals to take care of everything for them. And many more crafts workers are somewhere in between, relying on both

professional and self help. Your approach depends on how complex your tax affairs are and whether you have the time, energy and desire to do some or all of the work yourself.

Even if you are paying a professional to handle your taxes, you should read this chapter and familiarize yourself with basic tax rules. After all, your expenditures—and therefore potential deductions—will be occurring throughout the year. And the ultimate legal responsibility for your taxes lies with you, not your accountant. The more you know, the less chance there is that errors will slip by you—and the more you can save. This chapter covers a wide range of tax materials including:

- basic federal and state income tax rules (Sections A and B)
- what you can deduct (Section C)
- business use of your home (Section D)
- business assets and depreciation (Section E)
- car, travel and entertainment expenses (Sections F, G and H)
- deducting health insurance costs (Section I)
- deducting start-up costs (Section J)
- paying self-employment taxes (Section K), and
- paying estimated taxes (Section L).

Cross-references are provided throughout this chapter to IRS publications and other related reading. You can obtain IRS publications by calling the IRS at 800-TAX-FORM, visiting your local IRS office or downloading the publications at www.irs.gov. Other helpful tax sites are 1040.com (www.1040.com), offering state and federal links, and Tax Planet (www.taxplanet. com).

Much of the material in this chapter was written with the assistance of attorney Stephen Fishman, who drew from his research for his bestselling book, *Working for Yourself: Law & Taxes for Independent Contractors, Freelancers & Consultants* (Nolo).

This chapter is focused primarily on tax issues for self-employed individuals, that is, sole proprietorships. Many of the rules in this chapter will also apply if you operate your crafts business with someone other than your spouse—that is, if your business is a partnership or some other business form. For example, we offer some tax advice for owners of partnerships, corporations, limited liability companies and corporations. However, for specific tax advice for these business forms and regarding tax audits, consult a tax professional or review *Tax Savvy for Small Business* (Nolo) or *Stand Up to the IRS* (Nolo), both by Frederick W. Daily.

 For information regarding taxes for employees and independent contractors, see Chapter 5.

A. Federal Tax Basics

The federal government puts the biggest tax burden on self-employed crafts people. You'll be subject to:

- income taxes
- self-employment taxes
- estimated taxes, and
- employment taxes.

1. Income Taxes

Everyone who earns above a minimum number of dollars per year must pay income taxes. Unless you're one of the few self-employed crafts persons who have formed a C corporation, you'll have to pay personal income tax on the profits your business earns. Fortunately, you may be able to take advantage of a number of business-related deductions to reduce your taxable income. These deductions are discussed in Section C, below.

By April 15 of each year, you'll have to file an annual income tax return showing your past year's income and deductions and how much estimated tax you paid. You'll file IRS Form 1040 and include a special tax form in which you list all your business income and deductible expenses. Most self-employed crafts people use IRS Schedule C, Profit or Loss From Business.

Tax matters are more complicated if you incorporate your business. If you form a C corporation, it will have to file its own tax return and pay taxes on its profits. You'll be an employee of your corporation

and will have to file a personal tax return and pay income tax on the salary your corporation paid you.

2. Self-Employment Taxes

Self-employed crafts people are entitled to Social Security and Medicare benefits when they retire, just like employees. But just like employees, they have to pay into the Social Security and Medicare systems first, through self-employment (or SE) taxes. You must pay SE taxes if your net yearly earnings from your crafts business are $400 or more. When you file your annual tax return, include IRS Form SE, showing how much SE tax you were required to pay. Self-employment taxes are discussed in more detail in Section K, below.

3. Estimated Taxes

Federal income and SE taxes are pay-as-you-go taxes. You must pay them as you earn or receive income during the year. Unlike employees, who usually have their income and Social Security and Medicare tax withheld from their pay by their employers, a self-employed crafts worker normally pays these taxes—called estimated taxes—directly to the IRS. Estimated taxes are usually made four times every year: on April 15, June 15, September 15 and January 15. You'll use IRS Form 1040-ES. You will be responsible for figuring out how much to pay; the IRS won't do it for you. Estimated taxes are discussed in more detail in Section L, below.

4. Employment Taxes

If you hire crafts workers as employees to help you in your business, you'll have to pay federal employment taxes. These consist of half your employees' Social Security and Medicare taxes and all of the federal unemployment tax. You must also withhold half your employees' Social Security and Medicare taxes and all their income taxes from their paychecks. You must pay these taxes monthly, by making federal tax deposits at specified banks. You may also deposit them directly with the IRS electronically. When you have employees, you'll have to keep lots of records and file quarterly and annual employment tax returns with the IRS. Employment taxes are discussed in more detail in Chapter 5.

Tossing Your Tax Records

Have you been storing your cancelled checks from 1982 just in case the IRS audits you? Then it's time to climb up the attic stairs and get rid of that financial fire hazard. What tax records do you need to keep? Start with the basic rule that, with rare exceptions, the IRS is prohibited from asking you about returns that are more than three years old—that is, three years from the date of your last return. So you only need to keep records that relate to the last three years. Bear in mind that tax returns may be based on financial records that date back more than three years—for example, in the case of a five-year depreciation on business equipment. That means that you should keep records like these. For your personal income tax records, you will also need to hang on to information about capital gains and cost records for your house and improvements. There are also some exceptions to the three-year rule—for example, you can be audited for six years if you fail to report more than 25% of your gross income; or you can be audited without any time limits if you file a fraudulent return.

B. State Taxes

Life would be too simple if you were only required to pay federal taxes. States get into the act as well, imposing their own taxes to fund their governments.

1. Income Taxes

All states except Alaska, Florida, Nevada, South Dakota, Texas, Washington and Wyoming impose income taxes on the self-employed. New Hampshire and Tennessee impose income taxes on dividend and interest income only. In most states, you have to pay your state income taxes during the year in the form of estimated taxes. These are usually paid at the same time you pay your federal estimated taxes.

You'll also have to file an annual state income tax return with your state tax department. In all but six states—Arkansas, Delaware, Hawaii, Iowa, Louisiana and Virginia—the return must be filed by April 15, the same deadline as your federal tax return.

If you're incorporated, your corporation will likely have to pay state income taxes and file its own state income tax return.

Each state has its own income tax forms and procedures. Contact your state tax department to learn about your state's requirements and obtain the forms.

2. Employment Taxes

If you live in a state with income taxes and have employees, you'll likely have to withhold state income taxes from their paychecks and pay the money over to your state tax department. You'll also have to provide your employees with unemployment compensation insurance by paying state unemployment taxes to your state unemployment compensation agency.

3. Local Taxes

You might have to pay local business taxes in addition to federal and state taxes. For example, many municipalities have their own sales taxes, which must be paid to a local tax agency.

Some cities and counties also impose property taxes on business equipment or furniture. You may be required to file a list of such property with local tax officials, along with cost and depreciation information. Some cities also have a tax on business inventory. This is why many retail businesses have inventory sales: They want to reduce their stock on hand before the inventory tax date.

Calendar of Important Tax Dates

The following calendar shows you important state and federal tax dates during the year. If you're one of the few self-employed people who uses a fiscal year instead of a calendar year as your tax year, these dates will be different. If you have employees, you must make additional tax filings during the year. The dates listed below represent your last possible day to take the action described. If any of the dates falls on a holiday or weekend, you have until the next business day to take the action.

Tax Calendar

Date	Action
January 15	Your last estimated tax payment for the previous year is due.
January 31	If you hired independent contractors last year, you must provide them with Form 1099-MISC.
February 28	If you hired independent contractors last year, you must file all your 1099s with the IRS.
March 15	Corporations must file federal income tax returns.
April 15	You must make your first estimated tax payment for the year.
	Partnerships must file information tax return.
	State, individual income tax returns are due in all states except Arkansas, Delaware, Hawaii, Iowa, Louisiana and Virginia.
April 20	Individual income tax returns are due in Hawaii.
April 30	Individual income tax returns are due in Delaware, Iowa and Virginia.
May 15	Individual income tax returns are due in Arkansas and Louisiana.
June 15	Make your second estimated tax payment for the year.
September 15	Make your third estimated tax payment for the year.

C. Introduction to Income Tax Deductions

A deduction is an expense or the value of an item that you can subtract from your gross income to determine your taxable income—that is, the amount you earn that is subject to taxation. The more deductions you have, the less income tax you pay. When people speak of taking a deduction or deducting an expense from their income taxes, they mean they subtract it from their gross incomes.

Most of the work involved in doing your taxes is determining what deductions you can take, how much you can take and when you can take them. You don't have to become an income tax expert. But even if you have a tax pro prepare your tax returns, you need to have a basic understanding of what expenses are deductible so that you can keep proper records. This takes some time, but it's worth it. There's no point in working hard to earn a good income only to turn most of the money over to the government.

1. What You Can Deduct

Virtually any business expense is deductible as long as it is:

- ordinary and necessary
- directly related to your business, and
- for a reasonable amount.

You must be able to prove your expenses to the IRS. For that reason, reliable accounting software such as Intuit's QuickBooks (www.intuit.com), Peach-Tree's Complete Accounting (www.peachtree.com) or M.Y.O.B. Plus (www.myob.com) is well worth buying.

a. Ordinary and Necessary Expenses

An expense qualifies as ordinary and necessary if it is common, accepted, helpful and appropriate for your business or profession. An expense doesn't have to be indispensable to be necessary; it needs only to help your business in some way, even in a minor way. It's usually fairly easy to tell if an expense passes this test.

Example: Jill, a self-employed quilt maker, hires Sue to help her with the sewing and pays her $15 an hour. This is clearly a deductible business expense. Hiring such helpers is a common and accepted practice among professional crafters. Sue's wages are an ordinary and necessary expense for Jill's crafts business.

Example: Jill visits a masseuse every week to work on her bad back. She claims the cost as a business expense, reasoning that avoiding back pain helps her concentrate on her quilting. This is clearly not an ordinary or customary expense for a crafter, and the IRS would not likely allow it as a business expense.

b. Expense Must Be Related to Your Business

An expense must be related to your business to be deductible. That is, you must use the item you buy for your business in some way. For example, the cost of a personal computer is a deductible business expense if you use it to bill customers or keep track of inventory.

You cannot deduct purely personal expenses as business expenses. The cost of a personal computer is not deductible if you use it just to play computer games. If you buy something for both personal and business reasons, you may deduct the business portion of the expense. For example, if you buy a cellular phone and use it half the time for business calls and half the time for personal calls, you can deduct half the cost of the phone as a business expense.

However, the IRS requires you to keep records showing when the item was used for business and when for personal reasons. One acceptable form of record would be a diary or log with the dates, times and reason the item was used. This kind of record-keeping can be burdensome and may not be worth the trouble if the item isn't very valuable.

To avoid having to keep such records, try to use items either only for business or only for personal use. For example, if you can afford it, purchase two computers and use one solely for your business and one for playing games, writing to friends and other personal uses.

c. Deductions Must Be Reasonable

There is usually no limit on how much you can deduct, so long as it's not more than you actually spend and the amount is reasonable. However, certain areas are hot buttons for the IRS—especially entertainment, travel and meal expenses. The IRS won't allow such expenses to the extent it considers them lavish. (See Section H, below.)

Also, if the amount of your deductions is very large relative to your income, your chance of being audited goes up dramatically. One analysis of almost 1,300 tax returns found that you are at high risk for an audit if your business deductions exceed 63% of your revenues. You're relatively safe so long as your deductions are less than 52% of your revenue (though the IRS does choose some people for audit at random). If you have extremely large deductions, make sure you can document them in case you're audited.

You can unmix personal and business expenditures. If you incur a deductible expense and pay it personally—for example, with a personal credit card—reimburse yourself by making an expense report and writing yourself a check out of your business account.

d. Common Deductions for Crafts Artists

Self-employed crafts people are typically entitled to take a number of income tax deductions. The most common include:

- advertising costs—for example, the cost of an Open Studio advertisement or a promotional postcard
- attorney and accounting fees for your business
- bank fees for your business account
- business start-up costs
- car and truck expenses (see Section E, below)
- commissions and fees paid to sales representatives and the like
- costs of renting or leasing vehicles, machinery, equipment and other property used in your business

- depreciation of business assets (see Section E2, below)
- expenses for the business use of your home
- fees you pay to other self-employed workers you hire to help your business—for example, payments to a marketing consultant to advise you on how to get more online business
- gifts to customers and suppliers
- health insurance for yourself and your family (see Section I, below)
- insurance for your business—for example, liability, workers' compensation and business property insurance
- interest on business loans and debts—for example, interest you pay for a bank loan you use to expand your business
- license fees—for example, fees for a local business license or occupational license
- office expenses, such as office supplies
- office utilities
- postage
- professional or business books
- repairs and maintenance for business equipment such as a photocopier or fax machine
- retirement plan contributions
- software for your business (see Section E3, below)
- subscriptions for professional or business publications

- trade shows
- travel, meals and entertainment (see Sections F and G)
- utilities, and
- wages and benefits you provide your employees.

Inventory Is Not a Business Expense

If you make or buy goods to sell, you are entitled to deduct the cost of those goods that were actually sold. This is what you spent for the goods, or their actual market value if they've declined in value since you bought them.

However, this deduction is separate from the business expense deduction. Instead, you deduct the cost of goods you've sold from your business receipts to determine your gross profit from the business. Your business expenses are then deducted from your gross profit to determine your net profit, which is taxed.

Crafts businesses must determine the value of their inventories at the beginning and the end of each tax year using an IRS-approved accounting method. Conducting inventories can be burdensome.

For more information on inventories, see the Cost of Goods Sold section in Chapter 7 of IRS Publication 334, *Tax Guide for Small Businesses*; Publication 538, *Accounting Periods and Methods*; and Publication 970, *Application to Use LIFO Inventory Method*. You can obtain these and all other IRS publications by calling the IRS at 800-TAX-FORM, visiting your local IRS office or downloading the publications at www.irs.gov.

2. When to Deduct

Some expenses can be deducted all at once; others have to be deducted over a number of years. It all depends on how long the item you purchase can reasonably be expected to last—what the IRS calls its useful life.

a. Current Expenses

The cost of anything you buy for your business that has a useful life of less than one year must be fully deducted in the year it is purchased. This includes, for example, rent, telephone and utility bills, photocopying costs and postage and other ordinary business operating costs. Such items are called current expenses.

b. Capital Expenses

Certain types of costs are considered to be part of your investment in your business—the major costs of setting it up as opposed to the costs of operating it day to day. These are called capital expenses. Subject to an important exception for a certain amount of personal property (see Section E1, below), you cannot deduct the full value of such expenses in the year you incur them. Instead, you must spread the cost over several years and deduct part of it each year.

There are two main categories of capital expenses. They include:

- the cost of any asset you will use in your business that has a useful life of more than one year—for example, equipment, vehicles, books, furniture, machinery and patents (see Section E2, below), and
- business start-up costs such as fees for doing market research or attorney and accounting fees paid to set up your business.

3. Businesses That Lose Money

If the money you spend on your business exceeds your business income for the year, your business incurs a loss. This isn't as bad as it sounds, tax-wise. You can use a business loss to offset other income you may have—for example, interest income, or your spouse's income if you file jointly. You can even accumulate your losses and apply them to reduce your income taxes in future or past years.

 For detailed information on deducting business losses, see IRS Publication 536, *Net Operating Losses*. You can obtain this and all other IRS publications by calling the IRS at 800-TAX-FORM, visiting your local IRS office or downloading the publications at www.irs. gov.

a. Recurring Losses and the Hobby Loss Rule

If you fall into a pattern of incurring losses year after year, you risk running afoul of the hobby loss rule. This is no small risk—it could cost you a small fortune in additional income taxes.

The IRS created the hobby loss rule to prevent taxpayers from entering into ventures primarily to incur expenses they can deduct from their other incomes. The rule closes this potential loophole by allowing you to take a business expense deduction only if your venture qualifies as a business. Ventures that don't qualify as businesses are called hobbies—it's assumed that you're pursuing them for personal satisfaction, not for money. If the IRS views what you do as a hobby, there will be severe limits on what expenses you can deduct.

According to the IRS, a venture is a business if you engage in it to make a profit. It's not necessary that you earn a profit every year. All that is required is that your main reason for doing what you do is to make a profit. A hobby is any activity you engage in mainly for a reason other than making a profit—for example, to incur deductible expenses or just to have fun.

The IRS can't read your mind to determine whether you want to earn a profit. And it certainly isn't going to take your word for it. Instead, it looks to see whether you do actually earn a profit, or whether you behave as if you want to earn a profit.

b. Profit Test

You don't have to worry about the IRS labeling your business as a hobby if you earn a profit from it in any three of five consecutive years. If your venture passes this test, the IRS presumes it is carried on for profit.

You have a profit when the gross income from an activity rises higher than the deductions for it. You don't have to earn a big profit to satisfy this test. Careful year-end planning can help your business show a profit for the year. For example, if clients owe you money, press them for payment before the end of the year. Also, put off paying expenses or buying new equipment until the new year.

A loss for one or two years isn't fatal. But do everything possible to avoid showing losses for three consecutive years. This will definitely set the IRS computers to whirring and increase your chance of being audited. If you are audited, the hobby loss issue will definitely be raised.

c. Behavior Test

If you keep incurring losses and can't satisfy the profit test, you by no means have to throw in the towel and decide your crafts venture is a hobby. You can continue to treat it as a business and fully deduct your losses. However, you must take steps that will convince the IRS your crafts business isn't a hobby if you're audited.

You must be able to convince the IRS that earning a profit—not having fun or accumulating tax deductions—is the primary motive for your crafts. This can be particularly difficult for crafts artists. To the rest of the world, you're engaged in an activity that looks enjoyable. But don't give up. Crafts people who have incurred losses for seven, eight or nine years in a row have convinced the IRS they were running a business.

You must show the IRS that your behavior is consistent with that of a person who really wants to make money. There are many ways to accomplish this.

First and foremost, you must show that you carry on your enterprise in a businesslike manner. Some good indicators are that you:

- maintain a separate checking account for your business
- keep good business records
- make some effort to market your services—for example, have business cards, apply to crafts shows or create a website
- have business stationery and cards printed

- obtain a federal employer identification number
- secure all necessary business licenses and permits
- have a separate phone line for your crafts business if you work at home
- join crafts organizations and associations, and
- develop expertise in your crafts field by attending classes and similar activities.

It is also helpful to draw up a business plan with forecasts of revenue and expenses. This will also be a big help if you try to borrow money for your business.

For detailed guidance on how to create a business plan, see *How to Write a Business Plan*, by Mike McKeever (Nolo).

The more time and effort you put into the activity, the more it will look like you want to make money. So try to devote as much time as possible to your business, and keep a log showing the time you spend on it.

It's also helpful to consult with other crafts businesses and follow their advice about how to modify your operations to increase sales and cut costs. Be sure to document your efforts.

Example: Otto makes and sells rustic punched-tin ornaments. He has incurred losses from his business for the past three years. He consults with Cindy, a prominent art gallery owner, about how he can sell more of his work. He writes down her recommendations and then documents his efforts to follow them—for example, he visits crafts shows around the country and talks with a number of gallery owners about representing his work.

You'll have an easier time convincing the IRS your venture is a business if you earn a profit in at least some years. It's also very helpful if you've earned profits from similar businesses in the past.

d. Tax Effect of a Hobby Venture

If the IRS determines your venture is a hobby, you'll lose valuable deductions, and your income tax burden will increase. Unlike business expenses, expenses for a hobby are personal expenses that you can deduct only from income from the hobby. They can't be applied to your other income such as your or your spouse's salary or interest income.

Example: Bill holds a full-time job as a college geology teacher, and in his spare time constructs fanciful wooden weathervanes. The IRS has decided that making weathervanes is a hobby for Bill, since he's never earned a profit from it. In one year, Bill spent $2,000 on his weathervanes, but earned only $500. His expenses can only be deducted from the $500 income. This wipes out the $500, but Bill cannot apply the remainder to his other income. Because of the hobby loss rule, Bill has lost $1,500 worth of tax deductions.

4. Tax Savings From Deductions

Only part of any deduction will end up as an income tax saving—for example, a $5,000 tax deduction will not result in a $5,000 slice off your income tax bill. How much you'll save depends on your tax rate. The tax law assigns a percentage income tax rate to specified income levels. People with high incomes pay income tax at a higher rate than those with lower incomes. These percentage rates are called tax brackets.

To determine how much income tax a deduction will save you, you need to know your marginal tax bracket. This is the tax bracket into which the last dollar you earn falls. It determines the rate at which any additional income you earn would be taxed. The income tax brackets are adjusted each year for inflation.

For the current brackets, see IRS Publication 505, *Tax Withholding and Estimated Tax.* You can obtain this and all other IRS publications by calling the IRS at 800-TAX-FORM, visiting your local IRS office or downloading the publications at www.irs.gov.

The following table shows the tax brackets for 2002.

2002 Tax Brackets

Tax Bracket	Income If Married Filing Joint Return	Income If Single
10%	Up to $12,000	Up to $6,000
15%	$12,001 to $46,700	$6,001 to $27,950
27%	$46,701 to $112,850	$27,951 to $67,700
30%	$112,851 to $171,950	$67,701 to $141,250
35%	$171,951 to $307,050	$141,251 to $307,050
38.6%	All income over $307,050	All income over $307,050

To determine how much tax a deduction will save you, multiply the amount of the deduction by your marginal tax bracket. If your marginal tax bracket is 27%, you will save 27 cents in income taxes for every dollar you are able to claim as a deductible business expense.

Example: Barry, a single self-employed glass blower, earned $50,000 in 2002 and was therefore in the 27% marginal tax bracket. He was able to take a $5,000 home office deduction. His actual income tax saving was 27% of the $5,000 deduction, or $1,350.

You can also deduct most business-related expenses from your income for self-employment tax purposes.

The effective self-employment tax rate is about 12% on net self-employment income up to the Social Security tax cap ($84,900 in 2002).

In addition, you may deduct your business expenses from your state income tax. State income taxes rates vary, but they average about 6%. (However, Alaska, Florida, Nevada, South Dakota, Texas, Washington and Wyoming don't have income taxes.)

When we add the various taxes together, you can see the true value of a business tax deduction. For example, if you're in the 27% federal income tax bracket, a business deduction is roughly worth 27% + 12% + 6% = 45%. So you end up deducting about 45% of the cost of your business expenses from your state and federal taxes. If, for example, you buy a $1,000 computer for your business, you may deduct about $450 of the cost from your taxes. That's a whopping tax savings. In effect, the government is paying for almost half of your business expenses. This is why it's so important to take all the business deductions to which you're entitled.

D. Business Use of Your Home

If you elect to work from home, the federal government is prepared to help you out by allowing you to deduct your home office expenses from your taxes. This is so whether you own your home or apartment or are a renter. Although this tax deduction is commonly called the home office deduction, it is not limited to traditional home offices with desks, bookcases and potted ferns. You can also take the deduction if you have a crafts studio at home.

If you've heard stories about how difficult it is to qualify for the home office deduction and felt it wasn't worth the trouble involved, take a second look. Changes in the tax law that took effect in 1999 make it much easier for self-employed people to qualify for the deduction. Even if you haven't qualified for the deduction in the past, you may be entitled to it now.

Because some people still believe the home office deduction is an audit flag for the IRS—and preach that fear loudly—many self-employed people who may qualify for the deduction are afraid to take it. Although taking the home office deduction might increase your chance of being audited, the chances are still relatively small. Also, you have nothing to fear from an audit if you're entitled to the deduction.

However, if you intend to take the deduction, you should also make an effort to understand the requirements and set up your home office so as to satisfy them. Before you start moving your furniture around, read this section.

1. Regular and Exclusive Business Use

You can't take the home office deduction unless you regularly use part of your home exclusively for a trade or business.

Unfortunately, the IRS doesn't offer a satisfactory definition of regular use to guide you. The agency has decreed only that you must use a portion of your home for business on a continuing basis—not just for occasional or incidental business. You'll likely satisfy this test if you use your home office a few hours each day.

Exclusive use means that you use a portion of your home *only* for business. If you use part of your home as your business office and also use that part for personal purposes, you cannot meet the exclusive use test and cannot take the home office deduction.

> *Example:* Andrea uses her den to create miniature rock fountains. The den is furnished with a desk, chair, bookshelf, filing cabinet and bed. She uses the desk and chair for her work and for personal reasons. The bookshelf contains both personal books and examples of her rock fountains. The filing cabinet contains both personal and business files. Andrea can't claim a business deduction for the den since it is not used exclusively for business purposes.

You needn't devote an entire separate room in your home to your business. But some part of the room must be used exclusively for business.

> *Example:* Paul creates enameled plates in one part of his basement and uses that portion exclusively as his studio. The remainder of the basement—one-third of the space—is used to store personal household goods. Paul can take a home office deduction for the two-thirds of the basement used exclusively as a studio.

As a practical matter, the IRS isn't going to make a surprise inspection of your home to see whether you're complying with these requirements. However, complying with the rules from the beginning avoids having to lie to the IRS if you are audited.

This means, simply, that you'll have to arrange your furniture and belongings so as to devote a portion of your home exclusively to your home office. The more space you use exclusively for business, the more your home office deduction will be worth. (See Section D7, below.)

Although not explicitly required by law, it's a good idea to physically separate the space you use for business from the rest of the room. For example, if you use part of your living room as an office, separate it from the rest of the room with room dividers or bookcases.

2. Qualifying for the Deduction

Unfortunately, satisfying the requirement of using your home office regularly and exclusively for business is only half the battle.

It must also be true that:

- your home office is your principal place of business
- you meet clients or customers at home, or
- you use a separate structure on your property exclusively for business purposes.

Here are some ways to help convince the IRS you qualify for the home office deduction:

- Take a picture of your home studio or office and draw up a diagram showing it as a portion of your home.
- Have all your business mail sent to your home office.
- Use your home office address on all your business cards, stationery and advertising.
- Obtain a separate phone line for your crafts business and keep that phone in your home office. The tax law helps you do this by allowing you to deduct the monthly fee for a second phone line in your home if you use it for business. You can't deduct the monthly fee for a single phone line, even if you use it partly for business. However, you can deduct the cost of business calls you place from that line. Having a separate business phone will also make it easier for you to keep track of your business phone expenses.
- Encourage buyers, clients or customers to regularly visit your home office, and keep a log of their visits.

- To make the most of the time you spend in your home office, communicate with buyers, clients and customers by phone, fax or electronic mail instead of going to their homes or offices. Use a mail or messenger service to deliver your work to customers.
- Keep a log of the time you spend working in your home studio. This doesn't have to be fancy; notes on your calendar will do.

3. Home as Principal Place of Business

The most common way to qualify for the home office deduction is to use your home as your principal place of business. Indeed, due to the 1999 changes in the tax laws, most self-employed craft workers will be able to qualify for the home office deduction on this basis.

a. If You Do Most of Your Work at Home

If, like many self-employed crafts people, you do all or most of your work in your home studio or workshop, your home is clearly your principal place of business, and you'll have no trouble at all qualifying for the home office deduction.

b. If You Do Only Administrative Work at Home

Your home office will also qualify as your principal place of business even if you work primarily outside your home if:

- you use your home office to conduct administrative or management activities for your crafts business, and
- there is no other fixed location where you conduct such activities.

What this means is that, to qualify for the home office deduction, your home office need no longer be the place where you generate most of your business income. It's sufficient that you regularly use it to administer or manage your business—for example, keep your books, schedule appointments, do research and order supplies. As long as you have no other fixed location where you do such things—for example, an outside office—you'll get the deduction.

Based on these rules, most self-employed people qualify for the home office deduction. All you have to do is set up a home office that you regularly use to manage or administer your business. Even if you spend most of your work time away from home, you can still find plenty of business-related work to do in your home office.

4. Meeting Clients or Customers at Home

Even if your home office is not your principal place of business, you may deduct your expenses if a part of your home is used exclusively to meet with buyers, clients or customers. You must physically meet with them at your home—phoning them from home is not sufficient. And the meetings must be a regular part of your business—occasional meetings don't qualify.

There is no numerical standard for how often you must meet clients at home for those meetings to be considered regular. However, the IRS has indicated that meeting clients one or two days a week is sufficient. "Exclusive use" means you use the space only for business—for example, as a showroom devoted solely to selling crafts or taking custom orders. You are free to use the space for business purposes other than meeting clients—for example, for doing your business bookkeeping or other paperwork. But you cannot use the space for personal purposes such as watching television.

5. Using a Separate Structure for Business

You can also deduct expenses for a separate free-standing structure such as a studio, garage or barn if you use it exclusively and regularly for your business. The structure does not have to be your principal place of business or a place where you meet buyers, clients or customers.

As always where the home office deduction is involved, exclusive use means you use the structure only for business—for example, you can't use it to store gardening equipment or as a guesthouse. Regular use is not precisely defined, but it's probably sufficient for you to use the structure ten or 15 hours a week.

Example: Deborah has her main showroom and studio in an office building downtown, but also works every weekend in a small studio in her back yard creating her hooked rugs. Since she uses the back yard studio regularly and exclusively for her rugs, it qualifies for the home office deduction.

6. Storing Inventory or Product Samples at Home

You can take the home office deduction if you're in the business of selling retail or wholesale crafts products and you store inventory or product samples at home.

To qualify, you can't have a studio or office or other business location outside your home. And you must store your inventory in a particular place in your home—for example, a garage, closet or bedroom. You can't move your inventory from one room to the other. You don't have to use the storage space exclusively to store your inventory to take the deduction. It's sufficient that you regularly use it for that purpose.

Example: Janet sells her handmade rings door to door. She rents a home and regularly uses half of her attached garage to store her jewelry inventory. She also uses it to park her Harley Davidson motorcycle. Janet can deduct the expenses for the storage space, even though she does not use her garage exclusively to store inventory. Her garage accounts for 20% of the total floor space of her house. Since she uses only half of the garage for storing inventory, she may deduct one-half of this, or 10% of her rent and certain other expenses.

7. Amount of Deduction

How much you can claim toward your home office deduction depends on how much (what percentage) of your home you use as a home office or studio.

For example, if you use 20% of your home, you can allot 20% of your home office expenses to the home office deduction. The main expenses that qualify are:

- your rent if you rent your home, or
- depreciation, mortgage interest and property taxes if you own your home.

In addition, owners and renters may deduct this same percentage of other expenses for keeping up and running an entire home. The IRS calls these indirect expenses. They include:

- utility expenses for electricity, gas, heating oil and trash removal
- homeowner's or renter's insurance
- home maintenance expenses that benefit your entire home including your home office, such as roof and furnace repairs and exterior painting
- condominium association fees
- snow removal expenses
- casualty losses if your home is damaged—for example, in a storm, and
- security system costs.

You may also deduct the entire cost of expenses just for your home office. The IRS calls these direct expenses. They include, for example, painting your home office or studio or paying someone to clean it. If you pay a housekeeper to clean your entire house, you may deduct your business use percentage of the expense.

Taking the home office deduction won't increase your income tax deductions for these items, but it will allow you to deduct them from your self-employment taxes. You'll save $153 in self-employment taxes for every $1,000 in mortgage interest and property taxes you deduct. You'll also be able to deduct a portion of repairs, utility bills, cleaning and maintenance costs and depreciation.

8. Special Concerns for Homeowners

If you're not careful when you take the home office deduction, you may have to pay extra taxes when you sell your home.

Ordinarily, any profit you make when you sell your home is not taxable—up to $250,000 for single taxpayers and $500,000 for married taxpayers filing jointly. However, if you take the home office deduction, this rule does not apply to the portion of your house you use for business. Instead, your old house is treated as two separate properties for tax purposes.

You'll have to pay a 20% capital gains tax on the profit you earn from the portion of your house used as a home office. For example, if 20% of your house was used as a home office, you'd have to pay tax on 20% of the profit you earn when you sell your home. If your home has gone up in value dramatically since you bought it, you'll have a huge tax bill.

You'll also have to pay tax on any depreciation you took on your home office.

To avoid this tax trap, you must use your entire home as your principal residence for at least two of the five years preceding the year of sale. In other words, you can't take the home office deduction for those two years. So, if you plan on moving, it's best not to use a home office for least two years before the date of sale.

If you want to be able to move on short notice without worrying about taxes, don't take the home office deduction.

E. Deducting the Cost of Business Assets

One of the nice things about being a self-employed crafts worker is that you can deduct from your income taxes what you spend for things you use to help produce income. Booth canopies, engraving pens, computers, calculators and studio furniture may all be deducted. You can take a full deduction whether you pay cash for an asset or buy it on credit.

If you qualify for the Section 179 deduction discussed below, you can deduct the entire cost of these items in the year you pay for them. Otherwise, you have to deduct the cost over a period of years—a process called depreciation.

The rules for deducting business assets can be complex, but it's worth spending the time to understand them. After all, the U.S. government is in effect offering to help you pay for your equipment and other business assets. All you have to do is take advantage of the offer.

1. Section 179 Deduction

If you learn only one section number in the tax code, it should be Section 179. It is one of the greatest tax boons for small businesspeople. Section 179 permits you to deduct a large amount of your business asset purchases in the year you make them, rather than having to depreciate them over several years. (See Section E2, below.) This is called first year expensing or Section 179 expensing. It allows you to get a big tax deduction all at once, rather than having to mete it out a little at a time.

> *Example:* Ginger buys a $4,000 fusion welder for her crafts business. She can use Section 179 to deduct the entire $4,000 expense from her income taxes for the year.

It's up to you to decide whether to use Section 179. It may not always be in your best interests to do so. (See Section E2, below.) If you do use it, you can't change your mind later and decide to use depreciation instead.

a. Property That Can Be Deducted

You can use Section 179 to deduct the cost of any tangible personal property you use for your business that the IRS has determined will last more than one year—for example, computers, business equipment and office furniture. Special rules apply to cars. (See Section E3, below.) You can't use Section 179 for land, buildings or intangible personal property such as patents, copyrights and trademarks.

If you use property both for business and personal purposes, you may deduct under Section 179 only if you use it for business purposes more than half the time. The amount of your deduction is reduced by the percentage of personal use. You'll need to keep records showing your business use of such property. If you use an item for business less than half the time, you must depreciate it. (See Section E2, below.)

b. Deduction Limit

There is a limit on the total amount of business expenses you can deduct each year using Section 179. In 2002, the limit is $24,000. In 2003 and later it is $25,000.

If you purchase more than one item of Section 179 property during the year, you can divide the deduction among all the items in any way, as long as the total deduction is not more than the Section 179 limit. It's usually best to apply Section 179 to property that has the longest useful life and therefore the longest depreciation period. This reduces the total time you have to wait to get your deductions. (See Section E2c, below.)

> *Example:* In 2002, Ben, a self-employed jeweler, buys for his business a $2,000 faceting machine, a $4,000 engraving machine, a $3,000 electronic rolling mill, a $6,000 furnace, a $3,000 slab saw, a $4,000 computer, $3,000 in office furniture and a $1,000 printer. The total for all these purchases is $26,000—more than the $24,000 Section 179 limit for 2002. He can divide his Section 179 deduction among these items any way he wants. The printer and computer would have to be depreciated over five years, but the furniture over seven years. He should apply Section 179 to the furniture first and then to the computer or copier. Any portion of the cost of the copier or computer that exceeds the Section 179 limit can be depreciated over five years. This way, he avoids having to wait seven years to get his full deduction for the furniture.

c. Limit on Section 179 Deduction

You can't use Section 179 to deduct more in one year than your total profit from all of your businesses and your salary if you have a job in addition to your business. If you're married and file a joint tax return, your spouse's salary and business income is included as well. You can't count investment income—for example, interest you earn on your savings.

You can't use Section 179 to reduce your taxable income below zero. But any amount you cannot use as a Section 179 deduction you can carry to the next tax year and possibly deduct at that time.

> *Example:* In 2000, Amelia earned a $5,000 profit from her crafts business and $10,000 from a part-time job. She spent $17,000 for equipment. She can use Section 179 to deduct $15,000 of this expense for 2000 and deduct the remaining $2,000 the next year.

In the unlikely event that you buy over $200,000 of Section 179 property in a year, your deduction is reduced by one dollar for every dollar you spend over $200,000.

d. Minimum Period Of Business Use

When you deduct an asset under Section 179, you must continue to use it for business at least 50% of the time for as many years it would have been depreciated. (See Section E2c, below.) For example, if you use Section 179 for a computer, you must use that computer for business at least 50% of the time for five years, since computers have a five-year depreciation period.

If you don't meet these rules, you'll have to report as income part of the deduction you took under Section 179 in the prior year. This is called recapture.

For more information, see IRS Publication 334, *Tax Guide for Small Business*, Chapter 12, "Depreciation." You can obtain this and all other IRS publications by calling the IRS at 800-TAX-FORM, visiting your local IRS office or downloading the publications at www.irs.gov.

2. Depreciation

Because it provides a big tax deduction immediately, most crafts business owners look first to Section 179 to deduct asset costs.

However, you must use depreciation instead if you:
- don't qualify to use Section 179—for example, you want to deduct the cost of a building or a design patent, or
- use up your Section 179 deduction for the year.

Depreciation involves deducting the cost of a business asset a little at time over a period of years. This means it will take you much longer to get your full deduction than under Section 179. However, this isn't always a bad thing. Indeed, you may be better off in the long run using depreciation instead of Section 179 if you expect to earn more in future years than you will in the current year. Remember that the value of a deduction depends on your income tax bracket. If you're in the 15% bracket, a $1,000 deduction is worth only $150. If you're in the 30% bracket, it's worth $300. (See Section C4, above.) So spreading out a deduction until you're in a higher tax bracket can make sense.

Depreciation may also be preferable to using Section 179 if you want to puff up your business income for the year. This can help you get a bank loan or help your business show a profit instead of incurring a loss and avoid running afoul of the hobby loss limitations. (See Section C3, below.)

a. Items That Must Be Depreciated

Whether you must depreciate an item depends on how long it can reasonably be expected to last—what the IRS calls its useful life. Depreciation is used to deduct the cost of any asset you buy for your business that has a useful life of more than one year—for example, buildings, equipment, machinery, patents, trademarks, copyrights and furniture. Land cannot be depreciated because it doesn't wear out. The IRS, not you, decides the useful life of your assets. (See Section E2c, below.)

You can also depreciate the cost of major repairs that increase the value or extend the life of an asset—for example, the cost of a major upgrade to make your computer run faster. However, you deduct normal repairs or maintenance in the year they're incurred as a business expense.

b. Mixed Use Property

If you use property both for business and personal purposes, you can take depreciation only for the business use of the asset. Unlike for the Section 179 deduction, you don't have to use an item over half of the time for business in order to depreciate it.

Example: Carl uses his photocopier 75% of the time for personal reasons and 25% for his crafts business. He can depreciate 25% of the cost of the copier.

Keep a diary or log showing the dates, times and reasons the property was used, so as to distinguish between the two uses.

c. Depreciation Period

The depreciation period—called the recovery period by the IRS—begins when you start using the asset and lasts for the entire estimated useful life of the asset. The tax code has assigned an estimated useful life for all types of business assets, ranging from three to 39 years. Most of the assets you buy for your business will probably have an estimated useful life of five or seven years.

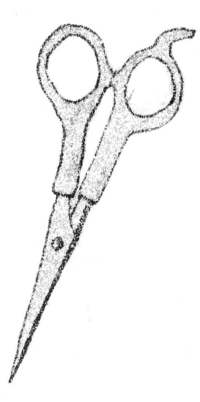

To find the depreciation period for an asset not included in this table, see IRS Publication 534, *Depreciation*, which contains a complete listing. You can obtain this and all other IRS publications by calling the IRS at 800-TAX-FORM, visiting your local IRS office or downloading the publications at www.irs.gov.

You are free to continue using property after its estimated useful life expires, but you can't deduct any more depreciation.

Depreciable Periods for Commonly Used Office Property

Type of Property	Recovery Period
Computer software (except software that comes with your computer, which is not separately depreciable unless you're separately billed for it)	3 years
Office machinery (computers and peripherals, calculators, copiers, typewriters)	5 years
Autos and light trucks	5 years
Construction and research equipment	5 years
Office furniture and any property that does not have an established IRS class life and has not been designated by law as being in any other class	7 years
Residential buildings	27 1/2 years
Nonresidential buildings purchased before May 12, 1993	31 1/2 years
Nonresidential buildings purchased after May 12, 1993	39 years

d. Calculating Depreciation

You can use three different methods to calculate the depreciation deduction: "straight line" or one of two accelerated depreciation methods. A brief introduction is provided here. (Review the IRS publications for more details.) Once you choose your method, you're stuck with it for the entire life of the asset.

In addition, you must use the same method for all property of the same kind purchased during the year. For example, if you use the straight-line method to depreciate a computer, you must use that method to depreciate all other computers you purchase during the year for your business.

The straight-line method requires you to deduct an equal amount each year over the useful life of an asset. However, you ordinarily deduct only a half-year's worth of depreciation in the first year. You make up for this by adding an extra year of depreciation at the end.

Most small businesses use one of two types of accelerated depreciation: the "double declining balance" method or the "150% declining balance" method. The advantage to these methods is that they provide larger depreciation deductions in the earlier years and smaller ones later on. The double declining balance method starts out by giving you double the deduction you'd get for the first full year with the straight-line method. The 150% declining balance method gives you one and one-half times the straight-line deduction.

In the wake of the 9/11 tragedy and the ensuing recession, Congress revised the depreciation rules to give businesses an additional depreciation deduction. Under these rules, taxpayers get an additional "bonus" 30% depreciation deduction for property purchased between September 11, 2001 and September 10, 2004 and placed into service (used in business) before 2005. The 30% is deducted from the "adjusted basis" (usually the cost) of the property and is in addition to normal depreciation.

For more information, see IRS Publication 534, *Depreciation,* and IRS Publication 946, *How to Depreciate Property.* You can obtain these and all other IRS publications by calling the IRS at 800-TAX-FORM, visiting your local IRS office or downloading the publications at www.irs.gov.

3. Cars, Computers and Cellular Phones

There are special rules for certain items that can easily be used for personal as well as business purposes.

These items are called listed property and include:

- cars, boats, airplanes and other vehicles (see also Section F for rules on mileage and vehicle expenses)
- computers
- cellular phones, and
- any other property generally used for entertainment, recreation or amusement—for example, VCRs, cameras and camcorders.

The IRS fears that taxpayers might use listed property items such as computers for personal reasons while claiming business deductions for them. For this reason, you're required to document your business use of listed property. You can satisfy this requirement by keeping a logbook showing when and how the property was used.

a. Exception to Recordkeeping Rule

You normally have to document your use of listed property even if you use it 100% for business. However, there is an exception to this rule: If you use listed property only for business and keep it at your business location, you need not comply with the recordkeeping requirement. This includes listed property you keep at your home office if the office qualifies for the home office deduction. (See Section D, above.)

Example: John makes ceramic tiles full time in his home studio, which he uses exclusively for his crafts. The studio is clearly his principal place of business and qualifies for the home office deduction. He buys a $4,000 computer for his business and uses it 100% for his crafts business. He does not have to keep records showing how he uses the computer.

b. Depreciating Listed Property

If you use listed property for business more than 50% of the time, you can depreciate it just like any other property. However, if you use it 50% or less of the time for business, you must use the straight-line depreciation method and an especially long recovery period. If you start out using accelerated depreciation and your business use drops to 50% or less, you have to switch to the straight-line method and pay taxes on the benefits of the prior years of accelerated depreciation.

F. Car Expenses

Most crafts makers do at least some driving related to business—for example, to visit buyers, trade shows or retail customers; to pick up or deliver work, to obtain business supplies; or to attend seminars. Of course, driving costs money—and you are allowed to deduct your driving expenses when you use your car, van, pickup or panel truck for business.

There are two ways to calculate the car expense deduction. You can:

- use the standard mileage rate—which requires relatively little recordkeeping, or
- deduct your actual expenses—which requires much more recordkeeping but might give you a larger deduction.

If you own a late model car worth more than $15,000, you'll usually get a larger deduction by using the actual expense method, since the standard mileage rate doesn't include enough for depreciation of new cars. On the other hand, the standard mileage rate will be better if you have an inexpensive or old car and put in a lot of business mileage.

Either way, you'll need to have records showing how many miles you drive your car for business during the year—also called business miles. Keep a mileage log book for this purpose.

Commuting Expenses Are Not Deductible

You usually cannot deduct commuting expenses—that is, the cost involved in getting to and from work. However, if your main office is at home, you may deduct the cost of driving to meet clients. This is one of the advantages of having a home office.

1. Standard Mileage Rate

The easiest way to deduct car expenses is to take the standard mileage rate. When you use this method, you need only keep track of how many business miles you drive, not the actual expenses for your car such as gas or repairs.

You can use the standard mileage rate only for a car that you own. You must choose to use it in the first year you start using your car for your business. In later years, you can choose to use the standard mileage rate or actual expenses.

Each year, the IRS sets the standard mileage rate—a specified amount of money you can deduct for each business mile you drive. In 2002, for example, the rate was 36.5 cents per mile. To figure your deduction, multiply your business miles by the standard mileage rate for the year.

Example: Ed, an expert in jewelry made from recycled materials, drove his car 10,000 miles for business in 2002. To determine his car expense deduction, he simply multiplies the total business miles he drove by 36.5 cents. This gives him a $3,650 deduction (36.5 cents x 10,000 = $3,650).

If you choose to use the standard mileage rate, you cannot deduct actual operating expenses—for example, depreciation or the Section 179 deduction, maintenance and repairs, gasoline and its taxes, oil, insurance and vehicle registration fees. These costs are already factored into the standard mileage rate.

You can deduct any business-related parking fees and tolls—for example, a parking fee you have to pay when you visit a client's office. But you cannot deduct fees you pay to park your car at your place of work.

2. Actual Expenses

Instead of taking the standard mileage rate, you can elect to deduct the actual expenses of using your car for business. To do this, deduct the actual cost of depreciation for your car, interest payments on a car loan, lease fees, rental fees, license fees, garage rent, repairs, gas, oil, tires and insurance. The total deductible amount is based on the percentage of time you use your car for business. You can also deduct the full amount of any business-related parking fees and tolls.

Deducting all these items will take more time and effort than using the standard mileage rate, because you'll need to keep records of all your expenses. However, it may provide you with a larger deduction than the standard rate.

> *Example:* Sam drives his $20,000 car 15,000 miles for his crafts business in 2002, and doesn't drive it at all for personal use. If he took the standard mileage deduction, he could deduct $5,475 from his income taxes (36.5 cents x 15,000 = $5,475). Instead, however, he takes the actual expense deduction. He keeps careful records of all his costs for gas, oil, repairs, parking, insurance and depreciation. These amount to $7,000 for the year. He gets an extra $1,525 deduction by using the actual expense method.

a. Mixed Uses

If you use your car for both business and personal purposes, you must also divide your expenses between business and personal use.

> *Example:* In one recent year Laura, a gallery owner, drove her car 10,000 miles for her business and 10,000 miles for personal purposes. She can deduct 50% of the actual costs of operating her car.

If you only own one car, you normally can't claim it's used only for business. An IRS auditor is not likely to believe that you walk or take public transportation everywhere except when you're on business. The only exception might be if you live in a place with developed transportation systems, such as Chicago, New York City or San Francisco, and drive your car only when you go out of town on business.

b. Expense Records Required

When you deduct actual car expenses, you must keep records of the costs of operating your car. This includes not only the number of business miles and total miles you drive, but also gas, repair, parking, insurance and similar costs. If this seems to be too much trouble, use the standard mileage rate. That way, you'll have to keep track of only how many business miles you drive, not what you spend for gas and similar expenses.

c. Limits on Depreciation Deductions

Regardless of how much you spend for an automobile, your depreciation deduction is strictly limited. For example, for cars purchased in 2000, the annual depreciation deduction is limited to a maximum of $3,060 the first year, $5,000 the second year, $2,950 the third year and $1,775 thereafter. These amounts change each year.

For cars purchased between September 11, 2001 and September 10, 2004 and placed into service (used in business) before 2005, the first year's deduction cap is $7,660 (a $4,600 increase over the old cap).

 For more information about the rules for claiming car expenses, see IRS Publication 463, *Travel, Entertainment, Gift and Car Expenses*. You can obtain this and all other IRS publications by calling the IRS at 800-TAX-FORM, visiting your local IRS office or downloading the publications at www.irs.gov.

G. Travel Expenses

If you travel for your crafts business—for example, you regularly attend crafts shows or visit reps or gallery owners—you can deduct your airfare, hotel bills and other expenses. If you plan your trip right, you can even mix business with pleasure and still get a deduction for your airfare. However, IRS auditors closely scrutinize these deductions, because many taxpayers claim them without complying with the copious rules attached to them. This is why you need to understand the limitations on this deduction and keep proper records.

There are two per diem rates, lodging and meals and incidental expenses (M&IE). If you are self-employed, you can use only the M&IE. If you pay for employees to travel, you can use both lodging and M&IE to account for their expenses. For example, if you were a self-employed crafts artist selling at the BMAC winter show, you could use the maximum Philadelphia per diem rates of $46 for meals and incidental expenses, and you would not have to keep track of your meal receipts while at the show.

If you claim per diems, you cannot also individually account for meals (you must use one system or the other). Also, any meal costs substantiated using the M&IE rate are subject to the 50% limitation on meal expense deductions discussed in Section H3, below. Using the per diem system may simplify your recordkeeping and reduce your tax bill while still permitting you to deduct other related travel expenses.

1. Travel Within the U.S.

Some people seem to think they have the right to deduct the cost of any trip they take. This is not the case. You can deduct a trip within the United States only if:

- it's primarily for business
- you travel outside your city limits, and
- you're away at least overnight or long enough to require a stop for sleep or rest.

a. Business Purpose of Trip

For your trip to be deductible, you must spend more than half of your time on activities that can reasonably be expected to help advance your business.

Acceptable activities include:

- visiting or working with clients or customers
- attending crafts or trade shows, or
- attending seminars or classes where the agenda is clearly connected to your crafts business.

Business does not include sightseeing or recreation that you attend by yourself or with family or friends, nor does it include personal investment seminars or political events.

Use common sense before claiming a trip is for business. The IRS will likely question any trip that doesn't have some logical connection to your business. For example, if you build houses in Alaska, an IRS auditor would probably be skeptical about a deduction for a trip you took to Florida to learn about new home air conditioning techniques.

To repeat, if your trip within the United States is not primarily for business, none of your travel expenses are deductible. But you can still deduct amounts you spend while vacationing that are directly related to your business—for example, the cost of making long-distance phone calls to your office or clients.

b. Travel Outside City Limits

You don't have to travel any set distance to get a travel expense deduction. However, you can't take this deduction if you just spend the night in a motel across town. You must travel outside your city limits. If you don't live in a city, you must go outside the general area where your business is located.

c. Sleep or Rest

Finally, you must stay away overnight or at least long enough to require a stop for sleep or rest. You cannot satisfy the rest requirement by merely napping in your car.

Example: Phyllis, a glass bead maker based in Los Angeles, flies to San Francisco to meet potential clients, spends the night in a hotel and returns home the following day. Her trip is a deductible travel expense.

d. Combining Business With Pleasure

Provided that your trip is primarily for business, you can tack on a vacation at the end, make a side trip purely for fun or go to the theater and still deduct your entire airfare. What you spend while having fun is not deductible, but you can still deduct your expenses while on business.

Example: Bill flies to Philadelphia for the BMAC winter crafts show, where he maintains a booth for every day of the show. He then spends two days in Philadelphia enjoying the sights. Since Bill spent over half his time on business—four days out of six—the cost of his flight is entirely deductible, as are his hotel and meal costs during the business meeting. He may not deduct his hotel, meal or other expenses during his two vacation days.

2. Foreign Travel

The rules differ if you travel outside the United States, and are in some ways more lenient. However, you must have a legitimate business reason for your foreign trip.

a. Foreign Trips Lasting up to Seven Days

If you're away no more than seven days, and you spend the majority of your time on business, you can deduct all of your travel costs.

However, even if your trip was primarily a vacation, you can deduct your airfare and other transportation costs, as long as at least part of the trip was for business. You can also deduct your expenses while on business. For this reason, it's often best to limit business-related foreign travel to seven days.

Example: Jennifer flies to Munich for a two-day crafts show. She then spends five days sightseeing. She can deduct the entire cost of her airfare, as well as the portion of her hotel and meals she spent while attending the meeting.

b. Foreign Trips Lasting More Than Seven Days

More stringent rules apply if your foreign trip lasts more than one week. To get a full deduction for your expenses, you must spend at least 75% of your trip on business matters.

If you spend less than 75% of your time on business, you must determine the percentage of your time spent on business by counting the number of business days and the number of personal days. You can only deduct the percentage of your travel costs that relates to business days. A business day is any day you have to be at a particular place on business or during which you spend four or more hours on business matters. Days spent traveling to and from your destination also count as business days.

Example: Sam flies to London and stays 14 days. He spends two days in the air, five days meeting buyers and attending a crafts show and seven days sightseeing. He therefore spends 50% of his time on business. He can deduct half of his travel costs.

3. Deductible Expenses During Foreign or Domestic Travel

You can deduct virtually all of your expenses when you travel on business, including:

- airfare to and from your destination
- hotel or other lodging expenses
- taxi, public transportation and car rental expenses
- telephone and fax expenses
- the cost of shipping your personal luggage or samples, displays or other things you need for your business
- computer rental fees

- laundry and dry cleaning expenses, and
- tips you pay on any of the other costs.

However, only 50% of the cost of meals is deductible. The IRS imposes this limitation based on the reasoning that you would have eaten had you stayed home.

You must keep good records of your expenses. You cannot deduct expenses for personal sightseeing or recreation.

H. Entertainment and Meal Expenses

Depending on the nature of your business, you may find it helpful or even necessary to entertain buyers, clients, customers, suppliers, employees, other crafts people, professional advisors, investors and other business associates. It's often easier to do business in a nonbusiness setting. Entertainment includes, for example, going to restaurants, the theater, concerts, sporting events and nightclubs; throwing parties; and boating, hunting or fishing outings.

In the past, you could deduct entertainment expenses even if business was never discussed. For example, if you took a client to a restaurant, you could deduct the cost even if you spent the whole time drinking martinis and talking about sports. This is no longer the case. To deduct an entertainment expense, you must discuss business either before, during or after the entertainment.

The IRS doesn't have spies lurking about in restaurants, theaters or other places of entertainment, so it has no way of knowing whether you really discussed business with a client or other business associate. You're pretty much on your honor here. However, be aware that the IRS closely scrutinizes this deduction, because many taxpayers cheat when taking it, and you'll have to comply with stringent recordkeeping requirements.

1. Discussing Business During Entertainment

You're entitled to deduct part of the cost of entertaining a client or other business associate if you have an active business discussion during the entertainment aimed at obtaining income or other benefits. You don't have to spend the entire time talking business, but the main character of the meal or other event must be business.

> *Example:* Ivan, a stoneware artist, takes a prospective client to a restaurant, where they discuss and finalize the terms of a commissioned work. Ivan can deduct the cost of the meal as an entertainment expense.

The IRS will not believe you discussed business if the entertainment occurred in a place where it is difficult or impossible to talk business because of distractions—for example, at a nightclub, theater, rave or sporting event.

On the other hand, the IRS will presume you discussed business if a meal or entertainment took place in a clear business setting—for example, a catered lunch at your office.

2. Discussing Business Before or After Entertainment

You are also entitled to deduct the full expense of an entertainment event if you have a substantial business discussion with a client or other business associate before or after it. This requires that you have a meeting, negotiation or other business transaction designed to help you get income or some other specific business benefit.

Generally, the entertainment should occur on the same day as the business discussion. However, if your business guests are from out of town, the entertainment can occur the day before or the day after.

The entertainment doesn't have to be shorter than your business discussions, but you can't spend only a small fraction of your total time on business. You can deduct entertainment expenses at places such as nightclubs, sporting events or theaters.

> *Example:* Following a licensing meeting at your rep's office, you take the rep to a soccer game to unwind. The cost of the tickets is a deductible business expense.

3. 50% Deduction Limit

You can deduct only those entertainment expenses you actually paid. If a client picks up the tab, you obviously get no deduction. If you split the expense, you may deduct only what you paid.

Moreover, you're allowed to deduct only 50% of your expenses—for example, if you spend $50 for a meal in a restaurant, you can only deduct $25. However, you must keep track of all you spend and report the entire amount on your tax return. The cost of transportation to and from a business meal or other entertainment is not subject to the 50% limit.

You can deduct the cost of entertaining your spouse and the client's spouse only if it's impractical to entertain the client without a spouse and your spouse joins the party because the client's spouse is attending.

If you entertain a client or other business associate while away from home on business, you can deduct the cost either as a travel or entertainment expense, but not both.

Champagne and Caviar Might Not Be Deductible

Your entertainment expenses must be reasonable to be fully deductible. You can't deduct entertainment expenses if the IRS considers them lavish or extravagant. There is no dollar limit on what is reasonable. Nor are you necessarily barred from entertaining at deluxe restaurants, hotels, nightclubs or resorts.

Whether your expenses will be considered reasonable depends on the particular facts and circumstances—for example, a $250 expense for dinner with a client and two business associates at a fancy restaurant would likely be considered reasonable if you closed a substantial business deal during the meal. Since there are no concrete guidelines, you have to use common sense.

 For additional information, see IRS Publication 463, *Travel, Entertainment and Gift Expenses.* You can obtain this and all other IRS publications by calling the IRS at 800-TAX-FORM, visiting your local IRS office or downloading the publications at www.irs.gov.

I. Health Insurance Deduction

Self-employed crafts artists must provide their own health insurance. If you don't make a lot of money, this can be tough. Fortunately, there are specific tax deductions designed to help you.

If you're a sole proprietor, partner in a partnership, owner of an S corporation or member of a limited liability company, you may deduct a portion of the cost of health insurance covering you, your spouse and your dependents. However, this deduction can't exceed the net profit from your business. The amount of this deduction is 70% of insurance costs in 2002 and 100% of such costs in 2003 and later.

You can't take this deduction if you're an employee and are eligible for health insurance through your employer. Nor can you take it if your spouse is employed and you're eligible for coverage through his or her employer.

If you form a C corporation, it may deduct the entire cost of the health insurance it provides you and any other employees.

J. Deducting Start-Up Costs

Expenses you incur before you actually start your crafts business—for example, license fees, fictitious business and domain name registration fees, advertising costs, attorney and accounting fees, travel expenses, market research and office supply expenses —are deductible from your federal income taxes. These expenses are called business start-up costs and must be deducted in equal amounts over the first 60 months you're in business, a process called amortization.

Example: Bill decides to start a crafts business to sell premium maple and cherry boxes. Before he opens his office and takes on any clients, he spends $6,000 on license fees, advertising, attorney and accounting fees and office supply expenses. He can't deduct all $6,000 in start-up costs at once. Instead, he can deduct only $100 per month for the first 60 months he's in business—that is, a maximum of $1,200 per year.

You can avoid having to stretch out these deductions over 60 months and instead deduct them all in the first year you're in business if you:

- delay paying start-up costs until you open your doors and start serving clients or customers, or
- start your business on a very small scale and avoid incurring start-up expenses until you've made some money; it doesn't have to be a lot.

For more information on business start-up costs, see IRS Publication 535, *Business Expenses*. You can obtain a free copy by calling the IRS at 800-TAX-FORM or by calling or visiting your local IRS office. You can also download a copy at www.irs.gov.

K. Self-Employment Taxes

All Americans who work in the private sector are required to pay taxes to help support the Social Security and Medicare systems. Although these taxes are paid to the IRS, they are entirely separate from federal income taxes.

Employees have their Social Security and Medicare taxes directly deducted from their paychecks by their employers, who must make matching contributions. Such taxes are usually referred to as FICA taxes.

But if you're a self-employed crafts artist, your customers will not pay or withhold your Social Security and Medicare taxes. You must pay them to the IRS yourself. When self-employed workers pay these taxes, they are called self-employment taxes, or SE taxes. This chapter shows you how to determine how much SE tax you must pay.

1. Low Income, No Tax

If your net income from your business for the year is less than $400, you don't have to pay any self-employment taxes, and you can skip this section.

For additional information on self-employment taxes, see IRS Publication 533, *Self-Employment Tax*. You can obtain this and all other IRS publications by calling the IRS at 800-TAX-FORM, visiting your local IRS office or downloading them at www.irs.gov.

2. Who Must Pay

Sole proprietors, partners in partnerships and members of limited liability companies must all pay SE taxes if their net earnings from self-employment for the year are $400 or more.

Corporations do not pay SE taxes. However, if you're incorporated and work in your business, you are an employee of your corporation and will ordinarily be paid a salary. Instead of paying SE taxes, you must pay FICA taxes on your salary just like any other employee. Half of your Social Security and Medicare taxes must be withheld from your salary, and half paid by your corporation.

3. SE Tax Rates

The self-employment tax consists of a 12.4% Social Security tax and a 2.9% Medicare tax, for a total tax of 15.3%. But, in practice, the bite it takes is smaller because of certain deductions. (See Section C, above.)

The SE tax is a flat tax—that is, the tax rate is the same no matter what your income level. However, there is an income ceiling on the Social Security portion of the tax. You need not pay the 12.4% Social Security tax on your net self-employment earnings that exceed the ceiling amount. If the ceiling didn't exist, people with higher incomes would end up paying far more than they could ever get back as Social Security benefits. The Social Security tax ceiling is adjusted annually for inflation. In 2002, the ceiling was $84,900.

However, there is no similar limit for Medicare: you must pay the 2.9% Medicare tax on your entire net self-employment income, no matter how large. Congress enacted this rule a few years ago to save Medicare from bankruptcy.

Example: Mona earned $150,000 in net self-employment income from her glassworks business in 2002. She must pay both Social Security and Medicare taxes on the first $84,900 of her income —a 15.3% tax. Her remaining $65,100 in income is subject to the 2.9% Medicare tax, but not to Social Security tax.

4. Earnings Subject to Self-Employment Tax

You pay self-employment taxes on your net self-employment income, not your entire income. To determine your net self-employment income, you first figure the net income you've earned from your business. Your net business income includes all your income from your business minus all business deductions allowed for income tax purposes. However, you can't deduct retirement contributions you make for yourself to a Keogh or SEP plan or the self-employed health insurance deduction. If you're a sole proprietor, as are most self-employed people, use IRS Schedule C, Profit or Loss From Business, to determine your net business income.

If you have more than one business, combine the net income or loss from them all. If you have a job in addition to your business, your employee income is not included in your self-employment income. Nor do you include investment income, such as interest you earn on your savings.

You then get one more valuable deduction before finally determining your net self-employment income. You're allowed to deduct 7.65% from your total net business income. This is intended to help ease the SE tax burden on the self-employed. To do this, multiply your net business income by 92.35% or .9235.

Example: Billie earned $70,000 from her hand-woven chenille crafts business and had $20,000

in business expenses, leaving a net business income of $50,000. She multiplies this amount by .9235 to determine her net self-employment income, which is $46,175. This is the amount on which Billie must pay SE tax.

The fact that you can deduct business expenses from your SE income makes them doubly valuable: They will reduce not only your income taxes, but your SE taxes as well. Your actual SE tax savings will be 15.3% of the amount of such deductions—for example, a $1,000 home office deduction will save you $153 in SE taxes.

5. Computing the SE Tax

It's easy to compute the amount of your SE tax. First, determine your net self-employment income as described above. If your net self-employment income is below the Social Security tax ceiling—$84,900 in 2002—multiply it by 15.3% or .153.

Example: Mark had $50,000 in net self-employment income in 2002. He must multiply this by .153 to determine his SE tax, which is $7,650.

If your net self-employment income is more than the Social Security tax ceiling, things are a bit more complicated. Multiply your income up to the ceiling by 12.4%, and all of your income by the 2.9% Medicare tax; then add both amounts together to determine your total SE tax.

Example: Martha had $100,000 in net self-employment income in 2002. She multiplies the first $84,900 of this amount by the 12.4% Social Security tax, resulting in a tax of $10,527. She then multiplies her entire $100,000 income by the 2.9% Medicare tax, resulting in a $2,900 tax. She adds these amounts together to determine her total SE tax, which is $13,427.

In another effort to make the SE tax burden a little easier for the self-employed, you're allowed to deduct half of the amount of your SE taxes from your business income for income tax purposes. For example, if you pay $10,000 in SE taxes, you can deduct $5,000 from your gross income when you determine your taxable income.

6. Paying and Reporting SE Taxes

Pay SE taxes directly to the IRS during the year as part of your estimated taxes. You have the option of either:

- paying the same amount in tax as you paid the previous year, or
- estimating what your income will be this year and basing your estimated tax payments on that.

When you file your annual tax return, you must include IRS Form SE, Self-Employment Tax, along with it. This form shows the IRS how much SE tax you were required to pay for the year. You file only one Form SE no matter how many unincorporated businesses you own. Add the SE tax to your income taxes on your income tax return, Form 1040, to determine your total tax.

Even if you do not owe any income tax, you must still complete Form 1040 and Schedule SE if you owe $400 or more in SE taxes.

L. Paying Estimated Tax

What many self-employed crafts artists like best about their employment status is that it allows freedom in planning and handling their own finances. Unlike employees, they don't have taxes withheld from their compensation by their clients or customers. As a result, many self-employed people have higher take-home pay than employees earning similar amounts.

Unfortunately, however, self-employed workers do not have the luxury of waiting until April 15 to pay all their taxes for the previous year. The IRS wants to get its money a lot faster than that, so the self-employed are required to pay taxes on their estimated annual incomes in four payments spread out over

each year. These are called estimated taxes and are used to pay both income taxes and self-employment taxes.

Because of estimated taxes, self-employed people need to carefully budget their money. If you fail to set aside enough of your earnings to pay your estimated taxes, you could face a huge tax bill on April 15—and have a tough time coming up with the money to cover it.

Most States Have Estimated Taxes, Too

If your state has income taxes, it probably requires the self-employed to pay estimated taxes. The due dates are generally the same as for federal estimated tax. State income tax rates are lower than federal income taxes. The exact rate depends on the state in which you live. Contact your state tax office for information and the required forms.

---

1. Who Must Pay

You must pay estimated taxes if you are a sole proprietor, partner in a partnership or member of a limited liability company and you expect to owe at least $1,000 in federal tax for the year. If you've formed a C corporation, it may also have to pay estimated taxes.

However, if you paid no taxes last year—for example, because your business made no profit or you weren't working—you don't have to pay any estimated tax this year no matter what your tax tally for the year. But this is true only if you were a U.S. citizen or resident for the year and your tax return for the previous year covered the whole 12 months.

2. How Much You Must Pay

You should normally determine how much estimated tax to pay after completing your tax return for the previous year. Most people want to pay as little estimated tax as possible during the year so they can earn interest on their money instead of handing it over to the IRS. However, the IRS imposes penalties if you don't pay enough estimated tax. (See Section L8, below.) There's no need to get excessively concerned about these penalties. They aren't terribly large in the first place, and it's easy to avoid having to pay them. All you have to do is pay at least the smaller of:

- 90% of your total tax due for the current year, or
- 100% of the tax you paid the previous year, or more if you're a high-income taxpayer (see Section L3, below).

You normally make four estimated tax payments each year. There are three different ways you can calculate your payments. You can use any one of the three methods and you won't have to pay a penalty, as long as you pay the minimum total the IRS requires, as explained above. One of the methods—basing your payments on last year's tax—is extremely easy to use. The other two are more complex, but might permit you to make smaller payments.

3. Payments Based on Last Year's Tax

The easiest and safest way to calculate your estimated taxes is to simply pay 100% of the total federal taxes you paid last year, or more if you're a high-income taxpayer, as described below. You can base your estimated tax on the amount you paid the prior year even if you weren't self-employed in business that year (but your return for the year must have been for a full 12-month period).

You should determine how much estimated tax to pay for the current year at the same time as you file your tax return for the previous year—no later than April 15. Take the total amount of tax you had to pay for the year and divide by four. If this comes out to an odd number, round up to get an even number. These are the amounts you'll have to pay in estimated tax. You'll make four equal payments throughout the year and the following year. (See the chart in Section B, above, for when you must make your payments).

Example: Gary earned $50,000 last year. He figures his taxes for the prior year on April 1 of this year and determines he owed $9,989.32 for the year. To determine his estimated tax for the current year he divides this amount by four: $9,989.32 divided by four equals $2497.33. He rounds this up to $2,500. He'll make four $2,500 estimated tax payments to the IRS. So long as he pays this much, Gary won't have to pay a penalty, even if he ends up owing more than $10,000 in tax to the IRS for the year because his income goes up, his deductions go down or both.

a. High-Income Taxpayers Must Pay More

High-income taxpayers—those with adjusted gross incomes of more than $150,000, or $75,000 if they're married couples filing separate returns—must pay more than 100% of their prior year's tax.

Your adjusted gross income or AGI, is your total income minus deductions for:

- IRA, Keogh and SEP-IRA contributions
- the self-employed health insurance deduction
- one half of your self employment tax, and
- alimony, deductible moving expenses and penalties you pay for early withdrawals from a savings account before maturity or early redemption of certificates of deposit.

To find out your AGI, look at line 33 on your last year's tax return, Form 1040. The estimated tax amount is 112% of the prior year's income for returns filed in 2002 and 110% for 2003 and later.

b. You May Owe Tax on April 15

Basing your estimated tax on last year's income is generally the best method to use if you expect your income to be higher this year than last year. You'll be paying the minimum possible without incurring a penalty. However, if you do end up earning more than last year, using this method will cause you to underpay your taxes. You still won't have to pay a penalty, but you'll have to make up the underpayment when you file your tax return for the year on April 15. This could present you with a big tax bill if your income rose substantially from last year. To make sure you have enough money for this, it's a good idea to sock away a portion of your income in a separate bank account just for taxes.

4. Payments Based on Estimated Taxable Income

If you're absolutely certain your net income will be less this year than last year, you'll pay less estimated tax if you base your tax on your taxable income for the current year instead of basing it on last year's tax. This is not worth the time and trouble, however, unless you'll earn at least 30% less this year than last.

The problem with using this method is that you must estimate your total income and deductions for the year to figure out how much to pay. Obviously, this can be difficult or impossible to compute accurately. And there are no magic formulas to look to for guidance. The best way to proceed is to sit down with your tax return for the previous year.

Take comfort in knowing that you need not make an exact estimate of your taxable income. You won't have to pay a penalty if you pay at least 90% of your tax due for the year.

> *Example:* Larry, a polymer artist specializing in corporate wall hangings, earned $45,000 last year and paid $10,000 in income and self-employment taxes. Larry expects to earn much less this year, because a key client has gone out of business. The lost client accounted for more than one-third of Larry's income last year, so Larry estimates he'll earn about $30,000 this year. The minimum estimated tax Larry must pay is 90% of the tax he will owe on his $30,000 income, which he estimates to be $6,000.

IRS Form 1040-ES contains a worksheet for use in calculating your estimated tax. You can obtain the form by calling the IRS at 800-TAX-FORM, visiting your local IRS office or downloading it at www.irs.gov. Or, if you have a tax preparation computer program, it can help you with the calculations. If you have your taxes prepared by an accountant, he or she should determine what estimated tax to pay. If your income changes greatly during the year, ask your accountant to help you prepare a revised estimated tax payment schedule.

5. Payments Based on Quarterly Income

A much more complicated way to calculate your estimated taxes is to use the annualized income installment method. It requires that you separately calculate your tax liability at four points during the year—March 31, May 31, August 31 and December 31—prorating your deductions and personal exemptions. You base your estimated tax payments on your actual tax liability for each quarter. (See the chart in Section B, above.)

This method is often the best choice for people who receive income very unevenly throughout the year—for example, if your crafts work is seasonal in nature. Using this method, you can pay little or no estimated tax for the quarters in which you earned little or no income.

If you use this method, you must file IRS Form 2210 with your tax return; this form shows your calculations.

You'll Need Help With the Math

You really need a good grasp of tax law and mathematics to use the annualized income installment method. The IRS worksheet used to calculate your payments using this method contains 43 separate steps. If you want to use this method, give yourself a break and hire an accountant, or at least use a tax preparation computer program, to help with the calculations.

See IRS Publication 505, *Tax Withholding and Estimated Tax*, for a detailed explanation of the annualized income method. You can obtain the form by calling the IRS at 800-TAX-FORM, visiting your local IRS office or downloading it at www.irs.gov.

6. When to Pay Estimated Tax

Estimated tax must ordinarily be paid in four installments, with the first one due on April 15. However, you don't have to start making payments until you actually earn income. If you don't receive any income by March 31, you can skip the April 15 payment. In this event, you'd ordinarily make three payments for the year starting on June 15. If you don't receive any income by May 31, you can skip the June 15 payment as well, and so on.

The following chart shows the due dates and the periods each installment covers.

Estimated Tax Due	
Income received for the period	**Estimated tax due**
January 1 through March 31	April 15
April 1 through May 31	June 15
June 1 through August 31	September 15
September 1 through December 31	January 15 of the next year

Your estimated tax payment must be postmarked by the dates noted above, but the IRS need not actually receive them then. If any of these days falls on a weekend or legal holiday, the due date is the next business day.

7. How to Pay

The IRS wants to make it easy for you to send in your money, so the mechanics of paying estimated taxes are very simple. You file federal estimated taxes using IRS Form 1040-ES. This form contains instructions and four numbered payment vouchers for you to send in with your payments. You must provide your name, address and Social Security number (or EIN if you have one) and amount of the payment on each voucher. You file only one payment voucher with each payment, no matter how many unincorporated businesses you have.

If you're married and file a joint return, the names on your estimated tax vouchers should be exactly the same as those on your income tax return. Even if your spouse isn't self-employed, he or she should be listed on the vouchers so that the money gets credited to the right account.

If you made estimated tax payments last year, you should receive a copy of the current year's Form 1040-ES in the mail. It will have payment vouchers preprinted with your name, address and Social Security number.

If you did not pay estimated taxes last year, get a copy of Form 1040-ES from the IRS. Do so by calling the IRS at 800-TAX-FORM, visiting your local IRS office or downloading it at www.irs.gov. After you make your first payment, the IRS should mail you a Form 1040-ES package with the preprinted vouchers.

Use the addressed envelopes that come with your Form 1040-ES package. If you use your own envelopes, make sure you mail your payment vouchers to the address shown in the Form 1040 ES instructions for the place where you live. Do not mail your estimated tax payments to the same place you sent your Form 1040.

You may pay all or part of your estimated taxes by credit card. (Visa, MasterCard, Discover Card or American Express Card are all accepted.) You must do this through one of two private companies providing this service. You'll have to pay the company a fee for this service, based on the amount of your payment. The fee does not go to the IRS. You can arrange to make your payment by phone or through the Internet. Contact these companies at:

PhoneCharge, Inc.
1–888–255–8299
www.1888ALLTAXX.com

Official Payments Corporation
1–800–272–982
1–877–754–4413 (Customer Service)
www.officialpayments.com

8. Paying the Wrong Amount

If you pay too little estimated tax, the IRS will charge you a penalty fee. If you pay too much, you can get the money refunded or apply it to your next year's estimated taxes.

a. Paying Too Little

The IRS imposes a money penalty if you underpay your estimated taxes. Fortunately, the penalty is not very onerous. You have to pay the taxes due plus a percentage penalty for each day your estimated tax payments were unpaid. The percentage is set by the IRS each year. The penalty was 8% in early 2002.

The penalty has ranged between 6% and 8% in recent years. This is the mildest of all IRS interest penalties. Even if you paid no estimated tax at all during the year, the underpayment penalty you'd have to pay would be no more than 5% to 6% of your total taxes due for the year.

To find out the current penalty, see the most recent version of IRS Publication 505, *Tax Withholding and Estimated Tax*. You can obtain the form by calling the IRS at 800-TAX-FORM, visiting your local IRS office or downloading it at www.irs.gov.

The penalty is comparable to the interest you'd pay on borrowed money. Many self-employed people decide to pay the penalty at the end of the tax year as an alternative to taking money out of their businesses during the year to pay estimated taxes. If you do this, though, make sure you pay all the taxes you owe for the year by April 15 of the following year. If you don't, the IRS will tack on additional interest and penalties. The IRS usually adds a penalty of ½% to 1% per month to a tax bill that's not paid when due.

The IRS will assume you've underpaid your estimated taxes if you file a tax return showing that you owe $500 or more in additional tax, and the amount due is more than 10% of your total tax bill for the year.

If you have underpaid, you can determine the amount of the underpayment penalty by completing IRS Form 2210, *Underpayment of Estimated Tax by Individuals*. Then pay the penalty when you send in your return. Tax preparation programs can do this for you. However, it is not necessary for you to compute the penalty you owe. The IRS will be all too happy to determine the penalty and send you a bill. If you receive a bill, you may wish to complete Form 2210 anyway to make sure you aren't overcharged.

b. Paying Too Much

If you pay too much estimated tax, you have two options: You can have the IRS refund the overpayment to you, or you can credit all or part of the money to your current year's estimated taxes. Unfortunately, you can't get back the interest your overpayment earned while sitting in the IRS coffers; that belongs to the government.

To take the credit, write in the amount you want credited instead of refunded to you on line 68a of your Form 1040. The payment is considered to have been made on April 15. You can use the entire credited amount toward your first payment, or you can spread it out in any way you choose among any or all of your payments. Be sure to take the amount you have credited into account when figuring your estimated tax payments.

It doesn't make much practical difference which option you choose. Most people take the credit so they don't have to wait for the IRS to send them a refund check. ∎

Appendix

A

How to Use the CD-ROM

7he tear-out forms in Appendix B are included on a CD-ROM in the back of the book. This CD-ROM, which can be used with Windows computers, installs files that can be opened, printed and edited using a word processor or other software. It is *not* a stand-alone software program. Please read this Appendix and the README.TXT file included on the CD-ROM for instructions on using the Forms CD.

Note to Mac users: This CD-ROM and its files should also work on Macintosh computers. Please note, however, that Nolo cannot provide technical support for non-Windows users.

How to View the README File

If you do not know how to view the file README.TXT, insert the Forms CD-ROM into your computer's CD-ROM drive and follow these instructions:

Windows 9x, 2000, Me and XP
1. On your PC's desktop, double-click the My Computer icon.
2. Double-click the icon for the CD-ROM drive into which the Forms CD-ROM was inserted.
3. Double-click the file README.TXT.

Macintosh
1. On your Mac desktop, double-click the icon for the CD-ROM that you inserted.
2. Double-click on the file README.TXT.

While the README file is open, print it out by using the Print command in the File menu.

Two different kinds of forms are contained on the CD-ROM:
- Word processing (RTF) forms that you can open, complete, print and save with your word processing program (see Section B, below), and
- Forms from the U.S. Copyright Office (PDF) that can be viewed only with Adobe Acrobat

Reader 4.0 or higher. You can install Acrobat Reader from the Forms CD (see Section C, below). Some of these forms have "fill-in" text fields, and can be completed using your computer. You will not, however, be able to save the completed forms with the filled-in data. PDF forms without fill-in text fields must be printed out and filled in by hand or with a typewriter.

A. Installing the Form Files Onto Your Computer

Before you can do anything with the files on the CD-ROM, you need to install them onto your hard disk. In accordance with U.S. copyright laws, remember that copies of the CD-ROM and its files are for your personal use only.

Insert the Forms CD and do the following:

1. Windows 9x, 2000, Me and XP Users

Follow the instructions that appear on the screen. If nothing happens when you insert the Forms CD-ROM, then:
1. Double-click the My Computer icon.
2. Double-click the icon for the CD-ROM drive into which the Forms CD-ROM was inserted.
3. Double-click the file WELCOME.EXE.

By default, all the files are installed to the \Crafts Business Forms folder in the \Program Files folder of your computer. A folder called "Crafts Business Forms" is added to the "Programs" folder of the Start menu.

2. Macintosh Users

1. If the "Crafts Business Forms CD" window is not open, open it by double-clicking the "Crafts Business Forms CD" icon.
2. Select the "Crafts Business Forms" folder icon.
3. Drag and drop the folder icon onto the icon of your hard disk.

B. Using the Word Processing Files to Create Documents

This section concerns the files for forms that can be opened and edited with your word processing program.

All word processing forms come in rich text format. These files have the extension ".RTF." For example, the form for the Partnership Agreement discussed in Chapter 1 is on the file Partnership.RTF. All forms, their file names and file formats are listed in Appendix B.

RTF files can be read by most recent word processing programs, including all versions of MS Word for Windows and Macintosh, WordPad for Windows and recent versions of WordPerfect for Windows and Macintosh.

To use a form from the CD to create your documents you must:

1. Open a file in your word processor or text editor.
2. Edit the form by filling in the required information.
3. Print it out.
4. Rename and save your revised file.

The following are general instructions on how to do this. However, each word processor uses different commands to open, format, save and print documents. Please read your word processor's manual for specific instructions on performing these tasks.

Do not call Nolo's technical support if you have questions on how to use your word processor.

Step 1: Opening a File

There are three ways to open the word processing files included on the CD-ROM after you have installed them onto your computer.

- Windows users can open a file by selecting its "shortcut" as follows:
  1. Click the Windows "Start" button.
  2. Open the "Programs" folder.
  3. Open the "Crafts Business Forms" subfolder.
  4. Open the "RTF" subfolder.
  5. Click on the shortcut to the form you want to work with.

- Both Windows and Macintosh users can open a file directly by double-clicking on it. Use My Computer or Windows Explorer (Windows 9x, 2000, Me or XP) or the Finder (Macintosh) to go to the folder you installed or copied the CD-ROM's files to. Then, double-click on the specific file you want to open.
- You can also open a file from within your word processor. To do this, you must first start your word processor. Then, go to the File menu and choose the Open command. This opens a dialog box where you will tell the program:
  1. the type of file you want to open (*.RTF), and
  2. the location and name of the file (you will need to navigate through the directory tree to get to the folder on your hard disk where the CD's files have been installed).

If these directions are unclear, you will need to look through the manual for your word processing program—Nolo's technical support department will *not* be able to help you with the use of your word processing program.

Where Are the Files Installed?

Windows Users
RTF files are installed by default to a folder named \Crafts Business Forms\RTF in the \Program Files folder of your computer.

Macintosh Users
RTF files are located in the "RTF" folder within the "Crafts Business Forms" folder.

Step 2: Editing Your Document

Fill in the appropriate information according to the instructions and sample agreements in the book. Underlines are used to indicate where you need to enter your information, frequently followed by instructions in brackets. *Be sure to delete the underlines and instructions from your edited document.* If you do not know how to use your word processor to edit a document, you will need to look through the manual for your word processing program—Nolo's technical support department will *not* be able to help you with the use of your word processing program.

Editing Forms That Have Optional or Alternative Text

Some of the forms have check boxes before text. The check boxes indicate:

- optional text, where you choose whether to include or exclude the given text
- alternative text, where you select one alternative to include and exclude the other alternatives.

If you are using the tear-out forms in Appendix B, simply mark the appropriate box to make your choice.

If you are using the Forms CD, however, we recommend that instead of marking the check boxes, you do the following:

Optional text
- If you *don't want* to include optional text, just delete it from your document.
- If you *do want* to include optional text, just leave it in your document.
- In either case, delete the check box itself as well as the italicized instructions that the text is optional.

Alternative text
- First delete all the alternatives that you do not want to include.
- Then delete the remaining check boxes, as well as the italicized instructions that you need to select one of the alternatives provided.

Step 3: Printing Out the Document

Use your word processor's or text editor's "Print" command to print out your document. If you do not

know how to use your word processor to print a document, you will need to look through the manual for your word processing program—Nolo's technical support department will *not* be able to help you with the use of your word processing program.

Step 4: Saving Your Document

After filling in the form, use the "Save As" command to save and rename the file. Because all the files are "read-only," you will not be able to use the "Save" command. This is for your protection. *If you save the file without renaming it, the underlines that indicate where you need to enter your information will be lost, and you will not be able to create a new document with this file without recopying the original file from the CD-ROM.*

If you do not know how to use your word processor to save a document, you will need to look through the manual for your word processing program— Nolo's technical support department will *not* be able to help you with the use of your word processing program.

C. Using U.S. Copyright Office Forms

Electronic copies of useful forms from the U.S. Copyright Office are included on the CD-ROM in Adobe Acrobat PDF format. You must have the Adobe Acrobat Reader installed on your computer (see below) to use these forms. All forms, their file names and file formats are listed in Appendix B. These form files were created by the U.S. Copyright Office, not by Nolo.

Some of these forms have fill-in text fields. To create your document using these files, you must:

1. Open a file.
2. Fill in the text fields using either your mouse or the tab key on your keyboard to navigate from field to field.
3. Print it out.

NOTE: While you can print out your completed form, you will *not* be able to save your completed form to disk.

Forms without fill-in text fields cannot be filled out using your computer. To create your document using these files, you must:

1. Open the file
2. Print it out, and
3. Complete it by hand or typewriter.

Installing Acrobat Reader

To install the Adobe Acrobat Reader, insert the CD into your computer's CD-ROM drive and follow these instructions:

Windows 9x, 2000, Me and XP:
Follow the instructions that appear on screen. (If nothing happens when you insert the Forms CD-ROM, then:

1. Double-click the My Computer icon.
2. Double-click the icon for the CD-ROM drive into which the Forms CD-ROM was inserted.
3. Doubleclick the file WELCOME.EXE.

Macintosh

1. If the "Crafts Business Forms CD" window is not open, open it by double-clicking the "Crafts Business Forms CD" icon.
2. double-click on the "Acrobat Reader Installer" icon.

If you do not know how to use Adobe Acrobat to view and print the files, you will need to consult the online documentation that comes with the Acrobat Reader program.

Do not call Nolo technical support if you have questions on how to use Acrobat Reader.

Step 1: Opening U.S. Copyright Office Files

PDF files, like the word processing files, can be opened one of three ways:

- Windows users can open a file by selecting its "shortcut" as follows:
  1. Click the Windows "Start" button.
  2. Open the "Programs" folder.
  3. Open the "Crafts Business Forms" subfolder.
  4. Open the "PDF" folder.
  5. Click on the shortcut to the form you want to work with.
- Both Windows and Macintosh users can open a file directly by double-clicking on it. Use My Computer or Windows Explorer (Windows 9x, 2000, Me or XP) or the Finder (Macintosh) to go to the folder you created and copied the CD-ROM's files to. Then, double-click on the specific file you want to open.
- You can also open a PDF file from within Acrobat Reader. To do this, you must first start Reader. Then, go to the File menu and choose the Open command. This opens a dialog box where you will tell the program the location and name of the file (you will need to navigate through the directory tree to get to the folder on your hard disk where the CD's files have been installed). If these directions are unclear, you will need to look through Acrobat Reader's help—Nolo's technical support department will *not* be able to help you with the use of Acrobat Reader.

Step 2: Filling in U.S. Copyright Office Files

Use your mouse or the Tab key on your keyboard to navigate from field to field within these forms. Be sure to have all the information you will need to complete a form on hand, because you will not be able to save a copy of the filled-in form to disk. You can, however, print out a completed version.

NOTE: This step is only applicable to forms that have been created with fill-in text fields. Forms without fill-in fields must be completed by hand or typewriter after you have printed them out.

Where Are the PDF Files Installed?

Windows Users

PDF files are installed by default to a folder named \Crafts Business Forms\PDF in the \Program Files folder of your computer.

Macintosh Users

PDF files are located in the "PDF" folder within the "Crafts Business Forms" folder.

Step 3: Printing U.S. Copyright Office Files

Choose Print from the Acrobat Reader File menu. This will open the Print dialog box. In the "Print Range" section of the Print dialog box, select the appropriate print range, then click OK. ∎

Appendix

B

Tear-Out Forms

The following forms are included as tear-outs in this Appendix and are on the CD-ROM in rtf format.

The following forms are on the CD-ROM in in Adobe Acrobat PDF format. Asterisks indicate forms with fill in text fields.

Form Name	File Name
Form VA (PDF)	FormVA.PDF*
Copyright Circular 40	circ40.PDF
Copyright Circular 40a	circ40a.PDF
Copyright Circular 12	circ12.PDF*
Copyright Circular 10	circ10.PDF

Partnership Agreement

Partners. _____
(the "Partners"), agree to the following terms and conditions.

Partnership Name. The Partners will do business as a partnership under the name of _____
_____ .

Partnership Duration. The partnership *[choose one]* ☐ began ☐ will begin on _____ .
It will continue:

   [Choose one]

   ☐ indefinitely until it is ended by the terms of this agreement.

   ☐ until _____, unless ended sooner by the terms of this agreement.

Partnership Office. The main office of the partnership will be at _____
_____ . The mailing address will be:

   [Choose one]

   ☐ the above address.

   ☐ the following address: _____
   _____ .

Partnership Purpose. The primary purpose of the partnership is_____
_____ .

Capital Contributions. The Partners will contribute the following capital to the partnership on or before
_____ .

   A. Cash Contributions

Partner's Name	Amount
_____	$ _____
_____	$ _____
_____	$ _____
_____	$ _____

   B. Non-Cash Contributions

Partner's Name	Description of Property	Value
_____		$ _____
_____	_____	$ _____
_____	_____	$ _____
_____	_____	$ _____

Capital Accounts. The partnership will maintain a capital account for each Partner. The account will consist of the Partner's capital contribution plus the Partner's share of profits less the Partner's share of losses and distributions to the Partner. A Partner may not remove capital from his or her account without the written consent of all Partners.

Profits and Losses.

A. The net profits and losses of the partnership will be credited to or charged against the Partners' capital accounts:

   [Choose one]

   ☐ in the same proportions as their capital contributions.

   ☐ as follows: _____

   _____

   _____ .

B. The partnership will only make distributions to the Partners if all the Partners agree.

Salaries. No Partner will receive a salary for services to the partnership.

Interest. No interest will be paid on a Partner's capital account.

Management. Each Partner will have an equal say in managing the partnership.

   [Choose one]

   ☐ All significant partnership decisions will require the agreement of all the Partners.

   ☐ Routine partnership decisions will require the agreement of a majority of the Partners. The following partnership actions will require the agreement of all the Partners:

      ☐ borrowing or lending money

      ☐ signing a lease

      ☐ signing a contract to buy or sell real estate

      ☐ signing a security agreement or mortgage

      ☐ selling partnership assets except for goods sold in the regular course of business

      ☐ other: _____

Partnership Funds. Partnership funds will be kept in an account at _____

_____, unless all Partners agree to another financial institution.

Partnership checks:

   [Choose one]

   ☐ may be signed by any Partner.

   ☐ must be signed by all the Partners.

   ☐ must be signed by _____ Partners.

Agreement to End Partnership. The Partners may unanimously agree to end the partnership.

Partner's Withdrawal.

[Choose one]

☐ The partnership will end if a Partner withdraws by giving written notice of such withdrawal to each of the other Partners.

☐ Upon the withdrawal of a Partner, the other Partners will, within 30 days, decide either to end the partnership or to buy out the withdrawing Partner's interest and continue the partnership. A decision to buy out the withdrawing Partner's interest and continue the partnership requires the unanimous consent of the remaining Partners.

Partner's Death.

[Choose one]

☐ The partnership will end if a Partner dies.

☐ Upon the death of a partner, the other Partners will, within 30 days, decide either to end the partnership or to buy out the deceased Partner's interest and continue the partnership. A decision to buy out the withdrawing Partner's interest and continue the partnership requires the unanimous consent of the remaining Partners.

Buyout. If the remaining Partners decide to buy the interest of a withdrawing or deceased Partner, the remaining Partners, within _____ days after that Partner's withdrawal or death, will pay the withdrawing Partner or the deceased Partner's estate:

[Choose one]

☐ the amount in the capital account of the withdrawing or deceased Partner as of the date of withdrawal or death.

☐ the fair market value of the interest of the withdrawing or deceased Partner as determined by the partnership's accountant.

☐ other: _____.

General Provisions.

Entire Agreement. This is the entire agreement between the parties. It replaces and supersedes any and all oral agreements between the parties, as well as any prior writings. Modifications and amendments to this agreement, including any exhibit or appendix, shall be enforceable only if they are in writing and are signed by authorized representatives of both parties.

Successors and Assignees. This agreement binds and benefits the heirs, successors and assignees of the parties.

Notices. Any notice or communication required or permitted to be given under this agreement shall be sufficiently given when received by certified mail, or sent by facsimile transmission or overnight courier.

Governing Law. This agreement will be governed by the laws of the State of _____.

Waiver. If one party waives any term or provision of this agreement at any time, that waiver will only be effective for the specific instance and specific purpose for which the waiver was given. If either party fails to exercise or delays exercising any of its rights or remedies under this agreement, that party retains the right to enforce that term or provision at a later time.

Severability. If a court finds any provision of this agreement invalid or unenforceable, the remainder of this agreement will be interpreted so as best to carry out the parties' intent.

Attachments and Exhibits. The parties agree and acknowledge that all attachments, exhibits and schedules referred to in this agreement are incorporated in this agreement by reference.

[Optional]

☐ **Arbitration.** Any controversy or claim arising out of or relating to this agreement shall be settled by arbitration in _____ *[county]*, _____ *[state]*, in accordance with the rules of the American Arbitration Association, and judgment upon the award rendered by the arbitrator(s) may be entered in any court having jurisdiction. The prevailing party shall have the right to collect from the other party its reasonable costs and attorney's fees incurred in enforcing this agreement.

Date signed: _____

By: _____

Printed Name: _____

Address: _____

_____

By: _____

Printed Name: _____

Address: _____

_____

By: _____

Printed Name: _____

Address: _____

_____

By: _____

Printed Name: _____

Address: _____

_____

Invoice

_____
_____
_____
_____
_____
_____

Bill to: _____ Ship to: _____

_____ _____

_____ _____

_____ _____

Date	Your Order #	Our Order #	Sales Rep.	Ship Via	Terms

Item Number	Description	Quantity Ordered	Quantity Shipped	Retail Price	Discount	Unit Price	Total

☐ If payment is late, interest shall accrue from the date the payment was originally due, and the interest rate shall be 1.5% of the unpaid balance.

☐ If this account is delinquent, it shall be referred for collection, and Buyer shall pay all collection fees and costs including reasonable attorney fees.

[Choose one]

☐ This order may not be canceled.

☐ In the event the order is canceled, there is a cancellation fee of _____% of balance due.

Subtotal	
Tax	
Shipping	
Miscellaneous	
Balance Due	

Consignment Agreement

_____ ("Artist")
is the owner of the original works and accompanying rights in the works listed in Attachment A (referred to as
the "Works"). Artist desires to have _____ (the
"Gallery") located at _____
_____ represent Artist with regard to the exhibition and
sale of the Works. From time to time, the parties may revise the list of Works specified in the inventory listing
and such revisions, if executed by both parties, shall be incorporated in this agreement.

Appointment of Gallery; Agency Relationship. Artist appoints Gallery as its: _[Choose one]_

☐ exclusive agent for the sale and exhibition of the Works in _____
(the "Territory").

☐ nonexclusive agent.

Gallery shall use its best efforts to promote and sell the Works and to provide attribution of the Works to Artist.

Fees and Payments. Gallery shall sell the Works at the retail prices established by Artist in this agreement. All
income paid as a result of the sale of any Works by the Gallery shall be paid directly to Gallery, and Gallery
shall issue payment to Artist within _____ days of Gallery's receipt of such income along with
any accountings, including identifying inventory numbers.

For sales of Works, Gallery shall receive a commission of _____ % of any sales income.

[Optional]

☐ Gallery shall keep accurate books covering all transactions relating to the Works, and Artist or Artist's
authorized representatives shall have the right, upon five days' prior written notice and during normal
business hours, to inspect and audit Gallery's records relating to the Works.

☐ No payments may be made on credit or approval without the permission of Artist.

☐ Gallery shall provide Artist with the name and contact information for purchasers of the Works.

Discounts.

[Choose one]

☐ Gallery will obtain Artist's approval before changing retail prices or offering the Works at discount.

☐ Gallery may offer discounts to selected customers up to _____% and Gallery and Artist will split the
discount equally, provided that Artist does not receive less than _____% of the sale price.

Custom Order Commissions.

[Choose one]

☐ In the event of custom orders resulting from exhibition at Gallery, Gallery shall receive a commission of
_____% of any sales income.

☐ Gallery shall not be entitled to any commission on custom orders resulting from exhibition.

Shipping.

[Choose one]

☐ Costs for shipping shall be as follows: _____.

☐ Costs for shipping: (a) from Artist to Gallery shall be paid by Artist; (b) from Gallery to Artist shall be paid by Gallery; and (c) from Gallery to anywhere other than Artist (for example, to customers) shall be paid by Gallery.

☐ Costs for shipping shall be as set forth in Attachment B.

Insurance. Gallery shall maintain adequate insurance for the wholesale value of the Works (the retail price minus potential commission) and shall pay all deductibles.

Termination. This Agreement may be terminated at any time on or after _____ at the discretion of either Artist or Gallery. This Agreement shall automatically terminate if Artist dies or if Gallery becomes insolvent, declares bankruptcy or moves from the Territory. In the event of termination, all Works in Gallery's possession shall be promptly returned to Artist at Gallery's expense.

Ownership; Loss or Damage; Security Interest. Gallery agrees and acknowledges that the delivery of the Works to Gallery is a consignment and not a sale of the Works to Gallery. As Artist's agent, Gallery shall have a duty to protect the Works and shall be strictly liable for any damage to the Works once in Gallery's possession and until returned to Artist. If Works are destroyed while within Gallery's possession, Gallery shall pay Artist the full value as established by the retail price. Artist shall retain full title to all Works consigned to Gallery and shall in no event be subject to claims by creditors of Gallery. Title of the Works shall pass directly from Artist to purchaser, and, in the event of default or breach by Gallery, Artist shall have all rights of a secured party under the Uniform Commercial Code and Gallery agrees to execute all forms necessary to perfect such interest.

☐ **Posting Consignment Notice.** Gallery agrees to prominently post the following notice in its gallery: "Crafts at this gallery are sold under the terms of a consignment agreement."

General Provisions

Entire Agreement. This is the entire agreement between the parties. It replaces and supersedes any and all oral agreements between the parties, as well as any prior writings. Modifications and amendments to this agreement, including any exhibit or appendix hereto, shall be enforceable only if they are in writing and are signed by authorized representatives of both parties.

Successors and Assignees. This agreement binds and benefits the heirs, successors and assignees of the parties.

Notices. Any notice or communication required or permitted to be given under this agreement shall be sufficiently given when received by certified mail, or sent by facsimile transmission or overnight courier.

Governing Law. This agreement will be governed by the laws of the State of _____.

Waiver. If one party waives any term or provision of this agreement at any time, that waiver will only be effective for the specific instance and specific purpose for which the waiver was given. If either party fails to exercise or delays exercising any of its rights or remedies under this agreement, that party retains the right to enforce that term or provision at a later time.

Severability. If a court finds any provision of this agreement invalid or unenforceable, the remainder of this agreement will be interpreted so as best to carry out the parties' intent.

Attachments and Exhibits. The parties agree and acknowledge that all attachments, exhibits and schedules referred to in this agreement are incorporated in this agreement by reference.

No Agency. Nothing contained herein will be construed as creating any agency, partnership, joint venture or other form of joint enterprise between the parties.

☐ **Attorney Fees and Expenses.** The prevailing party shall have the right to collect from the other party its reasonable costs and necessary disbursements and attorney fees incurred in enforcing this agreement.

☐ **Jurisdiction.** The parties consent to the exclusive jurisdiction and venue of the federal and state courts located in _____ [county], _____ [state], in any action arising out of or relating to this agreement. The parties waive any other venue to which either party might be entitled by domicile or otherwise.

☐ **Arbitration.** Any controversy or claim arising out of or relating to this Agreement shall be settled by arbitration in _____ in accordance with the rules of the American Arbitration Association, and judgment upon the award rendered by the arbitrator(s) may be entered in any court having jurisdiction. The prevailing party shall have the right to collect from the other party its reasonable costs and attorney's fees incurred in enforcing this agreement.

Signatures.

Each party represents and warrants that on this date they are duly authorized to bind their respective principals by their signatures below.

GALLERY:

_____
Signature

_____
Typed or Printed Name

_____
Title

_____
Date

ARTIST:

_____
Signature

_____
Typed or Printed Name

_____
Title

_____
Date

Attachment A

Title of Work	Inventory No./Description	Retail Price
_____	_____	$ _____
_____	_____	$ _____
_____	_____	$ _____
_____	_____	$ _____
_____	_____	$ _____
_____	_____	$ _____
_____	_____	$ _____
_____	_____	$ _____
_____	_____	$ _____
_____	_____	$ _____
_____	_____	$ _____
_____	_____	$ _____
_____	_____	$ _____
_____	_____	$ _____
_____	_____	$ _____
_____	_____	$ _____
_____	_____	$ _____
_____	_____	$ _____
_____	_____	$ _____
_____	_____	$ _____
_____	_____	$ _____
_____	_____	$ _____
_____	_____	$ _____

_____

Date

_____

Consignee

Attachment B (Optional)

Expenses. Gallery shall pay expenses as listed in this Attachment B. In the event that an expense shall be shared between Artist and Gallery, the relative percentage of Gallery's payment shall be set forth below, and Artist shall be responsible for the remainder. For any shared expenses, Gallery shall provide an estimate of the expense and, in the event the actual amount of the expense exceeds the estimate, Gallery shall pay the difference.

Expense	Percentage paid by Gallery	Estimate	Deductible by Gallery
Promotional mailing	_____	_____	☐ Yes ☐ No
Advertising	_____	_____	☐ Yes ☐ No
Party/event (opening)	_____	_____	☐ Yes ☐ No
Frames	_____	_____	☐ Yes ☐ No
Installations	_____	_____	☐ Yes ☐ No
Catalog*	_____	_____	☐ Yes ☐ No
Photographic reproductions	_____	_____	☐ Yes ☐ No
Shipping to purchasers	_____	_____	☐ Yes ☐ No
Shipping to artist	_____	_____	☐ Yes ☐ No
Other _____	_____	_____	☐ Yes ☐ No
Other _____	_____	_____	☐ Yes ☐ No
Other _____	_____	_____	☐ Yes ☐ No
Other _____	_____	_____	☐ Yes ☐ No
Other _____	_____	_____	☐ Yes ☐ No
Other _____	_____	_____	☐ Yes ☐ No
Other _____	_____	_____	☐ Yes ☐ No
Other _____	_____	_____	☐ Yes ☐ No

*Gallery shall furnish Artist with ten copies of catalog.

Commission Agreement

Number: _____ Job Number: _____

To: _____ ("Buyer")

From: _____("Artist")

Delivery Date(s): _____ Fee: _____

Job Description ("Work"):

_____

_____

_____

Payment. Buyer shall pay Artist as follows:

☐ An initial nonrefundable payment of $_____ upon signing this agreement and the remainder upon receipt of the Work.

☐ Payment in full within _____(_____) days of signing this agreement.

☐ **Additional Expenses:** Artist shall be remunerated for the following expenses:

_____

_____

_____

Buyer shall also pay all applicable sales taxes due on this assignment.

☐ **Credit.** All publications or displays of the Work by Buyer shall contain the following statement:

_____ .

☐ **Termination; Cancellation.** In the event this agreement is canceled by Buyer for any reason other than Artist's breach of this agreement or inability to complete the work as agreed upon, Buyer shall pay to Artist the cancellation fee of $_____ along with expenses incurred. In the event of termination by Buyer, Artist shall retain all works in progress and any payments already made.

Liability. Neither party shall be liable for incidental or consequential damages, nor for any claims in tort (or for punitive damages) which may arise from any breach of this agreement or any obligation under this agreement.

Reservation of Rights; Ownership of Original. Artist retains copyright and all other intellectual property rights in all artwork furnished under this agreement.

☐ **No Destruction or Alteration.** Buyer agrees not to intentionally destroy or modify the Work.

General Provisions

Entire Agreement. This is the entire agreement between the parties. It replaces and supersedes any and all oral agreements between the parties, as well as any prior writings. Modifications and amendments to this agreement, including any exhibit or appendix hereto, shall be enforceable only if they are in writing and are signed by authorized representatives of both parties.

Successors and Assignees. This agreement binds and benefits the heirs, successors and assignees of the parties.

Notices. Any notice or communication required or permitted to be given under this agreement shall be sufficiently given when received by certified mail, or sent by facsimile transmission or overnight courier.

Governing Law. This agreement will be governed by the laws of the State of _____.

Waiver. If one party waives any term or provision of this agreement at any time, that waiver will only be effective for the specific instance and specific purpose for which the waiver was given. If either party fails to exercise or delays exercising any of its rights or remedies under this agreement, that party retains the right to enforce that term or provision at a later time.

Severability. If a court finds any provision of this agreement invalid or unenforceable, the remainder of this agreement will be interpreted so as best to carry out the parties' intent.

Attachments and Exhibits. The parties agree and acknowledge that all attachments, exhibits and schedules referred to in this agreement are incorporated in this agreement by reference.

No Agency. Nothing contained herein will be construed as creating any agency, partnership, joint venture or other form of joint enterprise between the parties.

☐ **Attorney Fees and Expenses.** The prevailing party shall have the right to collect from the other party its reasonable costs and necessary disbursements and attorney fees incurred in enforcing this Agreement.

☐ **Jurisdiction.** The parties consent to the exclusive jurisdiction and venue of the federal and state courts located in _____ [county], _____ [state], in any action arising out of or relating to this agreement. The parties waive any other venue to which either party might be entitled by domicile or otherwise.

☐ **Arbitration.** Any controversy or claim arising out of or relating to this agreement shall be settled by arbitration in _____ [county], _____ [state], in accordance with the rules of the American Arbitration Association, and judgment upon the award rendered by the arbitrator(s) may be entered in any court having jurisdiction. The prevailing party shall have the right to collect from the other party its reasonable costs and attorney's fees incurred in enforcing this agreement.

Signatures

Each party represents and warrants that on this date they are duly authorized to bind their respective principals by their signatures below.

BUYER: ARTIST:

_____   _____
Signature   Signature

_____   _____
Typed or Printed Name   Typed or Printed Name

_____   _____
Title   Title

_____   _____
Date   Date

Account No. _____

Dear _____:

Our records show that you have an outstanding balance with our company of $_____.
This is for _____

_____

_____ *(describe the goods or services)*.

Is there a problem with this bill? If so, please call me so that we can resolve the matter. Otherwise, please send your payment at this time to bring your account current. I'm enclosing a business reply envelope for you to use.

Until you bring your account current, it's our policy to put further purchases on a cash basis.

Sincerely,

_____

P.S. Paying your bill at this time will help you to maintain your good credit rating.

Re: Overdue Bill ($_____)

Account No. _____

Dear _____:

Your bill for $_____ is seriously overdue. This is for the _____
_____

_____ (describe the goods or services furnished) we supplied to
you last _____ (state the month). More than 60 days have gone by since we sent
you our invoice. You did not respond to the letter I sent you last month.

We value your patronage but must insist that you bring your account up to date. Doing so will help
you protect your reputation for prompt payment.

Please send your check today for the full balance. If this is not feasible, please call me to discuss a
possible payment plan. I need to hear from you as soon as possible.

Sincerely,

_____

Re: Collection Action on Overdue Bill ($_____)

Account No. _____

Dear _____ :

We show an unpaid balance of $_____ on your account that is over 90 days old. This is
for the _____
that we supplied you over _____ days ago.

I have repeatedly tried to contact you, but my calls and letters have gone unheeded.

You must send full payment by _____ or contact me by that date to discuss your
intentions. If I do not hear from you, I plan to turn over the account for collection.

Work-Made-for-Hire-Agreement

This Work Made for Hire Agreement (the "Agreement") is made between _____
_____ ("Company"), and
_____ ("Contractor").

Services. In consideration of the payments provided in this Agreement, Contractor agrees to perform the following
services: _____
_____
_____

Payment. Company agrees to pay Contractor as follows: _____
_____

Works Made for Hire—Assignment of Intellectual Property Rights. Contractor agrees that, for consideration that
is acknowledged, any works of authorship commissioned pursuant to this Agreement (the "Works") shall be
considered works made for hire as that term is defined under U.S. copyright law. To the extent that any such
Work created for Company by Contractor is not a work made for hire belonging to Company, Contractor hereby
assigns and transfers to Company all rights Contractor has or may acquire to all such Works. Contractor agrees
to sign and deliver to Company, either during or subsequent to the term of this Agreement, such other documents
as Company considers desirable to evidence the assignment of copyright.

Contractor Warranties. Contractor warrants that the Work does not infringe any intellectual property rights or
violate any laws and that the Work is original to Contractor.

General Provisions.

Entire Agreement. This is the entire agreement between the parties. It replaces and supersedes any and all oral
agreements between the parties, as well as any prior writings. Modifications and amendments to this agreement,
including any exhibit or appendix hereto, shall be enforceable only if they are in writing and are signed by
authorized representatives of both parties.

Successors and Assignees. This agreement binds and benefits the heirs, successors and assignees of the parties.

Notices. Any notice or communication required or permitted to be given under this Agreement shall be sufficiently given when received by certified mail, or sent by facsimile transmission or overnight courier.

Governing Law. This agreement will be governed by the laws of the State of _____.

Waiver. If one party waives any term or provision of this agreement at any time, that waiver will only be
effective for the specific instance and specific purpose for which the waiver was given. If either party fails to
exercise or delays exercising any of its rights or remedies under this agreement, that party retains the right to
enforce that term or provision at a later time.

Severability. If a court finds any provision of this agreement invalid or unenforceable, the remainder of this
agreement will be interpreted so as best to carry out the parties' intent.

Attachments and Exhibits. The parties agree and acknowledge that all attachments, exhibits and schedules
referred to in this agreement are incorporated in this agreement by reference.

No Agency. Nothing contained herein will be construed as creating any agency, partnership, joint venture or other form of joint enterprise between the parties.

☐ **Attorney Fees and Expenses.** The prevailing party shall have the right to collect from the other party its reasonable costs and necessary disbursements and attorney fees incurred in enforcing this Agreement.

☐ **Jurisdiction.** The parties consent to the exclusive jurisdiction and venue of the federal and state courts located in _____ [county], _____ [state], in any action arising out of or relating to this agreement. The parties waive any other venue to which either party might be entitled by domicile or otherwise.

☐ **Arbitration.** Any controversy or claim arising out of or relating to this agreement shall be settled by arbitration in _____ [county], _____ [state], in accordance with the rules of the American Arbitration Association, and judgment upon the award rendered by the arbitrator(s) may be entered in any court having jurisdiction. The prevailing party shall have the right to collect from the other party its reasonable costs and attorney's fees incurred in enforcing this agreement.

Signatures

Each party represents and warrants that on this date they are duly authorized to bind their respective principals by their signatures below.

COMPANY:

_____

Signature

_____

Typed or Printed Name

_____

Title

_____

Date

CONTRACTOR:

_____

Signature

_____

Typed or Printed Name

_____

Title

_____

Date

Nondisclosure Agreement

This Nondisclosure Agreement (the "Agreement") is made between _____ _____ (the "Disclosing Party") and _____ (the "Receiving Party"). The Parties agree to the following terms and conditions. Receiving Party acknowledges that the following information constitutes confidential trade secret information ("Confidential Information") belonging to Disclosing Party: _____

_____ .

In consideration of Disclosing Party's disclosure of its Confidential Information to Recipient, Receiving Party agrees that it will not disclose Disclosing Party's Confidential Information to any third party or make or permit to be made copies or other reproductions of Disclosing Party's Confidential Information.

This Agreement does not apply to any information which:

(a) was in Receiving Party's possession or was known to Receiving Party, without an obligation to keep it confidential, before such information was disclosed to Receiving Party by Disclosing Party

(b) is or becomes public knowledge through a source other than Receiving Party and through no fault of Receiving Party

(c) is or becomes lawfully available to Receiving Party from a source other than Disclosing Party, or

(d) is disclosed by Receiving Party with Disclosing Party's prior written approval.

This Agreement and Receiving Party's duty to hold Disclosing Party's trade secrets in confidence will continue until the Confidential Information is no longer a trade secret or until Disclosing Party sends Receiving Party written notice releasing Receiving Party from this Agreement, whichever occurs first.

If any legal action arises relating to this Agreement, the prevailing party will be entitled to recover all court costs, expenses and reasonable attorney fees.

This is the entire agreement between the parties regarding the subject matter. It supersedes all prior agreements or understandings between them. All additions or modifications to this Agreement must be made in writing and must be signed by both parties to be effective.

This Agreement is made under, and will be interpreted according to, the laws of the State of _____.

If a court finds any provision of this Agreement invalid or unenforceable as applied to any circumstance, the remainder of this Agreement will be interpreted so as best to effect the intent of the parties.

Dated: _____

DISCLOSING PARTY

_____
Name of Business

_____
Signature

_____
Printed Name and Title

_____
Address

RECEIVING PARTY

_____
Name of Business

_____
Signature

_____
Printed Name and Title

_____
Address

_____

Copyright Assignment

I, _____ ("Artist"),

am owner of the work entitled _____

(the "Work") and described as follows: _____

_____ .

In consideration of $_____ and other valuable consideration, paid by _____

_____ ("Assignee"), I assign to Assignee and Assignee's

heirs and assigns, all my right title and interest in the copyright to the Work and all renewals and extensions of

the copyright that may be secured under the laws of the United States of America and any other countries, as

such may now or later be in effect. I agree to cooperate with Assignee and to execute and deliver all papers as

may be necessary to vest all rights to the Work.

Signature(s) of Artist(s):

_____

_____

_____

Artwork Assignment Agreement

This Artwork Assignment Agreement (the "Agreement") is made between _____ _____ ("Company"), and _____("Artist").

Services

Artist agrees to perform the following services: _____ _____ and create the following artwork (the "Art") entitled: _____ .

The Art shall be completed by the following date: _____ .

During the process, Artist shall keep the Company informed of work in progress and shall furnish test prints of the Art prior to completion.

Payment

Company agrees to pay Artist as follows:

$_____ for performance of the art services and acquisition of the rights provided below.

Rights

Artist assigns to the Company all copyright to the Art and agrees to cooperate in the preparation of any documents necessary to demonstrate this assignment of rights. Artist retains the right to display the work as part of Artist's portfolio and to reproduce the artwork in connection with the promotion of Artist's services.

Expenses

Company agrees to reimburse Artist for all reasonable production expenses including halftones, stats, photography, disks, illustrations or related costs. These expenses shall be itemized on invoices, and in no event shall any expense exceed $50 without approval from the Company.

Credit

Credit for Artist shall be included on reproductions of the Art as follows:_____ _____ .

Artist Warranties

Artist is the owner of all rights to the Art and warrants that the Art does not infringe any intellectual property rights or violate any laws.

General Provisions

Entire Agreement. This is the entire agreement between the parties. It replaces and supersedes any and all oral agreements between the parties, as well as any prior writings. Modifications and amendments to this Agreement, including any exhibit or appendix hereto, shall be enforceable only if they are in writing and are signed by authorized representatives of both parties.

Successors and Assignees. This agreement binds and benefits the heirs, successors and assignees of the parties.

Notices. Any notice or communication required or permitted to be given under this Agreement shall be sufficiently given when received by certified mail, or sent by facsimile transmission or overnight courier.

Governing Law. This Agreement will be governed by the laws of the State of _____.

Waiver. If one party waives any term or provision of this agreement at any time, that waiver will only be effective for the specific instance and specific purpose for which the waiver was given. If either party fails to exercise or delays exercising any of its rights or remedies under this agreement, that party retains the right to enforce that term or provision at a later time.

Severability. If a court finds any provision of this Agreement invalid or unenforceable, the remainder of this Agreement will be interpreted so as best to carry out the parties' intent.

Attachments and Exhibits. The parties agree and acknowledge that all attachments, exhibits and schedules referred to in this Agreement are incorporated in this Agreement by reference.

No Agency. Nothing contained herein will be construed as creating any agency, partnership, joint venture or other form of joint enterprise between the parties.

☐ **Attorney Fees and Expenses.** The prevailing party shall have the right to collect from the other party its reasonable costs and necessary disbursements and attorney fees incurred in enforcing this Agreement.

☐ **Jurisdiction.** The parties consent to the exclusive jurisdiction and venue of the federal and state courts located in _____ [county], _____ [state], in any action arising out of or relating to this Agreement. The parties waive any other venue to which either party might be entitled by domicile or otherwise.

☐ **Arbitration.** Any controversy or claim arising out of or relating to this Agreement shall be settled by arbitration in _____ [county], _____ [state], in accordance with the rules of the American Arbitration Association, and judgment upon the award rendered by the arbitrator(s) may be entered in any court having jurisdiction. The prevailing party shall have the right to collect from the other party its reasonable costs and attorney's fees incurred in enforcing this agreement.

Signatures

Each party represents and warrants that on this date they are duly authorized to bind their respective principals by their signatures below.

COMPANY

ARTIST(S)

_____
Date

_____
Date

_____
Name of Business

_____
Authorized Signature

_____
Signature

_____
Printed Name and Title

_____
Printed Name

_____
Address

_____
Address

_____

_____

Unlimited Personal Release Agreement

Grant. For consideration which I acknowledge, I irrevocably grant to _____
_____ ("Company")
and Company's assigns, licensees and successors the right to use my image and name in all forms and media, including composite or modified representations, for all purposes, including advertising, trade or any commercial purpose throughout the world and in perpetuity. I waive the right to inspect or approve versions of my image used for publication or the written copy that may be used in connection with the images.

Release. I release Company and Company's assigns, licensees and successors from any claims that may arise regarding the use of my image, including any claims of defamation, invasion of privacy or infringement of moral rights, rights of publicity or copyright. Company is permitted, although not obligated, to include my name as a credit in connection with the image.

Company is not obligated to utilize any of the rights granted in this agreement.

I have read and understood this agreement, and I am over the age of 18. This agreement expresses the complete understanding of the parties.

_____   _____
Signature   Witness Signature

_____
Name

_____
Address

_____

_____
Date

[Include if the person is under 18]

Parent/Guardian Consent. I am the parent or guardian of the minor named above. I have the legal right to consent to and do consent to the terms and conditions of this model release.

_____   _____
Parent/Guardian Signature   Witness Signature

_____
Parent/Guardian Name

_____
Parent/Guardian Address

_____

_____
Date

Limited Personal Release Agreement *[For Specific Uses Only]*

Grant. For consideration which I acknowledge, I grant to _____
("Company") and Company's assigns, licensees and successors, the right to use my image for the following purposes:

_____

in the following territory _____ for a period of _____ year(s) (the "Term").

I grant the right to use my name and image for the purposes listed above in all forms and media, including composite or modified representations, and waive the right to inspect or approve versions of my image used for publication or the written copy that may be used in connection with the images.

[Select if appropriate]

☐ **Payment.** For the rights granted during the Term, Company shall pay $_____ upon execution of this release.

☐ **Renewal.** Company may renew this agreement under the same terms and conditions for _____ year(s), provided that Licensee makes payment of $_____ at the time of renewal.

Release. I release Company and Company's assigns, licensees and successors from any claims that may arise regarding the use of my image, including any claims of defamation, invasion of privacy or infringement of moral rights, rights of publicity or copyright. Company is permitted, although not obligated, to include my name as a credit in connection with the image.

Company is not obligated to utilize any of the rights granted in this Agreement.

I have read and understood this agreement, and I am over the age of 18. This Agreement expresses the complete understanding of the parties.

_____   _____
Signature   Witness Signature

_____
Name

_____
Address

_____

_____
Date

[Include if the person is under 18]

Parent/Guardian Consent. I am the parent or guardian of the minor named above. I have the legal right to consent to and do consent to the terms and conditions of this model release.

_____   _____
Parent/Guardian Signature   Witness Signature

_____
Parent/Guardian Name

_____
Parent/Guardian Address

_____

_____
Date

Merchandise License Agreement

Introduction

This License Agreement (the "Agreement") is made between _____
_____ (referred to as "Licensor") and _____
_____ (referred to as "Licensee").

The parties agree as follows:

The Work. The Work refers to the work described in Exhibit A. Licensor is the owner of all rights to the Work, and Licensee shall not claim any right to use the Work except under the terms of this Agreement.

Licensed Products. Licensed Products are defined as the Licensee's products incorporating the Work specifically described in Exhibit A (the "Licensed Products").

Grant of Rights

Licensor grants to Licensee:

[Select one]

☐ an exclusive license

☐ a nonexclusive license

to reproduce and distribute the Work in or on the Licensed Products.

Licensor grants to Licensee:

[Select if appropriate]

☐ the right to modify the Work to incorporate it in or on the Licensed Products provided that Licensee agrees to assign to Licensor its rights, if any, in any derivative works resulting from Licensee's modification of the Work. Licensee agrees to execute any documents required to evidence this assignment of copyright and to waive any moral rights and rights of attribution provided in 17 USC § 106A of the Copyright Act.

☐ the right to publicly display the Work as incorporated in or on the Licensed Products.

☐ the right to publicly perform the Work as incorporated in or on the Licensed Products.

Sublicense.

[Select one]

☐ **Consent required.** Licensee may sublicense the rights granted pursuant to this Agreement provided Licensee obtains Licensor's prior written consent to such sublicense, and Licensor receives such revenue or royalty payment as provided in the Payment section below. Any sublicense granted in violation of this provision shall be void.

☐ **Consent to sublicense not unreasonably withheld.** Licensee may sublicense the rights granted pursuant to this agreement provided Licensee obtains Licensor's prior written consent to such sublicense, and Licensor receives such revenue or royalty payment as provided in the Payment section below. Licensor's consent to any sublicense shall not be unreasonably withheld. Any sublicense granted in violation of this provision shall be void.

☐ **No sublicensing permitted.** Licensee may not sublicense the rights granted under this Agreement.

Reservation of Rights: Assignment of Good Will. Licensor reserves all rights other than those being conveyed or granted in this Agreement.

Territory. The rights granted to Licensee are limited to _____
(the "Territory").

Term. The "Effective Date" of this Agreement is defined as the date when the agreement commences and is established by the latest signature date.

[Select one]

☐ **Fixed term.** This Agreement shall commence upon the Effective Date and shall continue for _____ unless sooner terminated pursuant to a provision of this Agreement.

☐ **Specified term with renewal rights.** This Agreement shall commence upon the Effective Date and shall extend for a period of _____ years (the "Initial Term"). Following the Initial Term, Licensee may renew this agreement under the same terms and conditions for _____ consecutive _____ periods (the "Renewal Terms"), provided that Licensee provides written notice of its intention to renew this agreement within thirty (30) days before the expiration of the current term. In no event shall the Term extend beyond the period of United States copyright protection for the Work.

☐ **Term for as long as Licensee sells Licensed Products.** This Agreement shall commence upon the Effective Date as specified in Exhibit A and shall continue for as long as Licensee continues to offer the Licensed Products in commercially reasonable quantities or unless sooner terminated pursuant to a provision of this Agreement. In no event shall the Term extend beyond the period of U.S. copyright protection for the Work.

☐ **Term with renewal based upon sales.** This Agreement shall commence upon the Effective Date and shall extend for a period of _____ years (the "Initial Term") and may be renewed by Licensee under the same terms and conditions for consecutive _____ year periods (the "Renewal Terms"), provided that:

(a) Licensee provides written notice of its intention to renew this Agreement within thirty days before the expiration of the current term, and

(b) Licensee has met the sales requirements as established in Exhibit A.

Payments. All royalties ("Royalties") provided for under this Agreement shall accrue when the respective Licensed Products are sold, shipped, distributed, billed or paid for, whichever occurs first.

Net Sales. Net Sales are defined as Licensee's gross sales (that is, the gross invoice amount billed customers) less quantity discounts or rebates and returns actually credited. A quantity discount or rebate is a discount made at the time of shipment. No deductions shall be made for cash or other discounts, commissions, manufacturing costs, uncollectible accounts or fees or expenses of any kind which the Licensee may incur in connection with the Royalty payments.

Fees.
[Select one or more provisions]

☐ **Advance Against Royalties.** As a nonrefundable advance against royalties (the "Advance"), Licensee agrees to pay to Licensor upon execution of this Agreement the sum of $ _____.

☐ **Licensed Product Royalty.** Licensee agrees to pay a Royalty of _____% percent of all Net Sales revenue of the Licensed Products ("Licensed Product Royalty").

☐ **Per Unit Royalty.** Licensee agrees to pay a Royalty of $_____ for each unit of the Licensed Product that is: *[select one]*

    ☐ manufactured.

    ☐ sold.

☐ **Guaranteed Minimum Annual Royalty Payment.** In addition to any other advances or fees, Licensee shall pay an annual guaranteed royalty (the "GMAR") as follows: $_____. The GMAR shall be paid to Licensor annually on _____. The GMAR is an advance against royalties for the twelve-month period commencing upon payment. Royalty payments based on Net Sales made during any year of this Agreement shall be credited against the GMAR due for the year in which such Net Sales were made. In the event that annual royalties exceed the GMAR, Licensee shall pay the difference to Licensor. Any annual royalty payments in excess of the GMAR shall not be carried forward from previous years or applied against the GMAR.

☐ **License Fee.** As a nonrefundable, nonrecoupable fee for executing this license, Licensee agrees to pay to Licensor upon execution of this Agreement the sum of $ _____.

☐ **Sublicensing Revenues.** In the event of any sublicense of the rights granted pursuant to this Agreement, Licensee shall pay to Licensor _____ % of all sublicensing revenues.

Payments and Statements to Licensor. Within thirty (30) days after the end of each calendar quarter (the "Royalty Period"), an accurate statement of Net Sales of Licensed Products along with any royalty payments or sublicensing revenues due to Licensor shall be provided to Licensor, regardless of whether any Licensed Products were sold during the Royalty Period. All payments shall be paid in United States currency drawn on a United States bank. The acceptance by Licensor of any of the statements furnished or royalties paid shall not preclude Licensor questioning the correctness at any time of any payments or statements.

Audit. Licensee shall keep accurate books of account and records covering all transactions relating to the license granted in this Agreement, and Licensor or its duly authorized representatives shall have the right upon five days' prior written notice, and during normal business hours, to inspect and audit Licensee's records relating to the Work licensed under this Agreement. Licensor shall bear the cost of such inspection and audit, unless the results indicate an underpayment greater than $_____ for any six-month (6-month) period. In that case, Licensee shall promptly reimburse Licensor for all costs of the audit along with the amount due with interest on such sums. Interest shall accrue from the date the payment was originally due, and the interest rate shall be 1.5 % per month, or the maximum rate permitted by law, whichever is less. All books of account and records shall be made available in the United States and kept available for at least two years after the termination of this Agreement.

Late Payment. Time is of the essence with respect to all payments to be made by Licensee under this Agreement. If Licensee is late in any payment provided for in this Agreement, Licensee shall pay interest on the payment from the date due until paid at a rate of 1.5 % per month, or the maximum rate permitted by law, whichever is less.

Licensor Warranties. Licensor warrants that it has the power and authority to enter into this Agreement and has no knowledge as to any third-party claims regarding the proprietary rights in the Work that would interfere with the rights granted under this Agreement.

Indemnification by Licensor.

[Select one if appropriate]

☐ **Licensor indemnification without limitations.** Licensor shall indemnify Licensee and hold Licensee harmless from any damages and liabilities (including reasonable attorney fees and costs) arising from any breach of Licensor's warranties as defined in Licensor's Warranties, above.

☐ **Licensor indemnification limited to amounts paid.** Licensor shall indemnify Licensee and hold Licensee harmless from any damages and liabilities (including reasonable attorney fees and costs) arising from any breach of Licensor's warranties as defined in Licensor's Warranties, above. Licensor's maximum liability under this provision shall in no event exceed the total amount earned by Licensor under this Agreement.

☐ **Licensor indemnification with limitations.** Licensor shall indemnify Licensee and hold Licensee harmless from any damages and liabilities (including reasonable attorney fees and costs) arising from any breach of Licensor's warranties as defined in Licensor's Warranties, above, provided:

(a) such claim, if sustained, would prevent Licensee from marketing the Licensed Products or the Work

(b) such claim arises solely out of the Work as disclosed to the Licensee, and not out of any change in the Work made by Licensee or a vendor

(c) Licensee gives Licensor prompt written notice of any such claim

(d) such indemnity shall only be applicable in the event of a final decision by a court of competent jurisdiction from which no right to appeal exists, and

(e) the maximum amount due from Licensor to Licensee under this paragraph shall not exceed the amounts due to Licensor under the Payment section from the date that Licensor notifies Licensee of the existence of such a claim.

Licensee Warranties. Licensee warrants that it will use its best commercial efforts to market the Licensed Products and that their sale and marketing shall be in conformance with all applicable laws and regulations, including but not limited to all intellectual property laws.

Indemnification by Licensee. Licensee shall indemnify Licensor and hold Licensor harmless from any damages and liabilities (including reasonable attorney fees and costs):

(a) arising from any breach of Licensee's warranties and representation as defined in the Licensee Warranties, above

(b) arising out of any alleged defects or failures to perform of the Licensed Products or any product liability claims or use of the Licensed Products, and

(c) arising out of advertising, distribution or marketing of the Licensed Products.

Intellectual Property Registration. Licensor may, but is not obligated to, seek in its own name and at its own expense appropriate copyright registrations for the Work. Licensor makes no warranty with respect to the validity of any copyright that may be granted. Licensor grants to Licensee the right to apply for registration of the Work or Licensed Products provided that such registrations shall be applied for in the name of Licensor and licensed to Licensee during the Term and according to the conditions of this Agreement. Licensee shall have the right to deduct its reasonable out-of-pocket expenses for the preparation and filing of any such registrations from future royalties due to Licensor under this Agreement. Licensee shall obtain Licensor's prior written consent before incurring expenses for any foreign copyright applications.

Compliance With Intellectual Property Laws. The license granted in this Agreement is conditioned on Licensee's compliance with the provisions of the intellectual property laws of the United States and any foreign country in the Territory. All copies of the Licensed Product as well as all promotional material shall bear appropriate proprietary notices.

Licensor Credits. Licensee shall identify Licensor as the owner of rights to the Work and shall include the following notice on all copies of the Licensed Products: "_____.
_____ All rights reserved." Licensee may, with Licensor's consent, use Licensor's name, image or trademark in advertising or promotional materials associated with the sale of the Licensed Products.

Infringement Against Third Parties. In the event that either party learns of imitations or infringements of the Work or Licensed Products, that party shall notify the other in writing of the infringements or imitations. Licensor shall have the right to commence lawsuits against third persons arising from infringement of the Work or Licensed Products. In the event that Licensor does not commence a lawsuit against an alleged infringer within sixty (60) days of notification by Licensee, Licensee may commence a lawsuit against the third party. Before filing suit, Licensee shall obtain the written consent of Licensor to do so, and such consent shall not be unreasonably withheld. Licensor will cooperate fully and in good faith with Licensee for the purpose of securing and preserving Licensee's rights to the Work. Any recovery (including, but not limited to, a judgment, settlement or licensing agreement included as resolution of an infringement dispute) shall be divided equally between the parties after deduction and payment of reasonable attorney fees to the party bringing the lawsuit.

Exploitation Date. Licensee agrees to manufacture, distribute and sell the Licensed Products in commercially reasonable quantities during the term of this Agreement and to commence such manufacture, distribution and sale by _____. This is a material provision of this Agreement.

[Optional]

☐ **Advertising Budget.** Licensee agrees to spend at least _____% of estimated annual gross sales for promotional efforts and advertising of the Licensed Products.

Approval of Samples and Quality Control. Licensee shall submit a reasonable number of preproduction designs, prototypes, and camera-ready artwork prior to production as well as preproduction samples of the Licensed Product to Licensor, to assure that the product meets Licensor's quality standards. In the event that Licensor fails to object in writing within ten (10) business days after the date of receipt of any such materials, such materials shall be deemed to be acceptable. At least once during each calendar year, Licensee shall submit two (2) production samples of each Licensed Product for review. Licensee shall pay all costs for delivery of these approval materials. The quality standards applied by Licensor shall be no more rigorous than the quality standards applied by Licensor to similar products.

Licensor Copies and Right to Purchase. Licensee shall provide Licensor with _____ copies of each Licensed Product. Licensor has the right to purchase from Licensee, at Licensee's manufacturing cost, at least _____ copies of any Licensed Product, and such payments shall be deducted from Royalties due to Licensor.

Confidentiality. The parties acknowledge that each may have access to confidential information that relates to each other's business (the "Information"). The parties agree to protect the confidentiality of the Information and maintain it with the strictest confidence, and no party shall disclose such information to third parties without the prior written consent of the other.

Insurance. Licensee shall, throughout the Term, obtain and maintain, at its own expense, standard product liability insurance coverage, naming Licensor as an additional named insured. Such policy shall provide protection against any claims, demands and causes of action arising out of any alleged defects or failure to perform of the Licensed Products or any use of the Licensed Products. The amount of coverage shall be a minimum of $_____, with no deductible amount for each single occurrence for bodily injury or property damage. The policy shall provide for notice to the Licensor from the insurer by registered or certified mail in the event of any modification or termination of insurance. The provisions of this section shall survive termination for three years.

Licensor's Right to Terminate. Licensor shall have the right to terminate this Agreement for the following reasons:

[Select one or more provisions]

☐ **Failure to make timely payment.** Licensee fails to pay Royalties when due or fails to accurately report Net Sales, as defined in the Payment section of this Agreement, and such failure is not cured within thirty (30) days after written notice from the Licensor.

☐ **Failure to introduce product.** Licensee fails to introduce the product to market by the date set in the Exploitation section of this Agreement or to offer the Licensed Products in commercially reasonable quantities during any subsequent year.

☐ **Assignment or sublicensing.** Licensee assigns or sublicenses in violation of this Agreement.

☐ **Failure to maintain insurance.** Licensee fails to maintain or obtain product liability insurance as required by the provisions of this Agreement.

☐ **Failure to submit samples.** Licensee fails to provide Licensor with preproduction samples for approval.

☐ **Termination as to unexploited portion of territory.** Licensor shall have the right to terminate the grant of license under this Agreement with respect to any country or region included in the Territory in which Licensee fails to offer the Licensed Products for sale or distribution or to secure a sublicensing agreement for the marketing, distribution and sale of the product within two (2) years of the Effective Date.

Effect of Termination. Upon termination of this Agreement ("Termination"), all Royalty obligations as established in the Payments section shall immediately become due. After the Termination of this license, all rights granted to Licensee under this Agreement shall terminate and revert to Licensor, and Licensee will refrain from further manufacturing, copying, marketing, distribution or use of any Licensed Product or other product which incorporates the Work. Within thirty (30) days after Termination, Licensee shall deliver to Licensor a statement indicating the number and description of the Licensed Products that it had on hand or is in the process of manufacturing as of the Termination date.

Sell-Off Period. Licensee may dispose of the Licensed Products covered by this Agreement for a period of ninety (90) days after Termination or expiration, except that Licensee shall have no such right in the event this agreement is terminated according to the Licensor's Right to Terminate, above. At the end of the post-Termination sale period, Licensee shall furnish a royalty payment and statement as required under the Payment section. Upon termination, Licensee shall deliver to Licensor all original artwork and camera-ready reproductions used in the manufacture of the Licensed Products. Licensor shall bear the costs of shipping for the artwork and reproductions.

Attorney Fees and Expenses. The prevailing party shall have the right to collect from the other party its reasonable costs and necessary disbursements and attorney fees incurred in enforcing this Agreement.

Dispute Resolution.

[Select one if appropriate]

☐ **Mediation and Arbitration.** The parties agree that every dispute or difference between them arising under this Agreement shall be settled first by a meeting of the parties attempting to confer and resolve the dispute in a good faith manner. If the parties cannot resolve their dispute after conferring, any party may require the other parties to submit the matter to nonbinding mediation, utilizing the services of an impartial professional mediator approved by all parties. If the parties cannot come to an agreement following mediation, the parties agree to submit the matter to binding arbitration at a location mutually agreeable to the parties. The arbitration shall be conducted on a confidential basis pursuant to the Commercial Arbitration Rules of the American Arbitration Association. Any decision or award as a result of any such arbitration proceeding shall include the assessment of costs, expenses and reasonable attorney's fees and shall include a written record of the proceedings and a written determination of the arbitrators. An arbitrator experienced in copyright and merchandising law shall conduct any such arbitration. An award of arbitration shall be final and binding on the parties and may be confirmed in a court of competent jurisdiction.

☐ **Arbitration.** If a dispute arises under or relating to this Agreement, the parties agree to submit such dispute to binding arbitration in the state of _____ or another location mutually agreeable to the parties. The arbitration shall be conducted on a confidential basis pursuant to the Commercial Arbitration Rules of the American Arbitration Association. Any decision or award as a result of any such arbitration proceeding shall be in writing and shall provide an explanation for all conclusions of law and fact and shall include the assessment of costs, expenses and reasonable attorney fees. An arbitrator experienced in copyright and merchandising law shall conduct any such arbitration. An award of arbitration may be confirmed in a court of competent jurisdiction.

No Special Damages. Licensor shall not be liable to Licensee for any incidental, consequential, punitive or special damages.

General Provisions.

(a) **Entire Agreement.** This is the entire agreement between the parties. It replaces and supersedes any and all oral agreements between the parties, as well as any prior writings. Modifications and amendments to this Agreement, including any exhibit or appendix hereto, shall be enforceable only if they are in writing and are signed by authorized representatives of both parties.

(b) **Successors and Assignees.** This agreement binds and benefits the heirs, successors and assignees of the parties.

(c) **Notices.** Any notice or communication required or permitted to be given under this Agreement shall be sufficiently given when received by certified mail, or sent by facsimile transmission or overnight courier.

(d) **Governing Law.** This Agreement will be governed by the laws of the State of

_____.

(e) **Waiver.** If one party waives any term or provision of this Agreement at any time, that waiver will only be effective for the specific instance and specific purpose for which the waiver was given. If either party fails to exercise or delays exercising any of its rights or remedies under this Agreement, that party retains the right to enforce that term or provision at a later time.

(f) **Severability.** If a court finds any provision of this Agreement invalid or unenforceable, the remainder of this Agreement will be interpreted so as best to carry out the parties' intent.

(g) **Attachments and Exhibits.** The parties agree and acknowledge that all attachments, exhibits and schedules referred to in this Agreement are incorporated in this Agreement by reference.

(h) **No Agency.** Nothing contained herein will be construed as creating any agency, partnership, joint venture or other form of joint enterprise between the parties.

☐ **Attorney Fees and Expenses.** The prevailing party shall have the right to collect from the other party its reasonable costs and necessary disbursements and attorney fees incurred in enforcing this Agreement.

☐ **Jurisdiction.** The parties consent to the exclusive jurisdiction and venue of the federal and state courts located in _____ [county], _____ [state], in any action arising out of or relating to this Agreement. The parties waive any other venue to which either party might be entitled by domicile or otherwise.

Assignability

[Select one]

☐ **Assignment requires licensor consent.** Licensee may not assign or transfer its rights or obligations pursuant to this Agreement without the prior written consent of Licensor. Any assignment or transfer in violation of this section shall be void.

☐ **Licensor consent not unreasonably withheld.** Licensee may not assign or transfer its rights or obligations pursuant to this Agreement without the prior written consent of Licensor. Such consent shall not be unreasonably withheld. Any assignment or transfer in violation of this section shall be void.

☐ **Licensor consent not required for assignment to parent or acquiring company.** Licensee may not assign or transfer its rights or obligations pursuant to this Agreement without the prior written consent of Licensor. However, no consent is required for an assignment or transfer that occurs: (a) to an entity in which Licensee owns more than fifty percent of the assets, or (b) as part of a transfer of all or substantially all of the assets of Licensee to any party. Any assignment or transfer in violation of this section shall be void.

Signatures. Each party represents and warrants that on this date they are duly authorized to bind their respective principals by their signatures below.

Each party has signed this Agreement through its authorized representative. The parties, having read this Agreement, indicate their consent to the terms and conditions by their signatures below.

LICENSOR: LICENSEE:

_____   _____
Date   Date

_____   _____
Licensor's Name   Licensee's Name and Title

_____   _____
Authorized Signature   Signature

Exhibit A

The Property _____

Licensed Products _____

Sales Requirements: $ _____ in Gross Sales per year.

Merchandise License Worksheet

Licensee

Name of Licensee Business _____

Licensee Address _____

_____

Licensee Business Form

   ☐ sole proprietorship   ☐ general partnership   ☐ limited partnership

   ☐ corporation   ☐ limited liability company

State of incorporation _____

Name and position of person signing for Licensee _____

Property Definition

Design Patent No. _____

Design Patent Application Serial No. _____

Copyrightable Features _____

_____

Copyright Registration No(s). _____

Trade Secrets _____

_____

Trademarks _____

_____

Trademark Registration No(s). _____

_____

Licensed Products Definition

Industry (Have you limited the license to a particular industry?) _____

Product (Have you limited the license to a particular product or products?) _____

_____

Territory

   ☐ Worldwide; or

   ☐ Countries _____

   ☐ States _____

Rights Granted *(check those rights granted to Licensee)*

☐ sell	☐ import	☐ advertise
☐ make or manufacture	☐ lease	☐ promote
☐ distribute	☐ right to improvements	☐ other rights _____
☐ use	☐ derivatives (copyright)	☐ other rights _____
☐ revise	☐ copy (copyright)	☐ other rights _____

Rights Reserved

☐ all rights reserved (except those granted in license)

☐ no rights reserved

☐ specific rights reserved

Have you signed any other licenses? ☐ Yes ☐ No   If so, do you need to reserve specific rights?

_____

Term

Have you agreed upon:

☐ a fixed term (How long? _____)   ☐ a term limited by design patent length

☐ unlimited term until one party terminates   ☐ an initial term with renewals (see below)

☐ other _____

Renewals

If you have agreed upon an initial term with renewals:

How many renewal periods? _____

How long is each renewal period? _____

What triggers renewal?

☐ Licensee must notify of intent to renew

☐ Licensor must notify of intent to renew

☐ Agreement renews automatically unless Licensee indicates it does not want to renew.

Net Sales Deductions

What is the Licensee permitted to deduct when calculating net sales?

☐ quantity discounts	☐ debts & uncollectibles	☐ sales commissions
☐ promotion and marketing costs	☐ fees	☐ freight & shipping
☐ credits & returns	☐ other _____	

Is there a cap on the total amount of the deductions? ☐ Yes ☐ No

If so, how much? _____

Royalty Rates

☐ Licensed Products _____%

☐ Combination Products _____%

☐ Accessory Products _____%

☐ Per Use Royalty _____% or Usage Standard _____

☐ Other Products _____ _____%

☐ Other Products _____ _____%

Do you have any sliding royalty rates?   ☐ Yes   ☐ No

Advances and Lump Sum Payments

☐ Advance $_____   Date Due _____

☐ Lump Sum Payment(s) $_____   Date Due _____

Guaranteed Minimum Annual Royalty (GMAR)

☐ GMAR $_____   Date Due _____

☐ Does the GMAR carry forward credits?

☐ Does the GMAR carry forward deficiencies?

Audit Rights

No. of audits permitted per year _____

No. of days' notice _____

Sales Representative Letter Agreement

Date: _____

Dear: _____

This letter sets forth the terms and conditions of the agreement (the "Agreement") between_____

_____ ("Artist") and _____

_____ ("Sales Representative"). Artist is the owner of all rights in certain crafts works (referred to as the "Works") and described more fully in Attachment A to this Agreement.

Appointment. Artist agrees to have Sales Representative serve as

☐ an exclusive   ☐ a nonexclusive

sales representative for the Works in the Territory to

☐ retail accounts   ☐ commissioned works, including: _____

☐ wholesale accounts   ☐ licensing rights for the following markets: _____

☐ trade (wholesale) sales of crafts work

Territory. Sales Representative will represent Artist in the following territory: _____

_____ (the "Territory").

[Optional]

☐ The accounts and companies listed in Exhibit A are excluded from this Agreement, and Sales Representative shall not call on these accounts and shall not be entitled to income from such sources.

[Optional (use only if Agreement is exclusive)]

☐ Artist may advertise via ☐ Internet ☐ mail   to accounts in the Territory. In that event, revenues from such sales shall be accounted for as follows: _____

_____ .

☐ Artist may attend trade shows or meet with accounts or collectors in the Territory. In the event that Artist obtains a sales order or agreement in the Territory from such solicitations, revenues shall be accounted for as follows: _____

_____ .

Obligations of Sales Representative; Disclaimer. Sales Representative shall use best efforts to contact and solicit sales or other sources of revenue, as described above, and present and communicate sales information between the parties. Nothing in this Agreement shall be interpreted by Artist or Sales Representative as a promise or guarantee as to the outcome of any solicitation or negotiation by Sales Representative on behalf of Artist or the Works. Any representations as to the likelihood of success regarding exploitation of the Works are expressions of opinion only. Sales Representative is free to conduct business other than on Artist's behalf, including business or agency relationships with other Artists.

[Optional]

☐ **Sales Representative Reimbursement.** Representative shall be reimbursed for the following expenses from any net revenue or net receipts as described in the "Payments" section, below (the "Work Income"). These reimbursements shall be deducted from Work Income before splitting the resulting revenues or receipts, provided that such expenses are solely for the purpose of promoting Artist:

☐ promotional mailings   ☐ paid advertising   ☐ shipping

☐ insurance   ☐ travel   ☐ telephone

Artist's written approval is required for any individual expense over $_____.

In the event that any such costs are incurred for the benefit of other clients of Sales Representative as well as for Artist, the expenses shall be prorated to reflect each client's actual expenses.

☐ Artist shall pay the following fees for showroom exhibit costs: _____
_____.

Obligations of Artist.

Artist will provide Sales Representative with:

☐ _____ samples of the Works, which samples shall remain the property of Artist and shall be returned upon termination of this Agreement or upon thirty (30) days' notice from Artist. Sales Representative shall have the limited right to display, copy and distribute the Works solely in conjunction with promoting the works and fulfilling obligations as set forth under this Agreement.

☐ printed materials as follows: _____
_____.

Artist shall also perform the following duties: _____
_____.

Payments. As compensation for the services provided above, Sales Representative shall receive the following compensation:

[Check and complete appropriate choices]

☐ _____% of net receipts from all sales made by Sales Representative to retail accounts.

☐ _____% of net receipts from all sales made by Sales Representative to wholesale accounts.

☐ _____% of net revenues from any licensing agreements for the Works.

☐ _____% of net revenues from any commissions obtained by Sales Representative.

Artist agrees that all income paid as a result of any sales or agreements solicited or negotiated by Sales Representative for the Works (the "Works Income") shall be paid directly to Artist. Works Income shall include, but not be limited to, advances, guarantees or license fees.

Artist shall issue payments to Sales Representative within ten (10) days of Artist's receipt of any Works Income along with any client accountings as provided by the licensee.

The party responsible for all billings and collections shall be:

☐ Sales Representative

☐ Artist

Each party shall keep accurate books of account and records covering all transactions relating to this Agreement, and either party or its duly authorized representative shall have the right upon five (5) days' prior written notice, and during normal business hours, to inspect and audit the other party's records relating to this Agreement.

Rights. Artist represents and warrants that Artist has the power and authority to enter into this Agreement and is the owner of all proprietary rights, whether they are copyright or otherwise, in the Works.

Advertising.

[Choose one]

☐ Sales Representative can use Artist's name, likeness, trademarks and trade names in Sales Representative's advertising and promotions.

☐ Sales Representative can use Artist's name, likeness, trademarks and trade names in Sales Representative's advertising and promotions, but must obtain Artist's prior approval for every such use.

Assignment. This Agreement shall not be assignable by either party without the written authorization of the nonassigning party.

Termination. This Agreement may be terminated at any time at the discretion of either Artist or Sales Representative, provided that written notice of such termination is furnished to the other party thirty (30) days prior to such termination.

[Optional]

☐ If this Agreement is terminated by Artist, and within _____ (_____) months of termination Artist enters into an agreement for assignments, sales or licenses with any client or company for whom Sales Representative had entered into agreements on Artist's behalf during the term of this Agreement, Artist agrees to pay Sales Representative the fees established in this Agreement. This obligation shall survive termination of this Agreement.

No Special Damages. Neither party shall be liable to the other for any incidental, consequential, punitive or special damages.

General Provisions

Entire Agreement. This is the entire agreement between the parties. It replaces and supersedes any and all oral agreements between the parties, as well as any prior writings. Modifications and amendments to this Agreement, including any exhibit or appendix hereto, shall be enforceable only if they are in writing and are signed by authorized representatives of both parties.

Successors and Assignees. This Agreement binds and benefits the heirs, successors and assignees of the parties.

Notices. Any notice or communication required or permitted to be given under this Agreement shall be sufficiently given when received by certified mail, or sent by facsimile transmission or overnight courier.

Governing Law. This Agreement will be governed by the laws of the State of _____.

Waiver. If one party waives any term or provision of this Agreement at any time, that waiver will only be effective for the specific instance and specific purpose for which the waiver was given. If either party fails to exercise or delays exercising any of its rights or remedies under this Agreement, that party retains the right to enforce that term or provision at a later time.

Severability. If a court finds any provision of this Agreement invalid or unenforceable, the remainder of this Agreement will be interpreted so as best to carry out the parties' intent.

Attachments and Exhibits. The parties agree and acknowledge that all attachments, exhibits and schedules referred to in this Agreement are incorporated in this Agreement by reference.

No Agency. Nothing contained herein will be construed as creating any agency, partnership, joint venture or other form of joint enterprise between the parties.

☐ **Attorney Fees and Expenses.** The prevailing party shall have the right to collect from the other party its reasonable costs and necessary disbursements and attorney fees incurred in enforcing this Agreement.

☐ **Jurisdiction.** The parties consent to the exclusive jurisdiction and venue of the federal and state courts located in _____ [county], _____ [state], in any action arising out of or relating to this Agreement. The parties waive any other venue to which either party might be entitled by domicile or otherwise.

☐ **Arbitration.** Any controversy or claim arising out of or relating to this Agreement shall be settled by arbitration in _____ in accordance with the rules of the American Arbitration Association, and judgment upon the award rendered by the arbitrator(s) may be entered in any court having jurisdiction. The prevailing party shall have the right to collect from the other party its reasonable costs and attorney's fees incurred in enforcing this Agreement.

Signatures. Each party represents and warrants that on this date they are duly authorized to bind their respective principals by their signatures below.

SALES REPRESENTATIVE   ARTIST

_____   _____
Signature   Signature

_____   _____
Printed or Typed Name   Printed or Typed Name

_____   _____
Title   Title

_____   _____
Date   Date

Attachment A

Description of Works:

_____

_____

_____

_____

_____

_____

_____

_____

_____

_____

_____

_____

_____

_____

_____

_____

_____

_____

_____

_____

_____

_____

_____

_____

_____

_____

Excluded Accounts:

_____

_____

_____

_____

_____

Index

Remember:

Little publishers have big ears.
We really listen to you.

Take 2 Minutes & Give Us Your 2 cents

Your comments make a big difference in the development and revision of Nolo books and software. Please take a few minutes and register your Nolo product—and your comments—with us. Not only will your input make a difference, you'll receive special offers available only to registered owners of Nolo products on our newest books and software. Register now by:

PHONE
1-800-728-3555

FAX
1-800-645-0895

EMAIL
cs@nolo.com

or **MAIL** us
this registration card

fold here

Registration Card

NAME _____ DATE _____

ADDRESS _____

_____

CITY _____ STATE _____ ZIP _____

PHONE _____ E-MAIL _____

WHERE DID YOU HEAR ABOUT THIS PRODUCT? _____

WHERE DID YOU PURCHASE THIS PRODUCT? _____

DID YOU CONSULT A LAWYER? (PLEASE CIRCLE ONE)   YES   NO   NOT APPLICABLE

DID YOU FIND THIS BOOK HELPFUL?   (VERY)   5   4   3   2   1   (NOT AT ALL)

COMMENTS _____

_____

_____

WAS IT EASY TO USE?   (VERY EASY)   5   4   3   2   1   (VERY DIFFICULT)

We occasionally make our mailing list available to carefully selected companies whose products may be of interest to you.

❑   If you do not wish to receive mailings from these companies, please check this box.

❑   You can quote me in future Nolo promotional materials.
     Daytime phone number _____.

VART 1.0

Nolo *in the* NEWS

fold here

Place
stamp here

Nolo
950 Parker Street
Berkeley, CA 94710-9867

Attn: VART 1.0